We Are What We Drink

We Are What We Drink

The Temperance Battle in Minnesota

SABINE N. MEYER

University of Illinois Press
URBANA, CHICAGO, AND SPRINGFIELD

Library of Congress Cataloging-in-Publication Data
Meyer, Sabine N., 1979–
We are what we drink : the temperance battle in
Minnesota / Sabine N. Meyer.
pages   cm
Includes bibliographical references and index.
ISBN 978-0-252-03935-5 (hardback)
ISBN 978-0-252-09740-9 (e-book)
1. Temperance—Minnesota—History—19th century.
2. Temperance—Minnesota—History—20th century.
3. Woman's Temperance Crusade, 1873-1874. 4. Women
social reformers—Minnesota—History. 5. Women
immigrants—Political activity—Minnesota—History.
6. Woman's Christian Temperance Union of
Minnesota—History.
I. Title.
HV5235.M6M49   2015
178'.10977657909034—dc23   2014046096

For Claudia Meyer
and
in loving memory of
Alois Peter Meyer
(1942–1994)

Contents

Acknowledgments

The seeds of this book were sown in Minnesota in 2002, when Rudolph J. Vecoli, then director of the University of Minnesota's Immigration History Research Center, encouraged me to pursue what was initially not more than a tangle of ideas. Until his death in 2008, Rudy provided me with constant intellectual support and tons of good food and wine. I wish he could read the finished version of the research that began under his able guidance many years ago.

My greatest debt is to my mentor, Alfred Hornung. Without his expert advice, long-term support, unflinching encouragement, and mentorship I would not be where I am today, and this book would not exist.

I am also deeply indebted to other academic teachers and numerous colleagues. Through his enthusiasm and ample knowledge, Winfried Herget sparked my love for the field of American Studies. His intellectual contributions to my research as well as his farsighted advice on the publication of this book have meant very much to me. Helmut Schmahl was the first to introduce me to the history of American immigration and thus laid significant intellectual foundations for this book. For thoughtful comments on portions of this manuscript circulated in draft or presented in various forms, I would like to thank Lizabeth Cohen, Donna Gabaccia, Kate Moran, Dirk Bonker, Mary Lethert Wingerd, Manfred Siebald, Nicole Waller, Melissa Weiner, Jatin Wagle, Eric Erbacher, as well as the anonymous reviewers. I am deeply indebted to Paul Spickard, whose penetrating questions and constructive feedback have contributed to the genesis and publication of this book. I have also greatly profited from working—and occasionally consuming the products from the "Land of Amber Waters"—with Doug Hoverson, one of the few people as enthusiastic about everything connected with the history of alcohol in the United States as I am. He has supported my project in ever so many ways, commenting on the manuscript, passing along relevant information and archival material, and sharing illustrations from his own book. Finally, I would like to thank Peter Schneck for granting me the time it took to get this book published and for having been a great source of strength, support, and expertise throughout the publication process.

My research would not have been possible without the financial support of several sponsors. I would like to thank the German Academic Exchange Service (DAAD) for financing my academic year as a graduate student at the University of Minnesota, Twin Cities. The most significant financial support for my project has come from the Cusanuswerk, which supported me with scholarships throughout my undergraduate and graduate study and during the PhD phase. In addition, the state of Rhineland-Palatinate generously contributed to my research. Finally, my participation in the Bucerius Seminar, sponsored by the Zeit Foundation, the German Historical Institute in Washington D.C., and the University of Chicago, allowed me to acquaint myself with the American archival landscape and to introduce my work to renowned scholars, such as Paul S. Boyer and Kathleen Neils Conzen, whose critical comments and advice proved immensely helpful in the shaping of this project.

Among the many librarians and archivists who have assisted my research, I am particularly indebted to the competent staff of the Minnesota Historical Society, who have not only supported me in ever so many ways but who have also made me a member of their team during my extensive research stays. From the staff members at the Minnesota Historical Society, I would like to single out Debbie Miller, whose enthusiasm about Minnesota history and whose immense knowledge about the collections were invaluable to me and my work; Nick Duncan, who invested large amounts of time to provide me with additional archival material across the Atlantic and the high-resolution reproductions of the newspaper cartoons in my book and who introduced me to the art of Juicy Lucies; Jennifer Huebscher, who took care of permission issues as efficiently and generously as one could imagine; and Val Brown, who always made me feel at home and took care that I ate, drank, and rested enough while digging through dusty collections.

Creating this book would have been impossible without the help of an efficient, competent, and enthusiastic acquisitions editor. I have been privileged to work with Dawn Durante of the University of Illinois Press, who guided the manuscript securely and expertly all the way to production—all the while being extremely professional, cordial, and highly enthusiastic.

My friends have supported and enriched me while working on this project. Writing this book would have been impossible without the deep affection I have developed for Minnesota and the Twin Cities ever since my first stay there in

2001. Without my American friends Janna Ibis, Luke Ibis, Jenny Zahn, Laura Vitko, Adam Burgstede, Mia Burgstede, Lisa Steidl, Doug Hoverson, Sharon Day, Mike Galegher, Carrie Jastram, Lili Korbuly-Johnson, Allie Long, Nick Duncan, Mary Chilvers, Julie Krueger, Karl Krueger, and Grandma Ruth, Minnesota never would have become the home for me that it is, and my research trips would have been only half as much fun. This book expresses my deeply felt gratitude to all of you and to the enthusiasm with which you have always welcomed, hosted, and sustained me. My German friends, Katrin Klonau, Manfred Tamm, Claudia Lieb, Kati Keuper, Britta Padberg-Schmitt, Christina Meyer, Lara Friese, Annette Steffers, and Annika Merk, have also been a constant and indispensable source of support for me throughout the research for and the publication process of this book.

This book would have been impossible without the bottomless moral, emotional, and material backing of my mother, Claudia Meyer. She has supported me in all my endeavors, which took me to faraway places and onto difficult professional terrain. Her caring love, sustaining faith, and unswerving loyalty mean more to me than I can express. My father, Alois Peter Meyer, was the actual source of inspiration for my later work. Eager to accumulate knowledge, enthusiastic about history, and a great lover of books and newspapers, he passed on his probing mind and intellectual passions to his daughter, who had the chance to pursue the academic career he would have wished for as a young man.

Abbreviations

AASPM	Archives of the Archdiocese of St. Paul and Minneapolis
ASL	Anti-Saloon League
CAAC	Constitutional Amendment Agitation Committee
CTAU	Catholic Total Abstinence Union
d	daily/*täglich*
DW	*Der Wanderer*
IOGT	Independent Order of Good Templars
IWW	Industrial Workers of the World
LTL	Loyal Temperance Legion
MN	Minnesota
MNCPS	Minnesota Commission of Public Safety
MNCR	*Minnesota Chronicle and Register*
MNHS	Minnesota Historical Society
MN SZ	*Minnesota Staats-Zeitung*
MN VB	*Minnesota Volksblatt*
MSA	Minnesota State Archives
MSTU	Minnesota State Temperance Union
MWSA	Minnesota Woman Suffrage Association
NB of America	*Deutsch-Amerikanischer Nationalbund von Amerika*
NWC	*Northwestern Chronicle*
P	*Pioneer*
PP	*Pioneer Press*
SP	St. Paul
SWHA	Social Welfare History Archives of the University of Minnesota
TLA	Trades and Labor Assembly

VZ	*Volkszeitung*
w	weekly/*wöchentlich*
WCTU	Woman's Christian Temperance Union
WTH	*Western Temperance Herald*
YMCA	Young Men's Christian Association
YWCTU	Young Women's Christian Temperance Union
ZB of Minnesota	*Deutsch-Amerikanischer Zentralbund von Minnesota*
ZB of St. Paul	*Deutsch-Amerikanischer Zentralbund von St. Paul*

We Are What We Drink

Introduction

On September 26, 1908, Eva Jones, one of Minnesota's best-known female temperance workers, opened her diary and began to write down a list of "59 Objectives" for the temperance work she was about to start in the state's capital, St. Paul. She knew that in order to "[stir] sentiment for prohibition of saloons and of all drink manufacture and traffic" effectively, she would have to become acquainted with every inch of the city. Therefore, as a first step, she divided St. Paul into small districts with definite boundaries, through which she would labor district after district by means of house-to-house canvassing and parlor meetings. Jones also decided to collect evidence for "official laxness and complicity" within the city and to study St. Paul's judicial and political structures. She further planned to gather support from workers and immigrants by "[sympathizing] with labor and trade unions," by visiting both "large employing plants" and "foreign speaking settlements," and by collaborating with the Minnesota's Irish Catholic temperance society, the Catholic Total Abstinence Union (CTAU). To understand the shape and degree of influence of the liquor[1] industry in the state capital, Jones set out to study the beer and whiskey businesses in town. Finally, to have an inkling of a chance against the liquor traffic, she would have to mobilize children and young people and to collaborate with all the city's churches, reform workers, and women's clubs and associations receptive to temperance reform.[2]

The significance of Eva Jones's diary rests in its writer's awareness of the complexities she would have to face if she aimed at successfully conducting temperance work in St. Paul. After years of laboring at the state level, Jones understood that efficient temperance work had to be conducted on the ground—by minutely studying and engaging with a particular locale and its residents—hence she rejected the position as State Organizer offered to her by Minnesota's Woman's Christian Temperance Union (WCTU). She also knew that each locale brought with it a different set of rules, shaped by its demographic, economic, and political outlook, as well as its history. Jones had long realized that the oppositional forces she would have to deal with in St. Paul were deeply engrained, manifold, and diverse, including, but not limited to, representatives and employees of the liquor industry, the city's legal and political establishment, and many members of the city's laboring and immigrant communities. The support of potential advocates of temperance reform—churchgoing St. Paulites, women, children, and young people—could not be taken for granted in a city like St. Paul either, as Jones's plan of intense campaigning among these groups signifies. Her diary reminds us that in order to fully understand the temperance movement[3]—America's largest and longest sustained reform movement, it is imperative to develop a holistic view. Such a view demands that we grasp the movement's complexity by uncovering not only one isolationist strand of identity but also the multiple identity discourses at play in its wake. It demands that we explore how these identity discourses were shaped and claimed by a diverse set of individual players and communities and how they interacted with each other, the parameters of the place they were negotiated in, and the historical context. It demands that we engage in a bottom-up, rather than a top-down, approach to the organizations, communities, and individuals involved in the fight for or against liquor so that we can begin to see what temperance reform—or the fight against it—meant to each of them. It demands that we refrain from conceptualizing temperance activism largely as a moral crusade pitting clearly demarcated, stable, and easily definable camps against each other: Protestant, middle-class Anglo-American women and men against working-class men, immigrants, racial minorities, lawless city bosses, and, of course, the liquor industry. Instead, we need to perceive temperance and anti-temperance as motifs around which a large variety of cultural agendas were arranged. These agendas were not stable but shifted according to the actors involved, as well as the historical forces they were confronted with and thus require careful deconstruction. Finally, we need to follow Eva Jones's lead and study in particular the groups and individuals opposing the temperance movement. Only by unraveling the cultures behind that opposition can we understand the internal history of the temperance movement and its reformers.

Inspired by such source material from the grass roots, this book intends to expand the analytical framework for writing the history of the American temperance movement. In the 1970s, scholars such as Joseph Gusfield and Ian R. Tyrrell primarily interpreted the temperance movement through the lens of class and status; in the 1980s, however, Jack S. Blocker insisted that the movement "has never been solely a mirror for the middle class" and could not be fully grasped by merely approaching it through one single category of identity. To Roy Rosenzweig, the temperance movement and the saloon were "intense battlegrounds buffeted by the powerful and complex forces of class, gender, and ethnicity."[4] Despite this call to engage with the movement's identitarian complexities, scholars have, by and large, continued to publish monographs that read the movement through one isolated category of identity and have neglected to integrate various analytical perspectives into a truly holistic approach toward temperance.[5] While acknowledging that temperance reform needs to be envisioned "as a mutable and complex set of ideas, rationales, and sources of identity, shaped and claimed by diverse, often competing groups and individuals over time, in different contexts, and for different purposes," those studies do not pay sufficient attention to the interplay of various identity categories in the development of the temperance movement from the nineteenth into the twentieth century.[6]

Rather than focusing on one strand of identity or presenting the various identities negotiated within the temperance movement as monolithic categories, this book sets out to uncover the myriad and ever-shifting ways that ethnicity, gender, class, religion, and place all interacted with each other in the temperance struggle, sometimes enabling the formation of coalitions, sometimes limiting groups' abilities to form them, sometimes interpenetrating one another as factors in politics and culture. While class and religion retain their significance and weave in and out of the story—sometimes central to the action, sometimes only a felt presence—my analysis will demonstrate that ethnicity, gender, and identity of place exerted an equal, if not at times more important, impact on contemporaries' attitudes toward temperance.

From Rosenzweig's list of forces buffeting the temperance battleground, ethnicity has been explored insufficiently so far. Scholars have explained the temperance movement largely from an Anglo-American perspective and have neglected to provide a nuanced reading of the involvement of immigrant communities. Irish and German Americans, in particular, have been homogenized with respect to temperance reform: Their supposed opposition has been interpreted as a given; patterns of German and Irish American advocacy of and resistance to temperance have neither been uncovered nor analytically framed. Besides failing to deconstruct this homogenization, scholars have so far not drawn a link between German and Irish American involvement in the temperance movement and immigrant identity formation.[7] Furthermore, not a single study examines the temperance movement from an interethnic perspective, analyzing the discourses, conflicts, compromises, and cooperations it engendered among the various ethnic groups, in particular within the realm of the American Catholic Church.

"Ethnicity," as Rudolph J. Vecoli argued, "can only be understood in the context of group interaction."[8] Through my careful deconstruction of the Irish and German ethnic positioning with respect to Anglo-American temperance activism, my book offers a different perspective on the movement and treats temperance history for the first time as (inter)ethnic history. I unravel the complexities of ethnic identity formation in the light of temperance reform and explore to what extent interethnic cooperations and tensions acted as a motor behind temperance and anti-temperance activism and provided catalysts of ethnic identity formation.

With respect to gender—more specifically, female identity—the book contributes to the gradual reinterpretation of female temperance history, which has taken shape largely within the last ten years with the aim of correcting earlier studies on women's temperance activism.[9] The majority of these earlier studies were deeply engaged in the rationale of feminist scholarship. In their analyses of the work and policies of the Woman's Christian Temperance Union (WCTU), their authors drew a connection between nineteenth-century female temperance activism and feminism, between female reform and feminist consciousness. Their general tendency was therefore to belittle the achievements of the WCTU and to emphasize what the WCTU was not rather than what it was. Whereas feminist scholars have generally defined the suffrage movement as the fullest embodiment of feminist concepts, they have depicted the temperance movement as seeking to reinterpret women's place within the private sphere and therefore as conservative. Even Ruth Bordin, the first temperance scholar to question the unease of feminist historians to place what they saw as an antilibertarian reform into the mainstream of their cause, has branded the WCTU's use of contemporary gender ideology as conservative and has continued to dichotomize the suffrage and temperance movements, thereby overlooking that there was a considerable overlap between the two causes.[10]

This book situates female temperance activism within the private-public paradigm and shows that, inspired by the state's leading female temperance workers, from the late 1880s on, an ever-increasing number of Minnesota's temperance women on the ground (and not only national leaders such as Frances Willard) engaged in grassroots and equal-rights feminism and reconceptualized the temperance movement as an identity political formation. By investigating the genesis, rhetoric, and activism of women's temperance organizations in Minnesota and the coalition work between them and state's suffragists, the book corrects the fairly recent scholarly claim that the female temperance workers entered collaborations with the suffragists mostly to realize their goal of alcohol prohibition and not necessarily to advance woman's suffrage.[11] It rather demonstrates that from the moment of the women's temperance movement's founding, an ever-growing cohort of women engaged in women's rights arguments and sought to make these compatible with traditional notions of femininity. The book thus offers a subtle corrective to the scholarly dichotomizing and hierarchizing between female temperance and suffrage activism and reforges the largely neglected, yet vital, link between them. In addition, it presents new source material shedding light on the Anglo-American temperance women's interaction with and attitude toward Minnesota's various immigrant communities, as well as Native and African Americans.

Besides reading temperance reform in the light of ethnicity and gender, I endeavor to make a meaningful argument about the power of place in the temperance movement and thus to introduce a new category of analysis into the study of temperance and a new dimension into the complex matrix of intersecting identities. While several books, such as Jed Dannenbaum's *Drink and Disorder*, Bruce Dorsey's *Reforming Men and Women*, or James E. Klein's *Grappling with Demon Rum*, succeed at exploring how the temperance movement played out in particular locales, they do not interrogate place as an analytical category. As I will demonstrate, temperance opponents and advocates were not only influenced by their class, gender, religious and ethnic identities but also by the culture of the place they resided in. By offering a close-grained study of the complex ways in which selected identities interact with and influence each other in one specific locale, my analysis sheds light on the connection between the temperance movement and processes of place-making as well as on the impact of people's identity of place on their attitude toward temperance reform.

Focusing on St. Paul—a city heavily invested in the opposition to temperance—finally allows me to pay particular attention to the deeply engrained, resilient, highly dynamic opposition to temperance and to draw a nuanced picture of the cultures behind that opposition. Temperance scholarship, in general, has not paid sufficient attention to and has often oversimplified the greatly heterogeneous and dynamic opposition to alcohol controls, temperance laws, the stigmatization of the liquor traffic, and the proposed culture of sobriety. The internal dynamics between reformers and opponents were tied to intersecting processes of identity formation as well as political and economic change over time. These dynamics need to be uncovered in order to write a balanced history of the American temperance movement.

Through its analysis of the interdependencies of place, gender, and ethnicity—alongside with class and religion—with respect to its actors' choices of beverage, alcohol or water, this book aims to come to a deeper understanding as to why the temperance movement mobilized people across class, sex, ethnic, racial, religious, and political lines. Rather than seeding the creation of clearly defined, stable camps, the temperance struggle provoked the formation of heterogeneous alliances, which shifted according to the involved actors' needs and interests. The book explores these multiple alliances and reads the movement against larger cultural and historical changes to highlight its contingent nature and to compellingly argue why prohibition in the end was doomed—at least in its perfectionist ends.

Rather than retelling the well-known national temperance narrative, this book tells a close-grained story about alcohol consumption from one point in space, Minnesota, by recognizing the multiple perspectives occupying and defining this point. At the same time, it further reduces the scale from the state level to a particular locale and zooms in on Minnesota's capital, St. Paul, the state's key battle site in the struggle about temperance.

In its multiscalar approach, the book deviates from the mainstream of temperance scholarship, which has focused on the development of the national alcohol discussion and related it to the larger workings of American culture, most notably the industrialization and urbanization of America and the emergence of a sizable middle class. The activism and policies of organizations such as the WCTU, the Anti-Saloon League (ASL), or the Prohibition Party on a national level, however, do not tell us anything about the experiences and interactions of temperance activists and opponents in specific settings and about the impact of the movement on their everyday lives. Moreover, the battle about prohibition at the national level was largely dependent on the outcomes of this battle in particular locales, as the three-fourths majority required for the ratification of the Eighteenth Amendment indicates. While (trans)national political, social, and economic developments, as well as the evolution of the national temperance movement, influenced local temperance activists, the temperance movement I portray through my close-grained analysis was an intensely local experience, inextricably intertwined and interacting with regional and local social, ethnic, economic, racial, and political structures.

But why look at Minnesota in particular? Minnesota is located in the midst of America's heartland, the Midwest, a region that has so far received only marginal attention by temperance historians.[12] This dearth of temperance historiography on the Midwest is all the more surprising because it is a region where the movement played an even more significant role than in the East. In the nineteenth century, Midwestern territories and states emerged as political units and underwent intense processes of regional identity formation, which pitted competing interests and visions against each other. The debates among, first and foremost, recently arrived New Englanders, Anglo-Americans from other parts of the Union, and immigrants from Germany, Ireland, and Scandinavia revealed the profound disagreements between these groups over the "meanings of places, over the relations of peoples in and with places, and over their often competing visions of the future." All these Midwestern actors attempted to make their specific cultural values the core of the dominant narrative of their respective state. The temperance movement was one of the cultural phenomena that gave settlers the opportunity to enter such conversations and debates about what it meant to be Minnesotan, Wisconsinite, Iowan, or South Dakotan. It allowed them to exchange ideas about material and moral development, the importation of New England traditions versus the collaborative creation of new traditions by the various local actors on the ground, the role of government, the terms of citizenship, and the limits of the public sphere.[13]

Minnesota lends itself well to a study focusing on the interactions and interpenetrations of various forms of identity within the temperance movement. It had an influential women's temperance movement, which rapidly grew in size and expanded its sphere of action over the years. It was the home of a wide range of religious denominations and sizable immigrant communities, most notably German, Irish, and Scandinavian Americans. These immigrants had a great say in the political, economic, and social workings of the state, and their specifically ethnic positions added spice to the initially largely Anglo-American temperance fare. Minnesota, specifically its capital St. Paul, was also a center of Irish Catholic temperance activism. Archbishop John Ireland, one of the state's most lucent and influential figures, was a—if not the most—prominent leader in the American Catholic temperance movement. He promoted the temperance cause despite the intense resistance of his German American flock, which led to an inner-Catholic schism that came particularly to the fore in Minnesota. And finally, what made the fight about liquor so intense in Minnesota were the deep roots the liquor industry had put down in the state, which is why Doug Hoverson has recently dubbed it the "Land of Amber Waters."[14]

In a recent contribution, Jessica Trounstine has employed the dictum "All Politics Is Local," most often credited to Thomas "Tip" O'Neill, to remind us of the significance of the study of local, substate politics. "Local politics," she has argued, "are American politics," as the "local contexts shape state and national politics" and "as the local level is charged with implementing many federal and state policies."[15] This holds particularly true for temperance reform, which grew out of and was most hotly debated in the cities, so that there is no uniform national story. In order to shed light on how individual communities were affected by and negotiated the temperance movement and how it influenced people's everyday lives, my book will time and again zoom in on one particular community—St. Paul, Minnesota's capital.

St. Paul offers distinct advantages for an examination of the value of place as an analytical category in temperance scholarship and the workings of the temperance movement on a local level. From its earliest days, its history, identity, and economic well-being were inextricably intertwined with alcohol consumption and production. The Catholic Church's solid presence and firm integration into the civic structure strengthened St. Paul's attitude toward liquor. Thus, a movement to restrict or prohibit the liquor traffic, fought with a particular fierceness in the state capital, shook both its economic and cultural foundations and forced city residents to negotiate their attitudes toward temperance reform within the contours of this particular place. St. Paul's local government, legally responsible for implementing the state and federal policies concerning liquor, developed its own strategies of law evasion that tested the limits of the decentralized structure of American government and determined the success or failure of such policies. In addition, St. Paul's proximity to its neighboring twin Minneapolis—a city whose founding history, demographics, and economic alignment greatly differed from those of the state capital—allows me to explore how particular geographical constellations can influence a city's self-definition and its response to the temperance movement.

Parts of the book thus tell the story about how one Midwestern American city responded to and made sense of a social movement that so contradicted its founding history and mentality, as well as its economic interests. Many of the questions that were debated in St. Paul in the context of the battle about temperance—questions touching upon the extent of civic home rule, the relation between the city's various interest groups, and the contours of the urban economy—were also discussed in other American cities, with the answers differing due to their formulation on the basis of locally specific parameters. While this story thus may not be representative, it provides a building block for future studies seeking to uncover the connection between temperance and place-making and making oneself in relation to place.

To put my analysis of ethnicity, gender, and place on a sound basis, I would like to discuss my approach to each of these categories of identity by reviewing and positioning myself with respect to the existing theoretical literature. "Identity" in its most basic sense refers to an individual's or a group's sense of self. People can draw their identities from an almost infinite number of sources. Identities can be: ascriptive (age, ancestry, gender, ethnicity [defined as extended kin], race); cultural (ethnicity [defined as a way of life], religion, language, nationality); territorial (village, city, country, continent); political (faction, clique, party); economic (job, occupation, profession); and social (friends, club, team). Identities are simultaneously essentialist and constructed, volitional and ascribed, and continually renegotiated and redefined. They are "produced in specific historical and institutional sites within specific discursive formations and practices." The debates about alcohol consumption and production were such discursive formations, in which identities are produced and negotiated.[16]

Viewing temperance as an (inter)ethnic issue, this book sets out to analyze the connection between the temperance movement and the construction of ethnic identities among Minnesota's Irish and German Americans.[17] It advances the premise that the temperance movement engendered processes of ethnicization and was strategically employed by German and Irish American leaders in order to promote the invention or renegotiation of these groups' respective identities, with drink acting as a marker of ethnic identity. This premise reveals that I conceive of ethnic identities as social constructions, which are, according to changing circumstances, constantly negotiated, defined, redefined, and sometimes dismantled over time. Ethnicity also draws heavily on contrastive strategies, relying on the constant contraction and expansion of group boundaries.[18] My claim that the temperance movement was often strategically exploited by ethnic leaders to construct an ethnic identity promoting their group's cultural and/or economic interests hints at the instrumentalist nature of ethnicity. Instrumentalists, such as Nathan Glazer and Daniel Patrick Moynihan, understand ethnicity as an instrumental and situational "interest group mentality." Abner Cohen also regards it as a political resource, helping competing interest groups to attain their collective goals.[19] While my book time and again points out how temperance reform was instrumentalized by leading community members for specific purposes, it also demonstrates that this is only part of the truth. My analysis also reveals that the arguments for or against liquor consumption were often "based in [certain] cultural lifestyles, communal arrangements, and shared memories and values" and thus constituted one of the most intimate forms of ethnic expression. Such findings stress the primordial character of ethnicity, that is, its connection to kinship, race, language, religion, customs, and tradition.[20] I will demonstrate throughout my book that ethnicity is based both on cultural experiences, memories, and values and on strategic decisions and maneuvering.

I combine this view of ethnic identity as both constructionist and essentialist with a theory of ethnicity developed by Kathleen Neils Conzen, Rudolph J. Vecoli, David A. Gerber, Ewa Morawska, and George E. Pozetta. Based on Werner Sollors's theory of "The Invention of Ethnicity," they produced a modified concept better suited to the study of American ethnic history. In response to changing realities both within the immigrant groups and the host society, the former continually reinvent themselves by redefining their identity, by creating new traditions and rituals, and by readjusting group boundaries. Within the realm of cultural construction, ethnicity can change, wane, or revive. However, Conzen and her colleagues reject Sollors's notion of ethnicity as a "collective fiction." Instead, they argue that a group's identity is based on real-life historical context and social experience and is expressed through shared worldviews, institutional structures, and behavioral patterns. Inventing or reinventing one's ethnicity actively involves the immigrants, who consciously decide to renegotiate their "traditions." While "[p]articular moments of societal crisis" can trigger the invention of ethnicity, "power relationships among the various players affect the process of negotiation." This process of negotiation takes place both between the immigrant groups and the dominant culture but also among the various immigrant groups. The dynamic process of ethnicization, that is, the development of a sense of ethnic identity, is central to this approach and is stimulated by contestation.[21]

In my analysis of German and Irish American identity constructions in the context of the temperance struggles, I will particularly focus on the motivations of these groups for the invention or renegotiation of ethnic identities. Did they seek to protect Old-World values and traditions or to realize ulterior goals, such as a socioeconomic and cultural repositioning? Did this invented or renegotiated ethnicity satisfy emotional longings and/or was it just a means to an end? Was it based on cultural essentials and/or on contrastive strategies? I will also investigate how the temperance movement influenced inner- and interethnic relations. Did it lead to cultural confrontations and clashes between the various ethnic groups and/or did it cause interethnic cooperation and the establishment of interethnic alliances? Did it lead to the strengthening and/or the weakening of social boundaries toward Anglo-American culture, that is, did it bring about integration or separatism? Finally, did the temperance movement cause the fragmentation or consolidation of ethnic groups?

My analysis of gender is based on sociologist Suzanne Staggenborg's claim that most social movements affect gender arrangements by altering men's or women's roles, by expanding the consciousness of movement participants, by introducing new organizational strategies and means of expression, and by creating new cultural practices and discourses. This book intends to unravel how the temperance movement in Minnesota became one factor which, alongside other reform movements and historical circumstances, greatly contributed to the construction of a female public identity.[22]

The term *female public identity* invariably evokes the concept of the two spheres. The notion of two separate gendered spheres of action, public vs. private, has been the focus of scholarly debate since the mid-1960s. The veracity, contents, and implications of the two-sphere concept have been questioned, confuted, affirmed, and redefined. Since the 1990s, numerous scholars have harshly criticized the public/private dichotomy for invoking a gap between theory and practice and have therefore even suggested its abandonment. I argue in favor of maintaining the private/public distinction, as I consider it a useful explanatory framework for an analysis of the connection between the temperance movement and women's gradual emancipation in the nineteenth and twentieth centuries. My sources reveal that the majority of women in nineteenth-century Minnesota were, both in theory and in practice, confined to the domestic sphere and contended with the ideological and real-life boundaries that the contemporary gender ideology imposed on them. However, since the public/private distinction was a social construct, it was subject to negotiation. Moreover, the boundaries between the public and private spheres were fluid and permeable and allowed for crossings between them and, at times, for their virtual dissolution. Despite being theoretically confined to the private sphere, women were often to be found outside this sphere, doing business, being part of the workforce, and engaging in religious activities or reform work. The discrepancy between the growing public visibility of women and a gender ideology seeking to keep them invisible contributed to great ambiguities of gender in nineteenth-century America and to contestations between the sexes.[23]

In order to situate the temperance movement within the public/private paradigm, I analyze the development of female temperance activism in Minnesota from its beginnings until the onset of prohibition. I explore the "types" of women who participated in the temperance movement, the activities those temperance women engaged in, and how far those activities changed over the years. I also investigate women's organizational structures, their relationship to the public sphere, and their emancipatory potential. It will be interesting to see how temperance women justified their increasing activism in favor of woman suffrage and women's rights, whether this political activism led to internal discrepancies within Minnesota's female temperance movement, and how the women negotiated different strands of opinions. I further wish to shed light on the relationship between a female public identity and the two-sphere ideology. Linda Kerber has rightly argued that "the ideology of separate spheres—like all ideology—is not frozen in time but in a constant state of refinement until it fits reality so badly that a paradigm shift in conceptualization is unavoidable."[24] Paradigm shifts occurred in the early decades of the twentieth century and reached their climax with the ratification of the suffrage amendment, the first legal proof that women had made inroads into, and become official players in, the dominant public sphere. I examine the effect of the female public identity created during the temperance movement on such paradigm shifts, the eventual erosion of the ideology of the two spheres, and the redefinition of gender roles.

I will read all female efforts in favor of temperance against the backdrop of the wide spectrum of female reform activism in the nineteenth and early twentieth centuries. Kerber justly calls the years between 1870 and 1920 the "high-water mark of women's public influence," hinting at the large variety of causes women engaged in, which all greatly contributed to the gradual paradigm shift in gender roles. The temperance movement is highly indebted to many of these female reform movements. There was also considerable interaction between them, especially between the temperance and the suffrage movements. I will explore the differences and similarities between the two movements by comparing their respective membership, strategies, methods, and coalition building and draw conclusions regarding the relative success of each in terms of female emancipation.[25]

Aside from the relationship between temperance and ethnic and female identities, this book also seeks to tackle the yet unexplored link between the temperance movement and place. Sociologists have pointed out that places have three necessary constituents. They are geographic locations; they are physical, that is, they consist of material form. Most importantly for this study, they are invested with meaning and value. "Without naming, identification, or representation by ordinary people, a place is not a place," Thomas F. Gieryn has argued. Places are thus "doubly constructed": They are both physically built but also "interpreted, narrated, perceived, felt, understood, and imagined." Despite its comparably durable materiality, the meaning and value of place is in flux, "flexible in the hands of different people or cultures, malleable over time, and inevitably con-tested."[26]

However, places are not merely subject to the various people and cultures settling them, but they are also, according to Mindy Thompson Fullilove, "a core element of identity formation," that is, they have the power to shape their residents' individual and collective identities. "Place," as Gieryn has illustrated, "is not merely a setting or backdrop, but an agentic player in the game—a force with detectable and independent effects on social life." It influences people's in-teraction, network-formation, and individual and collective action. It also "em-bodies and secures otherwise intangible cultural norms, identities, memories." In a study on the shape of liquor consumption, it is highly significant that place is "imbricated in moral judgments and deviant practices." Behavioral norms depend on where they occur, and acting against the normative order imposed upon by a place needs to be considered as an act of resistance. Places therefore also exert an enormous influence on their residents' emotions. While attach-ment to and identification with a place create a sense of well-being and security, loss of place exerts a tremendous toll on individual and collective identity and psychic health. The loss of place does not necessarily have to coincide with a physical displacement. Residents can feel displaced without going anywhere for various reasons, including their inability to identify with the values and behavioral norms of the place.[27]

This reciprocity between people and place plays an important role in a study on the temperance movement. The positioning of St. Paul as a civic entity and its residents as individuals with respect to the temperance movement, I argue, is a direct result of the constant interplay between the city's civic identity and that of its citizens. Whereas in most scholarship the term *civic identity* describes national identity, set apart from local identities or identities of place, numerous scholars, including myself, interpret it as local identity, constructed in local communities or cities, connected to, yet different from, national identity. "For the concept 'civic,'" John J. Czaplicka reminds us, "blends the political dimen-sion of citizenship rights and responsibilities . . . with the sense of belonging to a place and more specifically with the projection of locality often associated with the city." The term *civic identity* implies both the identity of a city and that of the majority of its residents. This double implication derives from the fact that civic identity emerges through the interaction of people and place.[28]

My understanding of civic identity draws on, yet significantly deviates from, Mary Lethert Wingerd's approach to civic identity. In her seminal study on St. Paul, Wingerd, a labor historian, conceptualizes civic identity as a "deep place-based loyalty" most critically shaped by a culture of insularity and by "contractual elements," that is, interior compromise in response to economic and social conditions. Consequently, in her analysis she foregrounds economic parameters rather than cultural values and marginalizes the "imagined components" of civic identity, as she calls them. To her, civic identity took the form of a "civic compact" resulting from successful economic "negotiations among a broad set of players." While I readily agree that St. Paul's unique tradition of problem solving and its reliance on civic compromises were inextricably intertwined with a dispersal of power deriving from a particular set of economic conditions, in my conceptualization of civic identity cultural and imagined elements take their place alongside contractual, and thus economic, factors. In line with other cultural historians, such as Timothy Gilfoyle, I consider the cultural values of city founders and later residents, as well as their identification with and their narrations about their place of residence, as vital to the development of a civic identity as economic and social structures.[29]

Civic identity should not be mistaken for civic peace and constant harmony. Wingerd points out that civic identity equaled consensus only at the level of rhetoric and that the "meanings, rights, and obligations embedded in this community compact were constantly tested, challenged, and negotiated."[30] Such a view of civic identity as being vigorously contested is compatible with recent scholarly conceptualizations of the city as a site of heterogeneity, confusion, and internal strife and dispels scholarly doubts concerning the existence of a group identity grounded in place. Notions of the city as a place of internal strife and the existence of a civic identity are complementary rather than mutually exclusive.[31]

To analyze the role of the temperance movement in the construction of St. Paul's civic identity, I reconstruct the making of St. Paul's civic identity before the arrival of this movement by focusing on the city's founding history and the ensuing foundational myth, its demographics, cultural specificities, and economic characteristics. With the influx of Anglo-American settlers from the East Coast, this civic identity came under attack. Inaugurated by the newcomers as one means of reshaping the city's identity in their own image, the temperance movement led to intense debates about St. Paul's civic identity. I will pay particular attention to the various urban factions that emerged in the context of the temperance movement, to their specific motives and goals, and to the strategies they employed to reach them. Through these debates, St. Paul increasingly emerged as an anti-temperance space, and aversion to temperance became an integral part of the self-understanding of the majority of city residents and thus of the city itself.

In my analysis, I focus on discourses and texts, and thus on printed city histories, political cartoons, newspaper coverage (in particular editorial comments and letters to the editor), political speeches, and other civic documents. While refraining from a survey of the city's material culture, its built environment and artwork (a survey that would have complemented the analysis yet not changed my overall findings), I also take into account its social geography, when I analyze the role of the "Midway" area, which emerged in the mid-1880s as St. Paul's only temperance enclave in opposition to the rest of the city. Finally, by dealing with German and Irish American associational, leisure, and drinking practices in the city, as described in print media, I reflect on the conceptualization of St. Paul by these immigrant communities and their uses of urban space. These avenues of analysis will demonstrate that civic identity was an organic creation of an urban community at large, and yet also the product of a deliberate strategy employed by community and business leaders to protect their own economic interests. But even as St. Paul's civic identity was strategically appropriated in the form of anti-temperance propaganda, this propaganda nonetheless reflected the prevalent culture of place. What else is successful propaganda but an intentional tapping into certain sets of long-held beliefs, notions, and ideas pertaining to a place and shared by the majority of city residents?

Aside from tracing the development of civic identity in the context of the temperance movement, this book also explores the impact of this civic identity on the city residents' attitudes toward the temperance movement. It identifies those residents who acted against the civic identity maintained and nourished by the majority of St. Paulites and untangles what consequences their actions had for their personal lives and their relationship to the community. Did their agitation against St. Paul's civic identity lead to a lack of identification, a sense of displacement, or even to the formation of counter-identities? All of this is not to say that St. Paulites would have reacted entirely differently to the temperance movement in a different place. Broad national trends, such as economic and political developments, affected many American cities in a similar way. Nevertheless, St. Paul's internal dynamics created unique local circumstances and experiences calling for unique reactions and solutions.

This study finally also analyzes the role of Minneapolis in the negotiation of St. Paul's civic identity with respect to the temperance movement. It thereby establishes a correlation between Minneapolitan views of temperance and St. Paulites' attitudes in the struggles about alcohol. Was Minneapolis for St. Paulites a point of reference or rather a foil against which to define themselves, that is, were the so-called "Twin Cities" ovular or rather biovular twins with respect to the struggle about temperance?[32]

Rather than viewing ethnic, gender, and civic identities as monolithic categories, interpreting them separately, this book intends to shed light on the interaction or intersection of the processes of identity formation under scrutiny. If one was, for instance, an Anglo-American female St. Paulite, how did these multiple levels of identification affect one's attitude toward the temperance movement? Since this study explores various parameters of identification, it is worth remembering that individuals hold multiple identities in the form of socially recognized categories. Identities, Stuart Hall argues, are "never singular but multiply constructed across different, often intersecting and antagonistic, discourses, practices and positions" and are thus "constantly in the process of change and formation." "The relative salience of these identities," as Samuel P. Huntington has argued, "can change from time to time and situation to situation, as can the extent to which these identities complement or conflict with each other." Moreover, individuals can add new identities to the ones they already hold and change their view of themselves. Rather than being distinct realms of experience, identities relate to and interact with each other. This view of identities as interacting and intersecting is essential when dealing with multiple identities in the context of the temperance movement. Within this realm of multiple identities, individuals or whole groups made strategic decisions of identification, emphasizing one identity over the other(s) or reformulating single identities. Such strategic repositioning, triggered by historical circumstance, often resulted in a changed or modified attitude toward the temperance movement.[33]

I would finally like to elaborate on the architecture of and the source materials used in this book. In order to illustrate the interplay between Minnesota's temperance movement and the formation and negotiation of various identities and their complex interactions in the light of historical developments, this book is organized chronologically, with each chapter tackling a significant time period in Minnesota's temperance history, beginning in the 1820s and ending on July 1, 1919, when Wartime Prohibition set in. Covering the full span of temperance activism in a particular locale without, however, losing sight of (inter)national developments allows me to reflect on continuities and changes and fosters an understanding of the multifaceted ramifications of the temperance movement in the state.

Each chapter comprises five subchapters, one tracing significant events in the history of Minnesota's (Anglo-American) temperance movement, the others shedding light on processes of civic, Irish and German ethnic, and female public identity formation and the interaction of these identities with each other and with class and religion within the temperance movement. Placing particular emphasis on the intersection of identities raises challenges and requires structural choices. Irish women's temperance activism could be grouped with Irish male temperance activism or with Anglo-American women's reform work. German women's anti-temperance activism, as rare as it was, could similarly be read as both an expression of ethnic and of female identity. The balance of my sources suggests, however, that Irish and German American women's expressions about temperance were fundamentally different from that of Anglo-American women. Not only did they emerge at a much later point in time, but they were, in general, characterized by an absence of the women's rights arguments present in Anglo-American female temperance work from the 1860s on. Hence my decision to place Anglo-American female temperance activism and the history of the largely Anglo-American Minnesota WCTU[34] in the chapters on female public identity, while I treat Irish and German American women's experiences in the chapters on the respective ethnic groups.

All of these chapters are based on thorough historical analyses of a wide range of multilingual archival source material. The most valuable source for my research on the temperance movement was the great number of newspapers published in Minnesota in German and English by a wide array of interest groups.[35] Aside from such newspapers, I used all available minutes of Minnesota's temperance organizations, religious bodies, and relied on the legislative proceedings of both the state legislature and the St. Paul City Council. This book sets out to pay particular attention to how the temperance movement influenced people's daily lives on the ground. Investigating individuals' private behavior—that is their relation to and practice of alcohol consumption—proves inherently difficult, however, as the majority of the actors of this study were fairly unknown outside their small communities and rarely left records behind that revealed their thoughts on and activities in the temperance movement. Whenever available, though, I inserted biographical anecdotes drawn from individuals' personal papers and connected their lives to the larger workings of the American temperance movement. All of the aforementioned source material is interpreted with a particular view through the theoretical lenses of ethnicity, gender, and civic identity.

We are what we drink. It has been my aim throughout this book to probe this statement and to shed light on the myriad and ever-shifting ways that identities intersect and interact with each other in the struggle about temperance. In order to fully grasp the complexity of Eva Jones's list of objectives, we must go back to Minnesota's preterritorial beginnings where the story about "the Jug of Empire" began to unfold.

1. "Westward the Jug of Empire"

The Emergence of a Temperance Movement in Minnesota (1819–1865)

Contested Good: Whiskey in Minnesota Country

Writing about his visit to St. Paul in 1882, Mark Twain muses upon the significance of whiskey for the settlement of the United States: "How solemn and beautiful is the thought that the earliest pioneer of civilization, the van-leader of civilization, is never the steamboat, never the railroad, never the newspaper, never the Sabbath-school, never the missionary—but always whisky! . . . Westward the Jug of Empire takes its way" (see figure 1.1).[1] Minnesota country was no exception to this pattern. It was flooded with whiskey by the traders, who not only consumed it themselves but who also used it to woo their Native American customers and to influence business transactions for their own benefit. For U.S. soldiers, whiskey became both a staple and leisure-time item that made their lives in the wilderness more worthwhile. Consequently, as this chapter will demonstrate, the temperance movement that was inaugurated in Minnesota country in those years was not merely an imitation and transplantation of Eastern anti-liquor activism but also a response to the rampant whiskey consumption that preceded and accompanied the process of settlement. Temperance, in the form of total abstinence, became a tool for securing Minnesota's transition from "wilderness" to "civilization." Through their reform efforts, in particular their fight for a Maine Law, Minnesota's early temperance activists attempted to make their specific cultural values the core of the region's dominant narrative.

Until well into the nineteenth century, when Minnesota country first attracted a sizable amount of settlers, the region was dominated by traders—first French, then British, and, from 1808 on, American. While the French traders had labored under a system of government monopolies, the large-scale entrance of the British into the trade from 1767 on, inaugurated an era of free trade. The Crown

THE FIRST ARRIVAL.

Figure 1.1. "Westward the Jug of Empire takes its way." Illustration from Mark Twain, *Life on the Mississippi* (Boston: Osgood, 1883) 587.

granted individual traders certain exclusive rights to a specific territory, which led to an intense competition among them for Native American customers. In such a competitive climate, "[a]lcohol," as Mary Lethert Wingerd has rightly claimed, "quickly became the pernicious glue that held trading relationships intact." Alongside food and tobacco, it soon turned into a token of "regard and metaphorical kinship." From its first introduction by the French traders on, Native Americans ascribed to alcohol's medicinal and spiritual qualities. It was believed to warm their bodies, to ease their physical pain, and to have the power to mentally connect the living with their deceased ancestors. Alcohol soon also came to play a significant role in Native kinship ceremonies and mourning rituals. While the French mostly traded with brandy and the British carried with them rum, American traders greatly relied on whiskey in their business transactions. With the intensification of competition among traders, "[v]irtual rivers of alcohol flowed into the region." Competition, and thus the significance of alcohol in the trading game, reached particular height when the fur trade came to be dominated by rivaling trading companies. In 1799, rivalries between the North West and the XY Companies resulted in annual shipments of more than twenty thousand gallons of spirits into Grand Portage, the access point to the region.[2]

Native American alcohol consumption led to the rise of the drunken Indian stereotype among the colonizers. The early records of Minnesota's history abound with stereotypical descriptions of Native American alcohol abuse. Colonel Josiah Snelling, who was sent to Minnesota by the U.S. military in 1820, related that "[h]erds of Native Americans [were] drawn together by the fascinations of whisky [*sic*]," exhibiting "the most degraded picture of human nature I ever witnessed."[3] Accounts such as Snelling's prompted the American government officials to devise various schemes of how to reduce the effects of whiskey on Native Americans on the frontier. Lawrence Taliaferro, the Indian agent at Fort Snelling, a military post on the western heights of the Mississippi River established in 1819 in order to protect the American fur trade, was Minnesota's first crusader against the traders' strong reliance on whiskey in their businesses. Determined to stop the incessant flow of whiskey, in 1826, with the support of policy makers in Washington, he tried to enforce an edict banning liquor from the trade with the Native Americans but the traders managed to evade this much-hated regulation by claiming the introduced liquor was for their own men. In 1834, Congress passed "An Act to Regulate Trade and Intercourse with the Indians and to Preserve Peace on the Frontiers," the first to regulate liquor consumption in Minnesota country and to forbid the disposal of liquor to the Native Americans. However, this law, as well as the others that would follow in its wake, could not be enforced due to the noncompliance of the traders.[4]

The 1837 land cession treaty with the Ojibwe and Dakota, opening all their lands east of the Mississippi to white settlement, made it even easier for Native Americans to obtain liquor and thus severely aggravated the situation. Whiskey traders opened "groceries" along the left bank of the Mississippi, opposite the Native villages. Since Native Americans could now cross the river to buy whiskey, the traders did not even have to break the 1834 Act and could therefore not be pursued legally. Native Americans also actively participated in the liquor traffic by transporting whiskey to their northern fellow tribes.[5]

The situation did not improve after 1849, even though Alexander Ramsey, the first governor and Superintendent of Indian Affairs of the newly founded Territory of Minnesota, explicitly declared his intention to enforce the federal laws related to Native Americans. He encouraged the first legislative assembly to pass "An Act to provide against the traffic in ardent spirits with the Indians." However, as in the 1830s, all federal and territorial statutes largely remained dead letters on Minnesota's frontier, as a number of traders continued to give out whiskey to the Native Americans, thus forcing all traders to distribute whiskey in order to remain competitive.[6]

While alcohol did indeed pose a severe danger to Native Americans at the time, scholars have recently found that Native American alcohol consumption "was neither uniform nor inevitable" but resulted from their exposition to "antisocial behavior associated with frequent high-dose drinking by soldiers, [and] *coureurs de bois* (fur traders) . . . notably, all self-selected communities of men, away from their families and from the reach of alcohol policies and other forms of social control."[7] Such constellations, inducing Native Americans to mimic drinking habits at the frontier, could also be found in Minnesota country. John Sayer's trading journal reveals that binge drinking was an inherent facet of the traders' daily lives at the frontier. One day he wrote that he had to postpone his departure "until the Afternoon my Men being all Drunk." Soldiers stationed at Fort Snelling also consumed large amounts of whiskey. In 1823, a soldier who had just arrived at the fort wrote: "Intemperance, among both officers and men, was an almost universal thing, and produced deplorable effects. I regret to say that the commandant [Snelling] was no exception to this rule."[8]

Fears of excessive intoxication among Native Americans—curiously not among soldiers and traders—led to the first temperance campaigns in Minnesota country. Missionaries and teachers stationed with the tribes worked with Indian agents and military officers to eliminate whiskey among Native Americans by teaching them the principle of total abstinence. The Catholic missionary Augustin Ravoux toiled among the Sioux in the mid-1840s. Robert G. Murphy, a subagent at Fort Snelling, quietly and efficiently carried on a temperance movement within that tribe between January and May 1849.[9]

Temperance reform also found its way to Minnesota through newspapers, literature, visitors from the East, and the large percentage of New Englanders who had settled there by the late 1840s. The campaign for a Maine Law, inaugurated in Minnesota in the early 1850s, demonstrates the close connection of temperance work at the frontier with that in New England and the transplantation of notions of temperance in the process of westward migration.

By the late 1840s, reformers all over the country considered all sorts of liquor—as well as the liquor trade—evil, began to question the usefulness of moral suasion, and increasingly advocated legal measures to outlaw alcohol. Major changes in American society, such as rapid urban growth, waves of foreign immigration, industrialization, and the emergence of a class of poor, transient laborers in the cities frustrated the temperance activists' belief that individual reform through argument, persuasion, and moral example could eradicate the curse of drink that allegedly led to burgeoning slums, the impoverishment of residents, and the increase in crime, particularly in the nation's cities. Moreover, reformers increasingly viewed alcoholism as a disease from which no one was safe. Finally, by midcentury the manufacture and trade of alcoholic beverages had become a constituent part of the American economy and was thus viewed by the reformers as the root of all social evil and disorder that could be ousted only through coercive laws.[10]

Even though Minnesota was still a territory and thus not yet affected by these social and economic changes, many of its settlers, in particular the New

Englanders, had been part of or closely followed developments in New England, where in 1851 the first prohibitory law—the Maine Law—was passed. Four years later, thirteen states and territories had adopted such a prohibitory law. Eager to partake in this national prohibitionist reform wave, temperance advocates from all over Minnesota held a General Territorial Temperance Convention at the Presbyterian Church in St. Paul on New Year's Day in 1852 in order to consider the best means for suppressing intemperance in the territory. The majority of those present were clergymen and New Englanders from St. Paul, Stillwater, and St. Anthony. The latter was the territory's center of the prohibition crusade; it was populated by many so-called Mainites, who had come to the town to work in the lumber business, had been the driving force behind the movement for a Maine Law in Maine, and were eager to pass a similar law in their new home. Moreover, some of the town's leading citizens—such as John W. North, a native of New York and the legal counsel of the milling entrepreneur Franklin Steele—aimed at turning St. Anthony into a model community, "a political make-weight to . . . the dissolute, ignorant, drunken, Democratic, pro-slavery capital city down the river [St. Paul]."[11]

The great presence of clergymen at the Territorial Temperance Convention indicates that in Minnesota, as in other states and territories, the temperance movement was initially mostly religiously motivated and owed its emergence and rapid growth to currents within Protestantism. It corroborates what Sydney E. Ahlstrom has called "the intimate association of evangelism in its broadest sense with moral reform and social benevolence."[12] The major supporters of temperance reform came from the Methodist, Baptist, and Congregationalist denominations. In both 1851 and 1852, when the Minnesota Territory was still part of the Wisconsin Annual Conference, the Methodist Episcopal Church spoke out against liquor, recommended its members to nominate and vote only for people who would pass and sustain prohibitory laws, and advised the use of unfermented grape juice for the communion. At their first meeting in St. Paul in 1852, the territory's Baptists adopted resolutions in favor of temperance; defined intemperance as a source of crime, poverty, and wretchedness; and spoke in favor of prohibition. In 1853, the Congregational Association of Minnesota officially declared in favor of a prohibitory law and defined intemperance a sin.[13]

Besides such evangelical leanings, a great number of temperance advocates in Minnesota, as well as in other parts of the nation, had a middle-class background. Sobriety was a core element in the ideology of self-control espoused by the middle class. According to the reformers, total abstinence, once established as a norm of behavior by the larger community, would help to control both self and society and thus mitigate social disorder. It would also lead to economic success and material prosperity and contribute to the growth of the market economy. Members of the working class—in particular foreign-born

workers—became the major objects of temperance reform, for middle-class reformers assumed that economic efficiency, productivity, and social health could
be increased only through the control of the working class and the eradication
of certain working-class habits, such as liquor consumption in saloons.[14]

Driven by religious motives and a firm belief in middle-class values, Minnesota's reformers decided at their New Year's meeting to form a Territorial
Temperance Society and to fight for a Maine Law in Minnesota. Through the
passage of a Maine Law, society members argued, they could make Minnesota
more attractive for the right kind of immigrants. The Maine Law agitation
was thus part of a greater project with the aim to transform Minnesota from
a fur-trading hub into an exemplary territory that would attract law-abiding
and industrious settlers, ideally from a middle-class background and of Anglo-
American ancestry.[15]

In order to demonstrate their strength, Minnesota's temperance societies organized a procession in St. Paul on February 16, 1852, the largest that ever turned
out in the territory, composed of about five hundred men and women from
various religious faiths, diverse professions, and nationalities. They marched to
the hall where the legislative assembly met and handed in a "monster petition"
in favor of a Maine Law, which had been signed by six hundred Minnesotans, all
"men and women of decision and deeds." The petitions in favor of a Maine Law
with the largest number of signatures came from St. Anthony, where 206 adult
males and 178 women had enlisted themselves against liquor. But a number of
petitions also came from St. Paul and were signed by the town's clergymen, such
as Chauncey Hobart and John G. Riheldaffer, but also by people from whom
opposition to alcohol was least expected, such as the fur traders Alexis Bailly,
Norman W. Kittson, and Joseph Rolette.[16]

Despite the many declarations in favor of the law, the debate in the legislative assembly was fraught with difficulties. Legislators discussed questions of
personal rights versus public morals and of justice versus practicability. Based
on these uncertainties, the House of Representatives asked Chief Justice Jerome
Fuller for his opinion as to the power of the legislative assembly to pass a prohibitory law. Without having seen the drafted bill, he considered such a law
possible as long as it did not contradict the U.S. revenue laws. After lengthy
debates, the legislators passed it by a two-thirds majority in the House and by
a three-fourths majority in the Council. Four of the legislators who had voted
against the measure were employed in the lumbering business and another in
the fur-trading business, with whiskey playing an essential role in both of them.
Another opponent of the bill was a tavern keeper from St. Paul.[17]

The "Act for the Restriction of the Sale of Intoxicating Liquors within the
Territory of Minnesota" prohibited the manufacture and sale of liquor except
for special agents appointed to sell it for mechanical and medicinal purposes.

Violators faced a $25 fine, and liquor sold illegally was to be seized and destroyed. The citizens of the territory were to decide on the first Monday in April whether or not the law should go into effect on May 1, 1852.[18]

In the weeks before the election, there was considerable excitement throughout the territory. Maine Law advocates held lectures and sermons and established a temperance newspaper in St. Anthony. Presbyterian, Congregationalist, Baptist, and Methodist clergymen, in particular, labored for the success of the election all over the territory. The newspapers claimed that a large majority of the people in the territory, first and foremost the women, were in favor of the law and that the clergymen were its major boosters by preaching the subject from their pulpits.[19]

Although most sources available were produced by temperance supporters and deliberately downplayed or outright ignored oppositional voices, a few documents indicate considerable opposition to a prohibitory law in the territory among fur traders, liquor dealers, and lumbering men. This opposition was led by Daniel A. Robertson, editor of St. Paul's Democratic newspaper, the *Minnesota Democrat*, who considered such a law difficult to enforce and did not deem the liquor traffic a proper subject for legislation.[20] Robertson was only one of many opponents. In a letter exchange, Louis Robert, a fur trader and commission merchant with a large liquor trade, asked the Irish Democratic lawyers William Pitt Murray and Bushrod W. Lott, later the mayor of St. Paul, to return to Minnesota quickly for the final vote to tip the scales against the law. Even though Murray's name had appeared on one of the early petitions in favor of a Maine Law, he seems to have switched to his friend Robert's anti–Maine Law camp. Shortly before the election in April, Governor Ramsey recorded in his diary that although the friends of the law seem to have had the majority so far, it now appeared probable that there would be "considerable opposition as the enemies are organizing their forces."[21]

Despite such attempts of the opposition to win the day, the temperance advocates successfully convinced the majority of Minnesota's residents of the usefulness of the law. On April 5, 1852, 853 Minnesotans decided for the law and only 662 against the law. The reformers' euphoria over this legislative success knew no bounds. James M. Goodhue, a New England–born journalist and editor of the *Minnesota Pioneer*, advised future immigrants "to whom liquor is essential, as an ingredient of comfort or of life" to refrain from coming to Minnesota and cordially invited those "whose liberty is not confined in bottles, casks and decanters" to make the territory their home. Such euphoria, however, did not prevail long. The opponents of the law created a test case, which they took to the Territorial Supreme Court. At the end of November, Chief Justice H. Z. Hayner declared the law unconstitutional because the legislature had passed it under the proviso that it should become law only if the voters of the territory approved of it. As the Organic Act vested legislative power in the assembly and in the governor, such a delegation of power to the people was unconstitutional.[22]

Hayner's verdict did not put a damper on the temperance activists' reform spirit. They continued to hold temperance conventions and inundated the legislative assembly with petitions in favor of a new Maine Law meeting all demands of constitutionality. By 1853, however, enthusiasm about a prohibitory law had vanished in the majority of Minnesota's communities except for in St. Anthony, whose residents would continue to struggle for prohibition. The Maine Law had proved difficult to enforce and had been a constant cause of civic strife. Moreover, the presence of an ever-increasing number of immigrants made the legislators skeptical of the supposed benefits of a prohibitory law for the budding territory. Therefore, in both 1853 and 1854, the territory's legislators refused to pass a Maine Law. Instead, they decided in favor of a stringent license law, requiring liquor sellers to acquire a license costing between $75 and $200 from the county commissioners and to file a bond of $5,000 with two more sureties. The license law also prohibited the selling of liquor on Sunday, the sale of liquor to any minor or Native American, and gambling in saloons. Its passage marked the end of the campaign for a Maine Law in Minnesota, as the politicians had decided for the regulation of the liquor trade rather than its prohibition.[23]

In the early 1850s, the temperance movement had not yet entered party politics in the territory. While the strongest opposition tended to come from the Democratic ranks, opposition to and endorsement of the Maine Law did not follow straight party lines at the time. The *Minnesotian*, a Whig newspaper, insisted that Minnesota's Whigs did not aspire to make the temperance question a party issue. Dragging the Maine Law into party politics was not feasible at all, its editor argued, as some of the "most prominent" Whigs were strongly opposed to prohibition in the territory and had cooperated with individual Democrats to avert the bill's passage. The *Minnesota Democrat* similarly claimed that the Democrats differed on the Maine Law and therefore refrained from including it in the party platform. The petitions in favor of a Maine Law indeed bore the signatures of prominent Democrats. In 1852, David Olmsted enlisted in favor of a Maine Law, and Henry M. Rice's signature can be found on a Maine Law petition from Fort Snelling dated 1853. However, these two men were no staunch prohibitionists. Only three years later, Olmsted and Rice ran for territorial delegate for Congress on an antiprohibition platform. While Olmsted was probably swept away by the initial Maine Law euphoria, Rice might have temporarily supported the law in order to satisfy his Anglo-American urban supporters, knowing very well that by 1853 the Maine Law did not have a realistic chance any more anyway.[24]

Due to the hesitancy of both Whigs and Democrats to make prohibition a party issue, in June 1853, Minnesota's temperance advocates for the first time seriously considered forming a "Republican Temperance Party." But because of fears that such an action would divide the friends of temperance and cause political prejudice, the idea was laid to rest again until July 1854, when men who had previously been active in both the Democratic and the Whig Parties met in St. Anthony to plan the creation of a new party.[25] The immediate reason for such a creation was the repeal of the Missouri Compromise of 1820 and the passage of the Kansas-Nebraska Act in March 1854, which greatly upset those opposing slavery's expansion and convinced them to organize politically. In Minnesota, the members of the movement for a new party were not only opposed to the extension of slavery but also zealous supporters of temperance.[26]

When the Republican Territorial Convention finally met on July 25, 1855, to officially found the Republican Party of the Territory of Minnesota, the prohibition plank caused severe debates between the "ideological fire-eaters" and the more practically minded politicians.[27] Even though some of those present argued that such anti-liquor sentiments could alienate many of the party's warmest supporters and thus weaken it in its fight against the extension of slavery, the Unitarian minister Charles G. Ames from St. Anthony, editor of the *Minnesota Republican*, the territory's major organ of temperance and abolitionism, insisted on the adoption of a resolution in favor of a Maine Law. He thus acted against the advice of Charles Sumner, a famous statesman and the leader of the antislavery forces of Massachusetts, who visited Minnesota in July 1855. In a conversation with Ames, he had urged him not to press the prohibition issue until the slavery question was settled. Even though Ames, in retrospect, considered this advice as presenting "the wiser instincts of the time," in 1855 it was difficult for him to accept such arguments for political expediency.[28]

Consequently, the eighth plank of the first platform of Minnesota's Republican Party said: "*Resolved*, That we regard the traffic in intoxicating beverages as a public evil without mixture of good; and that at our approaching fall election, we will do what we can to secure the choice of a Legislature which shall enact a constitutional law suppressing it, and to fill the county and precinct officers with men who will enforce such a law." The Convention also made sure to nominate a candidate as territorial delegate to Congress who would advocate prohibition. After Alexander Ramsey's refusal to run due to the radicalism of the platform, William R. Marshall, an ardent abolitionist and Maine Law advocate, accepted the nomination. Minnesota's Republican Party thus positioned itself explicitly as a coalition against slavery and the liquor traffic. For the first time in the history of the territory, temperance had made it onto the platform of a political party and influenced the outcome of an election. Marshall's advocacy of prohibition cost him his election, with the pro-slavery yet pro-liquor Henry M. Rice beating him by about 1,200 votes.[29]

By 1856, the territory's Republican Party had dropped its prohibitory plank for political expediency and focused solely on the slavery issue. It would maintain this stand until 1886, much to the dismay of its reform-minded supporters. Despite this political reorientation within the Republican Party, the consumption of liquor had become an integral part of party politics and one of the key issues shaping the political landscape and its actors.[30]

Alcohol and the Founding of St. Paul

In his 1912 *History of St. Paul and Vicinity*, Henry A. Castle draws a direct connection between the future history of a community and "the tendencies and traits of [its] people for several generations after" and "the impress given by a few of its first settlers." Writing on St. Paul, Castle thus acknowledges the significance of St. Paul's founding history for its civic development and its cultural identity. Excessive whiskey consumption and distribution were responsible for the founding of the frontier settlement that was to become the city of St. Paul. The peculiar circumstances of St. Paul's founding and the composition of its early population created an inextricable link between alcohol and the town's civic identity, a link that the New Englanders, who migrated there from the late 1840s on, desperately sought to erase by means of temperance agitation.[31]

From 1821 on, with the permission of the post commandant, a number of traders—half-caste French voyageurs who had retired from the fur trade—several discharged soldiers, and numerous impoverished Swiss refugees from the ill-fated Selkirk settlement near St. Boniface, Manitoba, settled in the vicinity of the military outpost of Fort Snelling. In 1837, with the land cession treaty with the Ojibwe and Dakota underway, the War Department decided to determine the precise boundaries of the military reserve that Zebulon Pike had negotiated from the Dakota more than two decades earlier. The secretary of war therefore asked Fort Snelling's new commandant, Major Joseph Plympton, to procure a map marking the boundaries of the reserve. Plympton had an axe to grind with the settlers around the fort who were "in no way connected with the military." Many of them passed themselves off as independent fur traders but were in fact mere whiskey sellers, freely distributing their liquid goods to the Native Americans and the fort's soldiers. When asked by the commandant to leave the boundaries of the military reserve, many settled on the east side of the river, believing it to be beyond the bounds of the fort, and continued to ply their trade. In 1838, the new boundaries of the military reserve were published, along with Plympton's order prohibiting any civilians to settle or cut timber on government lands. To the dismay of the settlers, however, the newly mapped reserve included substantial lands on the east side of the river, so that they had to face yet another eviction. Plympton had convinced the secretary of war to approve of his proposal by arguing that he needed to protect both Native Americans and soldiers from the traders, who continued to supply whiskey in defiance of his orders. His pleas to the War Department were underlined by the surgeon of the post, John Emerson, who described "the most beastly scenes of intoxication among the soldiers of the garrison and the Indians in the vicinity." Thus, in the spring of 1840, the squatters settled beyond the reserve on the site that would become St. Paul. This settlement soon became known to the Dakota Native Americans as "the place where they sell minne-wakan [liquor]." The history of its founding indicates that from the first moment of its existence the settlement that was to become St. Paul was inextricably intertwined with liquor and the liquor trade.[32]

St. Paul's civic identity greatly derived from how its first settlers perceived it and from the actors that initially populated it. Founded as a trading hub for furs and whiskey, the frontier settlement that would later become St. Paul was named "Pig's Eye," in honor of its most notorious whiskey trader, Pierre "Pig's Eye" Parrant, a Canadian voyageur. This choice of name underlines that St. Paul was originally established in a haphazard fashion. The traders, who had taken the jug westward, and the impoverished settlers shared an "aversion to the constraints of 'civilization'" and were "a footloose and independent lot." They did not intend to found a city and traded away the land for a few dollars. Pig's Eye, as Wingerd states, was "beyond the reach of formal mechanisms of order." Climbing the social and economic ladder was based on courage and physical strength rather than on ethnicity and social class. John Fletcher Williams, the first city historian and a staunch temperance advocate, sarcastically and scornfully pointed at St. Paul's beginning as a liquor den: "Thus was our city 'founded'—by a pig-eyed retailer of whiskey. The location of the future Capital of Minnesota was determined, not by the commanding and picturesque bluffs . . . not by the great river flowing so majestically in front of it . . . but solely as a convenient spot to sell whiskey, without the pale of law." The location of the settlement at the unruly frontier, the circumstances of its founding, the economic significance of liquor, and the mentality of its early settlers intertwined in the formation of St. Paul's civic identity. Revelry and liquor existed as defining features of this civic identity.[33]

St. Paul's identity was also greatly influenced by the vital role of the Catholic Church in the community. Until the influx of Anglo-Americans into St. Paul, French Canadians, most of them Catholics, constituted the largest part of the town's population, and the number of Protestant settlers was small. Catholic influence manifested itself in the renaming of the town. St. Paul derived its final name from its first Catholic church, built at Father Lucien Galtier's instigation in November 1841. Only in 1848 and 1849, several years after the establishment of the first Catholic church, were the first Protestant churches—Methodist, Baptist, and Presbyterian—established.[34] The name change from Pig's Eye to St. Paul suggests that Pig's Eye had changed from a trading post into a more stable settlement and that first attempts at municipal organization were underway. It also reflects the residents' enthusiasm about the construction of a church in their settlement. A contemporary newspaper editor commented: "One shudders to think of what the place would have come to if it had not been rebaptized." Another editor wrote: "Pig's Eye, converted thou shalt be, like Saul; / Arise, and be, henceforth, Saint Paul."[35] St. Paul's settlers, Protestants and Catholics alike, hoped that the authority and influence of Catholicism would promote social order and morality and leaned on the authority of the Catholic Church. They therefore greeted the formal establishment of the Diocese of St. Paul and the arrival of its first bishop, the French-born Joseph Cretin, in 1851, integrated the overwhelmingly French clergymen into St. Paul's upper ranks, and praised the network of schools, hospitals, orphan asylums, and charitable organizations the Catholic Church provided. St. Paul's dependence on the Catholic Church would grant it and its clergy an enduring influence on the civic life. This influence also contributed to the development of the town's attitude toward alcohol. Whereas Catholicism frowned upon the immoderate use of liquor, it did not oppose the consumption and sale of alcohol as did most Protestant denominations. In the social life of Catholic St. Paul, liquor consumption would continue to play a significant role.[36]

Despite having a moralizing influence on St. Paul, the Catholic Church lacked the power to entirely erase lawlessness and vice in this frontier town. By the mid-1840s, formal governance was still minimal, and the only consistent business in town was the booming liquor trade. St. Paul's reputation as a whiskey stronghold was consolidated after its establishment as the capital of the new territory in 1849. That year, the *Minnesota Register* deplored that St. Paul's number of saloons was "a LEETLE [*sic*] too great for a sound and healthy state of public morals. It is the subject of remark by strangers who come among us, and gives us a bad name at home and abroad, to say nothing on the evil effects upon society." Even decades later, William Pitt Murray, one of St. Paul's first settlers, remembered the important role of liquor in the town's early years. When he arrived in 1849, he was amazed at the atmosphere in the frontier town. All people knew each other and—just for sociability's and hospitality's sake—constantly invited each other for a drink. As a consequence, Murray felt constantly drunk during his first days in town.[37]

This dominant position of liquor and saloons and the moral laxness in St. Paul's early days caused great indignation among the New Englanders, who, together with immigrants from the Middle Atlantic states, settled in St. Paul from the late 1840s on, came to dominate the city socially and economically, and took the places of St. Paul's French Canadians who retreated north.[38] John G. Rice describes the New England culture as the most homogeneous of all the various Anglo-American cultures. Even though there were old animosities, for instance, between New England Presbyterians and Congregationalists, on the one hand, and New England Baptists, Methodists, Unitarians, and Universalists, on the other, these were often eroded when they came into contact with other groups, such as Southerners or immigrants. This New England culture was highly literate, strongly middle-class, and rooted in the nonconformist, Calvinist teachings that had gained strength in England in the seventeenth century. Since they tended to regard most Westerners as uneducated, lazy, irreligious and a threat to the most fundamental American values, the New Englanders believed it their duty to move west and spread their culture. "The cultural persistence of Yankees," as Susan E. Gray has stated, "depended upon self-replication over time and through space. Yankee culture was at base a culture of hegemonic aspirations."[39] Minnesota's New Englanders also displayed such hegemonic aspirations. At the first anniversary banquet of the New England Society of the Northwest in Minneapolis in 1857, members expressed their hope that the territory would

> imitate the heroic virtues of her foster mother, till New England industry, New England enterprise, and New England thrift shall build here a glorious super-structure of education and Gospel truth, till Sabbath bells shall echo from hill-top to hill-top, and forests now untrodden shall be filled with the murmur of the common school, ensuring the intelligence and integrity of our people, and making the land we live in like the land we left.[40]

They were convinced that through their efforts Minnesota would soon become a "New England of the West," as James M. Goodhue termed it. Minnesota was to turn into an improved version of the New England they had left behind.[41]

St. Paul's New Englanders wholeheartedly agreed with John W. North's assessment of their town as "dissolute, ignorant, drunken."[42] Reverend Edward Duffield Neill, the first missionary the American Home Missionary Society sent to Minnesota, strongly criticized the significance of liquor in the city. Despite Neill's respectful attitude toward the Catholics, he stated that in a stronghold of Romanism like St. Paul the work of the Protestant clergy was very complicated. He further described St. Paul as located on the "extreme verge of the civilized world" and populated by an "ignoble" crowd of profit-oriented men of big dreams and slim means, "the glittering dollar the star of [their] ambition." Joseph C. Whitney, the American Home Missionary Society's second minister, described St. Paul as a "citadel of the devil that *must* be taken."[43] The Protestant ministers' were greatly supported by newspaper editors such as James M. Goodhue, who played a major role in emphasizing one vision of St. Paul over potential other visions in order to attract certain kinds of settlers. In the columns of his newspaper, he constantly advocated "morality and religion" and supported the Protestant clergymen in the creation of a *"moral influence in St. Paul, as mighty as ever controlled a Puritan village."* Harriet E. Bishop, the first of a significant cohort of reform-oriented New England women and the city's first public school teacher, similarly considered St. Paul "a field to be cultivated; a garden of untrained flowers to be tended." All of these New Englanders aimed at creating a cohesive moral order in the city and at turning St. Paul into a morally impeccable town that would compare to reformist New England enclaves, such as the neighboring St. Anthony.[44]

By the early 1850s, the New Englanders dominated the city socially and economically, while most immigrants, Catholics in particular, could be found at the lowest occupational level. In comparison to foreign-born workers, native-born workers—particularly those born in New England—had a better chance to achieve prosperity. In 1850, New Englanders also owned more property than any other group in St. Paul.[45] Daniel J. Fisher, the first Catholic priest ordained in the town, characterized its economic and power structure in 1852: "The Catholics are very poor here—and what is worse very irreligious and indifferent—they are Half breeds, Canadians and Irish. The Yankees have all the influence, the wealth and the power, although they are not near as numerous as the others." These social and economic disparities as well as the New Englanders' reform spirit and their uncompromising advocacy of certain middle-class norms led to their unpopularity among the town's pioneer settlers. William Pitt Murray described the New Englanders' reputation in early St. Paul from hindsight: "If there was anything an old pioneer had but little respect for, it was a Yankee."[46]

Before long, the New Englanders' quest to redefine St. Paul's civic identity led to the establishment of a temperance movement in the city. Fighting against liquor was one means to impress New England standards of morality upon St. Paul so that it would become a city upon a hill displaying "sobriety and good order." The alcoholic binges in the frontier saloons signified uncontrollability, moral decline, disorder, and dissipation. Temperance activism would counter this immorality and unpredictability and guarantee that the West would develop according to Eastern standards. Reformers also believed that a regular and orderly workforce was a prerequisite for a city's eventual economic success.[47]

St. Paul's first temperance society was formed on March 9, 1848, under the auspices of Reverend Ezekiel G. Gear, the chaplain of the garrison at Fort Snelling. Many of the thirty young St. Paulites who had signed the pledge soon resumed their liquor consumption, and the society quickly disbanded.[48] A year later, at the beginning of May, seventeen St. Paulites decided to form a more permanent temperance society. Most of these men were carpenters, blacksmiths, saddlers, and wagon makers, joined by a few lawyers; came from New England and New York; and belonged to the Methodist and Baptist denominations, such as Benjamin F. Hoyt, the city's first Methodist lay preacher and a real estate dealer, and the Baptist Abraham H. Cavender, superintendent of the first Sunday School and a carriage maker. They organized the first division of the Sons of Temperance in the territory and affiliated with the national order.[49] The St. Paul society advertised itself as an "educational organization" for aspiring entrepreneurs seeking the "attainment of power in debate" and was thus geared toward upwardly mobile young and middle-aged men who tried to dissociate themselves from the notions of masculinity prevalent at the frontier.[50]

While the Sons aimed at attracting artisans from the lower-middle social strata, about two dozen community leaders and evangelical clergymen, mostly from St. Paul but also from Stillwater and Cottage Grove, organized a Territorial Temperance Society on October 30, 1849. The society insisted on total abstinence and was led by some of St. Paul's early luminaries, such as the Presbyterian missionary Gideon H. Pond and William R. Marshall, the owner of a hardware store and a budding politician.[51] Enthused about their newly established temperance movement in the city, members of these two organizations also established the Excelsior Club No. 1 of the Temperance Watchmen in the fall of 1849, a secret temperance society that had originated in Maine that year. Its more than one hundred members worked for the enforcement of the existing liquor laws and the enactment of strict temperance laws.[52]

Between 1848 and 1851, temperance societies flourished. But the transformation of the city from a rough frontier town to a "Puritan village" occurred very slowly, much too slowly for the taste of the increasing number of New Englanders. Due to the continued drinking binges, St. Paul's temperance reformers eagerly joined the prohibitionist crusade coming out of St. Anthony, seeing it as a potential cure to St. Paul's alcoholic image and as a means to "entirely change the character of our incoming population."[53] The prospect of a Minnesota Maine Law led to an upsurge of temperance activism in the town. Groups such as the Temperance Watchmen increased their membership, cooperated with the Sons of Temperance, and began to meet on a monthly basis. On January 24, 1852, thirty of St. Paul's temperance supporters founded an auxiliary to the Territorial Temperance Society. And the 1852 petition from St. Paul in favor of a Maine Law shows that a broad coalition made up by the "elite of the city," "respectable ladies," and "the friends of law and order" strongly supported such a law. The temperance activists' shift from voluntarism to legal intervention, however, turned St. Paul into a divided city and produced civic wars in town. The focus of these wars was not merely liquor, but the very character of the city's identity.[54]

The Maine Law election at the beginning of April proved that the radical and coercive temperance agitation had created a rift in the city over the liquor issue: 343 of the city's residents voted against and 331 in favor of the law. This rift became literal at the celebration of Independence Day in 1852: One-half of St. Paulites enjoyed a "wet" celebration on Sunday, in defiance of the Maine Law, whereas the other half observed the Sabbath and celebrated together with the temperate citizens from St. Anthony and Stillwater without liquor and under the auspices of the Sons of Temperance on Monday.[55]

St. Paul also became the territory's center of Maine Law evasion, which led to repeated conflicts and clashes between the law's advocates and opponents.

County commissioners gave out liquor licenses valid beyond May 1, 1852, even though this ran counter to the law's regulations. They also refused to appoint the required agent for selling liquor for medicinal and mechanical purposes. Moreover, several St. Paulites, such as commission merchant William Constans, ignored the law by storing large amounts of alcohol, which caused a riot between the factions. Therefore, after May 1, 1852, the liquor traffic in St. Paul "went on about as usual."[56]

Due to the great opposition to the Maine Law in Minnesota's capital, its repeal was celebrated fervently. Harriet E. Bishop described the atmosphere in the city after Hayner's decision: "On the night of the repeal, a large steamboat bell was mounted upon wheels, and attended by scores of miserable beings, went booming through the streets of the capital, proclaiming death to the temperance principles, and loud hurrahs for the movers of repeal." There was, however, more behind this victory than a mere celebration of repeal, and the victory was not only celebrated by "miserable beings," as Bishop put it. Bishop, as well as her fellow New Englanders, seemed unaware that they were not only fighting against the economic interests of a flourishing liquor business but against a civic identity that had emerged years before their arrival and that was cherished by many St. Paulites. The liquor trade and lax and excessive liquor consumption had been the raison d'être for St. Paul's emergence and were integral parts of a mentality that had convinced many people to settle in the town. The early agitation for prohibition in St. Paul was thus not only a fight against intemperance, but also a struggle about the town's civic identity and about who was to be the dominant factor in shaping it.[57]

By 1854, the New Englanders' hopes for a prohibitory law and thereby the immediate transformation of St. Paul into a "Puritan village" had been shattered. Evasion or outright flouting of the liquor laws became the St. Paulites' primary strategy to undermine the effect of liquor laws imposed upon them by the territorial legislature, such as the 1854 Sunday and midnight closing laws, which were treated as dead letters in St. Paul. From the mid-1850s on, the heavy influx of immigrants, mostly of German and Irish descent, further watered down the New Englanders' chances of reforming the city. Particularly German notions of sociability and conviviality were ideally suited to St. Paul's mentality. Therefore, in those years, St. Paul's civic identity established at its founding was greatly reinvigorated, shedding most of the vestiges of New England culture it had inhaled from the late 1840s to the early 1850s.[58]

In addition, the national financial panic of 1857, resulting from a mania of speculation and the failure of the Ohio Life Insurance and Trust Company of New York, leveled St. Paul's economic hierarchies and paved the way for socio-economic immigrant influence in the city. New business alliances were formed, and ethnic and religious prejudices were often set aside because the Anglo-

American merchant class, deeply harmed by the economic collapse, needed cash. The financial panic also further solidified the position of the Catholic Church in the city, as the struggling residents were greatly dependent on its aid. Thus, by the late 1850s, St. Paul had become a very attractive place for immigrants who aimed at advancing socially and economically. Due to their sheer numbers and their economic importance to the city, they could not be denied a say in its political, economic, and social affairs and took an active part in shaping St. Paul's civic identity. The lack of reform spirit in the city is nicely encapsulated by a temperance reformer, who, in the winter of 1857, assessed Minnesota's capital to be "rather an unpromising field" for temperance activities.[59]

St. Paul's (Irish) Catholics and the Maine Law

It would, however, be a gross simplification to claim that only New Englanders and other Anglo-American Protestants had taken part in the campaign for a Maine Law. St. Paul's Catholic community also joined the temperance movement, but for entirely different reasons. Rather than wanting to reform St. Paul and to change its incoming population, the city's (Irish) Catholics, or rather Bishop Joseph Cretin, strategically employed the temperance movement to advance his flock socially and economically and to keep abreast of Protestant efforts.

Only a small proportion of the total population of Irish immigrants reached the frontier in Minnesota, often after a staged migration. Because of their poverty after the potato famine in Ireland in the mid- and late 1840s, most of the Irish remained in the great cities of the East. As early as the 1840s, Irish lumberjacks were employed in Minnesota's St. Croix Valley. From 1850 on, southeastern Minnesota, especially the counties along the Mississippi and Minnesota rivers, became the first major region of Irish settlement in Minnesota. The Mississippi Valley farther south also turned into an area of Irish settlement. St. Paul, as the state capital, a Democratic stronghold, and the heart of a large Catholic diocese, evolved into the religious, political, and social center of the Irish in Minnesota. Even though most of St. Paul's Irish lived in the neighborhoods near downtown, they generally spread throughout the city and had no exclusively Irish wards. Wingerd interprets this pattern of residential dispersion as a key element of Irish influence. The Irish moved into every quarter of St. Paul and were thus capable of exerting their influence on a broad basis. Since they still maintained their ethnic ties, a complex set of ethnic networks developed. These strong ethnic networks also derived from the relative homogeneity of the Irish as a group. They were not divided by culture, language, geographical origin, religion, and political affiliation and therefore displayed a great degree of ethnic unity and solidarity.[60]

From a socioeconomic point of view, St. Paul's Irish were at a disadvantage compared to other immigrant groups, such as the Germans. The majority of them arrived without any capital and particular skills. In 1850, half of St. Paul's Irish worked as unskilled laborers. A decade later, the situation had not changed: Only 12 percent of the Irish were engaged in any trade, and few of them were involved in interethnic commercial enterprises. They also had to struggle against the derogatory stereotypes they had brought with them from the East. They were often seen as heavy drinkers, ignorant, ungrateful, impudent, dirty, manipulable, and narrow-minded.[61] As a result of their economic and social background, the Irish were not welcome in St. Paul, as an editorial statement in the *Minnesotian* demonstrates: "We hope to gracious none of the Paddies will hear where St. Paul is." One of Minnesota's legislators even called them "the worst class of citizens." Their low socioeconomic position and their bad reputation were the major reasons for Bishop Cretin to involve his (Irish) Catholic flock in the Anglo-American temperance movement.[62]

Catholic temperance activism was not without precedent, either in the United States or in Minnesota Territory. By the 1840s, Irish Catholic temperance societies had been established in various dioceses along the East Coast to counter the popularity of liquor among Catholics. In Minnesota, Catholic involvement in the temperance movement began as early as 1839. That year, Father Lucien Galtier, instigated by Bishop Mathias Loras of the Diocese of Dubuque to which Minnesota belonged at the time, formed a temperance society in St. Peter, the settlement adjacent to Fort Snelling. Lacking an agenda, however, the St. Peter organization soon became ineffective.[63]

Despite such Irish Catholic lay temperance activism, the American Catholic hierarchy remained ambivalent about the temperance movement. At their Fourth Provincial Council in Baltimore in 1840, the American bishops offered encouragement to temperance activists but did not speak out in favor of total abstinence. They felt that they could not recommend abstinence from a beverage "which the Sacred Scriptures do not prohibit, and of which the most holy persons have occasionally partaken." Three years later, they commended total abstinence but defended the moderate use of liquor and stressed that no person should feel obliged to become a total abstainer. They also cautioned those interested in total abstinence to stay away from non-Catholic groups.

Antebellum Irish temperance activism reached its climax when between 1849 and 1851 Father Theobald Mathew, the Capuchin temperance apostle from Ireland, visited twenty-five of the then thirty-one states and more than three hundred towns and administered the pledge to over five hundred thousand Irish Americans, that is, to about one-third of the total Irish population in North America. After Mathew's departure, however, many of those who had taken the pledge broke it, and the Irish American temperance movement declined in the 1850s and 1860s.[64]

Considering these historical circumstances, Cretin's decision to found a Catholic temperance movement to support Protestant prohibitionist efforts was unusual for a Catholic clergyman, especially since he had himself not been a total abstainer before migrating from France to America. Writing to his sister in 1841, he praised the success of the temperance movement in the United States. He told her about how he had taken the pledge and not touched any liquor during the past eight months. Both Bishop Loras's influence and the American drinking habits must have prompted Cretin to become a supporter of the movement. The poverty, low social status, and insobriety of the majority of his congregants in St. Paul and their social and economic domination by the Protestant New Englanders certainly also convinced him to labor for the eradication of alcohol. Cretin's support of the Maine Law agitation in Minnesota proves scholars, such as John F. Quinn, wrong who claim that no Catholic leaders took part in the Protestant drive for a Maine Law.[65]

Irish temperance activism in St. Paul began on the second Sunday in January 1852, when Cretin invited all of the city's Catholics to meet at his house to found the Catholic Temperance Society of St. Paul. Membership lists reveal that the majority of members were of French-Canadian and Irish descent and came from all walks of life. Every Catholic above the age of twelve could become a member, so entire families can be found within the society's ranks. Cretin knew from the start that it would be difficult to attract Catholics merely by endorsing the principle of total abstinence. Therefore, he included certain benevolent features, such as sick benefits, into the society's agenda. These benevolent features underline its focus on personal and economic advancement rather than on communal discipline.[66]

In February 1852, the Catholic temperance society decided to take part in the Protestant campaign for a Maine Law in order "not to stay behind." This argumentation illustrates that the majority of Catholics were generally not thoroughly convinced of the necessity of a prohibitory law but considered the fight for a Maine Law an opportunity to vie with the Protestants in their efforts against alcohol. In addition, Catholic leaders like Cretin might have seen Catholic participation as an opportunity to cooperate with the city's Protestant social and economic elite and thus as a chance for Catholics to move up the social ladder.[67]

The Protestant temperance activists were greatly surprised at the Catholic participation in their Maine Law campaign. John W. North wrote to his parents-in-law: "To the astonishment of everybody the French Catholics, with the Priests have come out actively and unitedly for the law." Eager for support, they invited

the Catholic society to partake in their parade in favor of a Maine Law, an invitation the Catholic temperance society accepted. On February 16, 1852, St. Paul's
Catholics headed the temperance parade, carrying a costly and elaborate banner
and wearing badges with their pledge attached to their clothes. Many Catholics also signed the petitions in favor of a Maine Law. Besides the signatures of
numerous members of Cretin's temperance society, there can be found that of
Richard Ireland, the father of Minnesota's future famous prelate and temperance
advocate John Ireland. After the passage of the law, the Catholic Temperance
Society also supported the Protestants in their law enforcement efforts.[68]

Since early Catholic temperance activism was rooted in strategic motives
rather than in moral ideals, the Catholic Temperance Society began to stagnate
shortly after the passage and ratification of the Maine Law. From April to June
1852, attendance at the monthly meetings was very low. On August 8, 1852, the
society split into two different branches, one for the Irish and one for the French
to ease language difficulties. Cretin seemed to have favored the split and urged
each group to acquire new members. He also erected two large scrolls in the
Cathedral with the names of all the society's members, probably as an incentive
to join the cause.[69]

Measures like these were geared toward keeping current members involved
and toward gaining new ones, which reveals that not all of St. Paul's Catholics
had joined Cretin's society. In fact, many of them strongly opposed prohibition.
In April 1853, there were about 800 Catholics in St. Paul. The only membership
list of the Catholic temperance society dates from March 1852 and records 145
people. Since membership in the Catholic Temperance Society began declining
a few months after its founding, it is safe to assume that it never had significantly more than 145 members. Accordingly, it can be concluded that about 650
Catholics were either children younger than twelve years, indifferent, or opposed
to the temperance cause. Furthermore, only about 30 percent of the 145 Irish
temperance advocates had taken the pledge for life. The other 70 percent had
apparently joined the society for more pragmatic reasons—social benefits and
social advancement—or out of spontaneous excitement.[70]

Due to a dearth of sources, the precise identity of the Catholic opponents to
the Maine Law is hard to reveal. In a letter to Archbishop John Ireland in 1895,
Father Georg Keller, the fifth priest to be ordained by Cretin, described how the
latter had been antagonized by St. Paul's German Catholics for his temperance
efforts. Once, Keller wrote, the bishop had been greatly insulted by a German
saloon owner, who had offered him a glass of beer. Had not Cretin intervened,
the Irish part of the congregation would have pulled the saloon down.[71] Many
French and Irish Catholics also refused to take part in the movement. Louis
Robert, the leader of the French population in St. Paul, protested his bishop's
temperance efforts by prohibiting him to ring the Cathedral bell—a donation

by Robert—after the ratification of the Maine Law. Robert's and many Irish names appear on petitions against prohibition.[72]

This strong opposition to temperance by a large number of Catholics made the Catholic temperance movement vulnerable. The membership drives inaugurated by Cretin throughout 1852 did not show the promised success, and the minutes of the French and Irish Catholic temperance societies increasingly reveal internal strife. Obviously, the Irish Catholic temperance advocates had been offended by the division of the society into two branches, feeling discriminated against on grounds of their nationality. Despite attempts to resolve such tensions, the decline in membership continued in 1853. In the middle of August, the two branches decided to reunite immediately to ensure continuity. After August 1853, there are no more minutes of the Catholic Temperance Society. In June 1854, Bishop Cretin tried to reorganize the society in vain.[73] Although Cretin continued to inculcate his ideals of temperance into his priests, he had realized that a total abstinence movement was impossible to maintain among his parishioners. In 1854, he gave Father Georg Keller the following advice: "You are going to your first mission. You will find there saloons and poor people supporting them—tell them that to take a glass of vine [sic] or beer or whisque [sic] is not a great sin may be no sin at all but it is a great virtue to abstain from taking it for charity sake and for the good example to keep away the poor people from the saloon." By 1857, the year of Cretin's death, all of his temperance efforts among Catholics had vanished. A visitor who came to St. Paul that year declared that among the Catholics of the city "there was no talk of temperance and the word 'total abstinence' was not known."[74]

The early Catholic temperance movement was not a success story. Initiated by Cretin for strategic purposes, it was joined by many French and Irish Catholics out of spontaneous excitement rather than from a deep desire to reform prevalent drinking patterns. Only by the 1870s would the Irish Catholic wish for social advancement become so pressing that a long-lasting and large-scale Catholic temperance movement emerged, seeking to negotiate Irish identity. Such middle-class aspirations, however, did not yet exist at midcentury.

German Americans and the Antebellum Temperance Movement

The years between 1855 and the Civil War laid the basis for the German American opposition to the temperance movement. German Americans learned to use their ever-increasing numerical strength to successfully put pressure on the Republican Party, the St. Paul City Council, and the state legislature. The temperance issue mobilized German Americans from a variety of different regional, religious, political, and social backgrounds. Interethnic clashes with the

Anglo-Americans, as well as intraethnic debates with the German Methodists, forced them to strengthen their ethnic boundaries and to define some of the cultural contents they enclosed. In the context of the temperance movement, St. Paul's newly emerging German American community identified its culture of drinking and relaxation as a core value that the majority of its members shared. Through this core value, St. Paul's German Americans developed the rudiments of an ethnic group consciousness, began to mobilize their compatriots all over Minnesota, and took the leadership in the fight against coercive liquor legislation. In the context of the temperance debates, German American leaders became increasingly aware of the potential value of the temperance movement with its strong Anglo-American underpinnings as a constitutive outside against which a wide array of St. Paul's heterogeneous German Americans could identify.

The German element in Minnesota was strong. In 1860, almost every seventh Minnesotan was either German-born or of German parentage; in 1880, it was almost every fifth.[75] At the turn of the century, the Germans were still the leading foreign-born group in the state, and even when foreign-born Germans dropped to second place behind the foreign-born Swedes in 1905, American-born Germans remained by far the largest ethnic group in Minnesota. Ramsey County housed more Germans than any other county, with most of them living in St. Paul. The German element in St. Paul was, however, not as dominant as it was in New Ulm or Stearns County, because the city was more ethnically mixed.[76]

As a group, the St. Paul Germans, like Minnesota's Germans in general, were very diverse. They came from all walks of life and belonged to different denominations. There were German Catholics, Lutherans, Baptists, Methodists, Presbyterians, Jews, and freethinking Turners in the city. In addition to their religious heterogeneity, German Americans also displayed a geographical diversity: They came from different regions in Germany, such as Bavaria, Prussia, the Eiffel region, Hanover, Baden, Hesse, Wuerttemberg, and Westphalia and therefore spoke different dialects, leading to a certain degree of linguistic diversity.[77]

Most of St. Paul's German Americans arrived in the city with a combination of skills and capital and were familiar with the rules of a capitalist economy. Many of them were artisans, shopkeepers, and landowning farmers rather than peasants or manual laborers. Since St. Paul needed immigrants with skills and capital, these Germans were received with open arms. St. Paul's *Minnesota Democrat* considered the German newcomers as a "valuable acquisition" and as "republican, moral, industrious, thrifty, law-abiding and intelligent." Due to such views, St. Paul's large German American community was from the start unusually well-integrated into the city's business class, which becomes evident by the fair amount of interethnic businesses. As early as 1860, German Americans had found their niches in St. Paul's economy: 26 percent of the German-born males were engaged in trade and service, another 27 percent were in manufacturing, and only 14 percent worked as common laborers. Their solid socioeconomic position was one of the various factors that shaped their attitude toward the temperance movement.[78]

In St. Paul, there were extensive insular German neighborhoods in the heart of the city. Germans settled along the Upper Levee, near West 7th Street, and across the Mississippi on the lower West Side. German Catholic families also concentrated near Dale and Thomas Streets in Frogtown. In those vibrant ethnic enclaves, German American ethnic culture rapidly developed. This culture was largely based on such essential features as the love Germans had for their language and traditions from their homeland. This common heritage inspired them to establish parochial and private nonsectarian schools, associations—some across, others separated along regional lines—and more than twenty German-language newspapers.[79]

German Americans were famous for their lifestyle. They had brought with them to America a delight in relaxation, a love of nature, strolls, comfortable picnics, songs, dances, and extravagant public feasts, all enjoyed with a glass of beer, wine, or schnapps. Drinking was associated with *Gemütlichkeit* (sociability), and taverns were seen as embodiments of this sociability. Beer was widely propagated and endorsed as the quintessentially German ethnic beverage due to its alleged nutritional value, its low percentage of alcohol, and its promotion of conviviality. In the process of German migration, the importance of *Gemütlichkeit* even increased. German Americans—especially those migrating because of the failed 1848 Revolution—were confronted with the task of creating a German American ethnic identity out of the various regional German cultures that were assembled in St. Paul. They did not have to start from scratch, however. Since the eighteenth century, there flourished among the intellectual elites of the German League (*Deutscher Bund*) a linguistic and cultural self-awareness, which peaked in the nineteenth century. Even though the establishment of a national identity had to wait until the founding of the German Empire in 1871, a cultural identity had begun forming much earlier.[80] A German American ethnic identity would have to be based on the "reconstruction of historical culture," that is, on certain core values dear to the majority of Germans. *Gemütlichkeit* was such a core value, uniting German Americans from different regions, religions, and social strata. It was cultivated in beer gardens, parlors, backyards, and taverns and included food, drink, fellowship, and festivity. For German Americans, Sunday was the quintessential day of relaxation and often celebrated with a keg of beer (see figure 1.2).

Their taverns and beer gardens became the social and cultural focal points of St. Paul's German American community. Taverns were often meeting places of various associations, and tavern keepers acted as counselors, located jobs, arranged land sales, and actively influenced politics. Located on the outskirts

Figure 1.2. German American St. Paulites celebrating their Sunday over a keg of beer, circa 1885. Courtesy of the Minnesota Historical Society.

of the city, near parks, or attached to breweries, beer gardens were even more popular than taverns. Whereas the American or Irish saloon was an exclusively male sphere, German beer gardens were open to all family members. They functioned as extensions of the home and embodied a connection between drinking, leisure time, and social life. For German immigrants, their taverns and beer gardens were an integral part of their culture, an essential feature of their ethnic identity, and maintained a certain unity among this otherwise diverse ethnic group. Therefore, they could not possibly accept an attack on those cultural institutions.[81]

The centrality of alcohol in their lives also led to the German Americans' strong presence in St. Paul's liquor business. The Bavarian Anthony Yoerg established the state's first brewery in St. Paul as early as 1849. Other German brewers, such as Martin Bruggemann, Gottfried Fleckenstein, and Christopher Stahlmann followed, only to name some of the German pioneer brewers. In 1865, Theodore Hamm took over Andrew Keller's Pittsburgh Brewery, which he turned into the state's largest brewery within two decades. Other Germans, such as Charles Rausch, Fred Luhrsen, and John Wagner, ran some of the city's earliest and most popular saloons, while many of their compatriots, such as John E. Haggenmiller, Franz A. Renz, and Georg Benz, engaged in the wholesale liquor trade and continuously expanded their businesses over the next decades. Alcohol was thus not merely cherished by German Americans for its cultural value, but it was also an indispensable source of economic profit.[82]

Organized German American opposition to the temperance movement emerged in the mid-1850s. Between 1850 and 1860 the number of German-born residents of Ramsey County grew from 27 to 1,851. Their increasing numerical strength allowed them to make their opinion felt. The 1855 election was the first occasion on which St. Paul's German Americans articulated their aversion to temperance and acted as an ethnic interest group. Both the newly founded Republican Party and the Democrats vied for the German vote. The majority of St. Paul's German Americans were in a quandary: Opposed to prohibition as well as to slavery, they could not vote consistently for any of the candidates—neither for the Republican William R. Marshall, who was opposed to the Kansas-Nebraska bill but a temperance man, nor for the Democrat Henry M. Rice, an opponent of a Maine Law but an advocate of the Kansas-Nebraska bill.[83]

At a loss about whom to vote for, about one hundred Germans met at St. Paul's Court House on August 21, 1855, organized a political club called "German Democracy," and unanimously declared to be opposed to nativism, a Maine Law, and the extension of slavery. While they decided to support a third candidate, David Olmsted, the candidate of the other Democratic wing, as he declared openly in favor of the German platform, a meeting of another two hundred and fifty Germans taking place a few days later, however, spoke out in favor of Rice, considering Olmsted unfit for office. The fact that the still relatively small number of the city's German Americans were unable to agree upon the same candidate reflects their divisiveness. However, the temperance movement facilitated a certain degree of political unity. Despite being divided about which Democrat, Rice or Olmsted, to support, all of them agreed that the Republican Marshall's leanings toward a prohibitory law made him ineligible and therefore did not give their votes to the Republican Party. When a newspaper editor asked a St. Paul German whom he favored in the coming election he answered: "[W]ell, sir, I will tell you what I honestly think. When you come to judge of the true merits of the men, Marshall, is in my opinion, decidedly the best man; but then you know there are considerations ahead, aside from this however, I don't like that Maine Law, but I like Mr. Marshall. He is an honest man." Opposition to temperance acted as a political unifier keeping Germans in Minnesota's Democratic Party even though many of them were opposed to the extension of slavery.[84]

Aside from these political quarrels, conflicts about temperance were often also of a religious nature. Scholars have long emphasized the close connection between people's religious identities and their attitudes toward the temperance movement. Paul Kleppner and Richard Jensen have identified two polar theological positions and have labeled them *pietistic* and *ritualistic* or *liturgical*. Pietists practiced a relatively informal form of worship, emphasized a personal and fervent faith in a transcendental God, and actively worked for conversion, change of heart, and personal piety. Ritualists stressed formal doctrine and held the church responsible for all matters concerning morality and salvation. With respect to the issue of temperance, pietists believed that the government had to remove institutionalized immorality, such as Sunday drinking, saloons, intemperance, and slavery, because it was a major obstacle to the purification of society through revivalist Christianity. Ritualists, by contrast, opposed Sunday Laws and prohibition and were afraid that the pietists would gain governmental control and impose their standards of morality on them. By the 1860s, the Methodists, Congregationalists, Disciples, United Brethren, and Quakers in the Midwest were predominantly pietistic, while the Episcopalians and Catholics were predominantly ritualistic. Both Presbyterians and Baptists were divided into pietistic and liturgical camps. The Lutherans, to whom many German and the later Scandinavian immigrants belonged, also had both liturgical and pietistic factions with most German Lutherans belonging to the former.[85]

Most of the German immigrants who poured into St. Paul in the 1850s were liturgical in outlook and thus strongly opposed to any coercive temperance efforts. Their religious identity greatly reinforced their aversion to temperance on ethnic and economic grounds. St. Paul's anticlerical Germans, especially freethinkers such as Samuel Ludvigh, the editor of St. Paul's *Staats-Zeitung*, abhorred all mingling of religion and politics, considered temperance reformers religious zealots, and were therefore strongly opposed to the temperance movement's entrance into politics. There were, however, also German pietists in the city. In the spring of 1851, Reverend Jacob Haas established the first congregation of German Methodists, numbering about forty congregants two years later. Their conversion to Methodism, which was unknown in Germany and had long held temperance as a key tenet, had already meant a renunciation of German traditions. Close links with the English-speaking Methodists further promoted cultural adaptation. Therefore, some of the early German Methodists, such as Ferdinand Knauft and Jacob Haas, can be found on the membership lists of temperance organizations or on the petitions for a Maine Law. These pietistic Germans emphasized their religious identity over their ethnic identity. Being Methodist meant being opposed to liquor, while being German generally implied cherishing liquor as part of one's culture. The temperance movement forced Methodist Germans to come down on one side of the fence, to declare one identity more salient than the other. Whether their decision in favor of religion was a strategic one, made in order to integrate themselves more easily into American society, or whether it was based on religious conviction cannot be determined. Their decision in favor of temperance, however, inevitably brought them into conflict with their liturgical and freethinking compatriots. In conflicts over the issue of temperance, Knauft, for instance, regularly sided with the Anglo-American Methodist ministers, even though the latter accused St. Paul's Germans of desiring lager beer and schnapps rather than religion.[86]

Aside from these occasional intraethnic quarrels, the temperance movement mostly led to interethnic debates. In the antebellum era, those debates primarily occurred between the liturgical and freethinking German Americans, on the one hand, and the large number of Anglo-American temperance advocates on the other. The issue of Sunday Observance, that is, the closing of saloons on Sunday, was the major point of contention between these ethnic groups. It offended class, religious, and ethnic sensibilities and triggered a struggle about St. Paul's civic identity and about who was to be the dominant factor in shaping it.

The conflict about Sunday liquor selling began in early March 1858 when, after a riot had occurred in a St. Paul saloon on Sunday, the editor of the *Minnesotian* provocatively asked whether there was no law regulating Sunday liquor selling. He thereby instigated a public controversy in the city about whether the Sunday Law, already on the statute books since 1854, was to be enforced. The inclusion of such a Sunday Law in St. Paul's statute books proves the New Englanders' dominance of the city in the late 1840s and early '50s. The fact that it had long not been enforced, however, reflects the waning influence of these New Englanders and the city's emerging strategy of law evasion. In the context of the saloon riot of 1858, however, Mayor Norman W. Kittson expressed his intention to enforce the city's existing ordinances concerning vice and immorality. On Sunday, May 23, 1858, all saloons had to be closed, with the measure strictly enforced by the police.[87]

On the one hand, the debate about the enforcement of the Sunday Law can be read as a class conflict. While drinking was a cross-class phenomenon, saloongoing was not. Members of the middle and upper classes mostly consumed alcohol at home, in private clubs, or in expensive hotels and restaurants. The laborers, by contrast, enjoyed their beer or whiskey in public drinking places. A complex interaction of social forces led to the saloon's prominence in working-class social life all over the country. From the 1830s on, employers increasingly issued rules against workday drinking and tightened discipline during working hours. Simultaneously, workdays were shortened, and the workers' wages increased. Alcohol, as labor historians have argued, played a significant role in the establishment of an integrative working-class culture and became a cherished consumer item associated with and affordable during leisure hours. Laborers spent much of their free time in saloons because they offered the basic amenities of home, such as drink, food, shelter, and companionship. Saloons thus became "the axis of the recreational world" of the workers and became commonly known as "the poor man's club." This latter moniker also characterized the saloon as a male preserve to which "respectable" women had no access. As they were excluded from the saloon, women's drinking remained largely invisible.

It elicited universal disgust, as it raised the specter of both sexual promiscuity and domestic neglect and thus posed a severe threat to the contemporary gender ideology. Therefore, contemporaries considered it taboo and avoided its discussion.[88]

Male working-class public drinking, by contrast, led to severe criticism by temperance reformers, most of them belonging to the middle and upper classes, for its detrimental impact on the productivity and social advancement of the workers and the economic efficiency of industrial America. By reforming the recreational practices of the working class, among them saloon-going on Sundays, temperance reformers, in cooperation with the Protestant industrial elite, sought to impose on them the work and leisure ethic of industrial America. This middle- and upper-class perspective is embodied in the *Minnesotian*. Instead of passing their time according to middle-class standards, enjoying "the more ennobling pleasures of the home circle, or the church, or a ramble amongst the silent lessons of Nature," workers often spent their whole week's wages in the saloon on Sunday. They also spent the limited leisure time they had with other men rather than with their wives and children.[89]

On the other hand, the debate about the enforcement of the Sunday Law was an ethnic as well as a religious issue. Nonpietistic or freethinking immigrants, such as Samuel Ludvigh, often perceived the Sunday Law as the last remnant of the tyrannical Puritan Blue Laws and considered the imposition of the Puritan Sabbath upon a free people against the spirit of freedom embodied by the American Constitution. Legal bodies, the freethinker Ludvigh naturally thought, should not interfere with religion, and religion should be limited to the individual.[90]

From August 1858 on, German protest against the Sunday Law mounted. Many of St. Paul's German clubs evaded the law by moving beyond the city limits for their celebrations. The Germania Club's picnic at the beginning of August was held in West St. Paul, where the Sunday Law was not enforced. German St. Paulites even drafted a petition against the law, which they handed to the city council. Their agitation, however, prompted the law's Anglo-American supporters to action, who drafted a petition remonstrating against its repeal. Both petitions were transferred to a special committee and were not heard of any more, and the Sunday Law remained on the statute books.[91]

The German petition against the Sunday Law provoked extensive debates in St. Paul's newspapers. These debates were not merely discussions about the workers' or immigrants' consumption of lager beer on Sundays but also about which policy to adopt toward the latter—one of tolerance or coercive assimilation. Whereas many native-born Americans believed that the German immigrants should adapt to American customs and traditions, some of them were critical of the Sunday Law and its suppression of foreign cultures. An

Anglo-American visitor expressed how shocked he was about the intolerance of many Anglo-American St. Paulites toward the city's German community. To him such intolerance was "entirely repugnant to the spirit of American liberty." He found that an "active class of this community" favored the Puritanical view of the Sabbath, but that this view should not be imposed upon everyone. As the Germans considered the Sunday Law a "galling tyranny," they should be granted the same social privileges they had enjoyed in their fatherland.[92]

Due to such irreconcilable views, the question of Sunday Observance could not be resolved and reemerged time and again in the years to come. The Sunday Law remained on the statute books without being strictly enforced. The inability of the Sunday Law advocates to have it enforced is another proof that historical realities—the change in demographics and socioeconomic hierarchies—had changed the city's internal dynamics. The immigrants, primarily the Germans, had become a force to be reckoned with when defining the outline of municipal policies.

German American influence also came to increasingly shape the politics of the state of Minnesota, which had been admitted to the Union on May 11, 1858. German brewers, especially those from St. Paul, made their influence felt in the legislature and lobbied for laws promoting their product. As the center of the state's brewing industry, St. Paul was the home of twelve breweries in 1858, with an average annual capacity of 1,250 barrels. Due to the significance of beer for Minnesota's budding industry, the legislative session of 1858 catered to the brewers' interests by passing a license act introducing a lower license and lower bond fees for beer than for other liquors. In 1860, the legislators even went one step further. They passed "An Act to encourage the manufacture of Pure Lager Beer, and to discourage the use of Alcoholic Liquors." This law provided that those saloon owners who sold beer manufactured in Minnesota did not have to pay for a license and punished anyone adulterating lager beer or other malt liquors. Rather than being an anti-temperance measure, the so-called Lager Beer Act sought to protect the state's brewers from competitors from other Midwestern states, especially from beer-brewing Wisconsin.[93]

The group unhappiest about the Lager Beer Act was the temperance reformers, who recognized that it contradicted their efforts to curb the sale of liquor. Aside from distilled liquors, beer had increasingly become the target of temperance activists in Minnesota. When the Minnesota Grand Lodge of the Independent Order of Good Templars was founded in 1857, its founders included malt liquors into their abstinence pledge, while it took the Grand Lodge of North America until May 1858 to consider the consumption of lager beer and cider a violation of the pledge.[94] Beer only became popular in the United States after the arrival of large numbers of Germans from the mid-1850s on. Contemporary Daniel Dorchester even spoke of a "beer invasion" that befell

America. Beer presented an even greater problem to the temperance forces than whiskey because its low alcoholic content made it socially far more acceptable than whiskey. The introduction of lager beer also provoked the development of a new saloon culture, which was more desirable than the older drinking shops. The lager beer saloon became a social institution, as it provided food and music along with beer.[95]

Due to the temperance reformers' sensitivity toward the dangers of beer, their reaction to the Lager Beer Act came promptly. Led by the Minnesota Annual Conference of the Methodist Episcopal Church, they organized a Minnesota Temperance Union in St. Paul on January 17, 1861, whose primary object was to promote the cause of temperance in Minnesota by repealing the act. In a memorandum to the legislature, they argued that beer corrupted the human system, led to immorality and dissipation, and fueled an appetite for strong drink. The memorandum also questioned Minnesota's strong economic reliance on the brewing industry. If the manufacture of alcohol became entrenched in the economic structure of the state, "a power would arise, trained around the precincts of thousands of liquor shops, controlling our politics and legislation, corrupting our judicial integrity, debasing the moral sentiment of society, staining our reputation, weakening our energy and blasting the fairest prospects that ever animated the hopes of an infant commonwealth." An influential beer industry would harm the moral and material advancement of the state and nip its "noble mission for mankind" in the bud. Such arguments reveal that the debate about the Lager Beer Act threw into sharp relief different moral and economic visions about the future of the recently admitted Minnesota and its function in the Union. While many settlers, led by the state's German American community, saw a flourishing brewing industry as one route to economic and social success as well as stability, others envisioned Minnesota as a morally impeccable "state upon a hill" that would counterbalance the social unrest and the immorality supposedly prevalent in many parts of the East. The temperance movement in the Midwest thus offered a stage for discussions about the social and economic parameters of the newly established states and about which ethnic and religious groups of settlers would have the major say in defining these parameters.[96]

The legislature, however, treated the memorandum jocularly and, after juggling it back and forth between various committees, refused to repeal the Lager Beer Act. The rationale behind the legislators' action is easy to explain: The majority of Minnesotans, especially the state's German community, were against the act's repeal. They considered lager beer a healthy alternative to distilled liquors and thought that locally manufactured lager beer should be promoted, as its manufacture could be controlled and the economic profits would be kept at home. Furthermore, after experiencing German voters' prompt reaction to attacks on their favorite beverage, both Republican and Democratic legislators handled the lager beer controversy with the greatest care and were careful not to offend any ethnic sensibilities.[97]

After another year of struggle and pressure by Minnesota's pietistic denominations, the pietists seemed to have succeeded. In 1862, the legislature amended the 1858 License Act, which amounted to a repeal of the Lager Beer Act. This new, modified License Act charged the same license and bond fees for malt and intoxicating liquors and drastically reduced those fees. However, the new License Act was supplemented by an amendment stating that "the provisions of this act shall not apply to the city of St. Paul." As a consequence, the St. Paul City Council decided to lower the license for selling beer from $50 to $25.[98]

Thus, the victory of the temperance forces was limited. Even though the Lager Beer Act was formally repealed, the brewers suffered little actual loss from the new License Act, as the required license fee was small and as the center of the beer brewing industry, St. Paul, was exempted from the law. German American political power, on both city and state levels, constantly worked against the reformers' temperance efforts and toward the consolidation of the brewing power in Minnesota. The lager beer controversy was one of the struggles over the competing visions of Minnesota's future, and Minnesota's German Americans had demonstrated that their voice in this debate could not be ignored any more.

By the beginning of the Civil War, a German American opposition to the temperance movement had formed, and the process of constructing a German American ethnic identity had been initiated. It was not until after the war, however, that the German intelligentsia exploited the movement's increasing radicalism to initiate the invention of a German American ethnic identity, which could then be exported to German American communities in the rest of Minnesota.

Women's Temperance Work until the Civil War

The temperance movement was the first major cause in Minnesota for which women left their homes. Women suffered disproportionately from alcohol abuse: While most of them were not intemperate themselves, they were often physically abused by their intoxicated husbands and had to bear the consequences from their husbands' inability to provide for the family. Legally disadvantaged, women could neither control their own—nor their husbands'—wages and were thus completely at their spouses' mercy. Alcohol embodied women's vulnerable position within the family and made it possible to talk about that vulnerability without challenging family structures or directly attacking men. Many women also greatly disliked the saloon, as it constituted an exclusively male public sphere they could not control and posed a danger to their families. The temperance movement also managed to mobilize women to an unprecedented degree, as its deep roots in American Protestantism enabled it to profit from already existing Protestant networks. Although thus initially not about identity politics, female reform work offered women the opportunity to carefully venture into and become acquainted with the workings of the public sphere and created a space in which women and men could debate their different understandings of gender.[99]

Bruce Dorsey has argued that in antebellum Philadelphia the temperance movement was a contest between competing versions of masculinity, which had derived from a generational conflict between fathers and sons. The latter distanced themselves from the intemperate habits of their fathers and thus declared their independence from a masculinity linked to drink. The reformers, Dorsey remarks, "constructed notions of manhood that were in opposition to other men rather than directly in opposition to the category of 'woman.'" Holly Berkley Fletcher similarly portrays the temperance movement as a means of resolving uncertainties about male gender identities. In the antebellum years, men were at once expected to embody the values of the marketplace and had to be affectionate members of virtuous homes. She argues that through their temperance activities middle-class men could reconcile these competing claims of masculinity. Temperance organizations thus "served a positive function for male gender identity" by promoting "the two basic claims of middle-class manhood—success in the marketplace and domestication at home."[100]

However, Dorsey writes about Philadelphia and Fletcher has no geographical focus; thus, they neglect regional and local differences. Minnesota's capital, St. Paul, was a newly established frontier town and differed widely from most settings in the East at that time. It attracted only those settlers who accepted its rough pioneer mentality, including a numerical under-representation of women and an over-representation of alcohol in daily life. Alcohol's popularity derived from the importance of the saloon, which proved an indispensable and multifunctional institution on the frontier. Until settlers established a government, banks, schools, hospitals, libraries, and other social, political, and economic institutions, the saloon served as a community center, club, hotel, information exchange, and gathering place. It was a place where business and money transactions were made and where boredom was alleviated through such entertainment as billiards. At the frontier, drinking also served as an undeniable feature of masculine identity and as a proof of the prevalent egalitarianism. Young and middle-aged men equally participated in this male frontier culture, so that one cannot speak of generational disagreements. This frontier mentality, almost entirely male in character, was challenged by the arrival of the New Englanders in the late 1840s and 1850s. They brought with them notions of a middle-class masculinity that contradicted the pioneer masculinity of St. Paul's early settlers. Whereas the former emphasized sobriety as a marker of masculinity, the latter celebrated alcohol consumption as an integral part of male identity. Rather than a struggle between generations or different notions of middle-class masculinity, the temperance movement in early St. Paul displayed a competition between a pioneer and middle-class New England masculinity.[101]

Interpreting the temperance movement as a struggle between different versions of masculinity makes it appear a primarily male experience. And to a great degree, this is what it was in Minnesota's early days. The antebellum temperance movement existed primarily as a male province, led and dominated by men. But this does not mean that women were invisible in the fight against alcohol and that this fight was not as essential to their femininity as it was to masculinity. Since the movement's beginning, women acted as supporters of the men, as shining examples of morality, or as the victim of the male drunkard's addiction. St. Paul's first temperance society was established with the support of a woman, Harriet E. Bishop. Women also contributed to the men's fight for a Maine Law by participating in demonstrations and processions, sewing banners, attending temperance conventions, preparing banquets, and signing petitions against the Maine Law. They were also present at all kinds of dry celebrations and even allowed to raise toasts—nonalcoholic ones, of course. Individual women played very prominent roles in the temperance campaigns. John W. North's wife, Ann, copied the Minnesota version of the Maine Law that was later handed to the territory's legislative assembly and wrote a speech for the presentation of the temperance banner. Irish Catholic and French Catholic women also contributed to the temperance cause. The membership list of St. Paul's Catholic Temperance Society shows that of the 145 members about 40 were women and girls above the age of twelve.[102]

The speeches of the territory's male temperance leaders reveal that they were aware that in order to secure the passage of a Maine Law they needed the women's support. Therefore, they declared temperance conventions open to both sexes and explicitly appealed to women for their numerical support and their moral authority.[103] Repeatedly, men expressed their joy about women's participation in the cause. At a temperance convention in St. Paul on February 22, 1853, male temperance leaders rejoiced: "The women are with us, and that proves that we are on the right side!" This quotation proves that "female aid," as Fletcher argues, "gave temperance forces an edge in what they saw as a moral conflict" and that "[w]omen were the secret weapon of the temperance movement" in the antebellum years. The presence of women with their redemptive qualities, such as virtue, morality, and self-sacrifice, gave moral sanction to the male-dominated temperance efforts and greatly promoted them.[104]

Women's visibility in St. Paul's antebellum temperance movement largely resulted from their social position and the great esteem in which they were held by the men. James M. Goodhue highly praised the presence of women in the city, whom he deemed necessary to civilize men and to get them away from "their idols, erected in . . . saloons." For women, moving to a frontier town meant to give up most amenities of life and demanded courage and idealism. At the same time, it provided them with unprecedented opportunities, such as a fuller participation in the public sphere. At the frontier, the demarcation between the public and private spheres was not as rigid as in many towns in the East. Therefore, from the start, St. Paul's men integrated women into their temperance efforts.[105]

Women's integration, however, had clear boundaries in those years. Even though women attended temperance conventions and participated in demonstrations, they played the bit parts rather than being protagonists. While the Catholic Temperance Society admitted women alongside men, all of St. Paul's early Anglo-American temperance societies were for men only. Female membership was never considered, which relegated Anglo-American women's work outside the temperance societies' organizational structures. This segregation of Anglo-American temperance societies along gender lines changed only with the founding of the Independent Order of the Good Templars (IOGT) in Minnesota in 1856.

The first society of the Order had been founded in Utica, New York, in 1851. Its most progressive feature, distinguishing it from all other temperance organizations, was its admission of women, not only as passive members but also as officers. Women could speak, vote, hold office, and participate in secret rituals. Their admission resulted from the Order's ideology of universalism, asserting that anyone was eligible for membership so long as they promised to be teetotalers and to support prohibition.[106]

The first IOGT society in Minnesota was founded in Winona on March 5, 1856. In May 1857, after the necessary seven lodges had been established in the territory's villages and towns, the Minnesota Grand Lodge was instituted. From the beginning, women eagerly joined the Order, so that by May 1857, 112 of its 392 members were women (~29 percent). In St. Paul's first Good Templar Lodge, established in October 1858, six of its fourteen officers were women, including Henry H. Sibley's daughter Helen. Such a strong presence of women in the St. Paul IOGT's leading positions, however, seems to have been the exception rather than the rule. Female membership in Minnesota's Grand Lodge remained far behind that of the men. Even though the IOGT promoted equality and increased cooperation between the sexes within the organization, women were dominated by and dependent on men. Equality in theory did not necessarily translate into equality in practice.[107]

Not only did men relegate women from or dominate them within their temperance organizations, but they also did not tire of voicing their precise ideas about the shape of women's temperance activism. Women were portrayed as either victims of male drinking or championed for their taming and redeeming influence on wayward husbands and sons. Therefore, their benevolent actions appeared justified and were heartily endorsed by most men as long as they took place within certain boundaries. Even John W. North, who delegated important tasks to his wife Ann, acted according to the separation of spheres. Whereas he was politically active and spent much time working for temperance in public, Ann's letters reveal that her tasks mostly revolved around the house or were typically female chores, such as sewing temperance banners.[108] Men voiced their criticism when women overstepped the boundaries of the private sphere. On July 24, 1853, the women from St. Anthony and the vicinity formed a union of the Daughters of Temperance. Even though the editor of the *St. Anthony Express* approved of their action, he cautioned them not to leave their sphere and to employ their power "not in the ostentation of public controversy, but in the exercise of that secret social influence they are so fitted to exert." In short, female temperance work was characterized by an inculcation of morality rather than by public and political activism, as the latter was clearly perceived as outside the province of women.[109]

In the early stages of female temperance activism, most women seem not to have minded their exclusion from the public sphere. The founding of the Daughters of Temperance, however, Minnesota's first all-female society in which women made all speeches and held all offices, can be read as the result of a desire for more agency and for a space in which to do women's work in women's ways. Men's unwillingness to grant them such agency underscored female dependency and male dominance and made women conscious of the oppressive nature of the existing gender ideology. Even though this ideology was often fiction rather than fact, especially in a frontier town like St. Paul, the aforementioned sources show that it governed people's mindsets, led to moral judgments of women's activism, and narrowed women's opportunities. The increasing politicization of the temperance movement deprived women even more of a meaningful task because they were barred from the polls. Even though they signed petitions for a Maine Law, they had to face the fact that their signatures were not worth a dime. This was verbalized by the temperance opponents, who argued that the petitions signed by women and children did not count, as these two groups could not be considered citizens. Forming their own temperance society meant for women to escape from men's institutional structures as well as from their notions of femininity, at least temporarily.[110]

The Civil War acted as a watershed for Minnesota's temperance movement. It disrupted Minnesotan life, and everything assumed secondary importance to the fight for the Union. Many of the temperance movement's leading clergymen received appointments as army chaplains, and many of its leading officers joined the military. Various newspapers reported that sentiment in favor of temperance was very low in Minnesota, and the Good Templars described the Order's condition in the state as "very low and crippled" and conceded a "lack of progress." In 1861, the IOGT had thirteen lodges with 528 members. By 1863, it had shrunk to five lodges with 284 members. It must be credited to Minnesota's women that the Order managed to keep alive throughout the war at all. Whereas the temperance movement had been male-dominated before the war, women became a powerful and indispensable force during the war. They increasingly replaced the men as officers in the Grand Lodge and local societies and thus, for the first time, assumed leadership positions on a large scale. Through these positions, they realized that they had the same capabilities as men and consequently gained more self-confidence.[111]

In this situation, to some of them at least, their total absence of political rights appeared hypocritical and strengthened their wish for equality. In June 1865, a St. Paul newspaper reported that the women "of some temperance organization" in Hennepin and Anoka Counties—most likely Good Templars—started circulating a petition asking for the political equality of men and women in the state constitution and for women's suffrage and the right to hold offices. The petition was signed by many men and women and addressed to both houses of the legislature. The signers justified their demands by citing the following reasons: First, women possessed individual mental, moral, social, and financial interests and should therefore participate in the passage of laws touching upon those rights. Second, women had to suffer from many evils that could be remedied if they had the right to vote. Third, the principle of "no taxation without representation" was applicable to women. Fourth, the appearance of women at the polls would have a purifying and refining influence on politics. Finally, as an example of woman's capabilities, the petitioners mentioned Queen Victoria of England. This petition demonstrates that there was a nascent link between female temperance activism and political emancipation, a link that would become ever more prominent in the decades to come.[112]

2. Organizing into Blocs

The Fight for or against Personal Liberty (1866–1887)

The Rise of a "Temperance Politics"

In the decades after the Civil War, Minnesota underwent tremendous demographic, social, and economic changes. Between 1870 and 1890 its population tripled due to the influx of major waves of Scandinavians, Irish, and Germans. The Twin Cities rapidly grew from about 33,100 residents in 1870 to about 298,000 twenty years later. Minnesota, like the rest of the Midwest, industrialized significantly and became part of a burgeoning international market. The presence of an unprecedented number of immigrants, the rapid growth of the state's urban areas, as well as the sharpening of class differences in the course of industrialization led to repeated clashes among the state's various interest groups. Once again, the struggle about liquor proved one arena in which debates about Minnesota's future course were carried out. While for some Minnesotans a more or less strict adherence to temperance principles was vital for the state's economic growth and social and moral health, others advocated personal liberty and the undisturbed coexistence of various ethnic and social practices. While the latter group largely advocated a government not interfering with people's personal habits, the former increasingly relied on the legislative power of the state government to realize its demands.[1]

It was this growing reliance on the state government that led to the intense politicization of Minnesota's temperance movement between the end of the Civil War and the passage of a High License Law in 1887, the first lasting temperance law in the state. More than ever, Minnesota's temperance activists pushed the temperance cause into the political arena, so that—what I would call—a temperance politics emerged. This phrase signifies the increasing prominence of the temperance issue in party, electoral, and state politics and its advancement to an object of mass cognition.

This chapter will highlight some facets of Minnesota temperance politics in those years. The popularity of the temperance cause forced both Republicans and Democrats to engage with the arguments of both temperance reformers and opponents and to carefully negotiate their position within the legal battles about alcohol. These debates led to a rejuvenation of the Democratic Party in the 1880s and, consequently, equilibrium between the parties. In addition, it provoked the founding of a third party solely geared toward the extinction of the liquor traffic. Within the legislative realm, temperance increasingly moved center stage. The discussions about an Ohio Liquor Law in the early 1870s, the struggle for a prohibitory constitutional amendment in the early 1880s, and a High License Law in the mid- and late 1880s exemplify that two legal approaches toward temperance can be distinguished in Minnesota in this time period. One set of legal reforms sought to impose restrictions on the retail branch of the liquor trade, in particular the saloons, and was pursued by a group of reformers Ann-Marie E. Szymanski has called "anti-liquor moderates"—middle-class reformers or wealthy business interests. In the course of industrialization and urban growth, these moderates came to perceive the saloon as a constant source of temptation to the working class and the immigrants, a hotbed of social and moral disorder and labor unrest, and thus an impediment to industrial efficiency and the establishment of a stable capitalist social order. In contrast to such a "moderate" reformist agenda, the "radicals," led by the third-party reformers, the Woman's Christian Temperance Union (WCTU), pietistic church leaders, and the fraternal lodges, viewed liquor consumption as harmful—irrespective of the social context of its consumption—and strove for the extinction of the liquor traffic. These two reformist camps sometimes fought with, at other times against each other. They had, however, one enemy in common: a growing opposition to temperance reform spearheaded by German Americans and representatives of the liquor industry.[2]

The IOGT, which had been able to survive the dearth of the war years through women's temperance activism, became the leading force in the politicization of the temperance movement in Minnesota and the state's most active temperance organization. With its fifty-six lodges with a membership of 4,500 in 1866, it became the motor behind the campaigns for temperance legislation and exerted much pressure on the existing political parties to garner partisan support for its reform projects. Together with other reformers, many of them members of the Minnesota Annual Conference of the Methodist Episcopal Church, the Good Templars attempted to force the Republican Party back into taking a firm stance against liquor. Minnesota's Republican Party found this anything but fortunate and refused to "hazard the success of the great Republican party" by promoting anti-liquor legislation.[3] In September 1867, much to the dismay of the coalition of reformers, Minnesota's Republicans even adopted an anti-temperance plank, stating that "the habits and customs of a people cannot be changed by pro-hibitory or sumptuary laws, and that the legislature cannot interfere with such habits and customs without transcending the legitimate sphere of the legislative power." This plank was the result of a coup planned by the fifteen German del-egates under the leadership of Albert Wolff, editor of St. Paul's *Staats-Zeitung*, and Oscar Malmros, one of St. Paul's leading German Republicans, in a secret meeting the night before the convention.[4]

The Democrats employed the debates about temperance to fashion themselves as the party of the liberal-minded and declared personal liberty as their motto. This phrase implied a government devoted to the limitation of its own pow-ers, refraining from regulating citizens' daily lives in order to maximize their personal liberty. Personal liberty became the glue that held the party's different subgroups of voters together: It resonated emotionally with the German Ameri-cans by constantly reminding them of the party's continuing commitment not to control the habits, tastes, and appetites of people. The slogan also struck a responsive chord among Catholic voters, as it emphasized the Democrats' sup-port of measures securing freedom of worship, such as the continued existence of parochial schools. Finally, personal liberty expressed values and emotions central to the party's small Southern constituency in Minnesota. It suggested that the Democratic Party guaranteed the absolute freedom from all interfer-ences by federal government officials.[5]

The intransigence of the Democratic and Republican Parties with respect to the reformers eventually led to the founding of Minnesota's first Temperance Party in St. Paul on October 6, 1869. The emergence of this party was imme-diately motivated by the founding of a National Prohibition Party in Chicago the previous month and by the contemptible treatment of the Minnesota Good Templars' envoy, Reverend C. G. Bowdish, at the 1869 Republican Party conven-tion. Similar to the National Prohibition Party, Minnesota's Temperance Party was initiated by the Good Templars and aimed at the passage of a prohibitory law and at the rigid enforcement of the Sunday Law.[6]

The 1869 election results, however, illustrate that the Minnesota Temperance Party's early foray into state politics was an utter failure, discouraging even its most enthusiastic supporters. Merely 3.2 percent of all Minnesota voters cast their ballot in favor of the party's gubernatorial candidate, the Methodist min-ister Daniel Cobb. With its single-issue approach, the Temperance Party was not able to mobilize the grass roots or to dissolve the existing party loyalties of those in favor of prohibition. In the 1871 election, party members added planks in favor of woman suffrage and against corporations to the platform in order to attract more voters. These innovations did, however, not halt the decline. Not only did all proposed gubernatorial candidates refuse to run, but the party also received merely 1.1 percent of all votes. These disastrous results led to the IOGT's decision in 1872 to renounce independent political action. While the Prohibition Party would resurface time and again, putting up tickets in state elections in the decades to come, until the 1910s its numerical and political impact was negligible. Its members clearly constituted the fringes of Minnesota's temperance movement.[7]

While third-party activism thus did not garner much support among reform-minded Minnesotans at the time, the 1870s and 1880s witnessed a proliferation of legal remedies to the consumption and sale of liquor, signifying the reformers' increasing willingness to rely on the state in their fight against alcohol. While Minnesota's anti-liquor moderates generally refrained from supporting a prohibitory constitutional amendment, they considered Ohio Liquor and High License Laws suitable means to respond to rampant fears about drunkenness, disorder, and economic stagnation. The radicals, by contrast, tended to support a large variety of coercive liquor laws, but most preferably prohibitory ones. All these multifaceted fights illustrate that during the 1870s and 1880s the temperance movement greatly diversified. By moving away from a single-issue radicalism, it facilitated the integration of less radical reformers, enlarged the spectrum of temperance activism, and led to the formation of a heterogeneous, dynamic, yet increasingly powerful and influential temperance bloc. It also boosted the formation of a temperance opposition, fighting with as much conviction and political expertise as the reformers. Temperance, these three examples demonstrate, had become an indisputable force in Minnesota's political landscape.

The Ohio Liquor Law had first been enacted in Ohio a few years earlier, then in Michigan and Illinois, and was being debated in Wisconsin and Missouri. Its major characteristic was the provision that a drunkard's closest relatives could sue the saloon owner for the material damages the drunkard had caused after leaving the saloon. The Ohio Liquor Law illustrates the reformers' view of legal responsibility: Instead of the individual alcohol consumer, the saloon owner—and thus, by implication, society conferring upon him social respectability and legal protection—was held responsible for intemperance and therefore became the reformers' major target. Moreover, this law posed a particular danger to the owners of working-class saloons who could not have possibly afforded such lawsuits.[8]

Minnesota's Good Templars had recommended the passage of an Ohio Liquor bill as early as May 1871. On November 16, 1871, the state's Baptists, Presbyterians, Congregationalists, and Methodists founded the Minnesota State Temperance Union (MSTU) in Owatonna in order to support the Good Templars' advocacy of an Ohio Liquor Law and began circulating petitions. This spasm of organizational activity in late 1871 evidences that a law such as the Ohio Liquor Law, restrictive but much less drastic than prohibition, was needed to form a sizable coalition of reformers. Even though Minnesota's Baptists had decided against resolutions in favor of prohibition, they willingly joined the agitation for an Ohio Liquor Law.[9]

Minnesota's 1872 version of the Ohio bill, the Child bill, named after its major advocate, Senator James E. Child from Waseca, even surpassed the original Ohio Liquor Law in stringency. In addition to the aforementioned compensation clause, it contained a provision for Sunday Observance and a Local Option clause allowing communities to decide against the sale of liquor. Finally, the Minnesota version asked saloon owners to furnish two or more bondsmen willing to stand surety for $5,000, a restriction that would make it well-nigh impossible for members of the working class to open a saloon. Such restrictions and the assertion of the editor of the *Western Temperance Herald* that "the better classes of people are longing for the law" prove that this law was explicitly drawn up by the largely middle-class and upper-class reformers to halt the proliferation of working-class saloons particularly in the state's rapidly growing cities. The radicalism of the Child bill led to insecurities among the temperance reformers and to the formation of an oppositional bloc among St. Paul's German Americans, who decried it as a class measure and as nativist in character, seeking to discriminate against the state's working-class and immigrant saloon culture. Over the next three years, first and foremost due to the German Americans' severe opposition and their political representatives' dexterous agitation, all Ohio Liquor bills were killed by Minnesota's legislators.[10]

The increasing politicization of the temperance movement and its imposition of coercive laws on the liquor retailers contributed to the formation of a thoroughly organized anti-temperance bloc consisting of German Americans, liquor producers and sellers, and other opponents of temperance. In 1873, the so-called liquor interests[11] founded the Minnesota Wholesale Liquor Dealers Association and in 1876 the Minnesota State Association for the Protection of Personal Liberty, both of which aimed at protecting its members from temperance measures and at exerting greater influence in politics. As the name of the second association suggests, in the 1870s the personal liberty slogan, which had been originally devised by the rhetoricians of the Democratic Party, was employed by all temperance opponents.[12]

The repeated failure of the Ohio Liquor bill fueled the reformers' zeal and heightened their activism, so that the second half of the 1870s witnessed an upsurge in temperance activism in Minnesota. The state's women consolidated their temperance activism by founding the Minnesota WCTU in 1877, which counted more than 1,000 members three years later. The Sons of Temperance also revived their movement and between February and May 1876 managed to establish twenty-three divisions in the state, comprising several hundred men and women. The IOGT prided itself of a membership of 10,350 in 1876. In addition, by 1876 about ten thousand Minnesotans had signed the pledge of the Minnesota Sunday School Temperance League, and representatives from numerous pietistic denominations continued to cooperate through the MSTU. Finally, in 1876 about 4,200 Irish Americans labored within Minnesota's temperance movement. In 1877, St. Paul's newspapers announced that Minnesota's corps of temperance laborers was larger and better organized than ever before.[13]

Such announcements convinced those reformers in the state who ultimately aimed at the prohibition of liquor to once again campaign for the passage of a prohibitory law. Between 1877 and 1881, they therefore attempted to secure the passage of various prohibitory bills for Minnesota. Yet time and again, legislators did not take these bills seriously, portraying them as the pipe dreams of a largely female and overly zealous corps of temperance workers.[14]

Radical temperance activism in Minnesota in the 1870s and 1880s was spearheaded by Methodist clergymen. The cause's most prominent representative was William Wilson Satterlee. Originally a native of Indiana with English ancestry and a Wesleyan Methodist, he came to Minnesota in 1863 and worked as a clergyman in various towns until he became minister of Minneapolis's First Methodist Church in the mid-1860s. In 1868, he was first reported to have given a speech at a Good Templars meeting in Waseca. Having been one of the founders of the state's Prohibition Party in 1869, he remained the party's secretary for many years, even serving as its gubernatorial candidate in 1879. He also engaged in the fight for an Ohio Liquor Law, was one of the founders of the MSTU, and served as its state agent, lecturer, and secretary for many years. By 1873, he had given up his ministry and devoted all his time to temperance work. Satterlee was commonly known as "the most prominent and active Prohibitionist in the Northwest." In February 1892, he even received a letter from national WCTU President Frances Willard, praising him as the most noble and able champion of the Prohibition Party on the American continent. From 1886 until his sudden death in 1893, he worked as an Associate Professor of Political Science and Temperance at Grant Memorial University, Athens, Tennessee.[15]

People like Satterlee, who could afford to labor for the temperance cause full time, usually belonged to pietistic denominations and carried membership cards of various temperance organizations. They dedicated most of their time to creating and maintaining strong networks between the various, and sometimes disparate, temperance organizations; to defining a common agenda and a set of strategies; and to exerting pressure on politicians and legislators. To promote a prohibitory constitutional amendment in Minnesota, Satterlee, together with the Methodist minister Chauncey Hobart from Red Wing, initiated the organization of a Constitutional Amendment Agitation Committee (CAAC) in St. Paul's Reform Club hall on February 14, 1882. This committee of five was to organize the state down to the township level, raise funds, put speakers in the field, distribute literature, call state and district conventions, and obtain pledges from all those seeking nomination that if elected to the legislature they would support such an amendment. While only a decade earlier most pietistic denominations had shied away from supporting prohibition, by the early 1880s the state's Congregational Association, Baptist Convention, and the Methodist Episcopal Conference declared in favor of constitutional prohibition and the use of the ballot to put prohibition into effect, which indicates a gradual radicalization of the state's temperance movement.[16]

Even though the CAAC received the support of the WCTU, the IOGT, and the Prohibition Party, its work did not show the promised effect. The 1883 legislature remained deaf to the pleas of the temperance coalition and defeated the bill for a prohibitory constitutional amendment in Minnesota. In the end, it was a Republican, Gordon E. Cole of Faribault, who delivered a brilliant speech against its passage. He interpreted the bill as a violation of natural rights and as an invasion of religion into politics. After all, the movement for a prohibitory constitutional amendment was spearheaded by the pietistic ministers and church bodies in Minnesota. Besides Cole, the Minnesota Association for the Protection of Personal Liberty greatly contributed to the bill's downfall. They later revealed to have spent $50,000 for their campaigns against prohibition, an extraordinary amount of money at the time.[17]

For many anti-liquor moderates, this radical temperance agitation seemed out of proportion. While a great number of them were total abstainers themselves, they were not against liquor consumption per se, as long as it took place in the home, in private clubs, restaurants, hotels, or well-ordered drinking establishments. Particularly the wealthier citizens feared the further encroachment of working-class saloons—to them the embodiment of disorderly drinking and social unrest—into their residential areas. The passage of a High License Law, which had first been adopted in Nebraska in 1881 and was debated in various other states at the time, seemed to be able to allay such fears. Apart from fixing high license fees, such laws required saloon keepers to give bond to conduct their businesses according to law and to pay damages accruing to individuals from the business. They also prohibited the sale of liquor on Sundays and to habitual drunkards and minors. From the perspective of the anti-liquor moderates, who called themselves the "friends of law and order," a High License Law seemed to have many advantages. It would make liquor selling more expensive and thus drive a great number of saloon owners out of business, especially the smaller working-class saloons at the outskirts of towns. If there were fewer saloons, the reformers reasoned, liquor consumption, especially among workers, would reduce greatly and the political power of the saloon would be curtailed. Many contemporaries claimed that the latter had drastically increased during the past decade and that a candidate could only be elected with the support of the liquor interests. The increasing activism of the liquor interests in the context of the

Ohio Liquor Law and the prohibitory constitutional amendment had proved that the reformers' fears were not entirely unfounded.

The legislative fight for High License threw the split of the temperance movement into a radical and a moderate camp into sharp relief. While a few prohibitionists endorsed High License, declaring it to be better than nothing, the majority of radical reformers, such as the leaders of the Minnesota IOGT, considered it "a political compromise." They argued that to license an evil meant to become part of it and therefore denounced the High License movement to be a "delusion and a snare." The Good Templars were supported by the WCTU and the Party Prohibitionists. High License, all of these groups argued, was the bait the Republicans offered to their pietistic-reformist constituency in order to satisfy its increasing demands for stricter temperance laws and to solve internal tensions.[18]

Whereas the struggle for High License did not manage to attract the majority of the radical reformers, it garnered support from a multitude of other groups. Several industrialists felt that a reduction of the number of saloons would lead to greater discipline among their workers, whereas the officials in numerous Minnesota towns and cities rubbed their hands at the thought of the financial gain such a law would bestow on their communities.[19] More significantly, however, the struggle about High License marked the entrance of the Irish Catholic reformers, who had been active in the state since 1869, into the political temperance movement. In the context of the High License debates, a number of Irish temperance activists joined the Anglo-American anti-liquor moderates in the formation of a Committee of Fifteen, which was to coordinate High License agitation. High License was the first legislative issue bringing about interdenominational and interethnic cooperation on a large scale.[20]

Both in 1883 and in 1885, however, High License did not have a chance. Many legislators opposed it due to "its unjust discrimination against the poorer class of people and our foreign population." To them, High License meant "that when the genial German or the Irishman or the Swede or Norwegian comes to Minnesota he shall leave his social customs behind him and shall adopt the straight-laced ideas of Puritanism." It meant "that the laboring man who likes his glass of ale or beer as he sits at his humble board by the cheerful glow of his own firelight, shall be deprived of that small enjoyment, while his richer neighbor shall have the pleasure of resorting to the club room or the gilded saloon and enjoy his whisky cocktails and fancy punches without restriction." Because of such pro-labor and pro-immigrant sentiments, a great number of legislators either refused to vote on the bill or simply stayed away when the ballot was cast—a strategy without precedent in Minnesota. In addition, the liquor interests were known to have spent about $20,000 for the bill's defeat.[21]

Not surprisingly, the election campaign of 1886 witnessed an even fiercer struggle for High License. Due to the high pressure exerted by the reformers, the Republican Party, after decades of pursuing a strategy of evasion, introduced a plank into its platform favoring High License, Local Option, and the enforcement of the existing liquor laws. Many of those Republicans who had been against constitutional prohibition, such as Gordon E. Cole, favored the passage of High License. Moreover, High License struck a chord with many Republicans with no penchant for reform, so that the party's support of the policy did not entail a loss of large parts of its constituency. By endorsing High License, the Republicans also hoped to attract the Irish Catholic temperance advocates, traditionally Democrats, into their fold.[22]

While some Irish Catholic reformers followed their Bishop John Ireland and voted Republican, the majority of Minnesota's Irish still considered the Republicans promoters of nativism and therefore intended to vote for the Democrats. The Democratic gubernatorial candidate, Albert A. Ames, was also supported by the state's liquor interests. German American Republicans ignored existing party loyalties and fervently fought for his election as well. Whereas the Republican Party had dominated state politics until the early 1880s, from 1883 on, the temperance issue contributed to an increase in the Democratic vote and to a tight partisan balance in the late 1880s. By the late 1880s, temperance issues greatly influenced party and state politics: Minnesota's politics had become temperance politics.[23]

In 1886, the electoral scale tipped in favor of the Republicans. After a Republican victory, the passage of a High License Law was a foregone conclusion. Political pressure, exerted by the High License advocates through mass meetings in St. Paul's Opera House and through their physical presence during the legislative debates, prompted rapid decision making. On the day of the bill's passage, there was such a large crowd of male and female High License advocates and opponents in the House that it would have made "a skillfully packed dozen or more sardines blush for having wasted room." The galleries were so overcrowded that they began to settle and had to be evacuated.[24] Minnesota's High License Law, passed at the beginning of February 1887, was to take effect in Minnesota on July 1, 1887, and in St. Paul on January 1, 1888. In cities with ten thousand and more inhabitants, it required liquor sellers to pay $1,000 a year for receiving a license—in smaller cities, $500. The money realized from this fee was to be given to the cities. Local Option decided whether liquor was to be sold at all, and the liquor sellers were punished by severe fines for violating any of the regulations.[25]

The degree of public agitation over the High License question demonstrates how much was at stake in Minnesota in the 1880s. The self-proclaimed friends of law and order responded to the rapid social and economic changes by attempting to order their allegedly disorderly environment through law. Through legally controlling the recreational practices of the workers and immigrants, they sought to enforce Protestant Anglo-American bourgeois values. While they continued to emphasize the significance of personal reform, the restriction of the liquor retail trade, in particular the introduction of legal hurdles to opening and running saloons, moved to the center of temperance work in those years. While many of these reformers were middle- and upper-class Anglo-American Protestants, a considerable number of Irish Catholics eagerly joined this coalition. This reform choir was complemented by radically reformist voices, arguing that any form of liquor consumption would hamper Minnesota's economic and moral development. This heterogeneous yet increasingly powerful reform bloc was countered by an anti-temperance coalition led by German Americans and people involved in the liquor business—all striving to protect their economic needs and celebrating cultural pluralism, equal rights for all social classes, and personal liberty. Whereas in the 1870s each of these oppositional blocs contained members of both major parties, by the mid-1880s they became largely split along partisan lines, with the Republicans advocating laws further restricting the liquor retail part and the Democrats emphasizing personal liberty and the absence of governmental intrusion. In the years to come, issue-related voting and swing-voting would increasingly replace traditional voting patterns and, in the long run, alter the political landscape.[26]

St. Paul—From Civic Compromise to Civic Wars

In St. Paul, struggles about temperance further consolidated the city's civic identity that had emerged over the previous decades from a specific set of demographic, geographical, social, and economic parameters and that had been continuously rehearsed through narrations by its prominent early urban architects. The 1860s and 1870s were largely characterized by civic compromise, with the mayors trying to keep peace between the numerically dominant urban antireformist and the much smaller, yet zealous reformist camps. By the 1880s, however, civic compromise gave way to frequent civic wars about the regulation of the liquor traffic in Minnesota's state capital and the implementation of existing civic and state liquor laws. St. Paul's anti-temperance faction numerically dominated these civic wars, so that efforts to realign the city with respect to reform were doomed to failure. Being opposed to temperance became an integral part of being a St. Paulite. Even attempts of the Irish American and Anglo-American temperance advocates to utilize the state government in order to discipline the unruly state capital were crowned with success only partially. They caused spite among the majority of city residents, who conceptualized their city as an anti-temperance space, a bulwark of liberality, and an ideological counterweight to the state of Minnesota. The temperance movement, as this chapter will demonstrate, did not only cause conflicts between temperance advocates and opponents, but it also led to a tug of war and trial of strength between different governmental units, with the central question of these debates being: Did the state government have the right to superimpose laws on cities that contradicted the prevalent urban sentiment?

With its focus on wholesale trade, distribution, and transportation, St. Paul reaped its profits from small enterprises and manufacturers. Its dependence on small businesses rather than on large industrial companies made power structures fluid and negotiable and St. Paul's civic identity inclusive. Social and economic power was dispersed, and citizens were greatly interdependent, which encouraged a negotiation of civic issues, such as temperance, by a wide array of St. Paulites. In the postwar years, temperance struggles in Minnesota's capital were resolved through dialogue and compromise, with the city's mayors often functioning as peacekeepers. Mediating between St. Paul's contending cultures became one of their major tasks, and their political success greatly depended on their mediation capabilities. Many of these civic debates centered upon the enforcement of the Sunday Law. Whereas the small group of reformers considered it a token of their cultural imprint on the city, to the majority of city residents it meant an encroachment upon their personal liberty. Peace between those factions could be preserved only through civic compromise.[27]

Jacob H. Stewart, a native of New York and the first Republican ever to win the mayor's seat in St. Paul, is a good example of successful mayoral mediation. When he came into office in 1864, many of his Republican supporters expected him to run the city according to reformist ideas of morality. He was to suppress prostitution, close the saloons on Sunday, and drive gambling out of the city. William Pitt Murray describes how Stewart, himself a pioneer settler and thus familiar with St. Paul's civic identity, understood his mayoral responsibilities: "Doctor Stewart was even then an old settler. He knew the people of St. Paul;—he had to govern a cosmopolitan city—many of her citizens of foreign birth, and he was satisfied that no drastic policy ought to be adopted." Rather than affronting the greater part of the city's residents, Stewart compromised his reform zeal and sought to mediate between the reformist and antireformist factions. After his inauguration, he had a conference with the city's saloon owners, in which he told them that some of his supporters demanded a rigid enforcement of the Sunday Law. He then suggested a compromise: He asked them to close their businesses on Sundays until two in the afternoon, so that the forenoon church services would not be disturbed. Afterward, they could open their saloons, provided that they ran their places in an orderly manner with their doors shut and curtains drawn. The saloon owners assented to this form of civic negotiation, and this compromise was kept up during Stewart's mayoralties, which lasted, intermittently, until 1875.[28]

While in the 1860s and 1870s St. Paul's municipal life thus remained largely unaffected by the clashes between reformers and temperance opponents on the state level, the late 1870s and 1880s witnessed an upsurge—by St. Paul's standards—in temperance activism and, as a consequence, a polarization of the temperance question and civic wars between the city's antireformist and reformist blocs. Civic compromise slowly gave way to civic wars on the liquor question.

According to the numbers given by the individual organizations, by the late 1870s there were roughly about two thousand temperance activists in St. Paul, that is, about 5 percent of the city's residents were enrolled in one, or several, temperance societies. Anderson H. Wimbish, a contemporary St. Paulite, roughly confirms this number, estimating that there were about 1,500 Anglo-American Protestant and 1,000 Irish Catholic temperance workers in St. Paul at the time. The temperance cause even attracted members of the city's small African American community, which would comprise just 1 percent of the city residents at the turn of the century. In June 1877, the first African American Good Templar Lodge was founded in the city with forty charter members. J. K. Hilyard, one of its founders, officers, and later the owner of *The Appeal*, the city's African American newspaper, seems to have been instrumental in spreading the temperance gospel among the city's African Americans. In October 1879, he organized the Hilyard Temple of Honor and Temperance, a temperance and benevolent society for African Americans. African Americans faced racial discrimination and were stuck on the city's lower socioeconomic levels. Hilyard might have considered temperance agitation as a means to uplift St. Paul's blacks socially and to make them more acceptable to whites.[29]

This small band of reformers, scattered all over the city, was confronted with an anti-temperance sentiment crystallizing all over the city. Two groups dominated this highly disparate anti-temperance camp. On the one hand, the city's German Americans, who constituted about 26 percent of the population of Ramsey County and who exerted a powerful economic and cultural influence on the state capital, were unwilling to make compromises concerning their lifestyle and livelihoods. On the other hand, opposition to temperance came from and was coordinated and sponsored by the city's liquor interests, a highly heterogeneous conglomerate of people involved in the sale and manufacture of liquor. These two groups were backed by a great number of St. Paulites who enjoyed the city's liquor culture or who had a stake in the continuous flourishing of St. Paul's liquor industry. In 1880, the brewing industry was one of the city's most significant employers with its eleven breweries having a combined capitalization of $371,500, surpassed only by the city's printing industry. Furthermore, by 1886, St. Paul was proud to have more than eight hundred saloons and taverns supporting many small proprietors and employees, creating huge profit margins for liquor distributors, and filling the city coffers through license fees. St. Paul's flourishing nightlife and vice economy—that is, liquor, gambling, and prostitution—were also important for attracting potential buyers and traveling salesmen.[30]

The mayoralty of Christopher D. O'Brien, son of the Irish temperance advocate Dillon O'Brien, exemplifies the growing polarization between these temperance and anti-temperance blocs in the 1880s and the increasing unwillingness to compromise with each other. It also proves that the anti-temperance faction in St. Paul was able to decide the political fate of reformers. O'Brien, a so-called reform Democrat, had been elected by both Anglo-American reformers and his own political party. Shortly after his election, he began to pursue a moral reform course and ignored the interests of St. Paul's anti-temperance camp. William Pitt Murray fittingly characterized O'Brien: "With his earlier education and habits of life, he believed that vice, immorality and intemperance had too great a hold on the city, and that these evils had to be suppressed or sequestered, and he thought it could be done as easily as he could sway a jury." O'Brien swore to faithfully carry out the ordinances relating to liquor selling, brothels, and gambling. In June 1883, he instructed the police to make sure that every saloon in St. Paul closed at midnight and that saloon owners shut their front doors on Sunday. He also enforced Ordinance No. 10 prohibiting the operation of brothels.[31]

His unwillingness to compromise his ideas of morality and to negotiate with the city's saloon and brothel owners put an abrupt end to his political career. When in March 1885 O'Brien's renomination was discussed, the heads of St. Paul's Democratic Party, first and foremost Carl H. Lienau and William Dawson, spoke out against O'Brien's renomination, arguing that his enforcement policy had made him ineligible for most St. Paulites. Other Democratic leaders, such as William Pitt Murray and William Hamm, agreed with Lienau and Dawson and forced O'Brien out of the race for the mayoralty. Even John G. Donnelly—despite his membership in two of the city's Irish temperance societies—supported his party colleagues. Lienau and Dawson's line of argumentation proves that O'Brien, with his policy of strict enforcement, had not only thwarted the financial and economic interests of the city's merchant class but had also alienated the majority of St. Paulites. Until the onset of prohibition, the story of O'Brien's political fate would be dug up by St. Paul's antireformist camp whenever a city official would show signs of collaborating with the reformers. It became a parable of what would happen to every man who endeavored to superimpose municipal reform on liquor-friendly St. Paul.[32]

O'Brien would not remain the only St. Paulite who aspired to morally reform the city and thereby incurred the wrath of the antireformist camp, but he was soon followed by urban reformers striving for High License. In the decade between 1880 and 1890, St. Paul, as many other American cities, experienced an enormous demographic expansion, with its population more than tripling and becoming increasingly multicultural and nonpietistic. Native-born pietists feared that this overly rapid urban growth would precipitate moral degeneration, which they sought to halt through temperance and other social reforms. Imposing a High License Ordinance on St. Paul was seen by the urban reformers as one way of counteracting such moral decay. The city's large anti-temperance faction, however, perceived such efforts as an economic and cultural attack on their city. Thus, the stage was set for civic wars about temperance between the reformist and antireformist camps.[33]

The leader of the city's High License movement was Bishop John Ireland, who had, as early as 1882, tried to convince the St. Paul City Council to considerably raise the existing $100 license fee but to no avail.[34] Two years later—encouraged by the passage of a High License Ordinance and the establishment of patrol limits in Minneapolis—a reform coalition made up of Protestant and Catholic temperance workers organized the largest temperance campaign in St. Paul since the fight for a Maine Law. This campaign was inaugurated on April 7, 1884, when 2,200 supporters of a $500 license attended a large mass meeting at Market Hall. In his speech about the evils of intemperance, Ireland expressed his conviction that High License would greatly benefit St. Paul's working class and deprive the whiskey ring of its power. He also argued that with a sound High License policy "the whole state will receive from its capital city inspiration and courage." The reformers then established a Committee of Thirty, which was to coordinate High License work in the city. About one-third of the committee's members were Irish Catholic temperance activists. The others were mostly native-born Protestants known for their temperance activism, such as Daniel W. Ingersoll and L. C. Quinby. Not only did the issue of temperance lead to interdenominational and interethnic cooperation but also to interracial cooperation. Soon after its founding, J. K. Hilyard also joined the committee.[35]

In Minneapolis the drive to restrict saloons found wide support among the business elite. With their city increasingly transforming into a manufacturing nexus for large-scale production and industrial capitalism, members of this elite were greatly concerned about the efficiency of their workers. Due to St. Paul's focus on trade and transportation, business branches not requiring the services of a large local labor force, St. Paulites did not see a temperate working class as essential to their economic survival; thus, a large number of the city's businessmen with much emphasis expressed themselves in favor of holding the High License question in abeyance for a time. They were joined by St. Paul's political parties whose members argued that High License would discriminate against the lower classes by favoring the rich over the poor saloon owners and grind down the German and Irish citizens. They thus opted for upholding staples of St. Paul's civic identity—a strong presence of saloons across social classes, a flourishing liquor culture, and cultural and ethnic openness—rather than accumulating civic revenues from license fees.[36]

Due to the Republicans' and Democrats' refusal to endorse High License, the High License advocates decided to nominate their own candidates for aldermen. Obviously, the Committee of Thirty seems to have had difficulties finding people who were willing to come out openly on a High License platform. Positioning oneself against a major constituent of St. Paul's civic identity—alcohol—could destroy political and professional careers, as Mayor O'Brien's fate had proved. In order to attract a greater number of people, the committee members decided to change the title of their platform from High License to "Municipal Reform." The new emphasis on municipal reform was to shift the focus away from the regulation of the liquor business toward a clean and capable city government, something no one could really be opposed to.[37]

Despite this tactical name change, however, the reformers left the battlefield empty-handed. In the election of 1884, the reform ticket was entirely defeated, and the Democrat C. D. Cummings, the candidate of the saloon owners, was elected over Edmund Rice, the candidate of the reformers. The majority of St. Paulites were simply not willing to have their city turned into a "narrow-minded nest of New-England temperance hypocrites," as a German newspaper phrased it. The High License campaign of 1884 had unified the anti-temperance camp, increased Democratic supremacy, and further consolidated the city's identity. In the years to come, the Democratic Party continued to dominate municipal politics despite the reformers' desperate attempts to bring about change, and the liquor laws were deliberately ignored. As the editor of the *Pioneer Press* put it: "No one need to be told that the laws relating to the liquor traffic in this city are wholly in abeyance, and that each saloon-keeper does, with conscious immunity, precisely that which is right in his own eyes."[38]

This—from a reformist position—deplorable state of affairs in St. Paul convinced the city's reformers to come up with new strategies on how to discipline the state capital. Since neither the city administration nor the majority of St. Paulites could be counted on when it came to liquor reform, other sources of support had to be mustered. Therefore, in the late 1880s, St. Paul's reformers tried to involve two other agents in their project of disciplining the wayward state capital: the city's courts as well as the state of Minnesota.

Taking those saloon owners who ignored the liquor ordinances to court and thereby enforcing the latter was the explicit goal of the Law and Order League, which was founded in St. Paul's Market Hall on March 29, 1886. Its main initiators were a great number of Catholic and Protestant clergymen and Rabbi Wechsler, the head of the Jewish Mount Zion Congregation. These ministers were supported by several well-known St. Paul businessmen, such as John Nichols, Peter Berkey, and William R. Marshall, who were business partners in the iron trade. Many of the League's members were active in the city's Irish Catholic temperance movement, such as Dillon O'Brien and William Louis

Kelly. James J. Hill, railroad magnate and John Ireland's confidant, acted as one of its vice presidents. Numerous Protestant temperance advocates, such as Henry J. Horn and Thomas Cochran, also joined, so that once again Catholics and Protestants worked hand in hand in their project of reforming St. Paul. John Ireland, elected first president, defined the major goals of the St. Paul Law and Order League: "The special object of our attentions . . . shall be the liquor traffic. We have but the one purpose to demand that the laws that are now on the statute book be enforced. . . . The league will seek to impose no new law, neither prohibition nor high license." Ireland's emphasis that the League did not want to work for new laws was an attempt to disentangle it from temperance activism and to make it acceptable to St. Paulites. Without such precautionary remarks, he must have felt, the project of law enforcement would be doomed to failure in a city like St. Paul.[39]

In the following weeks and months, the League appointed an agent, opened an office in the Sherman Block, and hired a spy to find out about any violations of the liquor laws. By October 1886, it had caused the arrest of twenty-nine saloon keepers on various charges and the conviction of eighteen for selling to minors and for violating the Sunday Law.[40] This was only a drop in the ocean considering the degree of liquor lawbreaking in St. Paul. The work of the Law and Order League was also severely hampered by the activities of the Columbia Association, which had been founded in March 1886 by the city's saloon owners, liquor sellers, and producers in order to counteract the work of the Law and Order League. The Columbia Association—whose membership had soon skyrocketed to more than seven hundred, including the brewer William Hamm, all of St. Paul's saloon owners, liquor dealers, many producers, and other "friends of personal liberty"—supported its members against the lawsuits imposed upon them by the Law and Order League by hiring a special attorney and by demonstrating presence in court trials. The fights between the Law and Order League and the Columbia Association hardened the fronts between the city's reformist and antireformist camps and, at least temporarily, affected the civic climate negatively by creating an atmosphere of suspicion.[41]

The League's mediocre successes in combination with the increased efforts for a High License Law on the state level convinced St. Paul's reformers that only through such a state law could their unruly city be whipped into line and the inextricable link between St. Paul and anti-temperance be broken. The plan seemed to work. Despite the opposition mounted by St. Paul's legislators, High License became a state law and thus also applied to St. Paul. However, shortly after its passage, the *Pioneer Press* reported that the majority of city residents of "saloon-ridden" St. Paul, including the city's Republicans and the municipal government, were "leagued in opposition to" the law and that with such a hostility to the High License Law, the city would soon be honeycombed with saloons running under the protection of the city authorities and the municipal court. The municipal courts, as this statement indicates, were also generally opposed to reform activities, which explains the Law and Order League's limited success. Without additional legislation aiding its enforcement, the editor surmised, the High License Law would prove a complete failure in Minnesota's capital due to its lack of enforcement.[42]

What then happened in St. Paul over the next few days demonstrates how much the implementation of temperance laws was dependent on the specific characteristics of a particular locale and subject to the negotiation among local actors. St. Paul, technically subsumed under the jurisdiction of the state of Minnesota, revolted against and severely questioned the latter's authority. The revolt was initiated by the city's Columbia Association, which put into place "a quiet system of boycotting." In secret meetings, the Association's members planned to persuade the city officials to adopt ordinances circumventing the law. They also considered taking out licenses shortly before the new law became effective, so that High License would become operative much later. The efforts of the Columbia Association seem to have succeeded. On March 1, 1887, the St. Paul City Council passed Ordinance No. 756 with the explicit aim to exempt the city from the state law. The Ordinance allowed the city clerk to issue $500 licenses valid for two and a half years to St. Paul license holders until Minnesota's High License Law would go into effect. Once more, St. Paulites had devised a strategy helping them to—at least temporarily—evade a temperance law that so flatly contradicted the economic interests of a flourishing liquor business and the cultural predilections of its residents. The council's decision is all the more astounding because the $1000 license would have created a huge profit for the city coffers.[43]

This ordinance was without precedent and caused much debate in St. Paul. William Pitt Murray, then St. Paul's City Attorney, assured city residents of the validity of the ordinance, arguing that the state High License Law could not affect licenses issued prior to that date. The liquor interests celebrated their power in the state capital. H. F. Notbohm, president of the Columbia Association, bragged: "The $1,000 license bill is not a law in St. Paul because the president of the Columbia association did not sanction the same." By contrast, High License activists, such as John R. Nichols, D. R. Noyes, and James H. Davidson, considered the council's "plain and undisputed attempt to defy the legislature, to circumvent and defy the law of the land" a "monstrous outrage." "The action of the council," Nichols said, "is about what I expected. The only thing that surprises me is that the aldermen did not extend the licenses for ten years." Not only should the councilmen "be ashamed of themselves," Davidson argued, but "the people of this city ought to bury them out of sight." But this, he claimed, would never happen in St. Paul: "[I]f a vote was to be taken to-day I am afraid the majority would be on the wrong side." This statement reveals that the council's actions were condoned, if not approved of, by the majority of St. Paulites, whose sense of self was deeply inflected by the normative order, the moral judgments, and deviant practices that had developed in the context of the city's formation. The High License Law thus contradicted not only the economic interests of a particular class of city residents but also the mindset of the majority of St. Paulites who equated being St. Paulites with being opposed to temperance reform. They therefore perceived the imposition of High License by the state as both in contradiction to St. Paul's civic identity, their own self-understanding, and as an outrageous interference of the state in municipal affairs.[44]

Since nothing was to be expected from city residents, the High License advocates surmised, the state legislature needed to take the city to task, "so that we may be able to see whether the state of Minnesota has as much power as the St. Paul city council, a mere creation of the state." And this request the state met. In response to Ordinance No. 756, Minnesota's legislators passed the Crandal bill ensuring the enforcement of the High License Law in all counties, towns, and cities. It also provided that all officials violating this enforcement law would be declared guilty of malfeasance in office. Some senators were so infuriated at the action of the St. Paul City Council that they introduced a bill amending the city charter in order to deprive the state capital's city council of the power to issue licenses. This bill, however, lost by one vote. Having barely escaped a severe loss of civic autonomy, St. Paul's city officials realized that they had overstepped the mark by their refusal to implement the state law and accepted that High License would go into effect in their city in January 1888. The reformers' idea to utilize the state in order to discipline the state capital had proved an effective tool, at least for the time being. Albert Wolff of the *Volkszeitung*, however, predicted that this was only a temporary victory and that the High License Law would soon become a dead letter. Wolff was partly correct. Even though the $1,000 license remained in effect in St. Paul, after the imposition of High License onto the city, its antireformist majority developed an unmistakable spite against any efforts of reforming St. Paul. From then on, Minnesota's capital celebrated itself as an anti-temperance space and a bulwark of liberality more fervently than ever before.[45]

John Ireland and Minnesota's Irish Temperance Movement

Joseph Gusfield has interpreted drinking and abstinence as symbols of social status in nineteenth-century America because "they indicated to what culture the actor was committed and hence what social groups he took as his models of imitation and avoidance." Total abstinence became a significant avenue for groups aiming to climb the social ladder and become part of the Anglo-

American middle class. Motivated by their strong middle-class aspirations, Minnesota's Irish American reformers strategically exploited the temperance movement with the aim of renegotiating Irish American ethnic identity "with respect to its own self-concept and its relation to other groups in society." They reconceptualized themselves as a transformed, regenerated ethnic group, whose inclination to liquor was replaced, ideally, by sobriety, or, at least, by a moderate and self-conscious consumption of liquor. Once this renegotiated ethnic identity was in place, Irish American reform leaders surmised, it would serve as a major stepping stone toward an adjustment to and embrace of Anglo-American culture and facilitate social uplift and integration into middle-class Anglo-American society. Irish American participation in the temperance movement and their negotiation of ethnic identity in its wake were therefore mainly based on in-strumentalist motives and strategic considerations and geared toward cultural accommodation and socioeconomic repositioning.[46]

Numerous scholars have shown that Irish drinking habits were forged from a combination of social changes in rural nineteenth-century Ireland and the reali-ties of immigrant life in the United States. By the nineteenth century, whiskey consumption in Ireland had increased dramatically, and alcoholic beverages were an integral part of everyday life, a staple diet and a cure-all; liquor had symbolic importance by conferring significance and solemnity upon various events, such as baptisms, funerals, and business transactions. Liquor and taverns held important social and economic functions in Irish society, were central to Irish leisure-time activities, and provided a means for establishing a collective Irish (male) identity.[47] Irish drinking habits were not merely transplanted to America but also intensified there in the course of the nineteenth century. The dominance of the bachelor group, which was the result of a primarily male immigration of single adults in the prefamine period, led to an increase in the consumption of alcohol. Moreover, whereas in Ireland drink was largely a sign of male identity, across the Atlantic it developed into one significant pole of Irish American identity. As Hasia R. Diner rightly put it, "[a]lcohol symbolized who they [Irish immigrants] were, and demonstrated Irish cultural distinctiveness." For Irish immigrants, saloons offered an escape from the hardships of work and fostered ethnic community building. Drinking became a cure-all against home-sickness and the difficulties they encountered in the New World, particularly in America's urban environment. It acquired "a spiritual value," as Richard Stivers has argued. Finally, liquor consumption also became a tremendous business opportunity for Irish immigrant men and their sons in the New World. Irish saloon owners played significant roles in Irish communities, wielding political and social influence and enjoying great respect.[48]

The significance of alcohol for the Irish community and identity—and even more so the stereotype of the "drunken Paddy" it had engendered within

American society—were major stumbling blocks in the achievement of middle-class status, which became very important to a large number of Irish Americans in the last third of the nineteenth century. Kathleen Neils Conzen and her coauthors have argued that "a significant influence in the shaping of ethnicities was changing perceptions of various immigrant groups by the dominant society and the stereotyping and labeling which ensued." This also holds true for the Irish. Many Irish American intellectuals sought to distance their ethnic group from the "drunken Paddy" stereotype and from the notions of crime, squalor, poverty, and violence it inhered. Temperance activism offered Irish Americans a way to shed ancestral drinking habits, to renegotiate their identity with respect to alcohol, and to "redeem themselves within the United States." Strongly encouraged by the American Catholic hierarchy, who termed the zeal for total abstinence "most praiseworthy" at their meeting in Baltimore in 1866, strong centers of Irish Catholic temperance activity sprang up in the Northeast, especially in Pennsylvania, as well as in the larger cities of the Midwest. One of the centers of Irish American temperance activism was Minnesota and, in particular, St. Paul.[49]

While Minnesota's first postwar Irish Catholic temperance society was established at Belle Plaine in November 1868, it took until January 10, 1869, when the state's most significant society, the Father Mathew Society of St. Paul, was founded with forty-two Irishmen signing the pledge. John Ireland, as he himself would later relate time and again, had been approached by seven drunken Irish St. Paulites, one of whom called on him at the Cathedral and handed him a petition saying "For God's sake, organize a temperance society."[50]

The Father Mathew Society was a strictly Catholic organization for men over fifteen years of age, which encouraged total abstinence from intoxicating drinks and provided for the temporal welfare of its members by affording relief in case of accident or sickness and by assisting in the burial in case of death. Its social welfare provisions exemplify that the society was geared toward the Irish working class. "Catholic temperance," as Deidre M. Moloney has rightly argued, "appealed to laborers and labor leaders in a way that other Catholic reform activities did not." Within three months, the new temperance society had more than three hundred members. Membership lists reveal that the majority of these men were middle-aged and Irish-born; second-generation Irish figured less prominently among its ranks. The majority of them were farmers, laborers, and artisans, with only a few of them working as lawyers and policemen. Many of them had worked their way up in St. Paul's society, which reflects their strong middle-class aspirations. Thirty-seven-year-old Michael Roche, born in Ireland and a long-term temperance advocate, started out in St. Paul as a journeyman in 1857, temporarily left the city because the 1857 panic had ruined him economically, and started to work as a contractor after his return.

"[H]e has worked his way up from a small beginning," his contemporaries said, praising his move up the social ladder. In order to attract more people like Roche, John Ireland went on a lecture tour through Minnesota, and soon temperance societies after the model of the Father Mathew Society of St. Paul were founded in many of the state's parishes.[51] St. Paul's Irish reformers also began to toy with the idea of establishing an Irish Catholic State Temperance Union. This plan was implemented at the third anniversary of St. Paul's Father Mathew Society, when the Father Mathew Union was founded. In 1873, its name was changed to Catholic Total Abstinence Union (CTAU) of Minnesota and another year later to CTAU of the Diocese of St. Paul in order to bind it more closely to the Catholic Church.[52]

John Ireland became and remained one of the major advocates of temperance within the United States and the driving force behind the Irish Catholic movement in Minnesota. His temperance work earned him high honor, even among Protestants, who considered him one of the five most important men in Minnesota and admired him for having done "more for the temperance cause in the State of Minnesota than any other man."[53] He himself had taken the pledge from Father Mathew as a boy. He had also belonged to the English-speaking temperance society founded by Cretin in the 1850s. His dislike of any sort of alcohol derived from his childhood experiences in St. Paul's poor Irish neighborhoods and from his time as an army chaplain during the Civil War. He insisted that drunkenness was a particular weakness among the Irish and that liquor was the Irishman's curse. At a temperance meeting in Minneapolis in 1882, he said: "Half a glass of whiskey will do an Irishman more harm than half a pitcher would other people. Irishmen are lighthearted; that's the very reason."[54]

First and foremost, Irish Catholic anti-liquor activism was to gain the Irish respect and to challenge negative hegemonic images of them by their embracing the middle-class and mostly Protestant value of temperance. Minnesota's Irish American temperance reformers consequently portrayed temperance as a path to spiritual and material self-improvement and as a means to transform the Irish from a degraded into a regenerate state. John Devereux of the *Northwestern Chronicle* argued that with the advent of the temperance movement among the Irish, "a new generation of Irishmen has sprung up at home and abroad." He also claimed that "Pat with a short dudeen in the band of his hat and a shillelah in his hand, breaking heads for pure friendship and the glory of old Ireland, has ceased to exist unless on the stage." Dillon O'Brien also stressed the idea of a transformed Irish ethnic identity. He asked all Irishmen to follow the model of the "sober Irishman" rather than to confirm existing stereotypes. The overall aim of Irish temperance work, he declared, was to create a "regenerated nation" of Irish. The Irish reform leaders thus aimed at a renegotiation of

Irish identity: Alcohol was to shed some, or ideally all, of its significance for the Irish American community and culture, and sobriety was supposed to take its place. While the "drunken Paddy" might still be found in theater performances, it was not to have a real-life equivalent any more. This newly envisioned Irish American identity combined primordial and instrumentalist aspects; it was based on ancestral Irish values and kinship ties but simultaneously served the realization of ulterior motives, the integration into and acceptance by American society.[55]

Temperance also appealed to many Irish Catholics for theological reasons. Irish Catholicism was deeply imbued with the spirit of Jansenism, which considered man utterly depraved and expressed a distrust of natural human instincts and desires, exalted the virtue of purity, and encouraged minute examination of one's own conscience. The doctrine of Jansenism, which was undoubtedly pervasive in Irish thinking in the late eighteenth and early nineteenth centuries, was quasi-pietistic and therefore closely akin to Calvinism. It greatly facilitated the ideological immersion of the Irish in a movement that was so disconcerting to other ethnic Catholics, who did not see alcohol per se as dangerous—after all, it played a central role in the Bible as well as in Catholic liturgy.[56]

The motivation for and reasons behind Irish temperance work prove St. Paul's Catholic temperance movement to have been a specifically ethnic endeavor. Rather than reflecting the wish to control others, Minnesota's Irish temperance movement embodied an attempt at Irish self-definition and social advancement. In their speeches, the Irish temperance leaders did not hesitate to emphasize the ethnic specificity of their cause.[57] The proceedings of the Father Mathew Society of St. Paul also illustrate the Irishness of the Catholic temperance movement. Of the hundreds of people who joined, resigned, or were expelled from the society, the majority had Irish surnames. Few members, such as William H. Forbes, a trader and one of St. Paul's pioneer settlers, and John B. Brisbin, former mayor of St. Paul and renowned politician, were of French and Scottish ancestry. Only three members were of German descent and thus belonged to the minute number of German Catholics who were interested in the cause. It is also telling that despite the enthusiasm of their Irish coreligionists, none of St. Paul's six German Catholic parishes founded a temperance society.[58]

The Irish Catholic temperance movement in St. Paul was largely dependent on John Ireland's activism and enthusiasm. He attended most of the Father Mathew Society's meetings, gave lectures, made suggestions for activities, and actively took part in the society's administration. In April 1873, Ireland organized the Cadets and the Crusaders in St. Paul to encourage children and upwardly mobile, American-born young men, respectively, to join the temperance movement. These groups would be the movers and makers of tomorrow's Irish American community and were therefore the apple of the reformer's eye. John Ireland additionally established literary and debating societies, free libraries, and club rooms and organized a variety of lectures. By providing such uplifting entertainment, he aimed at transforming the Irish youth into a new, moral generation and attracting a wide spectrum of city residents, who would then mingle with these "respectable" Irish, thus giving them the opportunity to make contacts. Networking, both intra- and interethnic, was an important aspect of Irish temperance activism, as it promoted social and professional advancement.[59]

Thanks to the temperance advocates' enticing educational, welfare, and cultural programs and Ireland's regular lecture tours through Minnesota, nearly every English-speaking Catholic parish soon had a temperance society. By 1876, there were fifty-five Catholic temperance societies throughout the state with an aggregate membership of 4,200.[60] St. Paul remained the center of Irish Catholic temperance activism in Minnesota. Besides supplying the CTAU of the Diocese of St. Paul with leading officials, the city's Irish temperance movement was the strongest in the state. In 1875, Minnesota's capital had five Irish temperance societies with a membership of 425; in 1876, the Irish Catholic temperance movement was estimated to have about 1,000 supporters. This meant that about 8.6 percent of St. Paul's Irish Americans were enrolled members of a temperance society.[61]

While the number of Irish American men enrolled in the Father Mathew Society was comparably small, the Irish Catholic temperance society still managed to receive much attention and to make its ideology and tenets known throughout St. Paul's Irish American community. One important factor contributing to the respect of the movement among St. Paul's Irish Americans was its support by members of the city's Irish American elite. Besides John Ireland, it was the aforementioned Dillon O'Brien who conferred upon Irish Catholic temperance activism prestige and reputation. Together with John Ireland, Irish-born O'Brien had founded the Minnesota Irish Immigration Society, tirelessly engaged in Irish colonization schemes in Minnesota, and become the initiator and first editor of the *Northwestern Chronicle*. Another renowned Irish American who regularly gave lectures at the Father Mathew meetings was Ignatius Donnelly, a second-generation Irish lawyer and politician, who would become Minnesota's most famous Populist leader. These prominent Irishmen's participation in and contribution to the temperance cause considerably increased its prestige, attractiveness, influence, and popularity.[62]

St. Paul's Irish American temperance reformers also heightened their visibility and popularity through their frequent participation in public parades. Immediately after their society's founding, the Father Mathew men began to take part in the annual St. Patrick's Day parades, the showpieces of St. Paul's Irish American community, and in patriotic events, such as the parade in honor of George Washington's birthday in 1886. They also regularly staged impressive temperance parades all over Minnesota during the annual conventions of the state CTAU. The parades served as a public stage on which Minnesota's Irish American reformers performed their newly envisioned ethnic identity. Through this highly symbolic gesture, they celebrated and popularized this renegotiated identity, both among their own countrymen and among the non-Irish. While they thus demonstrated their power to themselves and to Irish and non-Irish outsiders, the parades simultaneously affirmed their loyalty to the Irish American community. Irish American ethnic identity had been added a new moral dimension, but it had not been alienated from its Irish roots.[63]

The clout of the Irish temperance movement also derived from the fact that it forced a sizable number of St. Paul's Irish Americans to reflect on their patterns of alcohol consumption. The minutes of the Father Mathew Society illustrate that numerous members were admitted every week, but just about as many were reported to have broken their pledges or were expelled for not having paid their dues. On the one hand, this high turnover rate suggests the difficulties that the principle of total abstinence posed for many Irish Americans. On the other hand, it illustrates that the actual number of Irish Americans that had at least temporarily been enrolled in the Father Mathew Society and exposed to its temperance ideology was far higher than the actual enrollment numbers are able to indicate. At every meeting, much time was dedicated to investigating whether and why individuals had broken the pledge. Once accused of having broken the pledge, members had to procure a certificate from a physician stating that the illicitly consumed liquor had been consumed for medical purposes only. If they could not procure such a writ, they had to pay a fine or were expelled. From the summer of 1869 on, the Father Mathew Society even established an investigative committee whenever the person accused of having broken the pledge denied the charge. Sometimes the investigations turned out to be rather difficult. When in June 1870, Timothy Reardon, an Irish-born carpenter and contractor, was accused of having violated the pledge and most emphatically denied this, the society went so far as to send a committee to the saloon in which Reardon had been reported drinking. The saloon owner argued that Reardon had forbidden him to give any information, which made many of the society's members declare him guilty. After long debates and due to a lack of evidence, the matter was tabled, but a few weeks later—probably out of indignation— Reardon voluntarily resigned. The inquisitorial attitude in the Father Mathew Society created a new climate among the city's Irish Americans: Liquor—once celebrated as an emblem of Irishness—began being viewed critically, ethnic drinking customs were scrutinized, and their impact on the success of the Irish in America assessed. While the majority of Irish did not join the movement in person, it still had strong reverberations among the Irish as a group because it exposed a large number of them to discussions on group identity and on the meaning of liquor for this identity. It fractured long-held beliefs that excessive whiskey consumption was respectable and an inextricable constituent of Irishness.[64]

Despite the influence and visibility of the Irish temperance movement, by far not all Irish Americans were in favor of Irish temperance activism and agreed with its suggested renegotiation of Irish ethnic identity. Many of them disputed Bishop Ireland's claim that Irish had a particular weakness for drink, claimed that the Irish-drunkard stereotype was sheer exaggeration, and interpreted the Irish temperance movement as an attack on their cultural habits and on the saloon as the focal point of leisure time. Other Irish Americans, who in principle agreed with the need for Irish temperance activism, condemned individual Irish temperance leaders for their radicalism. Thus, they were indignant at Dillon O'Brien, who had claimed that temperate liquor consumption was worse than excessive drinking and drunkenness. They considered this statement too radical, untrue, and blasphemous, as even Jesus Christ had moderately consumed liquor. Those Irish Americans, who were involved in the liquor business on St. Paul's Minnesota Street, the center of the saloon trade, publicly declared never to yield to the influence of the Irish temperance movement and taunted its leader, John Ireland: "You can't touch Minnesota Street!" The attack on the consumption and sale of liquor meant both economic ruin and a loss of prestige to Irish publicans and grocers. Apart from such individual criticism, however, we do not know much about St. Paul's Irish opposition to their compatriots' temperance efforts. Since the only Irish newspaper in St. Paul was actively involved in the temperance movement, the Irish oppositional voices remained largely unrecorded.[65]

Moloney has portrayed Irish temperance activism as "a positive alternative to Protestants who supported compulsion over suasion," but her findings do not hold true for Minnesota's Irish temperance movement. While in its early years, the Irish Catholic movement shied away from influencing other people's lifestyles through law, adhered to the personal liberty principle, and therefore maintained its boundaries against the Anglo-American reformers, by the mid-1870s a gradual change toward greater political involvement manifested itself. At the annual convention of the CTAU in 1875, President C. M. McCarthy advised individual Irish Catholics to cooperate with the non-Catholic temperance societies and to make sure at the polls that neither liquor sellers nor drunkards were elected. He furthermore pointed out that legislation against the liquor traffic could have its merits. In 1883, the Irish Catholic temperance advocates acted as leaders in the agitation for a High License bill, a clear sign that they had left the path of moral suasion. This shift from moral suasion to legal coercion was officially announced at the annual convention of the CTAU of the Diocese of St. Paul in June 1884. After praising High License as a regulatory measure, John

Ireland announced: "Hitherto we have confined ourselves to moral suasion in the movement. . . . But moral suasion must not be the sole means employed. We must also do our duties as citizens and use our rights of citizenship. We must, as citizens, see that good, salutory [sic] laws are enacted, laws which will control if they do not suppress the evil of intemperance."[66]

This official change in policy led to a loosening of boundaries and increasing cooperation between the Irish Catholic and Protestant temperance reformers. Their coercive temperance activism, however, also led to quarrels with the German Americans and heightened interethnic, particularly inner-Catholic, suspicions and tensions. For as soon as the Irish Catholic temperance movement entered the political arena, it automatically lost its exclusively Irish character. This loss of Irish specificity is reflected in the temperance addresses of 1887: Instead of being exclusively directed at the Irish, they were geared toward all "fellow-citizens of Minnesota."[67]

The self-confidence displayed in addressing all Minnesotans, irrespective of ethnic heritage, was directly related to the success of the High License Law. John Ireland and his Irish American reformers were mainly held responsible for the eventual passage of the bill in 1887. Self-confidence also derived from the fact that Minnesota's Irish Catholic temperance movement exerted a great impact on Irish Catholics all over the country. Members of the CTAU of the Diocese of St. Paul held important positions in the national CTAU and directed the national Irish Catholic temperance movement according to Minnesota standards. Moreover, in March 1887, the Irish Catholic temperance supporters gained another vital victory: After many years of seeking the approval of the temperance movement by the Catholic hierarchy, Pope Leo XIII sent a brief to Bishop Ireland in which he encouraged and praised total abstinence and the work of the Catholic total abstinence societies. Until then, many opponents of the movement, within and outside the Irish American community, had argued that the Catholic Church itself had never approved of its flock's temperance activities. According to the *Northwestern Chronicle*, the pope's brief was "the strongest encouragement ever yet given to the holy cause of Temperance" and therefore an efficient means to quiet those oppositional voices.[68]

By the late 1880s, Irish American temperance activism was generally viewed as a success story in Minnesota. Irish newspapers reported on the great number of temperate Irish buying lots and constructing homes, the sober and increasingly religious way in which the Irish holidays were celebrated, and the "complete absence of Irish names from the 'drunk and disorderly' docket of St. Paul," and they ascribed these changes solely to John Ireland's temperance activities. Anglo-American sources confirm these Irish claims by singing praises of Irish temperance work and emphasizing its importance for the advancement of Minnesota's Irish. The *Pioneer Press* proudly announced that the temperance movement had effected "a radical change . . . in the habits, manners and condition of this portion of our population. From the most intemperate, disorderly, and unthrifty, they have, as a rule, become among the most temperate, orderly, industrious, thrifty and moral classes of the community." In St. Paul, Irish American temperance activism was particularly crowned with success: Through its promotion of solid intra- and interethnic networks, combined with the creation of a regenerated generation of Irish, it slowly but surely turned the city into an "Irish town."[69]

German Americans for Personal Liberty

While the Irish became the Protestant temperance reformers' closest allies in the fight for temperance, Minnesota's German Americans, led by St. Paul's German American community, became the core of the anti-temperance bloc. Already in the antebellum years, Minnesota's German Americans had increasingly positioned themselves in opposition to the temperance movement. By the mid-1870s, due to the growing radicalization and coerciveness of the temperance movement, their attitude toward temperance became more pronounced, as they perceived it as an attack on both their culture and livelihoods. The temperance campaigns became their major point of cohesion and thus an asset that was exploited by the German intelligentsia in order to promote German American unity, the preservation of German heritage, and the emergence of a German American ethnic identity. This ethnic identity was based on essentials, such as the German language, history, and cultural peculiarities, but its maintenance also heavily relied on common causes of cultural defense, such as their fight against the temperance movement, and the interethnic debates arising in its wake.[70]

When from the late 1860s on, the largely Anglo-American Protestant temperance activism increasingly entered the realm of politics and dominated public discourse, German Americans began to develop elaborate arguments for their opposition to the movement. While they agreed with temperance in the form of moderation, they considered the temperance reformers' tendency to demand complete abstinence from liquor an absurdity. They were against the intemperate consumption of schnapps but did not find their ethnic beverage, beer, harmful. On the contrary, they argued that beer was healthy and a blessing to the country because it was the only way to counteract the devastation caused by whiskey.[71]

Most German Americans considered the temperance reformers mere fanatics and "moral cowards," who were incapable of practicing moderate liquor consumption. The highly derogatory term "Mucker," which they began to use for the Anglo-American temperance reformers around the time of the Civil War, reflects their contemptuous attitude.[72] Their contempt also derived from their feelings of ethnic superiority. Only few Americans, the editors of St. Paul's

German newspapers argued, enjoyed a philosophical and scientific education comparable to that of most German Americans. St. Paul's German Americans, as most German Americans, looked down upon the alleged lack of tradition, education, and a distinct high culture in the United States. Their pride in their own European cultural achievements and their corresponding feelings of cultural and educational superiority to the Anglo-American society made a social and cultural integration into the American mainstream undesirable. While the Irish American reformers interpreted participation in the temperance movement as a social and cultural asset, most German Americans viewed it as beneath their dignity. More importantly, their socioeconomic position was so sound that they did not need a temperance movement for social and material advancement.[73]

Prior to the organized temperance activism for an Ohio Liquor Law, German opposition to temperance was rather sporadic, mostly limited to legislative activism of individual German representatives, occasional public protests, demonstrations, and interventions into party politics—for example, Wolff and Malmros's introduction of an anti-temperance plank into the Republican platform.[74] With the specter of an Ohio Liquor Law, however, St. Paul's Germans began to perceive the temperance movement as a large-scale attack on their ethnic culture with its emphasis on sociable liquor consumption and on their economic existence. By the 1870s, the German American presence in the liquor business had even intensified, particularly in St. Paul. In those years, St. Paul's German Americans took out 121 of the 187 retail liquor licenses issued to foreign-born citizens. During a five-month period in 1878, they held 54 of the city's 57 brewers' licenses and thus monopolized the city's brewing industry. In 1880, Germans owned the majority of all the 132 breweries in Minnesota. And in 1887–1888, 285 of St. Paul's 634 saloons were owned by German Americans (44.95 percent) as opposed to only 55 by Irish Americans (8.68 percent).[75]

The realization that an Ohio Liquor Law for Minnesota would strike at the heart of German liquor culture, both economically and culturally, helped them to overcome what German newspapers described as the "jealous fragmentation of the German element in [the] state and in the city of St. Paul itself." German American elites used the fight against the Ohio Law to promote the organization of a solid anti-temperance bloc and the construction of a coherent German American ethnic identity, which could then be utilized to attain collective goals. German Americans perceived the Ohio Liquor bill as a "legislative monstrosity," as unjust and unreasonable. It would destroy the saloons and the liquor trade by making the sale of liquor risky and unprofitable and by giving immoral people the chance to sue the saloon owners. Therefore, they thought that the law should be termed "A Law for the Promotion of Rip-Offs, Extortion, Hypocrisy, and Showing-Off."[76]

German American newspaper editors across political colors and religious affiliations also conceptualized the Ohio Liquor bill in terms of class and ethnic identity. On the one hand, by dealing a heavy blow at Minnesota's saloon culture, the Anglo-American middle and upper classes actually sought to regulate the workers' leisure practices. On the other hand, the Ohio liquor bill was a nativist attack on German cultural habits: "The project originates from a source the dubious content of which is made up of Muckerdom, ingrained tyranny, and nativism." "Yankeeism," German Americans found, aimed at ethnic exclusivity and at annihilating German American culture. The fact that the German Americans accused the temperance reformers of nativist sentiments demonstrates that from their point of view the fight against the temperance law was not merely a fight about liquor but rather a fight for the maintenance of their culture and against assimilation into Anglo-American culture.[77]

Finally, German Americans considered the Ohio Liquor Law to be in stark conflict with the ideas of liberty and freedom delineated by the founders of the Republic. Personal liberty increasingly became their motto. In order to enjoy unrestrained liberty, they argued, they had sold their property, left their home country, and migrated to America. They had also shed their blood in the Civil War to uphold this personal liberty. After all these sacrifices, the majority of German Americans were not willing to accept the curtailment of that liberty that had made America so attractive to them. The personal liberty slogan was strategically appropriated by St. Paul's German American intelligentsia to promote greater cooperation within the German community. Only by appealing to values common to the majority of German Americans—all embodied by the personal liberty slogan—and by emphasizing the threat posed by the "fanatical enemy" could German American feelings of solidarity be strengthened and a common identity be invented. Personal liberty was what Joane Nagel has termed a *cultural construction*, a shared symbolic value promoting collective mobilization, group solidarity, and collective action.[78]

German American leaders worked hard to stir up oppositional spirit among their compatriots and to channel their anger into organized anti-temperance activism. On January 27, 1872, Theodor Sander of the *Minnesota Staats-Zeitung* asked all German opponents of the temperance movement and friends of personal liberty to come to Henry Orlemann's saloon to discuss countermeasures. He demanded resistance to the Ohio Liquor bill and provocatively asked: "Do you want to be put into a straightjacket without at least telling your rapists that you know that the law is a straightjacket and that you despise it as such?" Most of those attending the meeting at Orlemann's saloon belonged to St. Paul's German American elite, which indicates that the opposition to the temperance movement was not only led by German American liquor producers, sellers, and members of the working class—traditionally perceived as the major supporters of saloons—but also by the city's richest and most influential German American citizens. Ferdinand Willius, a prominent bank owner, chaired the meeting. Gustav Willius, his brother and co-owner of the bank; Albert Wolff, former editor of the *Minnesota Staats-Zeitung*; Carl H. Lienau, former editor of the *Volksblatt* and Democratic politician; John Haggenmiller, owner of the very popular Pittsburg Lagerbier-Saloon in St. Paul; and finally Theodor Sander himself were among those present. The participants drafted a petition that was to be circulated in St. Paul and beyond.[79] They also attempted to mobilize German Americans across Minnesota: Together with well-known German American leaders, such as William Pfänder from New Ulm and Henry Poehler from Sibley County, they invited "representatives of liberal ideas from German communities all over the state" to a mass convention of the "friends of progress" in St. Paul at the end of February. The goal was to organize Minnesota's "liberal German element" and to spread "light and enlightenment."[80]

The German American efforts at collaboration proved to be highly efficient. German petitions, secret arrangements, and the agitation of German political representatives prevented the Ohio Liquor bill from becoming law. The threat of an Ohio Liquor Law had acted as a wake-up call; from 1872 onward, one can truly speak of the existence of an anti-temperance coalition in Minnesota under the leadership of St. Paul's German Americans.[81] Within this newly emerging anti-temperance coalition, German American newspaper editors and politicians played a major role alongside German American liquor sellers and brewers. The debates about the Ohio Liquor bill convinced Minnesota's German American liquor sellers and producers of the need for organizational structures that could accumulate funds and lobbying power. In the course of three years, they founded two powerful associations: In 1873, wholesale liquor dealers from the Twin Cities, many of whom had German roots, founded the Minnesota Wholesale Liquor Dealers Association. In circulars, which they distributed throughout the state, the members of this new organization emphasized the legality of their business and their willingness to pay taxes and to obey the state's existing liquor laws. They also distanced themselves from the ongoing "fanaticism" seeking to ostracize their businesses and to dictate what people should eat and drink. The Minnesota State Association for the Protection of Personal Liberty, founded by St. Paul's saloon owners and brewers in 1876, proved to be far more powerful than that of the wholesale liquor dealers. They hired lawyers to protect their members in trials, influenced elections by informing voters about the candidates' attitudes toward liquor and "unjust class legislation," and put legislators under pressure. The Association's organizational structure was dominated by Germans, most notably by alcoholic heavyweights such as William Hamm and Georg Benz, one of the city's most wealthy liquor wholesale dealers and the Association's president. Benz, an immigrant from Hesse-Darmstadt who had come to St. Paul in 1856, was at the heart of St. Paul's liquor industry. While first having run a small business with the later brewer F. A. Renz, he then collaborated with J. C. Becht and from 1878 rapidly expanded his business with his sons. He was also a member of the legislature between 1873 and 1875 and greatly influenced legislative processes. The activities of these organizations reveal that the German American opposition to the temperance movement was not solely motivated by ideas of personal liberty or Old-World nostalgia but also by the fear of economic loss or ruin. The liquor dealers' and producers' economic interests greatly reinforced their ethnic interests: For them, personal liberty implied the freedom not only to act out their cultural habits but also the ability to conduct their businesses without restriction.[82]

German American anti-temperance activism and ethnic group building reached their first climax during the 1880s, when party politics and the legislative halls were infiltrated by the struggles for a prohibitory constitutional amendment and High License. In the context of these fights, articles in the German American press reveal a sense of group unity. When the prohibitory constitutional amendment was lost in the 1883 legislature, a German reader sent a poem to the *Volkszeitung*, which illustrated the German American community's malicious joy at the failure of the amendment. The poem's refrain is quite remarkable, suggesting that no matter what mission the temperance reformers will embark on, "amongst us we will continue to guzzle." The use of the word "us," referring to all German Americans, and the rigid separation of us versus them suggest that in the context of the coercive temperance efforts of the 1870s and 1880s, German Americans had come to see themselves as an ethnic group and had strengthened their social boundaries in order to protect—to echo Fredrik Barth—the "cultural stuff" they enclosed. With the help of the temperance movement, they had turned from an "unfinished ethnic group," as Heinz Kloß has called them, to a rather stable ethnic entity. This process of ethnicization was also an effective defense against rapid absorption by the Anglo-American society. The announcement that they would continue their drinking in spite of all temperance efforts suggests both ethnic consciousness and ethnic persistence.[83]

Of course, their rigid opposition to temperance brought them into conflict with other ethnic groups, notably the Anglo-American temperance advocates and the temperate Irish. After the Republican Party had adopted the "German" anti-temperance plank in 1867, Minnesota's Good Templars—most of them Anglo-Americans—accused the German American Republicans of having drafted the plank to pledge the Republican Party against all legal barriers to secure the proper observance of the Lord's Day. To them, the struggle about temperance signified a "great battle between German infidelity and American Christianity." "Abrogation of the legalized sanctity of the Sabbath," they argued, "is a part of the infidel Germans' political creed. . . . Until last Wednesday no American body has endorsed their views. To first bow down before them and to yield in the fullest manner to their insulting terms was reserved to the Republican State

Convention of the State of Minnesota." This statement is one of the few sources openly voicing the temperance advocates' anger about and contempt for the German Americans and their ideas of personal liberty, which they equated with anti-Christianity. The interethnic tensions caused by the temperance debates led to a tightening of group boundaries between German American temperance opponents and Anglo-American reformers.[84]

The most severe interethnic clashes, however, occurred between St. Paul's German American Catholics and their Irish coreligionists because they were inevitably confronted with each other within the realm of the Catholic Church. Due to the temperance activism of John Ireland and part of his Irish Catholic flock, German American Catholics found themselves in a quandary between their American Catholic and ethnic identities. Whereas the former obliged them to be loyal to their bishop and to live according to his guidelines, the latter made them cherish personal liberty and called for support of their countrymen in the fight against temperance. Furthermore, the Roman Catholic Church as such was not opposed to alcohol consumption, which strengthened the German American Catholics' opposition to temperance reform.[85] In the 1880s, St. Paul's German Catholics decided to emphasize their German American (and Roman Catholic) over their American Catholic identities, identifying with their countrymen rather than with their Irish coreligionists. The tensions arising from this decision were regularly fought out on the pages of St. Paul's German and Irish Catholic newspapers, *Der Wanderer* and the *Northwestern Chronicle*. After a particularly nasty exchange between these newspapers in the context of the High License debate, the German Catholic editor Hugo Klapproth concluded that, due to their fundamentally different opinions about High License, an agreement between the German Americans and the Irish American and Anglo-American reformers seemed unlikely.[86]

Conflicts also arose between the non-Catholic German Americans and the Irish American reformers, with the former especially enraged about the interference of the American Catholic Church, particularly John Ireland, in politics. They thought that Ireland should limit himself to influencing the affairs of his church and leave secular concerns to others. They believed that the church should restrict its activities to those people who needed its support, notably the Irish Americans, and should not worry about other nationalities whose liquor consumption did not have disastrous results. Furthermore, due to the long history of liquor in Germany, German Americans felt superior and more experienced with regard to the issue of liquor consumption and thus considered it a shame to be taught by Irish priests.[87]

In the wake of these manifold interethnic conflicts, ethnic persistence became the watchword of German American leaders in those years, and German beer was increasingly interpreted as a means of ethnic preservation. Minnesota's

Germans emphasized that "their share of the general sinfulness of human beings would not be lessened by means of High License," or, to put it more bluntly, that they did not intend to change their patterns of liquor consumption. Beer was, to them, not only a tasty and refreshing beverage promoting sociability, but it also served a significant "mission": It was a "great lever in the Germanization of the American." Considering their culture superior to the American way of life, Minnesota's German Americans felt the necessity to germanize their new home country. Beer was seen as a representative of German culture, a germanizing tool powerful enough to penetrate the wall of American narrow-mindedness. Thus, despite the temperance reformers' growing strength, the state's German Americans continued to promote their way of life and withdrew even more into the "closed cultural world" of their neighborhoods and associations.[88]

The Emergence of a Women's Temperance Movement

The years after the Civil War were finally characterized by the emergence of a thoroughly organized, largely Anglo-American women's temperance movement in Minnesota. During the war, women had acquired a taste for the public sphere that would translate into increasing female demands for greater political rights in postbellum Minnesota. Moreover, economic and social changes allowed middle- and upper-class women to engage in reform efforts. Developments within the national temperance movement, such as the Woman's Crusade as well as the founding of the national WCTU, also encouraged Minnesota's women to expand their temperance activism and to establish all-female temperance societies. The founding of a state WCTU can be considered one of the landmarks in the history of the temperance cause and woman's emancipation in Minnesota. With its strategic appropriation of the contemporary gender ideology, the WCTU served as what Nancy Fraser has called a "subaltern counterpublic," one of those "parallel discursive arenas where members of subordinated social groups invent and circulate counterdiscourses, which in turn permit them to formulate oppositional interpretations of their identities, interests and needs." "On the one hand," Fraser has argued, "they function as spaces of withdrawal and regroupment; on the other hand, they also function as bases and training grounds for agitational activities directed toward wider publics." From this subaltern counterpublic, women increasingly ventured into the male public and political spheres as speakers, lobbyists, and agitators. Minnesota's WCTU women's agitation for female suffrage, their involvement in the founding of the Minnesota Woman Suffrage Association (MWSA), as well as their successful fight for a Scientific Temperance Instruction Law in 1887 demonstrate the intertwining of the temperance and suffrage causes and women's increasing politicization. Through the work of the WCTU, the boundaries between the public and private spheres became increasingly fluid, and the public sphere was greatly democratized.[89]

Immediately after the Civil War, male temperance advocates reassumed control in Minnesota's temperance organizations, and it first appeared as if women's temperance activism would take the shape of the antebellum years. Instead, however, there developed a powerful women's temperance movement in the state. The reasons behind the emergence of such a movement were diverse. It has been widely acknowledged by scholars that the women's wartime work had changed their consciousness, convinced them of their manifold capabilities outside the domestic sphere, and led to the destabilization of the public/private dichotomy. This change of female consciousness immediately found expression in an emergence of female activism in favor of the ballot in Minnesota's legislature between 1865 and 1871. Even though all of the bills for woman suffrage were either killed by the legislators or vetoed by the governor, the stage was set for discussions of women's greater involvement in the workings of the state.[90]

Changes in middle- and upper-class women's lives in the second half of the century also facilitated their extensive engagement in temperance work. After the Civil War, homemaking and childcare became the major occupation for many middle-class women, whereas before many of them had had to contribute to the family income. The declining birth rate allowed women more leisure time, which they could use for reform work. Additional factors facilitating female temperance work were the increasing urbanization of the United States and the concomitant congregation of women in the cities, which made collaboration and interaction for a common cause easier. Finally, universal education was also responsible for the mass growth of a female temperance movement and provided for the necessary leadership.[91]

National developments within the temperance movement also affected female temperance work in Minnesota. Between 1873 and 1874 the so-called Woman's Crusade swept the country. Having originated in Ohio and New York State, it spread to more than nine hundred communities in thirty-one states and territories. Its principal strategy was a public march by groups of a few to several hundred women to the communities' saloons. Through prayers, songs, arguments, and pleas, the women then tried to persuade or coerce the owners to give up their businesses. Although the "Woman's War," as the Crusade came to be called, had only temporary results, it unleashed emotions similar to a conversion experience. It also led to the creation of an organization that would become one of the major forces in the fight against alcohol and one of the major vehicles for women's emancipation: the Woman's Christian Temperance Union (WCTU), established by Anglo-American temperance women in Cleveland, Ohio, on November 18, 1874.[92]

Even though the state's newspapers reported almost daily about the women's raids in Ohio and Indiana, Minnesota was barely touched by the Crusade. In

Figure 2.1. In 1873, women crusaders held a vigil in front of a saloon in Anoka. The saloon owner's wife, seen in the second floor window, prepared to rout the ladies by throwing a pan of water on them. Courtesy of the Minnesota Historical Society.

some smaller towns, such as Anoka, Howard Lake, and Hutchinson, women banded together and marched against the saloon (see figure 2.1). St. Paul, as well as the state's other towns, was spared such agitation despite individual female efforts "to inaugurate the Woman's Ohio war upon the saloons in this city," as the *Pioneer Press* reported. Numerous Minnesota men and women publicly spoke very negatively about this form of female temperance activism, deriding the Crusaders as "excited and silly females" and as "praying Amazons," and thus might have intimidated those women who had announced their intention to crusade.[93] Rather than causing actual saloon raids across the state, in Minnesota the Woman's Crusade led to the founding of women's temperance societies and to a discussion of women's roles within the temperance movement. Thus, as a response to the Woman's Crusade, Woman's Temperance Leagues were founded in St. Paul and several other towns in Minnesota in 1874 and 1875. The Woman's Crusade and its impact on the shape of female temperance activism in Minnesota were also debated at the State Temperance Convention in Red Wing on September 2, 1874. While sources remain silent about whether this form of female temperance work met the approval of those present, both male and female reformers agreed on the great encouragement the Crusade was to Minnesota's female reformers and emphasized that female reform work had increased in the wake of events in Ohio. In order to give an example of what women could do, the female delegates of the convention founded another temperance society, the Minnesota Sunday School Temperance League, with the goal of instilling temperance principles into the minds of Sunday School students.[94]

While the Sunday School temperance movement thus flourished in Minnesota, it took Minnesota's women until April 27, 1875, to establish the state's first WCTU chapter in St. Paul. The officers of this first WCTU were the wives of the city's most prominent citizens and temperance workers. Caroline Murray, one of the organization's vice presidents, was William Pitt Murray's wife, and Emilie Cochran, the wife of the temperance advocate Thomas Cochran, was one of its founding members. Harriet E. Bishop, St. Paul's first schoolteacher and female temperance worker, became the organization's president. Many of these women had previously been active in the temperance movement, particularly in the IOGT.[95]

The founding of the first WCTU chapter was an important step in the history of woman's emancipation in Minnesota. Women had developed from mere supporters of male temperance activism to major protagonists and organizers in their own right in the fight against alcohol. This new organizational structure also allowed women to do independent temperance work according to their own fashion. As Harriet E. Bishop argued at the St. Paul WCTU's charter meeting, "the work should be done by women in women's way," and no men should be enlisted under the WCTU's banner. Not surprisingly, within the organization men could neither vote, hold office, nor participate in debate. Within two years, the women involved in the Minnesota Sunday School Temperance League, who already closely cooperated with the national WCTU and who were, in 1877, for the first time asked to send a delegate to its annual convention, decided to found a state WCTU in Minneapolis's Westminster Presbyterian Church on September 6, 1877.[96]

The state WCTU was the first all-female organization at the state level. Most of its members were Anglo-American, pietistic, middle-class women. Their ethnic, class, religious, and gender identities reinforced each other and their enthusiasm about the temperance movement. Over the next years, its leaders learned to coordinate women's work in the local chapters effectively and to channel their influence, and thus turned the Minnesota WCTU into a powerful interest group. Women's agitation in the organization enabled them to function as organizers, speakers, political activists, and lobbyists and facilitated their meaningful participation in a movement that had come to rely predominantly on legal coercion. The WCTU managed to reach out to a comparably large number of women by allowing the coexistence of a multitude of positions on women's rights questions within the organization, which becomes clearly visible in its leaders' annual addresses. In her address at the second annual meeting in Owatonna, WCTU President "Mrs. Wilson Holt," the wife of the pastor of the Presbyterian Church in that city, clearly defined how she viewed the nature of the organization. Even though she considered the WCTU an outgrowth of the Woman's Crusade, she viewed it as "the crusade modified, made practical, more adapted to woman's nature and woman's work. It is a *gospel* temperance work, largely carried on by prayer." Holt mentioned how she herself had struggled to accept the office of president and encouraged those women who still quarreled with the idea of doing public work to become active. She also clearly stated that, as an organization, the WCTU was not fighting for the ballot. Her conceptualization of the WCTU was, however, not shared by all of its members. On the second evening of the convention, Sarah Burger Stearns, secretary of the Duluth WCTU and a well-known suffrage advocate, asked for the prohibition of the liquor traffic through the votes of men and women. To Stearns, prohibition could be achieved only by giving women the ballot, as the male prohibitionists were numerically too weak to overcome the state's anti-temperance forces. She furthermore stressed that women should move toward greater self-reliance and mutual helpfulness and should feel free to do anything that promoted the temperance cause. Stearns, however, knew that a number of WCTU members were opposed to her ideas of equality, and she asked them to give her speech a second thought.[97]

While Holt represented the more traditional women in Minnesota's WCTU, Stearns's address embodied its progressive strand that was present since the organization's founding and that gained strength over the next decades. In between these two extreme standpoints, there were all sorts of nuances. In order not to scare off their more traditional members, the progressives among Minnesota's WCTU leaders carefully fused concerns about domesticity and traditionalism with those about individualism and equal rights. The home-protection slogan, which had been introduced into the WCTU of America by then-secretary Frances Willard and was picked up by Minnesota WCTU women such as Stearns, exemplifies such pragmatism and strategic thinking. In the aforementioned address, Stearns took pains to point out that Minnesota's women needed the ballot not for the sake of individual rights but in order to protect the home from the liquor trade. By connecting it to traditional concepts of domesticity, she defused the radicalism of the suffrage ideology. Such a strategic appropriation of existing notions of femininity in order to undermine the ideology of the two spheres justified women's entrance into public and political life and built a stepping stone for those WCTU members who were not yet ready to question their socially ascribed role. As historian Elaine Frantz Parsons has noted, "it was precisely reformers' insistence that their ultimate goal was to return to the home that made the WCTU so successful in convincing moderate women to embrace their radical, invasive tactics." The concept of home protection drove multitudes of gospel temperance women into the WCTU's fold, where they were gradually exposed to and made receptive of ideas of female equality. Without this gradual politicization of a mass of women, the suffrage movement of the twentieth century would not have had the same amount of female support. Suffrage organizations, like the MWSA, failed to attract the grass roots to their movement, as their demands for the ballot on grounds of the equality of the sexes alienated the majority of women at the time. The WCTU leaders, by contrast, picked up women where they were and slowly moved them along the path of emancipation.[98]

The Minnesota WCTU's involvement in the founding of Minnesota's first state suffrage association underlines that its compromising attitude on the subjects of woman suffrage and women's rights was a pragmatic decision and not the result of an inherent conservatism. The records of the founding of the MWSA in 1881 reveal that at least five of the MWSA's fourteen charter members were standard-bearers in the WCTU. What is more, the MWSA was founded in the context of the WCTU's annual convention. Since the temperance women were dissatisfied with the repeated failure of a constitutional amendment allowing women to vote on liquor issues, they adjourned in order to organize a woman's organization that would spearhead suffrage as its single goal.[99]

The Minnesota WCTU's intentional ideological openness also impacted its structural and methodological alignment. Despite the strength of the state organization, the WCTU emphasized the autonomy of its local chapters, which were free to determine their activities, program, as well as the methods they employed in their fight against liquor. This structural and methodological autonomy was so important to the state's WCTU leaders that it was presented in the form of a resolution, which was passed at the Minnesota WCTU's annual meeting in 1879: "Resolved, That unanimity of spirit and unity of method in action, is always desirable in any organization, provided they may be secured without sacrifice of truth, justice or efficiency; but that it is better to agree to disagree than for any to be found recreant to individual conviction of right and duty." "To agree to disagree" became the guideline of the Minnesota WCTU and was one of its major assets. It took into account the heterogeneity of nineteenth-century women's mindsets, allowed women to develop new conceptions of femininity at their own speed, and thus facilitated the gradual creation of a separate female public sphere. In this exclusively female sphere, women could enhance their skills, learn about political realities, and become conscious of the oppressiveness of the ideology of the two spheres. Only through the gradualism of such an intermediate public could the wish to negotiate and finally erode the boundaries between the private and public spheres be generated.[100]

In order to allow the local chapters to choose from a broad spectrum of activities and methods and to satisfy the diversity of outlooks represented in it, the Minnesota WCTU implemented Frances Willard's demand for a "Do-Everything Policy" and established committees comprising most areas of social life. As early as 1880, it had standing committees on Temperance Literature and Publications; Press; Sunday School Work; Unfermented Wine; Work among the Foreign Population; Finance; Temperance Schools; Instruction in Schools; Juvenile Work; Young Ladies' Unions; Gospel Temperance; Fallen Women; Enforcement of Law; Prison Reform; Memorials to Ecclesiastic, Scientific and Other Bodies; and To Secure a More Favorable Legislation on Temperance. In addition, the WCTU proudly reported having various kinds of organizations for children and young girls with a large membership, such as the Young Woman's Christian Temperance Unions (YWCTU), the Bands of Hope, and the Loyal Temperance Legions (LTL). This wide range of activities signaled the WCTU's shift from a movement solely devoted to temperance to a women's reform movement, made it attractive to a great number of women, and led to a steady increase in membership. The latter rose from 23 unions with 696 members in 1879 to 202 unions with 3,826 members in 1887.[101]

Upon becoming members in the WCTU, many of these women were drawn into state politics and into struggles for greater political rights for women. The Minnesota WCTU collaborated with other temperance advocates in their campaigns for temperance laws and prohibition, collected thousands of signatures in favor of prohibition, and regularly showed physical presence in the state capitol. From 1877 on, the organization also fought for woman suffrage, initially for "the temperance ballot," that is, women's right to vote on matters pertaining to temperance. From 1881 on, they fought for "unlimited suffrage." By thrusting women into the public sphere, Minnesota's WCTU and its local chapters became springboards for political activism and motors of change in the existing gender ideology. In addition, the organization's support of suffrage yet again demonstrates the congeniality and overlapping of the temperance and suffrage causes.[102]

With the exception of the small number of third-party temperance activists who greeted women's political activism and inserted a suffrage plank into their party's platform describing "the enfranchisement of woman as an important stepping stone to the success of our cause," most men were initially hostile toward women's intrusion into their sphere and showered them with ridicule and contempt. In 1878, when a group of women appeared before the House to argue in favor of the temperance ballot, the speaker Charles A. Gilman became so abusive and insulting in his address that no papers dared to print it. The women quietly sat through the insults. Legislators also time and again reminded them that their assigned place was the domestic sphere. Instead of striving for the ballot and collecting signatures, they should rather educate their children not to become drunkards. Anglo-American women's temperance activism provoked conflicts between the sexes and harsh reactions from those men who were unwilling to renegotiate existing gender roles.[103]

Such hostilities did not discourage Minnesota's WCTU women from expanding their political involvement, which culminated in the passage of a Scientific
Temperance Instruction bill in 1887. Its passage concluded the first stage of the
WCTU's politicization, a process that taught a large number of women, who had
previously had little experience in the political arena, the practice of politics.
Scientific temperance instruction can be defined as the mandatory teaching of
the physiological consequences of alcohol consumption by means of scientific
data and statistics. By legally implementing temperance into the curricula of
Minnesota's public schools, the law shaped the generation of pupils that later
fought for the adoption of the National Prohibition Amendment in 1919. Even if
the law itself dealt with an acknowledged woman's issue—child education—and
was thus rooted in the female private sphere, the political process connected with
its passage was located in the male public sphere. And it was the circumstances
of the bill's passage that taught the women the rules of the political sphere.[104]

As early as 1885, the Minnesota WCTU women had presented a compulsory
temperance instruction bill to the chairman of the educational committee and
supplied both houses of the legislature with temperance lesson books. Two years
later, from hindsight, the superintendent of the Minnesota WCTU's Committee
on Temperance Textbooks, Charlotte S. Winchell, critically analyzed her own
and the other WCTU women's behavior: "[T]he women sat still at home and
anxiously waited for the announcement that the bill had become a law, when as
the session neared its close inquiry was made and it was learned that it had been
indefinitely postponed or something; indeed, we found it difficult to ascertain
what ever became of it. We had learned again that 'Success does not happen, it
must be won.'" Political success, the women had realized, could not be achieved
by moderation and reticence but only through agitation and lobbying. The motto
of WCTU leader Frances Willard encapsulates this lesson.[105]

This newly learned lesson was applied in the 1887 fight for a Scientific Temperance Instruction Law. This time, Minnesota's women did not quietly wait but
actively campaigned for the law by drafting a memorandum to the legislature,
holding various meetings in order to raise money, and collecting thousands of
signatures in favor of such a law throughout the state. The WCTU leaders also
studied the laws of various states, consulted a lawyer, and finally drafted a bill
containing the best features of all these laws. When the legislators juggled the
bill back and forth to prevent its passage, the WCTU asked two hundred of its
members to inundate them with letters. This flood of letters and the pressure
the women exerted in the legislature led to the passage of the law. The temperance women rejoiced and sent bouquets of flowers tied with white ribbons to
the governor and both Houses. On March 1, 1887, in the presence of the WCTU
women, Governor Andrew R. McGill signed the bill into law, presenting the
women his pen as a gift.[106]

The temperance women's degree of political activism displays how much their perception of themselves had changed. They had moved from supporting temperance campaigns largely led by men to initiating and drafting a law themselves and maneuvering it successfully through the Minnesota legislature. In the context of the Scientific Temperance Instruction Law, a sizable number of Minnesota's WCTU women were ready to transcend the boundaries of their designated sphere and the counterpublic that had developed within the WCTU and entered the political sphere wholeheartedly. Of course, it was easier for many women to fight for a law affecting the educational sector rather than for a prohibitory law and woman suffrage, both of which aimed at severely redefining the male sphere. Similarly, for men, the WCTU's involvement in favor of scientific temperance instruction was easier to digest than attacks on their saloons and political prerogatives. Nevertheless, the support and respect the women received from many legislators also indicate that the boundaries between the spheres had gradually begun to become more permeable and that an expansion and democratization of the public sphere was under way. This expansion and democratization was mostly due to the work of the WCTU, which had managed to "replace prayer as woman's answer to distress" by social and political action.[107]

3. "Talking against a Stonewall"

The High License Consensus (1888–1897)

Futile Fights for County Option and Prohibition

The decade after the passage of the High License Law was characterized by an almost complete standstill of temperance reform in Minnesota due to the existence of a High License consensus. The moderate reformers, the leaders of the Republican Party, and even many of the law's opponents argued in favor of maintaining it—all, of course, for different reasons. Except for occasional laws regulating the specifics of the liquor sale, stringent temperance reform in the form of County Option Laws and prohibition did not have the slightest chance. The agreement on the effectiveness of High License was so strong that the *Western Leader*, a temperance newspaper published in Minnesota, even went so far as to speak of a "conspiracy of silence" with reference to more stringent temperance legislation.[1] This situation did not change when two groups of Minnesotans joined the radical reformist camp: Minnesota's Scandinavian American community and the members of the state's Populist movement. The consensus also prevailed against attempts by the liquor interests to repeal the existing High License Law. Ironically, this High License consensus resulted in greater cooperation among the law's opponents and in the founding of the Minnesota Anti-Saloon League (ASL), the temperance organization that would eventually be mainly responsible for the passage and ratification of the National Prohibition Amendment in 1919.

According to its broad set of supporters, the greatest success of the High License Law was the reduction of the number of saloons. In his final message, Governor McGill proudly announced that High License had reduced the number of saloons in Minnesota by one-third, increased the revenue from the licenses by one-fourth, and decreased drunkenness. Newspapers confirmed that especially the smaller saloons and "immoral dives" located at the outskirts of the cities could not afford the high license fees and went bankrupt. The centralization of the saloon business, the law's advocates argued, resulted in a better surveillance of saloons by the police and in a greater observance of the law.[2] These enthusiastic accounts, however, have to be questioned with respect to their accuracy. The annual statistics published by the City of St. Paul suggest that while the High License Law had indeed reduced the number of saloons from 763 in 1887 to 361 in 1888, law observance, drunkenness, and morality had not improved and liquor consumption had not diminished significantly in its wake. After the High License Law became effective in St. Paul, the arrests for drunkenness and disorderly conduct even increased, and while the production of malt liquors slightly diminished, the production of distilled spirits rose.[3]

At the time, however, most reformers only saw the numerical reduction of saloons, were satisfied with their progress, and therefore had no need to advocate more restrictive measures. Many Minnesotans who had originally been skeptical of High License joined this consensus, praised the High License Law for its effectiveness, and proclaimed that further measures restricting the liquor trade had become unnecessary. Minnesota's Republican Party in particular felt that through its fight for High License it had done justice to the temperance element in its ranks and in its 1888 platform unanimously spoke out in favor of the continuation of the High License policy. Only two groups were actually opposed to the continuation of High License. On the one hand, the liquor sellers and producers, in particular the German brewers, worked for the abolition of High License because it seriously hampered their businesses. German Americans, who had a great stake in the production and sale of liquor and could not reconcile with the law for cultural reasons either, also agitated for its repeal. On the other hand, the radical temperance reformers—such as the Prohibition Party, the IOGT, and the WCTU, and a large number of Baptists, Congregationalists, Methodists, and Presbyterians—condemned High License as a halfway measure, arguing that only prohibition could efficiently oust liquor.[4]

While this latter group ideally wished for the immediate prohibition of liquor, its members were realistic enough to know that chances for prohibition were not particularly high at that moment. Besides campaigning for prohibition, they therefore also set their hopes on County Option. Replacing the Local Option Law of 1870, such a law would enable the voters of a county to decide for or against the sale of liquor within the county limits and enable the reformers to dry up the state gradually. County Option was not only debated in Minnesota but also in a large number of other states, such as Nebraska, Iowa, Montana, and New Jersey. It empowered the county's rural areas to decide on the fate of the liquor business in its larger towns or cities. It thereby violated the traditional governmental principle of home rule cherished by many native-born Americans and immigrants alike. From its first introduction into the Minnesota legislature in 1889 until its eventual passage in 1915, the County Option bill caused battles even more fervent than the fights about High License in the previous decade.[5]

In the course of several decades, Minnesota's radical temperance reformers developed a variety of arguments in favor of County Option. From an economic standpoint they argued that while all county taxpayers paid for the crime, insanity, and poverty resulting from saloons, it was only the towns and cities that benefited from their presence. They also interpreted County Option as boosting democracy because all people—not only those living in villages and towns—could decide on the liquor traffic. Besides these arguments relating specifically to County Option, there was, of course, the reformers' general tendency to portray liquor and the saloons as promoters of crime and immorality and to conceptualize County Option as the only way, short of prohibition, to curb these evils efficiently.[6]

In their fight for County Option, these reformers received support by the state's Scandinavian American community, which, by 1885, was estimated to constitute one-third of Minnesota's entire population and whose growing influence at the polls was a frequent topic of debate among contemporary Minnesotans. While the majority of Minnesota's Scandinavian Americans did not advocate total abstinence, sources reveal that a growing number of them collaborated with the Anglo-American reformers in their agitation for more stringent temperance laws. By 1890, the Scandinavian membership of the IOGT had increased so rapidly that the Grand Lodge could afford to establish a Scandinavian district covering the entire state and consisting of eighteen lodges with 641 members. This new ethnic district started holding its own annual sessions and established a monthly newspaper, the first Scandinavian IOGT newspaper in the country. In August 1892, Minnesota's Scandinavian Good Templars even founded their own "Junior Grand Lodge." Besides organizing within the IOGT, Scandinavian Americans founded prohibition clubs and circulated petitions asking for the further restriction of the liquor trade. Prominent Scandinavian American County Optionists, such as Falk Gjertsen, Soren Listoe, and Sven Oftedahl, also engaged in futile attempts to commit the Republican Party to County Option. In July 1892, Scandinavian American leaders put pressure on the Republicans' gubernatorial candidate Knute Nelson, assuring him that an overwhelming majority of Scandinavian Lutherans favored total prohibition as the ultimate solution to the liquor problem. While they did not expect him and his party to go so far, they considered a plank in favor of County Option a "stern necessity" if the party wished to secure Scandinavian support in the coming elections.[7]

The County Optionists were also strengthened through the rise of the Populist movement, which emerged in the Midwest as an economic protest movement against agrarian grievances and mainly aimed at ending the alleged corporate dominance of the government and at nationalizing monopolies, such as the railroad and the telegraphs. Many Populists endorsed the dry cause; they considered the liquor interests one of those corporate interests dominating politics. With its shifting of political power from the cities to the rural areas, County Option, in particular, was greatly in accordance with the Populist antiurban agenda. Not surprisingly, Populist leaders, such as Sidney M. Owen and William R. Dobbyn, as well as a great number of their Scandinavian American supporters, openly aligned themselves with the dry cause. In the early 1890s, legislators of Minnesota's two Populist parties, the Farmers' Alliance and the People's Party,[8] repeatedly endorsed County Option bills in Minnesota's legislature. The People's Party even considered absorbing the Prohibition Party due to their partial overlap of interests. While they refrained from advocating prohibition in order not to alienate their voters, in 1892 and 1894 they added the "nationalization of the liquor industry and its management by the state without profit" to their antimonopoly plank. The Prohibition Party, however, wholeheartedly rejected this plank, as it fell short of prohibition. On the need to eradicate liquor there was no compromise.[9]

The agitation of these groups of reformers time and again led to intense temperance debates in the legislature, such as the "great temperance debate" in the House of Representatives in 1889, which lasted for seven hours. But such debates, in which the reformers mustered all their strength, could not belie the fact that the majority of Minnesotans were strongly in favor of upholding the 1887 High License Law and that the radical reformers constituted merely a minority within the state's population. In 1889, only one out of every ninety Minnesotans declared to be in favor of County Option or prohibition. Due to such a distribution of power, which would not change significantly during the next years, County Option was defeated time and again in the legislative sessions throughout the period.[10]

The High License consensus also undermined all efforts to get rid of the High License Law. The Columbia Association's attempts at repeal had been thwarted as early as 1889. In 1894, upon his election as senator, saloon owner Nicholas Pottgieser of St. Paul vowed to introduce a bill reducing the license fee to $500 everywhere in Minnesota. He kept his promise and was supported by the Twin Cities' liquor interests. After much turmoil in the legislature, the legislative delegations of Ramsey and Hennepin Counties decided that it was unwise to attack the High License Law, as this would benefit the radical reformers. Their decision against pushing this bill through was indeed a wise one. Shortly after its introduction, the legislature received a petition of the members of the House of Hope Presbyterian Church against the Pottgieser bill, arguing that rather than being reduced the license fee should be raised to $2,000.[11]

The only temperance bills with a chance of success at the time were those that sought to regulate specifics of the liquor sale rather than curtail the manufacture or sale of liquor. One of these bills, the Sullivan, or Anti-Growler, bill, deserves particular mention, as it highlights the temperance movement's objective to forcibly change working-class drinking habits. While on the surface aiming at the prohibition of the sale of liquor to minors, this bill, introduced into the 1893 legislature by Dennis M. Sullivan, actually sought to undermine the practice of "rushing the growler," that is, sending one's child to the saloon with an empty pitcher to buy alcohol. Representative John H. Ives, who represented a working-class district and was the salaried attorney of a St. Paul brewery, accused Sullivan, one of St. Paul's Irish Republicans and the Superintendent of the Minnesota Transfer Company, of seeking to harm the working class with his bill. Unlike the residents in Sullivan's district, Ives argued, his constituents could not afford to store wine and beer in their cellars but instead had to send their children to the saloon after a day of hard work to fetch them. Among the businessmen, by contrast, the Sullivan bill found great support. The Democratic Irish Representative Patrick H. Kelly, founder of the Kelly Mercantile Company in St. Paul, argued that the bill would save children from "the curse of drunkenness" and "from that of prostitution." The Republican Representative John E. Holmberg, a Swedish businessman from Minneapolis, argued that it greatly benefited the workers and therefore should be endorsed. The bill was subsequently passed, but, at least in Minnesota's capital, its success was limited. St. Paul's courts circumvented it by arguing that if the children carried with them written orders from their parents, the state law would not be violated.[12]

The repeated failure of more stringent temperance reform in Minnesota's legislature convinced the radical reformers that greater organizational collaboration was required if the High License consensus was ever to be overcome. A first step in this direction was the founding of the Minnesota County Option League at the end of 1896—most notably by members of the WCTU, the Scandinavian Total Abstinence Societies, the Christian Endeavor Societies, and the Epworth Leagues[13]—under the auspices of the Good Templars. Although the League, in cooperation with the WCTU, then convinced more than seventy thousand people to sign petitions in favor of County Option—a heretofore unrivaled amount of signers—the County Option bill was defeated in the House and smothered in the Senate in the 1897 legislative session. Mrs. A. C. Curdy of the WCTU, who had given a speech in support of the bill, later told her WCTU colleagues that she had felt as if she was "talking against a stone wall." Even then, when about one out of twenty Minnesotans had signed petitions in favor of County Option, Minnesota's legislators unwaveringly insisted on the continuance of the High License Law, feeling confident that they were representing the will of the majority of Minnesotans.[14]

Despite this setback, the radical reformers did not give up. At the annual convention of the IOGT in June 1897, Grand Chief Templar N. J. Bray resolved that
due to the rising interest in County Option the IOGT was to hold a temperance
mass meeting in Minneapolis at the beginning of September. At such a meeting,
he argued, temperance advocates were "to perfect a permanent organization in
the nature of a State Anti-Saloon League, that the sentiment already aroused
may be crystallized into some tangible form." This resolution, which was adopted and put into action in the months to come, marked the birth of the most
powerful temperance organization in Minnesota, the Minnesota Anti-Saloon
League (ASL). It was to become the first long-lasting temperance organization
that would assemble under its roof most of the state's temperance reformers,
irrespective of their religious background or political creed. Through its organizational strength and strategic skills, it would move Minnesota down the road
toward prohibition.[15]

St. Paul—"As Dead as a Door Nail"

The passage of the High License Law in 1887 and, even more importantly, the
state's intervention for its enforcement in St. Paul were milestones with regard
to the city's attitude toward temperance and reform. The law, heralded by Minnesota's temperance reformers as a means to discipline their capital city, was
perceived by many St. Paulites as a straitjacket and as a contradiction to their
own and their city's culture and identity. The majority of the city's residents were
against the $1,000 license, and even among the city's Republicans the attitude
prevailed that a $500 license would have been sufficient and easier to enforce
as it would have corresponded to the public sentiment in St. Paul. The *Pioneer
Press* soon foresaw that the municipal authorities and courts might cater to the
public sentiment and protect the liquor business against what was commonly
perceived as an outrageous invasion of the state into St. Paul's civic affairs.[16]

This was exactly what happened in St. Paul in the 1890s. As they were forced
by the state to enforce the High License Law and could not effect its repeal on
the state level due to the High License consensus, the only option St. Paul's
antireformist residents had left was an even more fervent and spiteful resistance to all further attempts made by the reformers to convert the city to their
moral values. Such collective action against a powerful enemy, as Geneviève
Massard-Guilbaud has argued, "can reinforce solidarity and develop a sense of
belonging to a social entity." This also held true for St. Paul. By fighting tooth
and nail against reformist attacks, St. Paul's antireformist camp banded together
more closely, with its members' civic identification and loyalty heightening. Not
surprisingly, when "Temperance Evangelist" Thomas N. Doutney returned to St.
Paul in 1891, after almost fifteen years of absence, he pointed out that the public

sentiment toward temperance had declined since his last visit. He accused the city authorities of not implementing the liquor laws and the public of silently tolerating this and described St. Paulites to be "as dead as a door nail to the importance of this subject."[17]

Due to this intense aversion to reform, it is surprising that the city's temperance movement survived at all in those days. While John Ireland and his Irish, the WCTU, and Good Templar lodges continued their work, the reform activism in this decade was spearheaded by people who had neither been born nor raised in the city. They were outsiders, often from the East Coast, who had arrived in St. Paul after the Civil War. Riding "the wave of moral reformism and 'civic uplift' zeal" flooding middle-class urban America in the 1890s, they perceived St. Paul as a den of iniquity and felt the mission to reform it. They were either not familiar with or oblivious to the city's founding history, its civic identity, and the resulting normative order. Instead, they used it as a foil, a constitutive outside, and defined themselves against its cultural implications. This counter-identity caused a lack of identification with the city and a sense of alienation.[18]

Thomas Cochran was one of these temperance leaders from out of town. Born in Brooklyn, New York in 1843, he had moved to St. Paul in 1869 after graduating from Columbia Law School. In St. Paul, he established himself in the real estate and insurance businesses, was an elder and teacher in the House of Hope Presbyterian Church, a member of the city's Chamber of Commerce, and one of the major promoters of St. Paul's YMCA. Cochran and his wife had been active in the temperance movement since their arrival in the city and thus resisted its normative order. Emilie Cochran acted as one of the vice presidents of St. Paul's first WCTU. Cochran himself promoted all kinds of reforms in St. Paul and Minnesota, such as fights for Sunday Observance, the enforcement of liquor laws, a prohibitory constitutional amendment, and High License. He also closely cooperated with Archbishop Ireland, both in reform and business matters.[19]

The prevailing anti-temperance sentiment in the city and the lawlessness it fostered deeply alienated Cochran. He publicly condemned St. Paul for its godlessness and immorality and threatened that he would have to leave town, as he could not provide his children with a moral upbringing there. Cochran suspected a conspiracy in the city between municipal authorities, newspapers, and residents. As he considered the local newspapers subsidized by immoral interests and therefore biased, he published his harangue against St. Paul in the Chicagoan newspaper *Inter-Ocean*. In an interview, he explained that St. Paul's municipal authorities were protectors of vice and that its population was "benumbed by having seen for a while law violated without protest, and thus having become indifferent as well as discouraged." This analysis is clearly that of an outsider: Deeply alienated himself by the lack of law enforcement in the city, Cochran mistook St. Paulites' acquiescence of law violation as indifference but failed to see that their behavioral norms and moral judgments had emerged in interaction with a particular place. Rather than interpreting the normative order in St. Paul as an interaction between people and place, Cochran ascribed it to one individual, Democratic mayor Robert A. Smith, the "chief abetter of all the lawlessness of which this city abounds." Unable to place the city's normative order within his framework of identities, Cochran defined himself against it, greatly emphasized his religious identity, and began to initiate a variety of reforms that aimed at bringing St. Paul more in line with his pietistic-reformist ideas.[20]

Foreseeably, Cochran's attempts to secure the enforcement of the Sunday Law through the Chamber of Commerce, which had become the mouthpiece of the city's Anglo-American reformers, and through the reinvigoration of the Law and Order League in July 1891 were blighted, both by Mayor Smith and the majority of city residents. Smith spoke out against Cochran's and the League's doings. Having been mayor in St. Paul since 1887, and returning to office time and again in the years to come, he increasingly became the spokesperson and icon of the anti-temperance St. Paulites. Smith was one of St. Paul's pioneer settlers and emphasized his thorough understanding of the city's character and traditions. Conceptualizing the city as a haven of liberality, he spoke out against the reformers' activism and their tendency to bad-mouth the city. Smith claimed that St. Paul was the best policed and most orderly city of its size in America and that it was good for the city that not all liquor laws were enforced.[21]

Smith's words are certainly propagandistic, instrumentalizing St. Paul's cultural identity to ward off Cochran's reform efforts and to protect his own person. But by tapping into long-held civic discourses and narrations shared by the majority of St. Paulites, he secured himself the political support he needed. A great number of St. Paulites condemned Cochran's "blind and hot-headed recklessness of vilification," his intense moralism, and his slandering of St. Paul in a Chicagoan newspaper. To them, he was an "enthusiast," with whom it was impossible to cooperate. They thought that Cochran's campaign for Sunday Observance was "of unprecedented malignance" and polluted the atmosphere in the city. They further threatened that those officials who decided to cooperate with the reformers would suffer the same fate as Mayor Christopher O'Brien in the early 1880s and would not be reelected. This was a serious threat reminding the municipal authorities that the antireformist camp numerically dominated St. Paul and could therefore determine political careers.[22]

Such threats did not discourage some members of another group of St. Paul's latecomers to increasingly support the temperance reformers' desperate attempts to reform the capital city. Since their massive arrival in St. Paul in the 1880s, there had emerged among the city's growing number of Scandinavians an ethnic temperance movement. Scandinavian temperance reformers figured particularly prominently in the city's IOGT, where they had established two Scandinavian lodges with about 230 members. Many Scandinavian women also readily responded to the Anglo-American female reformers' wooing and joined the city's WCTU chapters. Scandinavian male and female reformers campaigned for High License, prohibition, and Sunday Observance. They also expressed their sympathy with the Law and Order movement and wanted to secure John Ireland and other members of the new Law and Order League as speakers. However, these numbers, the presence of a plethora of saloons on the city's Scandinavian East Side, and the employment of a great number of Scandinavian workers by the city's liquor industry suggest that only a part of St. Paul's Scandinavian community stood solidly behind temperance reform.[23]

Jørn Brøndal has shed light on the interplay between the temperance movement and the emergence of Scandinavian American identities in Wisconsin. First, Scandinavian Americans used the movement to align themselves with the temperate old-stock Americans and to distance themselves from German and Irish Americans. Second, by engaging in the temperance cause, Scandinavian Americans nurtured their intraethnic networks and those across the Atlantic.[24] In Minnesota's wet capital—a Catholic, Democratic stronghold, in which the Irish had a large say—the Protestant, Republican Scandinavians' radical attempts at municipal reform resulted in the exclusion from municipal power. Their aim to clean up the capital and their unwillingness to obey the rules of the "civic game," as Wingerd has called it, added a cultural separation from the rest of the city to their geographical, religious, and political aloofness. On the state level, by contrast, they increasingly turned into major political players, both in the Republican and Prohibition Parties.[25]

Over the years, the aversion to any kind of reform by the majority of St. Paulites and the long Democratic rule fostered a certain degree of lawlessness and corruption in the city. The city's municipal authorities interpreted liberality and personal liberty as noninterference with the doings of the city's vice and liquor industries. The liquor dealers and manufacturers as well as the saloon and brothel owners rejoiced at this policy of noninterference and heavily supported the Democratic government. Cries of bossism and of the existence of a "Democratic machine" became loud. In 1892, these fears of corruption and lawlessness led to the election of an outsider with a penchant for reform to the mayor's seat, the Republican Frederick P. Wright, one of St. Paul's most successful businessmen and a native of Pennsylvania, who had resided in St. Paul since 1872. Republican leaders had presented Wright as the embodiment of moral order and law enforcement and as the direct opposite of Smith, whom they had accused of supporting the widest of wide-open policies. The *St. Paul Daily Globe* constantly dubbed Wright "the Prohibition candidate," and the city's German Americans portrayed him as a zealous reformer and a nativist and claimed that "only the most stupid calves elect their own butchers." Despite such negative criticism, a sufficiently large number of St. Paulites, including the city's Irish Catholic temperance advocates, agreed on the need for reform, were frustrated about the city's debts, and therefore voted for Wright.[26]

Wright is a good example of how ethnic and religious identities—he was an Anglo-American Presbyterian—were negotiated in the context of place. Soon after his inauguration, Wright began his reform work. At the beginning of July 1892, he initiated the passage of an ordinance prohibiting winerooms, private compartments used for gambling purposes or the introduction of women, mostly prostitutes, into saloons. Men and women often resorted to these compartments in order to sexually engage with each other. He also ordered all saloons to close after midnight and directed the chief of police not to allow saloon owners to sell liquor to minors. Wright made sure that the liquor laws were implemented and lawbreakers punished: He revoked two saloon licenses, the one due to noncompliance with the wineroom ordinance and the other as a reaction to a petition signed by eighty-eight property owners against a saloon in which a serious Sunday row had occurred.[27]

St. Paul's Anglo-American and Irish Catholic temperance advocates endorsed Wright's strictness, which encouraged him to go one step further. He asked for the dismissal of three popular and time-honored members of the city's police force, who had been accused of helping notorious saloon owners get licenses by confirming that their saloons were run in an orderly manner. The mayor's action was a sensation and without precedent in the city's history. Despite the unpopularity of his decision, the assembly and the Council of Aldermen, after several weeks of debate, decided to confirm the dismissal, a sure sign that during the Wright mayoralty the reformers temporarily held sway over St. Paul's municipal government.[28]

In this temporary climate of reform, the city's reformist faction, led by Cochran and a number of Catholic priests and Protestant ministers, saw yet another chance to realize its long-cherished goal, the enforcement of the Sunday Law. John Ireland gave a speech in which he emphasized why Sunday Law enforcement was so vital in St. Paul: "The people of St. Paul have a special responsibility resting upon them. They are the people of the Capital City. Other parts of the state look to us; people from other parts come to us and observe us. If the law is not observed in St. Paul, what probability can there be of its observance in other parts of the state."[29] For the temperance advocates St. Paul was to be a city upon a hill for the rest of the state and the Northwest, a paragon of morality and temperance. It was envisioned as what Paul Boyer has called a "virgin interior" providing an ethical counterweight to the cities in the East. To the opponents of temperance, however, St. Paul had a similarly exceptional position. A German from Carver County emphasized that "all our eyes are constantly directed at St. Paul" and that all Germans "were proud of their liberal capital." To them, St. Paul acted as a bulwark of liberality, ethnic pluralism, and heterogeneity and therefore as a ray of hope. Thus, both camps, reformers and opponents of reform, claimed that the outcome of the temperance struggle in St. Paul would carry weight for at least the rest of the state, if not the whole Northwest. In the context of the temperance movement, the city became a microcosm, in which large-scale problems as conceptions of assimilation versus cultural heterogeneity and a variety of social, cultural, and political ideologies were debated. These broader perceptions explain the fierceness and seriousness with which St. Paulites fought about the issue of temperance.[30]

While he emphasized that he personally would love to see the Sunday law enforced, Mayor Wright decided not to cater to the reformers' wishes. On the one hand, strict Sunday law enforcement, he argued, would be impossible in a city like St. Paul and would destroy civic peace and order. On the other hand, he could not afford to further affront the city's saloon owners, who had become an indispensable source of income since the introduction of High License. By 1905, for instance, license fees would amount to $384,000 and were thus the second largest source of revenue for the city, constituting 86 percent of all licensing revenues and 7 percent of the total revenue.[31]

Wright's reaction to their pleadings demonstrates St. Paul's moderating influence on many out-of-town reformers. Although he himself was in favor of strict law enforcement, as his early law enforcement campaigns show, he had compromised these personal beliefs by the time the debates about the Sunday Law set in. Wright refrained from action due to his knowledge of the mentality of St. Paul's citizens. He also knew that St. Paul's business community had no desire to curtail the city's economically highly profitable liquor and vice industries. Whereas radical reformers, such as Cochran, defined themselves in opposition to St. Paul's civic identity, more moderate temperance advocates, such as Wright, time and again stepped back from their ideals, realizing that compliance with them was irrational in a city like St. Paul and that political pragmatism was the only sensible approach.

However, Wright's final leniency did not save the Republicans from defeat in the municipal election of 1894. To St. Paul's antireformist coalition, Wright had become ineligible after his law enforcement campaigns, his revocation of licenses, and his dismissal of policemen. Therefore, in 1894, Robert Smith, the icon of the city's "liberals," was reelected mayor of St. Paul. As in the case of Christopher O'Brien, St. Paulites had dismissed a reform mayor after only one term in office and rejoiced at the return of the Democratic Party and a mayor in favor of personal liberty.[32]

By the late 1890s, St. Paul's municipal authorities, either Republican or Democratic, had turned into the reformers' major targets. Backed by the great number of city residents opposed to reform, city officials brushed aside any efforts against lawlessness in the city and often showered the reformers with ridicule. When in 1897 Reverend David Morgan—another latecomer to St. Paul—and his Christian Citizenship League[33] tried to prevent the granting of licenses to certain saloon owners, St. Paul's aldermen simply ignored his pleas and granted the licenses in question. Personal conviction, political expediency, as well as the moderating influence of St. Paul's civic identity guided their course of action. In the summer of 1897, St. Paul's Irish Catholic reformers concluded that there was not much sympathy for the temperance cause in St. Paul. Even after another decade of intense temperance activism, St. Paulites were still "as dead as a door nail" with respect to municipal reform.[34]

Irish Women's Temperance Activism

In the decade after the passage of the High License Law, the Irish reformers' pet measure, and the endorsement of Irish Catholic temperance activism by the pope, Minnesota's Irish Catholic temperance movement was at the height of its bloom. Irish male temperance reformers received support from Irish women, who from 1886, but in particular since John Ireland's endorsement in 1889, began to form their own societies and to devise their own programs. Irish women's temperance work gave Irish men and women the opportunity to socialize on equal terms and to discuss existing gender ideologies. While Irish women greatly admired their Protestant sisters' reform activism, they distanced themselves from the WCTU's women's rights rhetoric and activism in the public sphere and emphasized their own continued adherence to the concept of the two spheres. Women's entrance into the movement inaugurated a new phase of Irish temperance work in Minnesota. Irish temperance societies solidified their position in the state's social life, enjoyed great popularity, and put a great emphasis on their members' intellectual and professional advancement. Around 1894, however, Irish temperance leaders were faced with the first harbingers of decline.

Minnesota was a latecomer with respect to Irish female temperance agitation. While the national CTAU had endorsed the formation of women's total abstinence societies as early as 1874, it would take until 1876 before Bishop John Ireland, in the context of the Paulist Fathers'[35] missions in the diocese, for the first time administered the pledge to women. This practice was soon taken up all over the state, and Irish women enthusiastically supported the temperance cause. They were, however, allowed to disseminate total abstinence principles only in the home, their designated sphere of action. Female temperance societies or membership in male temperance societies were not envisioned by Minnesota's Catholic Church leaders at the time. Independent Irish female temperance activism emerged in 1886, once again during the parish mission of the Paulist Fathers in the state. The Paulists' visit led to the founding of the Sacred Thirst Ladies'

Society of St. Paul, which had a membership of 850 two years later and would remain the state's most active women's society. Other societies soon followed, so that by 1887 there were three women's temperance societies in St. Paul with a membership of 1,200. Most of these societies joined the Minnesota CTAU, which in 1888 had six women's societies with 1,576 members, an incredible number when taking into account that the Union's male members added up to only 2,249 at that time. That year, Irish women also first appeared as delegates at the Union's annual convention, and the Minnesota CTAU elected a woman to represent the organization at the convention of the national CTAU in Boston. In addition, CTAU President John O'Brien, encouraged the founding of more women's societies. In 1889, for the first time in the CTAU of St. Paul's history, an Irish woman gave a speech at the annual convention. After the initial enthusiasm had faded, the number of female members in the CTAU fluctuated between 250 and 760.[36]

While John Ireland had been hesitant for several years to speak out in favor of independent Irish female temperance work outside the home, in spring 1889 he announced his shift in opinion during an informal talk at a temperance meeting in Stillwater and appealed to Catholic women to found their own temperance societies and to mingle with the male societies. At the annual convention in 1889, he hailed women's temperance activism and asked Minnesota's Irish women to found societies in all parishes. According to Ireland, female temperance activism would not only promote the movement as such but also women's talents. In comparison to Anglo-American Protestant women, the prelate argued, Irish American women were too timid. With reference to the temperance movement, Ireland was correct. In contrast to the Protestant women, who had founded the WCTU on their own account, Irish Catholic women's temperance agitation only emerged at men's initiative. The major reason why Minnesota's Irish American women joined the temperance cause only after the Paulist Fathers, the CTAU president, or John Ireland had asked them to was the centrality of the Catholic Church in their lives and their fierce loyalty to that Church. The teachings of the Church frowned upon married women engaging outside the home. As Irish female temperance workers were predominantly married women, they joined the movement only upon male invitation.[37]

The admission of Irish women rang in a new era of Irish Catholic temperance activism in the Archdiocese of St. Paul, which had been established in May 1888 with John Ireland as its religious leader. The male reformers emphasized the opportunities such female activism offered to their movement. In 1889, CTAU President O'Brien stated: "May our combined efforts serve to build this union to the high standard of usefulness which so long has been its ambition, and may the accession to our ranks of the good Catholic women of Minnesota mark the beginning of an end—the complete reclamation of all of our people from the effects of the great evil of intemperance." Irish American Catholic leaders were enthusiastic about Irish women's participation in the temperance cause because it led to greater numerical strength and efficiency. At the annual convention of the CTAU in 1891, male temperance leaders even suggested organizing mixed societies and praised women as the key to success for the cause.[38]

Why did it take Minnesota's Irish temperance reformers almost two decades to integrate Irish women into their work? Before the mid-1880s, Irish Catholics had defined their temperance movement as a largely male endeavor in order to challenge the negative stereotypes of Irish men that resulted from their status as members of a religious and ethnic minority group. The masculine character of Irish temperance societies often revealed itself through their military drill and distinguished them from Anglo-American temperance societies. Only as growing numbers of Irish Catholics attained middle-class status and Irish women began to be involved in other social reform efforts in the Catholic Church was there a slow shift in opinion about the role Irish Catholic women could play in the movement. In addition, as John Ireland himself had admitted, Protestant women's temperance activism encouraged Irish temperance leaders to seriously consider the possibility of Irish female temperance work. Once again, the Irish were not to stay behind Protestant efforts.[39]

This shift in opinion became visible on the pages of St. Paul's *Northwestern Chronicle*. In a letter to the editor, an Irish man accused Irish American women of considering the fulfillment of their domestic duties as a sufficient contribution to the temperance cause. He then contrasted their lacking engagement with the activism of the WCTU women. The response from an Irish woman illustrates that the major reasons for their missing activism were the absence of male encouragement and the imposition of a domestic ideology on Irish women by Irish men. She stated that, in contrast to Anglo-American men, Irish American men had never encouraged Irish American women to take part in the temperance movement but had rather excluded them from it. She also complained that Irish men had long simply ignored Irish women or merely allowed them to "sing a sentimental song," by which she alluded to Irish men's belief that women could best contribute to the temperance cause by exerting influence on their male relatives in the home rather than by agitating in the public sphere. This and subsequent articles demonstrate that the relationship between Irish men and women was, at times, rather strained and that by far not all Irish men agreed with our male letter writer on the degree and shape of Irish women's temperance agitation. Seen from this perspective, the meetings and CTAU conventions and the mixed Irish temperance societies that were occasionally established offered a rare opportunity for Irish American men and women to socialize on equal terms, to discuss existing gender ideologies within the Irish Catholic community, and to fight for a common goal—the uplift of the Irish and the curbing of intemperance.[40]

Besides Irish men's encouragement, Irish female temperance reformers also received inspiration from the Anglo-American Protestant women's agitation. At the annual convention of the CTAU of St. Paul in 1892, the Irish Catholic speaker expressed her admiration for the WCTU women's zeal. The WCTU, she argued, proved that "women in society exert a great influence over men" and that "they should use this influence and make it extend as far as possible to suppress this great evil of intemperance." In contrast to the WCTU, she hastened to add, Irish women "are not invited to unseemly employment, are not called to act as legislators or to mingle in the whirlpool of political strife." Instead, Irish women should use their influence "at home, at the social gathering, in banquet hall." In contrast to the Anglo-American Protestant women, with very few exceptions, Irish Catholic women shied away from leaving their designated sphere and from encouraging other Irish women to do so. Their reform efforts remained couched in terms of domestic ideology, and women's rights arguments hardly ever found their way into Irish female temperance activism.[41]

Irish women's temperance activism contributed to the flourishing of Irish temperance activism in Minnesota in the late 1880s and early 1890s. St. Paul's Irish societies serve as a case in point. Between 1888 and 1891, the membership of the city's eight to fourteen Catholic temperance societies fluctuated around 1,257 members, including women, and they had developed into an integral part of the city's social life.[42] A look at the programs of the city's various Irish temperance societies makes their popularity understandable. They offered activities that were morally uplifting, educative, intellectually stimulating, and very appealing. In 1888, St. Paul's Father Mathew Society, with its membership of two hundred, gave weekly meetings at Market Hall during Lent; several hundred people attended and received the pledge. Not all of these people were enrolled members of temperance societies, but they still enjoyed these social events and the mental inspiration derived from them. Moreover, the Father Mathew Society provided a library with four hundred volumes and planned to construct a hall with a reading room, a gymnasium, and billiards. In order to create better job opportunities for its members, it established a Labor Committee with a special emphasis on securing employment for the society's unemployed members. The good reputation and prominence of the Father Mathew Society became evident at its twentieth anniversary in 1889, when a large audience consisting of legislators, Protestant clergymen, and members of the city's social and economic elites attended the festivities and celebrated Irish temperance efforts.[43]

The Crusaders' Temperance Society seems to have done even more effective work than the Father Mathew Society. They were St. Paul's most active and fastest growing temperance society and were claimed to be the largest Catholic temperance society in the country west of the Alleghenies. While in 1888 the society had 148 members, it would add two hundred names to its membership rolls within the following year. The Crusaders claimed greater heterogeneity than any other Catholic organization. Even though they catered mostly to young Irish American men between the age of sixteen and thirty, they prided themselves in representing eight different nationalities and in 1889 happily announced that two African Americans had joined their ranks. The fact that St. Paul's Irish included African Americans into their uplifting programs attests to the degree of their self-confidence and social power. The Crusaders had their own Crusaders' Dramatic Club, and their programs abounded with theater performances, lectures, intellectual debates, and socials, all geared toward improving their members' morality, knowledge, reputation, and rhetorical skills. On the first floor of Cretin High School, the society had its own meeting hall and a club room, which was open every evening and which contained nice furniture, a piano, a pool table, a refreshment stand, weekly papers, and magazines. It also had its own library of five hundred volumes and a small gymnasium and posed a real alternative to the saloon as the only focal point of leisure time. Prominent Irish St. Paulites, such as the lawyer James Manahan and Judge William Kelly, were active in the society and frequently gave inspiring talks to young people. St. Paul's business elite rewarded these activities. From the 1890s on, newspapers increasingly reported that membership in the society expanded job opportunities, as employers preferred the Crusaders to regular young men. St. Paul's Irish temperance societies served as educational centers and facilitated intra-Irish networking and professional advancement. Even those Irish Catholics in St. Paul who were not supporters of the temperance cause—in St. Paul's Irish American Club, for instance, whiskey continued to be served—applauded their countrymen's efforts because they boosted the ethnic group as such. Their socially uplifting work with its entertaining and intellectual features pushed Irish American reformers to the core of the city's power structure.[44]

In the summer of 1890, Irish reform leaders congratulated themselves on having successfully uplifted their countrymen "by organizing and fostering schools of thought and discussion which have given untold knowledge to their attendants" and by inculcating "valuable lessons of morality through the adoption of systematic efforts tending to intellectual culture, social purity."[45] This exuberance, however, became soon overshadowed by feelings of gloominess. In 1894, the CTAU of St. Paul for the first time recorded a considerable loss in membership. Between 1888 and 1894, membership in the organization had dropped from 3,825 to 1,963. Even though the Union was in a better shape again the following year, CTAU leaders inaugurated a membership drive to overcome the dearth of the mid-1890s. They offered their members premiums for winning new members, appealed to all clergymen to encourage the organization of temperance societies in their parishes, and tried to boost the founding of new societies by charging no admission fees and by paying the incidental expenses occurring in the organizational process. In 1897, Minnesota's Irish temperance leaders attempted to attract younger people to the temperance movement by founding the Catholic Total Abstinence Benefit Association, which gave benefits in case of death to all of its members' families. To receive such benefits, however, one had to be a member of a Catholic total abstinence society and to be younger than fifty years.[46]

All these measures showed the desired effect. Between 1895 and 1900, the CTAU's membership steadily rose again and hit the three thousand mark around the turn of the century. At the time, Irish leaders thought that they had successfully averted the danger of gradual decline. During the next decade, however, the downward trend would intensify, and Irish temperance activism would slowly but surely be relegated to the realm of nostalgia.[47]

German Americans Caught between Ethnicity and Religion

Minnesota's German Americans were less successful than their Irish fellow immigrants at using the temperance movement in order to strengthen their ethnic position in American society. Although their fight against radical temperance laws and the Americanizers in the American Catholic Church would at first prove a point of cohesion, in the long run divisiveness prevailed among them. The German American ethnicity invented in the context of the temperance movement turned out to be fragile. This was especially due to the intersection of ethnic and religious identities. Whereas German American pietists had long valued their religious affiliation more highly than their ethnic traditions, in the 1890s German American Catholics made a similar decision. The temperance movement created a schism in the American Catholic Church to such a degree that even German American bishops appealed to their flock not to simply brush the total abstinence activism of their Irish American brothers and sisters aside. Considerations like these inaugurated the demise of the German American anti-temperance front and the fragmentation of the newly invented German American ethnic identity.

The years immediately following the passage of the High License Law were characterized by a strengthening of the German American anti-temperance bloc. The agitation against High License had led to a temporary consolidation of the German American ethnic identity and a strengthening of social boundaries toward Anglo-American and Irish American temperance reformers. The idea to found a German Society in St. Paul on October 7, 1889, was the result of both ethnic self-confidence and offended cultural sensibilities. Its major purposes were to take care of the incoming German immigrants, to do charitable work among the poor, and to emphasize "through unified action" German American demands concerning infringements on their perceived rights, an obvious allusion to the temperance movement. The society represented most of St. Paul's German American leaders, such as Carl H. Lienau, Georg Benz, Ferdinand Willius, and Albert Scheffer, all of whom were also active in the fight against temperance. The founding responded to the German Americans' desire to cooperate more closely in order to make their ethnic position felt. Such intraethnic cooperation also acted as a remedy against the slow decline of the German American associational world, which began in the 1890s and was caused by the dwindling number of immigrants from Germany and by the rise of the second generation.[48]

German American cohesion was also heightened by the increasing influence of the Americanization movement within the American Catholic Church. The Americanizers sought the approval of Anglo-American Protestants by accommodating the American Catholic Church to the prevailing American Protestant culture and society. Irish Catholic and German Catholic drinking habits rendered such accommodation difficult, which is why Catholic temperance activism was one central element of John Ireland's plan to Americanize the American Catholic Church. At a Catholic state temperance meeting, he argued: "Non-Catholics admire us: they hail us as the leaders, the heroes in the cause of Total Abstinence, and in presence of our Total Abstinence Societies, their prejudices against our holy Church fall to the ground." Dedication to the temperance cause was thus seen as a means of challenging the negative stereotypes that Protestant Americans held and of making Catholicism more popular. Ireland's intention to adapt the American Catholic Church to American society and culture flatly contradicted German American ideas of Catholicism and ethnicity and caused much dissension between him and his German American flock. German Americans were convinced that the survival of the Catholic faith in the New World largely depended upon maintaining their cultural and linguistic heritage. They accused the majority of Irish American Catholics of "having a feud with the German-American Catholics of this country" and of "seeking to deprive them of their ecclesiastical and linguistic autonomy." The dispute about Americanization raged fiercely from the mid-1880s until the mid-1890s.[49]

One of the areas in which the struggle about Americanization played out in the everyday lives of Minnesota's Catholics was the temperance movement. John Ireland regularly affronted the ethnic, cultural, and professional sensibilities of his German American flock by accusing all those who sneered at temperance of violating the rules of the Catholic Church and of not being true Catholics. As the Church detested intemperance, Ireland argued, the liquor business, and all those involved in it, had to be considered disreputable. Due to such accusations, Minnesota's German American Catholics denounced Irish Catholic temperance activism in the same breath as the Irish Americanization efforts. While initially, they argued, the "praiseworthy goal [of Irish temperance societies] had been the fight against the Irish whiskey-devil, they had gradually moved into an evil prohibition fury" and were employed "for abominable attacks on German Catholics." Not surprisingly, the German American Catholics' "spirit of contradiction" made them highly unpopular with their English-speaking coreligionists and widened the gap within the American Catholic Church.[50]

The Americanization debate also manifested itself in the school question, which, to German Americans, was just another facet of Ireland's attack on their drinking customs. The school question appeared in the form of the so-called Bennett Law, which was first debated in Wisconsin and then spilled into Minnesota and other states from the late 1880s on. It mandated compulsory school attendance for children between the ages of eight and fourteen as well as the teaching of classes in English. While Minnesota's legislature refrained from passing such school bills due to the German American opposition, Ireland, who had been in favor of these bills, devised the so-called Faribault School Plan. Through this plan, Ireland and the pastor of the Immaculate Conception Parish of Faribault attempted between August 1891 and May 1892 to secure a form of state support for parochial schools in dire financial straits. They rented Faribault's parochial school to the city's Board of Education for a nominal fee of one dollar, provided faculty for it, and guaranteed that no religious instruction would be given during school hours. Whereas the board unanimously accepted the proposal, Minnesota's German Americans did not see the Faribault School Plan as a model of cooperation between church and state. They rather interpreted it as an insidious trick of the Irish prelate with the aim to eliminate all German parochial schools from his diocese and stood up against Ireland's policy of coercive Americanization.[51]

They also interpreted Ireland's Faribault School Plan as a weapon in his campaign to root out German American drinking habits. German parochial schools, Minnesota's German American Catholics surmised, were considered by Ireland as hotbeds of future anti-temperance agitation. By forcing German American children to go to public schools, which were subject to the WCTU's Scientific Temperance Instruction Law, Ireland aimed at indoctrinating them with temperance and thereby effectively sought to crush the German American opposition to the temperance movement in the long run. "The Bennett Law," the German Catholic *Der Wanderer* sarcastically commented, "is the first wedge to the higher civilization of prohibition and abstinence." Its editor claimed that "grim hatred of anything German" was the source for both temperance and school laws and that the Republican Party was the originator of all those nativist ideas. This perception of a connection between the school question and temperance agitation was not entirely unfounded. Both the advocacy of temperance and the public school model were based on the same premise: the willingness to increase the power of the state over the life of the individual.[52]

Despite effecting greater cohesion, the cooperation in the fight against the temperance movement and Americanzation did not manage to entirely erase the divisiveness among German Americans and to turn them into a solid ethnic bloc. *Der Wanderer* mentioned that the German Protestants were "separated from us through such a deep gulf of religious fraternal strife . . . that even in the school-question they seem hardly to want to strike wholeheartedly and strongly in the hand proffered to them." Even though German Protestants and Catholics were equally opposed to the attacks on their parochial schools, religious differences could not be forgotten. This quotation—one of the rare examples documenting interdenominational strife among the state's German Americans—demonstrates that the coalition between the various German American subgroups, built in the context of the temperance movement, was fragile and that the newly invented ethnic identity did not succeed at holding together all these different groups permanently. Minnesota's German American Catholics were especially predestined to break out of this coalition, as their situation was the most difficult one. Their ethnic self-conception and the contents of their religion, especially as shaped by John Ireland, increasingly clashed. Due to their great loyalty to the hierarchy of the Catholic Church, Minnesota's Catholic German Americans felt constantly torn between their archbishop's endorsement of the temperance movement and Americanization and their own ethnic sensitivities and needs. In the long run, they had to decide which of their identities, religious or ethnic, they valued more highly. The fact that their Roman Catholic faith itself did not see liquor consumption as problematic but that it was their Irish archbishop who reinterpreted it as such greatly complicated this decision. Whereas Irish Catholics had long served as constitutive outside for German American Catholics, increasing interethnic strife within the archdiocese called for a strategic repositioning of German American Catholics.[53]

These complications arising from the clashing of ethnicity and religion intensified in the mid-1890s through events occurring in other states. In March 1894, Bishop John A. Watterson of Columbus, Ohio, introduced a decree announcing that he would withhold his approbation from every society in his diocese that had a liquor dealer or a saloon owner among its officers and would suspend such a society from the rank and privileges of a Catholic society. As a reaction, a German American Catholic society in Columbus protested and wrote a petition to Francesco Satolli, first Apostolic Delegate to the United States. In July, Satolli, to much surprise, approved of Watterson's decision, arguing that the bishop had decreed what he considered important for the welfare and honor of Catholic societies. He also stated that the liquor traffic, especially the way it was conducted in the United States, was the source of much evil and that Watterson acted within his right when he sought to restrict it. John Ireland and his Catholic temperance reformers expressed their joy at Satolli's decision, which was a high-water mark of ecclesiastical support of the movement. St. Paul's *Der*

Wanderer quickly understood that this decree greatly strengthened the position of the English-speaking Catholic temperance advocates and made the German American Catholics' opposition to and condemnation of Catholic temperance activism increasingly untenable.[54]

Other German Americans shared *Der Wanderer's* apprehensions. At the German American Catholics' Day (*Katholikentag*) in Louisville, Kentucky, in the fall of 1894, Bishop Sebastian Messmer of Green Bay, Wisconsin, gave a speech about temperance that needs to be read as a response to the Satolli decision. Messmer argued that the question of temperance had become so prevalent in America that German American Catholics had to take a more careful stand. He regretted the sole interpretation of temperance as total abstinence but asked German American Catholics to respect and even support all efforts based on wisdom and justice. He appealed to them not to condemn total abstainers and prohibitionists and claimed that everyone's personal liberty had to be sacrificed if the welfare of the state was threatened. With the latter claim, he invalidated the German Americans' personal liberty argument against temperance laws and fell in line with the Anglo-American interpretation of the relationship between individual liberty, public welfare, and state intervention. Absolute personal liberty, Anglo-American reformers argued, was not congenial to a civilized state of society, and the individual had to surrender certain natural rights for the general good, which gave the state the right to prohibit the manufacture and sale of liquor. Messmer finally also appealed to the honor of German American Catholics, who were accused of upholding the power of the saloon: "Do you, as German Americans, want to silently accept such ignominious insults?" A few months later, Messmer even went one step further, proposing a great national Catholic Temperance League, in which all Catholics could work together for a more temperate society.[55]

Satolli's decision and Messmer's words must have been very hard to digest for German American minds. Naturally, they did not cause immediate change within Minnesota's German American community. Over the next decade, however, these arguments, also propagated on other occasions, slowly settled into the German American Catholic consciousness and would lead to a strategic repositioning of German American Catholics and their emphasis of religious over ethnic identity.

Other groups of German Americans preceded German American Catholics in their decision to emphasize religion over ethnicity. Aside from the state's German Methodists, who had endorsed the fight against alcohol since the 1850s, the state's German Evangelical churches, all of whom were members of the largely German Minnesota Conference of the Evangelical Association, allied with the Anglo-American Evangelical churches on the topic of temperance. In 1873, the Conference decided for the first time to use its influence against Sabbath desecration and intemperance in any legitimate way possible. In 1875, it even imputed bad intentions to its non-Evangelical German American countrymen by insinuating that they used the personal liberty slogan only as a strategic tool to fight against temperance. From the 1880s on, the Conference resolved to "convince" its members that total abstinence was the only path leading to morality and happiness. The fact that the organization felt the need to convince its members of total abstinence shows that at that time many German Evangelicals obviously endorsed temperance in the form of moderation but were not necessarily against the consumption of alcohol and thus steered a middle path between their ethnic proclivities and their religion. By 1889, Minnesota's Evangelical Germans fully fell into line with the Anglo-American radical reformers. That year, they openly supported prohibition and asked their coreligionists to fight for a constitutional amendment at the polls, from the pulpit, and with all legislative means possible.[56]

Even though the German American pietistic denominations are noteworthy for their willingness to adapt to pietistic American values and traditions at the expense of their ethnic heritage, their influence on the overall German American attitude toward temperance must not be exaggerated. St. Paul's City Directory of 1890 lists the estimated membership of the single German churches in St. Paul. The city's 150 German Baptists, 700 German Methodists, 390 German Evangelicals, and a few German Presbyterians were faced with 6,700 German Catholics and about 5,000 German Lutherans. Thus, roughly, about every ninth or tenth churchgoing German American was a member of a church endorsing temperance and prohibition. Membership in such a church, however, did not automatically imply wholehearted support of total abstinence. More importantly, this calculation does not take into account the great number of freethinkers, most of them solidly in the anti-temperance camp. In addition, St. Paul's small German American Jewish community joined their Catholic, Lutheran, and freethinking brothers and sisters in their anti-temperance agitation. Therefore, the actual number of "temperance Germans" was much lower, and German pietistic temperance advocates were a noteworthy exception rather than the rule. They certainly did not have the numerical strength, visibility, and clout—neither in St. Paul, nor in the rest of Minnesota—to change the image of German Americans as *the* oppositional force against the temperance movement. This image would not even change when, in 1900 and 1911, the WCTU and the IOGT would succeed at convincing a small number of German Americans to found two short-lived and barely visible nondenominational German total abstinence societies. German Americans would always constitute the heart of the anti-temperance camp. Despite their increasing repositioning within the temperance debate, the state's German American Catholics would ideologically always remain attached to this camp.[57]

The WCTU's Fight for Women's Rights
and against the Evils of Humanity

The introduction of a Scientific Temperance Instruction Law in 1887 rang in a
new era of the Protestant women's fight against liquor. The law's passage had
shown them that they were as capable of agitating in the political sphere as men,
and their cooperation with various state agencies in the process of pressuring the law through had enhanced their political expertise and lobbying skills.
Therefore, from the late 1880s on, the Minnesota WCTU, both its leaders and
rank and file, openly addressed the question of women's rights and suffrage and
demanded their realization. In fact, the WCTU leaders' teachings influenced an
ever-increasing number of temperance women, who joined them in the fight
for greater equality and women's access to the public and political spheres. In
order to achieve these ends and to enhance their clout and reputation, they
cooperated with other organizations, particularly with the Prohibition Party
and the IOGT. Such willingness of cooperation, however, stood in stark contrast
to the WCTU women's dealing with immigrants and racial minorities, whom
they considered uncivilized and inferior.

President Harriet Hobart's speech, given at the Minnesota WCTU convention
in 1891, embodies the state organization's shift from appropriating contemporary
notions of gender in order to justify women's public and political agitation to
openly fighting for women's rights and the equality of the sexes. Hobart defined
the Minnesota WCTU's major purpose not as the promotion of temperance, but
as the development of the female character. Woman, she argued, had so long
been "dominated and subjugated by the cruelty and lust of man," had so long
been "kept in ignorance of her birthright and of her powers, that there has been
danger of the world's forgetting that *God* made woman; that He made her in
his own image; endowed her with dominion and sovereignty—man's co-equal."
Moreover, as man and woman fell together, only together "they are to rise to
the stature of perfect manhood and womanhood. Neither bond nor free—neither male nor female. One in Christ, two halves of a perfect whole. With equal
prerogatives and powers, equal in civil, political, judicial and industrial rights.
One in Church and State and home." Hobart thus spoke out against the rigid
separation between the genders, rather imagining them as two sides of the same
coin. She implied that the ideology of the two spheres was man-made and a
social invention rather than a biological reality or a religious tenet. Such a view
of gender deprived gender inequalities of any legitimacy. With her speech, she
wanted WCTU women to realize that it was woman's natural right to leave her
designated sphere, to develop a female consciousness, and to become acquainted
with all areas of public life, especially with politics.[58]

Due to its increased self-confidence, embodied in the speeches of Hobart and others, Minnesota's WCTU—consisting of 4,179 adult and young adult members and 5,099 children in 1891—significantly broadened its agenda. Rather than focusing on the liquor question, the WCTU women wanted to work against the "evils of humanity" and turn the world into a better place, especially for women. While the agitation for stricter temperance laws remained at the center of the Minnesota WCTU's agenda, the Union moved to the forefront of legislative campaigns seeking to improve women's economic and social situation. Thus, they fought for the appointment of women as school directors and police matrons, convinced the Minnesota legislature to raise the age of consent from ten to sixteen years, and asked for bills making both parents—and not only fathers—the legal guardians of their minor children and improving women's situation in case of their husbands' deaths.[59]

Woman's suffrage moved to the center of the Minnesota WCTU's work in those years. By the late 1880s, the ideology of the two spheres had become unacceptable to many WCTU women, and they were ready to move out of their female counterpublic and into the male public sphere. In 1888, the WCTU State Superintendent of Equal Suffrage reported that many unions were becoming "deeply interested in the subject of Equal Suffrage" and that many members claimed to have changed their views on the issue over the past months. Two years later, the State Superintendent announced that the support for franchise within the ranks of the WCTU had again increased, with about 75 percent of the unions having Superintendents of Franchise and about 60 percent having sent reports favorable to suffrage. Furthermore, a growing number of temperance women defined suffrage as "a measure of justice," a basic right that every educated human being should possess.[60]

The WCTU women took active steps for the political implementation of female suffrage. They knew that suffrage work had to take place on two planes: First, voters had to be convinced of the expediency and necessity of woman suffrage. Second, the legislators had to be pressured into submitting such an amendment to the people. In order to accomplish the first goal, the WCTU women sought to increase the general sentiment in favor of suffrage by staging essay contests on the topic "Why Women Want to Vote," which were to inspire public debates on the pros and cons of the woman's ballot. In order to influence the political process, they engaged in petition drives in favor of municipal suffrage and tried to put pressure on the legislators by attending legislative sessions. However, between 1891 and 1895, all bills in favor of woman suffrage were killed or indefinitely postponed. The strongest opposition to the suffrage bills came from the ranks of the German Americans, who claimed that only a minority of women wanted the right to vote and that it was merely a strategy for attaining prohibition. Moreover, the liquor interests spent large amounts of money lobbying against suffrage, which they considered a danger to their trade.[61]

Julia Bullard Nelson, who had moved from Connecticut to Minnesota in 1857, was one of the state's most ardent temperance and suffrage advocates. At the head of Minnesota's suffrage and temperance movement since the early 1870s, in 1886 she even attracted nationwide attention at a national suffrage convention in Washington, D.C. In her speech addressing the House Judiciary, she asked the legislators to remove the barriers restraining women from equal opportunities and privileges with men. Back in Minnesota, she became an indispensable link between the temperance and suffrage causes. Not only had she been one of the founding members of both the state WCTU and the MWSA, but during the years to come she continuously split her time between both organizations. Between 1886 and 1890, she acted as vice president of the Minnesota WCTU and in that function labored in South Dakota's campaign for woman suffrage. From 1890 until 1896, she served as president of the MWSA and simultaneously as the Minnesota WCTU's Superintendent of Franchise (1893–1896). Arguing that the WCTU was far better organized than the MWSA, Nelson was eager to use its broad membership network as an operational base for her campaigns for suffrage. During her six-year presidency of the MWSA, she petitioned every legislative session for woman suffrage. Simultaneously, she greatly enhanced the Minnesota WCTU's involvement in the campaigns for suffrage by integrating temperance women into the massive petition drives and by influencing them through her contributions as editor of the *Minnesota White Ribbon* (1903–1906), since 1890 the organ of the Minnesota WCTU. In these contributions, Nelson questioned the widely held notions of gender at the time, in particular the two-sphere concept, and argued in favor of gender equality.[62] Such feminist texts encouraged and empowered their female readers, expanded their vision, and helped them to imagine new identities for themselves. Their publication and circulation in the Minnesota WCTU's newspaper reveals that the WCTU was one of the major forces shaping such new identities. A statement by the later Minnesota WCTU president, Bessie Laythe Scovell, illustrates the WCTU's success in this endeavor. In 1900, Scovell described how the organization had helped her to develop a female consciousness and generated a wish for emancipation: "I caught a larger vision here that gave me greater faith in all womanhood and quickened my love for God's whole family." Julia Bullard Nelson's activism yet again calls into question long-held scholarly dichotomies between the temperance women's "domestic" feminism and the suffragists' "proper" feminism. In Minnesota, there was not only a strong overlap in membership and a close cooperation between both organizations but by the 1890s the Minnesota WCTU voiced demands as radical as those of the suffragists.[63]

Although not all of Minnesota's WCTU women endorsed goals as radical as Nelson's and Hobart's, sources illustrate that a great number of local unions adored them for their inspiration and viewed their visions as the guidelines for their programs. The women residing in the state's urban areas were particularly receptive to the WCTU leaders' women's rights arguments. Minnesota's large cities abounded with a great number of so-called New Women, a special cohort of educated women emerging in the 1880s and 1890s, who asserted their right to a career, a public voice, and visible power and thus contributed to the symbolic death of the earlier female subject, the refined and confined Victorian woman.[64]

In Minnesota's capital, for instance, a small but determined band of one to two hundred women, organized into five to eight unions, aimed at infiltrating and redefining typically male spheres. In 1896, for example, St. Paul's temperance women founded a Rescue League whose members entered disorderly houses and saloons twice a week in order to check whether they were observing the liquor laws. In the spring of 1896, S. V. Root, one of the leaders of the Ramsey County WCTU, and Mrs. Murphy of the Hamline Union entered the saloon of Edward L. Murphy, one of those Irish Americans who did not care about the temperance movement. They accused him of operating winerooms in his saloon and brought him to trial. The case caused quite a stir because Murphy was an alderman in the city council and thus part of the municipal government. The lawsuit against Murphy was the topic of daily conservations among St. Paulites, and a great number of them, including Mayor Robert A. Smith, took their stand in Murphy's favor. To everyone's surprise, the jurors fined Murphy one hundred dollars and closed his saloon and several other winerooms. While St. Paul's municipal authorities and Grand Jury usually brushed off the demands of male temperance reformers, they obviously had difficulties denying the women's requests. Not only had the WCTU women's saloon visits stunned St. Paul's establishment, but they had also greatly disturbed a large number of men who perceived them as an intrusion into the male public sphere. These women not only transcended contemporary notions of gender but, through their activism, questioned these notions and "challenged the dominant, idealized sexual division of urban space."[65]

Besides depriving the saloon of its status as a largely male preserve, St. Paul's WCTU women also forced their way into other urban institutions, such as prisons and the police force. Since 1886, one of their goals was the appointment of a matron for the city prison. The sheriff was unwilling to grant this request, as hiring a matron meant women's intrusion into a sphere so far dominated by men, and even forbade them to hold their services in the jail. After considerable protest and pressure by the women as well as the female prisoners, he gave in and hired a prison matron. In 1892, after much petitioning and lobbying among the municipal authorities, St. Paul's WCTU women also managed to convince the St. Paul City Council to appoint a police matron. The installment of both police and prison matrons reflects the respect the city fathers had developed toward women's work and proves their lobbying and pressuring skills. The public sphere had ceased to be an exclusively male preserve.[66]

Despite their successes, both on the local and on the state level, Minnesota's WCTU women knew that in order to implement women's political rights more effectively, they needed greater support from men. In the 1890s, they therefore developed a remarkable willingness to cooperate with like-minded—that is, largely Protestant, middle-class, white—male temperance organizations. Relations were especially hearty with the Prohibition Party. While remaining officially nonpartisan in order not to lose its Republican members, the Minnesota WCTU, under the leadership of President Harriet A. Hobart, promised to support "that party that was fighting for prohibition and woman suffrage," thus de facto endorsing the Prohibition Party. Hobart's strong third-party leanings and her advocacy of independent political action naturally caused conflicts within the WCTU of Minnesota. In August 1889, a number of women found that Hobart was ruining the state WCTU with her partisanship and established the Non-Partisan WCTU of Minneapolis. Hobart's reaction was harsh: Even though the defectors wanted to remain auxiliary to the Minnesota WCTU, she refused to admit them if they kept the adjective "Non-Partisan" in their name. Besides collaborating with the Prohibition Party, the WCTU women also kept in close contact with the IOGT: They sent delegates to each other's conventions, cooperated in various petition drives, and had a considerable overlap in membership. The Minnesota WCTU women's large-scale cooperation with the IOGT and the Prohibition Party and their effective political and social agitation greatly enhanced their reputation in Minnesota and convinced the male temperance advocates of their capabilities and importance for the cause. As a result, the majority of male temperance reformers were strongly in favor of granting them more political rights.[67]

The WCTU women also cooperated with and labored among those ethnic groups whose members displayed a penchant for reform and strong middle-class aspirations—in case they had not yet made it into the middle class. While they had never made any efforts to work among the Irish Catholic women or to integrate them into their Protestant reform networks, they greeted the emergence of an Irish Catholic women's temperance movement with enthusiasm. Following the lead of their national leader Frances Willard, they claimed to embrace ecumenism, invited and heartily welcomed members of the Irish Catholic women's temperance societies to their conventions, and sent their own delegates to the CTAU conventions. In 1894, they even passed a resolution hailing the day when the Sacred Thirst Society, the CTAU, and the WCTU would unite their forces.[68]

Minnesota's temperance women were also enthusiastic about Scandinavian Americans, whom they hailed as the "Yankees of Europe," as they found them to be "more like the Americans than any other nationality that comes to our shores." "They seek a greater diversity of professions, trades and occupations generally than others; are a staunch, honorable, progressive people." Due to their massive arrival in Minnesota since the 1880s, the WCTU women found it strategically wise to win the female members of this group over to the temperance cause. Scandinavian American women, they surmised, could help them win the state for prohibition. Thus, they made sure to translate temperance literature into the Scandinavian languages, tried to make contact with Scandinavian American ministers, and sent lecturers into the Scandinavian American communities. By 1886 there were three and by 1891 five unions entirely composed of Scandinavian women, and some Scandinavian women had joined English-speaking WCTUs.[69]

In contrast to Scandinavian Americans, Minnesota's WCTU women considered German Americans hopeless cases with regard to temperance due to their ethnic proclivities. Minnesota's German American representatives, politicians, and press missed no opportunity to ridicule the "overstrung" "temperance dames" and to bad-mouth and oppose their reform goals, which greatly offended the WCTU women and increased their prejudice. Aside from their occasional work among German Methodists, the Minnesota WCTU neglected work among this nationality group. This absence of work among German Americans runs all the way through the Minnesota WCTU's history. The Minnesota WCTU thereby deviated from the course of the national WCTU, whose foreign work largely consisted of work among German Americans.[70]

While work among immigrant communities was clearly located at the sidelines of the Minnesota WCTU's broad spectrum of activities, racial minorities attracted even less of the women's attention. As a state union, the Minnesota WCTU did not make any organized attempts to draw African Americans into its fold. Even though in 1898 the Union finally established a Department of Work among Colored, this department would never rise to prominence. Only individual unions or members worked among African Americans and initiated the founding of African American WCTU chapters, mainly in the Twin Cities, where most of the state's African Americans resided. A similar lack of activism can be found with regard to Minnesota's Native Americans. Only in 1901 did the WCTU women finally establish a Department of Work among Indians, but its progress was meager. Year after year, Superintendent Frances A. Wright regretted the lack of work on the reservations.[71]

A closer engagement with immigrants and the racial other would have meant for the women to socialize across class, ethnic, and color lines, an idea that many of them obviously found disturbing. Moreover, many WCTU women, especially those in the rural areas, seem to have been afraid of ethnically, racially, and socially different groups. Such fears mostly resulted from conceptions that were not uncommon at the time but that can be considered nativist and racist. Even comparably progressive leaders, such as President Bessie Laythe Scovell, repeatedly stressed that immigrants were objects of reform and that they needed to be assimilated as quickly as possible. According to Scovell, the WCTU's major work was to "meet the foreigners early and give them our customs before they have established theirs of the old world upon us" and "to get them to love clear brains better than beer." She also hoped that "the time will come soon when we shall recognize no difference, when all people coming to America will speedily learn the language of the country and all will be Americans." Anglocentrism, feelings of cultural superiority, as well as fears of cultural domination by the immigrants peek through these quotations. WCTU leaders seem to have seen assimilation as the only way of how to deal with the "immigrant problem."[72]

With respect to racial minorities, such as African and Native Americans, the majority of WCTU women were thoroughly in line with the racial taxonomies and stereotypes prevalent at the time. When Scovell, a university-educated woman, opened the 1900 convention in Mankato, she mentioned the great number of Native Americans that had been executed in that city after the Sioux War in the 1860s. She then established a connection between the executed and the liquor evil: "There is an enemy in the land more stealthy than the Indian, more deadly in its work—the alcoholic liquor traffic. . . . We toil and sacrifice to-day to hasten the to-morrow when this enemy will be executed upon the gibbet of public opinion, and the liquor traffic be as dead as the Indians buried in yonder mound." Similarly racist ideas were expressed by I. F. McClure and Frances A. Wright, Superintendents of Work among Indians. They perceived Native Americans as an idle and uncivilized race, which relished "depending on the bounties of the United States." Wright justified the WCTU women's reluctance to engage in work among them by pointing at the difficulty of the task to "bring out the natural good traits [in the Indian] and suppress the bad, and put self and love in the labor of teaching him to be a true man." Such derogatory attitudes toward non-WASPs illustrate that the WCTU's progressive attitudes toward gender did unfortunately not translate into progressive notions on ethnicity and race. Even though single members, such as Julia Bullard Nelson, ardently worked for the promotion of other racial and ethnic groups, the majority of WCTU women were not eager to extend their services to them.[73]

The Minnesota WCTU's deep engagement in women's rights and politics throughout the 1890s did, of course, not suit everyone and at times evoked great resistance. Besides the aforementioned internal dissensions on the question of partisanship, the WCTU's greater emphasis on suffrage than on temperance alienated many women. Increasing criticism also arose from outside the organization. Many people thought that the WCTU had done great work until it wandered off into politics and "got out of its true place." Even the members of the Prohibition Party, most of them longtime advocates of woman suffrage, debated the question of whether it would be wise to admit women as delegates. They feared that the other political parties could be offended by such a step and therefore decided to merely grant WCTU members freedom of speech in their meetings. All these comments, arguments, and debates reveal how much resentment against and insecurity about women's rights the WCTU's agitation provoked. Many men and women seem to have felt that the contemporary gender ideology had become vulnerable and that a redefinition of gender roles was at hand. Such gender insecurities caused many people, men and women alike, to desperately cling to the traditional concept of the two spheres, embodied by the aforementioned emphasis on woman's "true place."[74]

WCTU President Hobart constantly encouraged the women to ignore such criticism and ridicule from outside and to continue their fight for temperance and women's rights. She and other WCTU leaders praised women's rights activists, such as S. V. Root, at the annual conventions and celebrated them as role models other women could aspire to and as examples of what could be achieved with the right mixture of idealism, motivation, courage, and creativity. Only in their fight against temperance and all the other evils of humanity, Hobart's successor Susanna Fry argued, woman "found her own limitations and threw herself against them."[75]

4. "Putting on the Lid"

The Anti-Saloon League and Its Impact on the Dry Movement (1898–1915)

Progressivism, the Anti-Saloon League, and the Fight for County Option

The turn of the century witnessed a nationwide expansion of temperance activism. The tenets of Progressivism combined with the work of the Anti-Saloon League (ASL) boosted the passage of County Option Laws all over the country, including Minnesota. The activism of the state's ASL and its intense collaboration with the Prohibition Party and other reformers led to liquor law enforcement campaigns and slowly increased the general sentiment in favor of County Option. Due to severe resistance to County Option, particularly by the politically powerful liquor interests, but also by German Americans, workers, and other opponents of reform, it took until 1915 until the reformers' combined efforts showed the promised effect. In Minnesota, the fight against liquor continued to alter the political and legislative landscape. Not only did the temperance movement lead to the adoption of new political strategies, but it also contributed to the loosening of party ties and the development of the state's nonpartisan legislature. The individual candidate and his opinion on temperance became much more important than his party affiliation. By 1915, political realities in Minnesota had changed, and the temperance movement was one of the great motors of change.

The year 1898 marked a turning point in Minnesota's temperance history. The election of the Democratic gubernatorial candidate John Lind, a Swedish immigrant, inaugurated the Progressive era in Minnesota. Historians have called Lind's inaugural address to the legislature "an inventory of Minnesota life and problems at the turn of the century." It also served as a blueprint of Progressive reform for the years to come. Progressivism inherited a significant legacy from the Populist era and the economic depression of the 1890s. It addressed agrarian grievances and adopted a broadened conception of government's role in dealing with the social consequences of the growing power of big business and the mounting discontent among the urban-industrial workers. Whereas Populism's support had been almost exclusively rural, Progressivism catered to larger segments of the population. It attracted all those who feared a conspiracy of wealth and industrial forces and its social by-products, such as immigration, urban growth, the concentration of corporate power, and the widening of class divisions, and therefore found wide support in small towns and large cities. Metropolitan business communities, however, were afraid that overly enthusiastic reform might create a climate unfavorable to commerce and industry and remained skeptical of the movement. Progressivism never constituted a cohesive movement with a unified program either but was rather a mosaic of reforms, which often overlapped but sometimes diverged. Reform efforts ranged from campaigns for stricter business regulation and reform of governmental structures to activism for laws restricting immigration, protecting workers, and abolishing prostitution and the saloon. This wide spectrum of measures attracted a diverse lot of reformers. Along with the native-born middle class—the major advocates of Progressive reforms—urban immigrants and the working class also provided critical support to specific reform efforts.[1]

Based on a strong belief in the perfectibility of humanity, Progressivism was heavily influenced by nineteenth-century American Protestantism. Its strong moral commitment and its Protestant heritage led to an inextricable connection between Progressivism and temperance reform. Both reform movements drew on the same moral idealism and sought to deal with the same basic problems. Of course, not every Progressive was a temperance reformer, but the climate of Progressive reform enabled the temperance activists to integrate their single-goal cause into a larger pattern of reforms and to lend it more strength. The temperance movement also profited from Progressivism's emphasis on a scientific approach to social problems. Progressives believed that the scientific and technological expertise that underlay the new industrial order would help to solve the social problems caused by industrialism. Therefore, they employed social research, statistical data, and expert opinion to support their wide range of reform efforts. Temperance reformers began using this scientific approach as well. It led to a more efficient organization of the temperance movement and—through its emphasis on facts rather than on religious arguments—cleansed it to some extent of its evangelical flavor. Intemperance also came to be viewed as the product of an urban environment and less as the personal failings of individuals. Such views and methods increased the credibility and strength of the temperance movement and allowed a greater range of people to identify with it.[2]

In Minnesota, the control of the sale and consumption of alcohol was an integral part of the Progressive agenda. Most of the state's Progressives were hostile toward alcohol as it threatened the family, the supposed bedrock of nineteenth-century society. They also argued that it created anchorless men and women, whose political attitudes could easily be manipulated by the large corporations, first and foremost the liquor industry, and who were not able to contribute to the state's economic and moral development. In typical fashion, Minnesota's Progressives identified the cause of alcohol abuse as external to the individual and consequently considered the prohibition of the sale of liquor as an effective way to eradicate the liquor evil.[3]

Along with the introduction of Progressivism into Minnesota politics, the founding of the Minnesota ASL—a federation of the various churches against the saloon—on January 1, 1898, also made the year a turning point in the state's temperance history. The League succeeded in federating the state's moderate and radical reform forces by adopting goals and strategies on which everyone could agree. Its motto, "The Saloon Must Go," indicates that it worked against the saloon rather than against liquor consumption as such, because, in a truly Progressive manner, it defined the saloon, and not the individual, as the root of intemperance (see figure 4.1). The League also aimed at County Option instead of prohibition, did not require a total abstinence pledge as a prerequisite for membership, and focused on individual localities rather than on state or national levels of government. Its single-issue policy, its gradual and local approach—termed "local gradualism" by Ann-Marie E. Szymanski—and its strictly nonpartisan character made the ASL attractive to a wide variety of Minnesotans. If one considers women's central role in the temperance movement at that time, it is surprising that the ASL—despite its close cooperation with the WCTU and its rhetorical support of women's enfranchisement—was a men's organization. Even though ASL members welcomed women's support in demonstrations and other public events, all League professionals were men, and the place of women in the League was never a subject of debate.[4]

Similar to its national counterpart, Minnesota's ASL excelled in terms of efficiency and professionalism over any other of the state's temperance organizations. All of its leaders were paid staff, who dedicated their entire time to building up and running the organization. The League's most prominent figure was its superintendent and founder, the Congregational minister and Good Templar Richard H. Battey. Many other ASL members had similarly started out in the IOGT but resented the fact that the order relied too heavily on ritualistic ceremony rather than on political agitation. The ASL's efficiency also derived from its structure as a business corporation. A board of trustees directed the funds and policy of the organization. Funds—always tight in the state's other temperance organizations—were solicited systematically by establishing a net-

Figure 4.1. The button from a temperance parade in Minnesota in May 1910 shows that the anti-saloon forces denounced the saloon as the root of intemperance and the destroyer of the home and family life. Courtesy of the Minnesota Historical Society. Photograph by Robert Fogt.

work of donors. Minnesota's ASL also started publishing its own newspaper from the spring of 1898 on, which enabled its leaders to communicate with the subordinate branches and to give organizational and tactical advice. By 1900, *The Minnesota Issue* already had a circulation of nine thousand.[5]

The League's leaders made other organizational decisions that would guarantee the organization's success. First, they established close contact with the ministers of the state's numerous churches. By encouraging local pastors to enroll their congregations, the League organized at the grass roots. Soon, a large number of Minnesota's religious bodies, its Congregational, Methodist, Evangelical, and Baptist conferences in particular, actively supported the ASL's work. Second, the League selected Minneapolis as its headquarters, an intelligent choice indeed. Since the 1880s, Minneapolis, with "her very exceptional record in the efforts to suppress the saloon," had developed a reputation as a comparably reform-minded city, and a great number of its residents were supportive of the

League's work. The majority of the League's officials came from Minneapolis, while only a handful came from St. Paul and other towns.[6]

In the years to come, the ASL perfected its organizational structure and delineated its methods of agitation. Most significantly, its leaders decided in favor of branching out across the state. By the end of 1899, the ASL had held meetings in sixty-five of the state's then eighty-two counties and established from one to six local leagues or preliminary committees in almost each of them. In the summer of 1900, it employed a brigade of about sixty male students to elicit interest in about half of the state's counties. Students were to become one of the ASL's main assets, intellectually capable yet cheap laborers. In order to organize this student workforce, ASL leaders had established an intercollegiate branch in February 1900, representing the League at the state's educational institutions. Aside from heightening its presence in all parts of the state, the ASL also emphasized that its agitation was to be constant, as its goals, law enforcement and the gradual drying up of the state, could not be achieved through a "short and spirited campaign lasting about two weeks or seven days just before the election." This consistency distinguished the ASL from most other temperance organizations and greatly contributed to its success over the next two decades.[7]

The ASL's constant agitation was multifaceted. In order to promote better knowledge of the existing laws and to facilitate law enforcement, it published and distributed a booklet compiling all liquor laws of Minnesota. In several towns, it hired detectives investigating violations of these laws and made county or city attorneys prosecute the liquor sellers. In later years, the League would even send attorneys to prepare and try the cases for low or no fees at all. With the League's support, many towns voted out saloons under the 1870 Local Option Law, which allowed the voters of each municipal township to decide on whether or not liquor licenses were to be given out in their locality. Minnesota's ASL also sought to influence elections by publishing detailed information on the candidates' voting behavior in temperance matters. Many candidates even asked the League for help and support in their campaigns.[8]

By the turn of the century, the ASL had developed into a powerful and well-respected lobby group, which came to play a significant part in the political game. In 1901, Lieutenant Governor Lyndon A. Smith invited Superintendent Battey to consult with him on whom to appoint as a member of the Senate Temperance Committee. From 1900 on, the ASL also regularly lobbied for a Speaker of the House who was in favor of temperance and was thus the first temperance organization to realize the significance of this office to the temperance cause. Elected by the House members, the Speaker was responsible for appointing the House Temperance Committee, which decided on whether or not to recommend bills relating to liquor for passage—a decision with considerable influence on the vote of the House. The liquor interests had long realized the Speaker's vital position and similarly tried to get their candidates elected for that position. The attempt of pro- and anti-liquor activists to secure the position of the Speaker resulted in fierce speakership fights from 1907 on.[9]

The Progressive era's emphasis on efficiency and professionalism as well as the ASL's meticulously planned activism also rubbed off on the work of Minnesota's Prohibition Party. Between 1900 and 1912, the party worked hard to expand its voter base. Due to its clever nomination of Reverend B. B. Haugan, a Norwegian Lutheran minister of Fergus Falls, in 1900, it attracted more Scandinavian Americans to its ranks than ever before, all fervently in favor of County Option and prohibition. In 1902, under Willis G. Calderwood's leadership, the party decided to use more systematic and efficient methods of campaigning in order to cut a better figure in the elections. Calderwood was of the opinion that "[t]he party has been conducting a sentimental campaign for thirty years and we deem it time to attempt to crystallize this sentiment." The State Prohibition Committee rented the biggest automobile ever seen in the Northwest and went on an eight-week stumping tour carrying two or three speakers, a male quartet, and a brass band. It also put a great number of people in the field driving around in tallyhos—carriages drawn by four horses—and giving addresses several times a day.[10] Similar to the ASL, the Prohibition Party tried to win more young people to their cause by collaborating with youth organizations, such as the Epworth League, the Baptist Union, and the Christian Endeavor Societies, and by holding conventions at the state's various colleges. In 1907, the party had the largest war chest since its founding—$10,000—and used it to hire a brigade of young college students for "gumshoeing"—house-to-house canvassing—the state. In the end, the Prohibition Party's improved campaign methods and the inclusion of standard Progressive reform into its party program paid off. In 1912, for the first time in its history, Minnesota's Prohibition Party earned nearly a double-digit percentage of the vote in the election (9.38 percent).[11]

Before 1905, the Prohibition Party refused to cooperate with the ASL, as it considered the latter's nonpartisanship an insurmountable obstacle in the fight against liquor. The years between 1905 and 1915, however, witnessed an increasing amount of collaborative efforts between the two organizations, within and outside the state's legislative halls, which culminated in their campaign for the so-called Indian lid.[12] The Indian lid referred to the prohibition of the sale of liquor on land ceded by Native Americans through treaties as well as in "Indian country"—i.e., land on which Native Americans actually resided and land allotted to them but sold to whites in the meantime. As early as September 1905, newspapers reported that the Department of the Interior might proceed to confiscate liquor and close several hundred saloons in Minnesota as they were located on territory covered by three different Indian treaties, the 1851 Traverse des Sioux Treaty and the 1855 and 1863 Chippewa Treaties. While the Treaty of

1855 provided that no liquor was to be sold in the ceded parts "until otherwise provided by Congress," the treaties of 1851 and 1863 gave the president the authority to remove the alcohol ban. If these treaties were enforced, two-thirds of Minnesota—excluding St. Paul but including parts of Minneapolis—would have gone dry. It was not clear who had initiated this government investigation, but it ignited a fierce battle in Minnesota and Washington, D.C. between 1909 and 1915, fought by the state's Prohibition Party, the ASL, the lawyers of the breweries and distilleries, the special agents of the Indian bureau, Congress, Presidents William Howard Taft and Woodrow Wilson, and the courts. The Minnesota ASL and the Prohibition State Committee considered the legal debate about the Indian lid as a great chance to use the federal government as a tool to introduce prohibition into parts of Minnesota, against the will of the state government. The conflict even brought William Eugene "Pussyfoot" Johnson to Minnesota, who was a special agent of the Indian bureau since 1906, an ASL member, and a fervent advocate of prohibition. He raided saloons and confiscated large amounts of liquor, mostly in northern Minnesota. At the beginning of 1911, President Taft finally issued an order modifying the two treaties he could and recommended that Congress repeal the treaty of 1855. Johnson continued his work in the territory of the 1855 treaty until he was stopped by an injunction effected by Minnesota's brewers and distillers. In October 1914, the U.S. Supreme Court dissolved the injunction and confirmed the Indian bureau's right to close the saloons in the areas covered by the 1855 treaty. Consequently, Johnson's successors made five counties and parts of nine others saloonless.[13]

As the campaign for an Indian lid in Minnesota has demonstrated, the ASL's and Prohibition Party's campaigns and lobbying efforts were countered by the doings of brewers, distillers, wholesale liquor dealers, and retailers, whose political power had increased tremendously in the wake of the High License Law. The dependence of the cities on the high license fees had enhanced the liquor retailers' influence in local politics and had led to a certain deference of municipal authorities to them. The high license Law had also greatly changed the structure of the liquor business itself. On the one hand, it fostered blind pigging, that is, selling liquor without a license, as some saloon owners could not afford to pay the license fees and chose to go underground instead. On the other hand, High License transformed the liquor producer into the most central figure in the liquor business. Before its introduction, the two segments of the liquor business, the manufacturers and the retailers, had operated largely independently. The $1,000 license fee forced many saloon owners to ask the manufacturers, mostly the brewers, for financial support. In 1912, a Senate investigation found out that in St. Paul the brewers paid and took out 60 to 75 percent and in Minneapolis more than 40 percent of all licenses, mostly in a bulk, and had their renters pay weekly or monthly installments for building, fixtures, and the license fee. This so-called tied-house system increased the number of saloons, made competition keener, and profit making more difficult. It also heightened the brewers' interest in local and state politics. Their greater financial involvement in the sale of liquor—that part of the liquor trade that was most vulnerable to the temperance reformers' attacks—put them at the forefront of political anti-temperance activism. By means of extensive political maneuvering and lobbying, they sought to avert the blows destined to ruin their financial enterprises.[14]

The liquor interests' involvement in Minnesota's political life deeply concerned the state's Progressives. Lynn Haines, a native of Minnesota and a reform-minded journalist and political commentator, revealed how corporations in general and the liquor interests in particular were involved in the establishment of the legislatures and in the election of the Speakers, and through which means they controlled individual legislators and the legislation process. Haines, as his contemporaries, never differentiated between producers of beer, hard liquor, and sellers when disclosing their political lobbying, lumping them together as "allied liquor forces" or "liquor interests." While unwilling—or unable—to make a distinction between the various branches of the liquor business, he repeatedly singled out the brewery machine as constituting the head of the liquor industry. To Haines, it was the most "compact and perfectly operating organization," surpassing all other interest groups in "profligacy and unscrupulous practices" and thereby exerting "an immeasurably evil influence in Minnesota politics." His writings stirred up the reformers who vented about the "monstrous brewery conspiracy" and the "Hamm-strung legislators," that is, the legislators bribed by brewers such as William Hamm. Naturally, the liquor interests undermined any of the Progressives' legislative attempts to curb their political power.[15]

In their anti-temperance agitation, the liquor interests were supported by the state's German Americans and by Minnesota's labor organizations, which, for the first time in the state's history of organized labor, took a firm stance against temperance. While class is, besides gender, ethnicity, religion, and civic identity, a significant and complex factor in the battles around liquor, these battles, were, however, too complex to follow straight class lines. Whereas a great number of workers perceived the temperance movement as an attack on their values and lifestyle as well as their economic security (see figure 4.2), time and again workers could be found fighting along with the middle-class reformers or their employers against saloons. The Knights of Labor, one of the most important labor organizations in the nineteenth-century United States, maintained a close relationship with the WCTU. The Knights, under the leadership of the Irish American Terence V. Powderly, urged their members to abide by temperance principles, classed saloon keepers as social parasites, and banned them from their ranks. The relation between social class and temperance was further complicated when ethnic concerns intersected with

Figure 4.2. The brewery workmen's unions were at the forefront of the workers' fight against County Option and other prohibitory laws. The German banner in the photograph, displaying the 1901 Labor Day meeting of the Minneapolis union of brewery workmen, asks God to preserve hops and malt ("Hopfen und Malz, Gott erhalt's!") and thus visualizes the deep intertwining of economic and ethnic concerns in the production of beer. From the Collection of Steve Ketcham. Photograph by Robert Fogt.

class. Many Irish workers joined the CTAU of St. Paul and collaborated with the Protestant reformers in order to move up the social ladder and to improve the reputation of the Irish as a group. Finally, religion was another factor that further muddied the picture and could exert a larger influence on the workers than their class background. Workers belonging to pietistic denominations were generally more inclined toward the temperance movement than workers belonging to liturgical ones.[16]

It might have been their awareness of these manifold intersections and conflicting identifications that deterred Minnesota's labor organizations from taking an active part in the fight against temperance. It was only in May 1908, in the context of the ASL's law enforcement campaigns, that the St. Paul unions of cigar makers, bartenders, beer bottlers, cabinetmakers, coopers, brewers, and ice wagon drivers convinced the St. Paul Trades and Labor Assembly (TLA) to pass a resolution condemning sumptuary laws. The latter, they argued, impaired people's legal and constitutional privileges, violated the very essence of civil liberty, and constituted "the very pinnacle of governmental paternalism." The advocates of the prohibition movement, the TLA claimed, were "the same in character and purpose, if not in personality, as those who have so bitterly fought throughout the years against the shortening of the hours of labor or the increase of the standards of wages for fear the laboring people would . . . immerse themselves in the filth of profligate living." It thus implied that the temperance reformers did not want to promote the general welfare of the working class but intentionally aimed at keeping it down to retain their own standards.[17]

While this resolution was unanimously passed in liquor-friendly St. Paul, it caused considerable strife in the Minnesota State Federation of Labor, since 1890 the umbrella organization of all the state's workers. At its annual meeting in Winona on June 8, 1908, the Federation's anti-temperance camp found itself confronted with a small, yet determined, group of members who insisted that the Federation should take no stance on temperance at all. After much debate, the representatives agreed upon a relatively moderate compromise resolution stating that sumptuary legislation would disturb and disrupt industrial conditions and declaring the enforcement of the existing liquor laws to be sufficient. The Federation also pledged its moral support to all affiliated unions who were making an effort to prevent the passage of County Option or prohibitory laws but refrained from engaging itself in the struggle about temperance. The Minnesota Federation of Labor did not even depart from this policy of reticence when the passage of a County Option bill was dawning on the horizon. In 1914, an attempt of the Federation's anti-temperance faction to secure the passage of a strong resolution against prohibition and County Option once again divided the convention. It took several days of heated debate until a sufficient amount of representatives could be secured who supported such a resolution. Due to the hesitancy of the Minnesota State Federation of Labor to position itself and to become politically active in the fight against stringent temperance laws, the St. Paul Brewery Workers' Union No. 97 and the Beer Bottlers' Union No. 343 initiated the founding of the Minnesota Trade Union League to Prevent Unemployment and Promote the Principle of Home Rule, the state's first workers' anti-temperance organization, in May 1915. The League, which soon represented about forty organizations, pledged itself to support the antiprohibition movement in all its forms. The available sources, however, remain silent about the League's activism.[18]

Not only did the debate about County Option cause debates among the ranks of organized labor, but it also affected Minnesota's political landscape. Aside from the aforementioned speakership fights, which regularly poisoned the state's political climate, the issue of County Option contributed to the loosening of party ties and affected voting behavior. The 1910 election, for instance, entirely revolved around the issue of County Option and turned voting patterns upside down. While the Republicans had ignored the demands of the ASL, decided against a County Option plank in their platform, and nominated Adolph Olson Eberhart, the incumbent and a strong opponent of County Option, as a gubernatorial candidate, the Democrats' Progressive wing managed to line up the party in favor of County Option. John Lind, the Democrats' strongest gubernatorial candidate, announced early that he would accept the nomination only if the Democrats introduced a County Option plank into their platform. Despite such announcements, the Democratic convention in late July unanimously decided against County Option but still nominated Lind, who did not react to this nomination for about three weeks. Only then did he decline his nomination in a letter to Frank A. Day, who did not pass it on until early September. With almost no time left for the search for and appointment of another candidate, the Democrats had to pick James Gray as a replacement for Lind despite the former's endorsement of County Option. Contemporaries later claimed that Gray's nomination had been the plan of the party's small County Option faction all along and that Lind's late decline was part of a great conspiracy to force the Democrats into endorsing County Option.[19]

Thus, Minnesota's electorate were faced with an entirely new situation. The Republicans, traditionally more inclined toward reform, had chosen a gubernatorial candidate against County Option, while the Democrats, the longtime opponents of reform, had put a temperance reformer at the head of their ticket. This constellation produced new voting patterns. Most temperance advocates, led by the ASL, supported the Democratic candidate Gray. The Traveling Men's Liberty League, founded by the liquor interests in the context of the County Option movement, worked throughout the state and actively campaigned for Eberhart. Even William Hamm, one of the state's staunchest Democrats, endorsed the Republican gubernatorial candidate. Eberhart also received the votes of two immigrant groups. Under the leadership of the recently founded German-American Central Alliance of Minnesota (*Deutsch-Amerikanischer Zentralbund von Minnesota*, ZB of Minnesota), Minnesota's German Americans forsook the Democratic Party in favor of the Republicans.[20]

With its designated fight against machine politics, Progressivism had greatly strengthened the trend to vote for the man rather than the party, which had begun around the turn of the century. The fight about County Option hastened the increasingly nonpartisan sentiment in Minnesota, as both the ASL and the opponents of temperance forced candidates to voice their opinion on County Option, published this opinion, and encouraged the state's electorate to ignore party lines and to judge the individual candidates merely upon the basis of their statements. Such developments toward nonpartisanship would culminate in the banning of state legislators' party designations in 1913, a measure celebrated by the rejoicing temperance reformers as "the most important and revolutionary political reform in the last half century." Voters would from then on be released from their traditional obligation to their parties and could support legislators on the basis of local issues.[21]

Eberhart's fulminant victory in 1910 demonstrated that County Option had again not been an option or at least not the priority for the majority of Minnesota's electorate. It would take another four years until County Option had a realistic chance in the "Land of Amber Waters." Several factors moved the state down the path toward County Option. After a decade of work, the ASL's strategic gradualism slowly showed its desired effect. By holding Local Option elections regularly and by working for its enforcement, the ASL had, according to its own records, succeeded in making 160 of the state's 525 municipalities dry. Moreover, the League emphasized that of the state's 1,800 townships, 1,200 were without saloons, and 400 allowed saloons only in the incorporated villages. In 1913, the legislature passed a bill extending Local Option, which had so far applied only to towns and villages, to fourth-class cities with a population of less than ten thousand and thus created even greater room for temperance activism. Up to the introduction of County Option, the number of the state's dry municipalities had increased to 254, and the state's dry territory was greatly expanded through the enforcement of the Indian lid. With large numbers of Minnesotans living in dry areas, County Option did not appear so far-fetched and drastic any more.[22]

The years of 1913 and 1914 also witnessed the most intense cooperation between the ASL, the Prohibition Party, the IOGT, and the WCTU, who combined their human power, organizational structures, and information channels to heighten public sentiment in favor of County Option and to exert pressure on the legislators. These efforts culminated in the formation of the Cooperative Temperance Council of Minnesota in February 1914, which was composed of two members of the WCTU, the Prohibition Party, and the ASL, and one delegate of the young people's church organizations. The Council's designated goal was to fight for the nomination of pro-temperance legislators.[23]

Finally, another development also increased the temperance supporters' strength in the 1915 legislature. By staging an "anti-machine republican [*sic*] conference" in Minneapolis in March 1914, the Progressive faction of the Republican Party managed to avert Eberhart's renomination and to place William E. Lee, a Progressive and a strong advocate of County Option, in the field. While the ASL and the other temperance forces supported Lee, many Eberhart supporters decided to give their votes to the Democratic nominee, Winfield S. Hammond. Whereas Lee promised to push for the enactment of County Option, Hammond indicated that he would sign such a bill if the legislature passed it.

This slight difference in attitude toward County Option was virtually the only distinction between the two candidates. Progressives claimed that "no State election in years has been so vital for the future of Minnesota." To them, the real issue of the election was: "Shall the liquor interests dominate the politics of Minnesota?" They portrayed the brewers as the force standing in the way of progress and the County Optionists as the vanguard of good government. The Progressive reform element thereby artfully turned the question of County Option into a question of morality versus immorality, of good government versus bad government. County Option acquired a moral aura that made it hard for legislators to decide against it yet again.[24]

Hammond won the election, successfully attracting voters opposed to County Option, while allowing County Option supporters who preferred him to Lee to vote for him knowing that he would not block this temperance measure. Recognizing the signs of the times, Hammond, in his inaugural gubernatorial address, pleaded for an early resolution of the question, which, he maintained, had aroused "bitterness entirely unwarranted by its importance from a temperance standpoint or from any other standpoint." After the Senate passed the bill (36:31) on February 4, 1915, all eyes were directed to the House, which was to decide on County Option twenty days later. Excitement in St. Paul was tremendous. Crowds of people wandered to the Capitol, "thronged and shoved each other in the corridors, rushed like a mad mob to the galleries and even tried to trespass into the lower part of the assembly hall. . . . Numerous women showed up as early as 8am, armed with lunch baskets." After nine hours of debate, the House passed the bill (66:62), and Hammond signed it on March 1, 1915. The temperance advocates happily proclaimed that the County Option Law was "the first radical measure aimed at the liquor business in Minnesota which has passed the Legislature since the High License Law was enacted more than a quarter of a century ago." After decades of struggles, the High License consensus had finally been shattered.[25]

The adoption of County Option can be considered a major step toward prohibition, as it gradually dried the state up and encouraged public sentiment in favor of ousting liquor altogether. Within thirty days after the passage of the bill, temperance advocates in fifty counties started preparing County Option elections. The County Option Law required that 25 percent of the registered voters from the previous general election sign a petition requesting a special election in a county concerning the licensing of saloons. Such an election could take place every three years. The ASL and other temperance organizations did everything in their might to help local groups to work successfully in favor of a dry county. Between April and August 1915, forty-four of Minnesota's counties were voted dry, with the law giving the saloon owners six months to clean up their businesses. Therefore, by late summer, fifty-one out of Minnesota's eighty-six counties were dry through County Option elections and through enforcement of the old Indian treaties. In December 1915, the *Bemidji Daily Pioneer* stated that within the previous two years about two hundred saloons had been closed by the Indian bureau, while about twice as many had fallen victim to a dry vote in the County Option elections.[26]

In 1915, no one in Minnesota would have believed that only four years later national prohibition would become a reality. Similar to the sentiment in the aftermath of the passage of the High License Law in 1887, there was a broad consensus in favor of the maintenance of County Option and against the introduction of prohibition, which is why legislators swiftly killed the prohibition bill. With the exception of the state's radical reformers, contemporaries seem to have been glad that the fierce battles about County Option were over. Even the ASL considered prohibition premature at that point. Unbeknown to them, however, the war in Europe, which had begun in 1914, would soon prove to be the major catalyst of prohibition in Minnesota as well as in the rest of the United States.[27]

St. Paul and Minneapolis—"Two Cities . . . So Unlike"

After one year of reform work in the Twin Cities, ASL leaders concluded the following:

> The fact that the two cities are so unlike in all matters relating to agitation, legislation and law enforcement, owing to the different character of the nationalities of the citizens and other reasons together with the fact that there is and always has been a disposition to avoid doing in one city in municipal affairs what has been done in the other, or that each city seems inclined to hew out its own path, renders the situation complicated.[28]

This statement reveals that contemporaries were conscious of the striking differences between—and the contrasting self-conceptualizations of—these two neighboring cities. From Minneapolis's incorporation in 1856 onward, St. Paul and its upstream neighbor competed with each other for economic supremacy. Despite being geographic neighbors, as Wingerd has argued, "the cities increasingly regarded themselves as worlds apart." Their different civic identities resulted from their varying founding histories, demographics, and economic structures. In contrast to St. Paul, Minnesota's ethnically diverse pioneer settlement and whiskey distribution center, Minneapolis had been established as a milling town, and its early population consisted primarily of Protestant New Englanders. The city was soon declared to be a "New England of the West," a long cherished yet unattainable goal in St. Paul. In the years to come, Minneapolis's New Englanders continued to constitute the city's economic and social elite. Catholic Pig's Eye–St. Paul and the Protestant "city of waters" also differed economically. Wingerd succinctly summarizes these differences: "commercial versus industrial capitalism, trade versus manufacture, independent enterprise versus corporate combination."[29]

By the end of the nineteenth century, the battle lines between the culturally and economically disparate cities had hardened. The census of 1880 and the so-called Census War of 1890 made it evident that Minneapolis had outpaced St. Paul in terms of residents. In addition, Minneapolis emerged from the depression of the 1890s stronger than ever, with its sawmill industry on the verge of becoming the largest producer in the country. The city had also developed into the country's major center for wheat and reduced St. Paul to a regional distribution center, which increased St. Paulites' ill feelings toward Minneapolitans. St. Paulites portrayed Minneapolis as a heartless industrial machine with a top-down hierarchy, whereas they saw their own city as an actual community, in which small businesses and manufacturers were highly valued and unionism was encouraged. Minneapolitans, in turn, stressed their economic, cultural, and moral superiority.[30]

Contemporaries codified the "almost polar cultural configurations" of the two cities both verbally and visually. Its civic leaders and the city's press fashioned Minneapolis as an "amalgamation of a New England town and the second largest Scandinavian town in the world, the one representing justice and sobriety and the other temperance." Such self-characterizations were readily picked up and perpetuated by outsiders, such as the muckraking journalist Lincoln Steffens, who imagined Minneapolis as a "Yankee with a round Puritan head, an open prairie heart, and a great, big Scandinavian body," known for his hard work, financial efficiency, and sobriety.[31] St. Paulites, in turn, hailed their city as the state's bulwark of liberality and personal liberty and celebrated its joie de vivre. Contemporary cartoonists from both cities incorporated these contrasting civic identities into their work. Whereas they portrayed Minneapolis as the elegant, chaste, and well-dressed woman "Minne," they depicted St. Paul as the plump, happy-go-lucky monk St. Paul. The halo on his head signified hypocrisy rather than sanctity (see figures 4.3 and 4.4).[32]

Not only were the cities' polar cultural configurations a topic among contemporary journalists and cartoonists, but they also played out in the everyday lives of city residents. The temperance movement was one such arena in which these cultural differences manifested themselves and were reified. The way in which both cities handled demands for reform—such as the campaigns for an anti-wineroom ordinance—reveals their "disposition to avoid doing in one city in municipal affairs what has been done in the other," as the ASL so keenly observed. St. Paulites, in particular, strictly refused to be identified with Minneapolis. The upstream city provided the ideal foil, the constitutive outside, against which St. Paul's identity could be negotiated. St. Paulites' tendency toward othering made life hard for the residents of St. Paul's only reformist enclave in its history, the Midway area, which was founded in the 1880s. The "Midway War"

Figures 4.3 and 4.4. "St. Paul" and "Minne" as conceptualized by contemporary cartoonists. Cartoons from the *Daily Pioneer Press* [St. Paul] 22 Apr. 1897: 1, and reprinted in *The Minnesota Issue* [St. Paul] July 1907: 2. Courtesy of the Minnesota Historical Society.

between Midway residents and "real" St. Paulites sheds light on the consequences of a suburb's resistance to the normative order of a place. The celebration of St. Paul's oppositional disposition with respect to temperance appeared to have come to a sudden end, when in 1906 the state of Minnesota, through the force of its legal apparatus, coerced its capital into emulating its far more temperate neighbor. However, below the surface, difference prevailed.

The ASL, whose major target was the state's cities, began its grass roots reform work in St. Paul as early as 1899, when State Superintendent Battey visited over a dozen of St. Paul's evangelical churches in order to introduce the organization and its work. Whereas in Minneapolis the ASL had been immediately able to notch up successes, such as the enforcement of the Sunday Law, in St. Paul its work had no immediate effect.[33] This lack of success cannot merely be ascribed to St. Paul's cultural and demographic peculiarities but also to its specific economic situation at that time. In 1899, the total manufacturing output for St. Paul was $30,060,000, as opposed to Minneapolis's $94,410,000. While St. Paul still possessed immense wholesaling operations at the end of the nineteenth century, its wholesaling market was shrinking. In order to halt or, at least, slow down this decline, the business classes heavily invested in and relied on a thriving vice industry (gambling, saloons, prostitution), which was to keep their city attractive to potential buyers.[34]

Predictably, the ASL's campaign against winerooms in St. Paul met with resistance, as it sought to erase facets of immorality that were quite desirable to St. Paul's business elites as well as the city administration. In early 1900, the Minneapolis ASL, supported by various reform groups and churches, started a campaign for the closing of the city's winerooms. Its attorney drafted an anti-wineroom ordinance, which was, without much ado, passed in April 1900 and signed by Mayor James Gray a short time later. Due to the ASL's successful enforcement campaign, between June and August of 1900, Minneapolis's saloon owners removed 1,200 to 1,300 winerooms, stalls, and booths from their saloons.[35]

Encouraged by this success, the ASL attempted a similar anti-wineroom campaign in St. Paul. When the ordinance was introduced in November 1900, it was buried by the Committee on License, with city politicians arguing that St. Paul was simply not Minneapolis, and while the latter might need such an ordinance, the former certainly did not.[36] After juggling the ordinance from committee to committee, perpetually postponing action, in June 1901, the assembly finally passed the anti-wineroom ordinance and handed it to the Board of Aldermen. Instead of acting right away, the aldermen referred it once more to the Committee on License, where it remained for almost half a year. Only on January 21, 1902, due to the upcoming election, the aldermen recalled the ordinance from the committee and passed it, expecting Mayor Smith's veto, which promptly followed. After two more anti-wineroom ordinances failed to become law, both chambers of the city council eventually adopted an ordinance, which had many loopholes and was not enforced by the police. It had taken St. Paul almost one and a half years to adopt an ordinance much more moderate in character than the one adopted in Minneapolis within a few weeks. The refusal of St. Paul's city officials to pass an ordinance in their city that had previously been passed in Minneapolis also demonstrates how much St. Paulites at the time defined themselves in opposition to their neighbors upstream.[37]

St. Paulites' conceptualization of their city as an anti-temperance space and their tendency to define themselves in opposition to their neighbors were responsible for an inner-city war between them and the residents of the Midway area. Located midway between Minneapolis and St. Paul, the area's residents identified with the former while belonging to the latter. The Midway area was St. Paul's only reformist enclave, a residential suburb differing from the rest of St. Paul in the character of its population, its mindset, and its moral outlook. Like in the case of St. Paul, the Midway area's identity and its attitude toward alcohol were to a great degree based on its founding narrative. Previously a vast open space, sparsely settled by farmers, the completion of the interurban railroad in 1880 made the Midway area an attractive place for settlement. Right from the start, its major promoters—many with a pietistic background—conceived of it as a village for wealthy businessmen and white-collar workers. As late as 1969, newspapers still described the Hamline neighborhood as "prim, straight-laced, conservative."[38]

The Midway area soon turned into an important educational center, attracting institutions such as Hamline University and Macalester College. Luminaries such as John Ireland and Thomas Cochran also greatly boosted it by buying real estate and working for an improvement of electrification and transportation. Because of such economic growth, St. Paul cast greedy eyes on the flourishing Midway area and was granted the right to annex it by the 1885 legislature. Legislators, however, prohibited the city council from issuing licenses for saloons within a circuit of four and a half square miles, of which Merriam Park was the center. Founder John L. Merriam strongly advocated the prohibition of liquor in the area, and the presence of several educational institutions underlined such advocacy.[39]

This legislative ousting of liquor attracted reformers to the area who enjoyed being outside the city proper, which was steeped in anti-temperance sentiment. However, it did not prevent blind piggers from pitching their tents in the Midway area in order to meet the demands of customers from both Minneapolis and St. Paul. Midway residents started campaigning against these illegal liquor outlets from the early 1890s on, but the city's police force either refused to interfere or tipped off blind piggers. St. Paul's License Inspector, Grand Jury, Corporation Attorney, and city council, in turn, repeatedly claimed that these blind piggers were a chimera of Midway residents and simply did not exist. St. Paulites in general felt that the Midway residents deserved the strong presence of immoral saloon owners. After all, with the help of Minneapolitan legislators, they had time and again thwarted attempts of St. Paul's legislators to deprive the Midway area of its status as a prohibitory district and had thus decided against the establishment of a legal saloon culture.[40]

After more than a decade of futile campaigning and petitioning, the Midway residents decided to ask outsiders for support in their fight against St. Paul's normative order. They established a Citizens' Committee in order to gather evidence against the Midway blind pigs and passed this evidence onto the Ramsey County authorities. The result of these actions was the biggest raid against blind pigs that had ever taken place in Minnesota up to that point, termed by contemporaries the "Midway War." On April 15, 1904, at 7:30 P.M., a number of Midway citizens set up pickets east and west of University Avenue Bridge, while Ramsey County Sheriff Philip C. Justus and his men raided the blind pigs, arrested seven blind piggers, and confiscated two vanloads of liquor. The county attorney had issued the search warrants a few days prior to the raid. The success of the operation derived from the fact that all those involved had managed to keep it a secret from the St. Paul police and city authorities, so they could not tip the blind piggers. The timing of the raid was certainly not coincidental either. By placing it shortly before the municipal election, the raiders hoped to bring down Mayor Smith and to ensure the election of the Republican reformer Frederick P. Wright, a clever but ultimately unsuccessful strategy.[41]

The Midway War displays the Midway residents' degree of alienation from their city of residence. Their negative perception of St. Paul and their emphasis on "the enormity of the immorality of the city" led to the formation of a counter-identity. They found the conditions in the city "obnoxious" and were so suspicious of St. Paul's authorities that they relied instead on help from outside in their attempts to fight against the wet status quo. The fact that St. Paul's newspapers severely criticized the Midway reformers and always referred to them as the "residents of the prohibited district"—never as St. Paulites—suggests that they did not view them as proper city residents. Minneapolitan newspapers, by contrast, consistently endorsed their attempts to cleanse the area of blind pigs.[42]

Through their agitation in favor of temperance, the Midway residents had widened the rift between them and the majority of St. Paulites. St. Paul would remain their constitutive outside, everything they did not want to be. The ongoing tensions between the factions sometimes even unleashed violence. In late April 1904, shortly after the first raid, unknown persons, supposedly agents of the blind piggers, smashed a large plate glass window in the residence of F. W. Buswell, a member of the Midway citizens' Vigilance Committee. This was the revenge for trying to change St. Paul's civic identity and to emulate upstream Minneapolis—a painful lesson St. Paul's temperance suburb had to learn.[43]

The year 1905 constituted the height of St. Paul's blatant opposition to Minneapolis in terms of liquor law enforcement and reform. The immediate cause for the events that year was Albert Alonzo "Doc" Ames's two-year mayoralty of immorality and corruption in Minneapolis between January 1901 and August 1902.[44] Not only did his rein cause tremendous frustration among Minneapolitans and ended with his conviction, but it also gained Minneapolis the unjustified reputation of being a perpetual den of iniquity through an article by Lincoln Steffens, which appeared in *McClure's Magazine* in 1903. In order to restore the city's former reputation, acting Mayor David P. Jones took over the reins and started cleaning up the city, regulating prostitution and enforcing all liquor laws to the letter, including the Sunday Law.[45]

St. Paul rejoiced when Minneapolis was "put on a lid." The Sunday closing of saloons in Minneapolis from November 5, 1905, on offered great economic opportunities to the "Saintly City"—an ironic moniker common among contemporaries—with about $20,000 going from Minneapolis to St. Paul every Sunday. Soon St. Paul achieved national renown as "Sunday Jag Headquarters." Even a newspaper from Northampton, Massachusetts, reported that every Sunday about forty thousand Minneapolitans, that is, about 15 percent of the city's residents, came to St. Paul in order to evade the lid.[46] The *Minneapolis Journal* reported "startling stories of unrestrained debauchery and bacchanalian Sabbaths at St. Paul." The newspaper continued sarcastically: "Whether the downriver town sees in the present situation an opportunity to win undying fame as a lusher's paradise and thereby to grow is not known, but certain it is that the city is known in the cast as a place where the lid has been destroyed and where unlicensed alcoholic carnivals are weekly occurrences." St. Paulites, by contrast, were very satisfied with the situation. The *Pioneer Press* indeed perceived Minneapolis's dry Sunday as a chance for St. Paul to overtake its neighbor and to win back its reputation as the largest and most prosperous city in the state. Its editor claimed that the strict law enforcement during Christopher D. O'Brien's mayoralty in the 1880s had been the reason why Minneapolis had overtaken St. Paul in the first place and now it was time to make up for this loss. In the mind of many St. Paulites, the enforcement of the liquor laws was not only associated with dreariness, religious zeal, and cultural narrow-mindedness, but also with economic decline. St. Paul could survive only if its liquor culture flourished.[47]

St. Paul's Sunday business probably would have gone on for a good while, had not the state again intervened—this time through its highest legal authority, the Supreme Court. In 1906, in the context of a trial between the ASL and St. Cloud's Mayor John E. C. Robinson over the latter's refusal to enforce the Sunday Law, the state's highest court emphasized that state laws were superior to municipal charters and ordinances. The court also declared it the duty of the attorney general to remove from office any city officials who failed to enforce these laws.[48] This decision was a heavy blow for St. Paulites and many other Minnesota city residents who had been striving for home rule in the state for more than a decade. After in 1897 an amendment had been adopted enabling Minnesota's cities to frame their own charters, St. Paul's new charter, which went into effect on June 1, 1900, made the city a "self-governing autonomy, with all necessary powers . . . vested in the people of the city for managing their own affairs." St. Paulites felt that their new charter would "avoid the evils which fall upon unlimited special legislation by the legislature, and at the same time enable each city . . . to secure that government which was best adapted to its needs." Just like in the context of the High License debates, however, the state outlined the extent of its legislative authority and thus set clear limits to the practice of home rule.[49]

St. Paul's temperance reformers were not worried about this limitation of home rule but celebrated this decision as the "greatest victory" that "has been accomplished in the Northwest in years." For the first time in the history of the state, they had been given a legal club enabling them to discipline their city. If St. Paul's city officials continued refusing to enforce the state law, the temperance reformers would appeal to Attorney General E. T. Young, who would then remove them from office. Since St. Paul's Board of Police Commissioners did not want to risk removal from office, it decided to enforce the Sunday Law strictly. Thus, in June 1907, the highly profitable Sunday sale in St. Paul came to a halt, with the state forcing St. Paulites to emulate their neighbors' reform eagerness.[50]

Figures 4.5 and 4.6. Cartoons commenting on the contradictory reactions of Minneapolis and St. Paul to the "lid." Cartoons reprinted in *The Minnesota Issue* [Minneapolis] 7 July 1907: 2, 3. Courtesy of the Minnesota Historical Society.

Minneapolis's editorials abounded with malicious joy. The *Minneapolis Journal* published a cartoon portraying Attorney General Young holding the Sunday Law umbrella over happy "Minne" and dumbfounded St. Paul to make them dry. While "Minne" seems very content, St. Paul vents his despair about the lid, saying: "Water, water everywhere but not a drop to drink!" (see figure 4.5). The second cartoon emphasizes that while St. Paul's lid came directly from the "State Millinery Shop," that is, it was imposed upon the city by the state, Minneapolis wore a "home-made" lid, once again directly pointing at the cities' contrasting mentalities (see figure 4.6).

In St. Paul, spirits were low. The *Tägliche Volkszeitung* reported—with elegiac sadness—that St. Paul offered a sorry sight on Sundays: people standing at street corners in groups, looking in vain for an open saloon. "One could not detect satisfaction in people's faces. Even the sky had put on a grim face: It opened the floodgates, sent down lightning, and, through the growling thunder, clearly voiced its anger about St. Paul's alienation from its destiny as a liberally governed city. The 'dry Sunday' was the general topic of conversation yesterday, which was not always treated with the most refined expressions." Such statements illustrate that St. Paul's strong advocacy of liquor and its opposition to temperance were not merely the result of the city's economic needs, but were deeply connected to its civic identity, which had emerged through the interaction of people and place at a particular point in time and had been defended and consolidated over many decades.[51]

The Sunday lid was followed by the 11 P.M. lid on December 20, 1907. Whereas since 1878 state law had fixed 11 P.M. as saloon closing time in the state, Minnesota's large cities had always allowed saloons to remain open until midnight. Once again, the city of Minneapolis acted as a vanguard. Its ministers, backed by large parts of the city's population, convinced Mayor J. C. Haynes to enforce the earlier closing time. St. Paul's ministers as well as its Baptist and Methodist youth seized the opportunity and put St. Paul's city officials under pressure by contacting Attorney General Young.[52] Young remained deaf to the entreaties of a committee of St. Paulites, who tried to explain to him that the enforcement of all these strict temperance laws was "against the public sentiment." He notified St. Paul's officials that they must enforce the state law or bear the consequences and thus put another lid on St. Paul. The cartoon from the *Minneapolis Journal* reflects St. Paul's unhappiness about such "enforced saintliness" and depicts the felt violence with which Young imposed this second lid on the city. The cartoonist comments: "Poor old St. Paul gets a new halo from the state authorities" (see figure 4.7). Through this halo, St. Paul was to become more like Minneapolis.[53]

Such alikeness, however, existed only in the realm of artistic imagination. While Minneapolis's authorities made efforts to enforce the lids, St. Paulites

ENFORCED SAINTLINESS.
Poor old St. Paul gets a new halo from the state authorities.

Figure 4.7. Attorney General Young enforcing the 11 P.M. closing law in St. Paul. Cartoon from *Minneapolis Journal* 18 Dec. 1907: 1. Courtesy of the Minnesota Historical Society.

consulted over possible escape routes out of this unfortunate situation. Between 1909 and 1913, the city's legislators tried to effect the repeal of the 11 P.M. closing law for Duluth, Minneapolis, and St. Paul. All of these bills, however, failed due to the agitation of the ASL, the Prohibition Party, and many legislators from Minneapolis. St. Paul's political representatives were furious and swore never to support any issue dear to Minneapolitans any more. One thousand Swedes from St. Paul also spoke out against the lifting of the lid, which did not make them any more popular in the city.[54] In order to satisfy their liquid needs while fighting for a legal solution against the lids, St. Paulites did what they had become very skilled at over the years: They simply ignored the state laws. In those days, the *Tägliche Volkszeitung* mused, St. Paulites could quench their thirst at all times in a wide variety of establishments. Now, with the two lids placed upon St. Paul, appearance became more important than reality. It appeared as if the city was peaceful and quiet. However, in reality those with "local knowledge" had many opportunities to fight "demon thirst." Due to his "common sense," Chief of Police John J. O'Connor allowed some establishments to ply their trade. While the state of Minnesota had set clear limits to the practice of home rule, St. Paulites on the ground had yet again found their own ways to satisfy their own and their city's needs and to celebrate their civic particularities.[55]

Throughout the 1910s, St. Paulites continued to do the exact opposite of what Minneapolis did. During the Senate Committee's investigation of brewery-owned saloons in 1912, St. Paul's city officials refused to appear before the committee while Minneapolis's municipal authorities complied. The tendency to act in opposition to Minneapolitans even manifested itself in St. Paul's militia. When in 1914 Minneapolis's companies of the state militia decided to close their army canteen in the coming maneuver and asked their St. Paul counterparts to follow suit, the latter stubbornly refused.[56] Due to such polar cultural configurations, it did not come as a surprise that the question of County Option elicited very different responses in both cities. While in 1915, Hennepin County managed to procure 29,334 (out of 68,671) votes in favor of County Option in its special election, in St. Paul the temperance reformers had to realize that they would never be able to find the sufficient number of petitioners needed for such a special election to take place. More than ever, in 1915, St. Paul and Minneapolis represented two divergent mindsets. For young Harrison E. Salisbury, who grew up in Minneapolis in the 1910s, St. Paul was "a sink of iniquity," "a haunt and a dive, populated, in large part, by politicians (a very lowly breed indeed), Democrats (even more lowly), Irish (another step down), and drunks." "Drunkenness" he believed, "was the normal condition of the wretched St. Paulites. . . . To my boy's eye, once the magic line between the two cities was crossed, one entered . . . a region of dismal slums, alien people, narrow streets, saloons, and God-alone-knew-what evils." The so-called Twin Cities were not twins at all, as contemporaries keenly observed, but rather "two cities . . . so unlike."[57]

The Demise of Irish Catholic Temperance Activism

The story of the Irish Catholic temperance movement in Minnesota between 1898 and 1915 is one of demise. Irish temperance activism had always been tied to a particular objective—the social uplift of the Irish as a group. Once this uplift was perceived as largely having been accomplished, Irish temperance work had fulfilled its designated purpose and was deprived of its raison d'être. Most Irish temperance societies lost large parts of their membership, while others increasingly turned into social and educational clubs, in which the fight against liquor was relegated to the margins. The CTAU of St. Paul faded from the temperance scene and lived on the memory of old times rather than on active work. This downward trend was accelerated by the pope's criticism of the Americanist agenda, of which temperance was an integral part, and by the inability of the movement to adapt to the Progressive spirit of the time. St. Paul's Sacred Thirst Society was one of the few Irish temperance societies in the state that continued its work. While Irish temperance women at large did not question the gender ideology espoused within the Catholic Church and the Irish community, the exceptional record of Margaret J. Kelly from St. Paul demonstrates that individual Irish American women indeed foregrounded female identity construction in their temperance activism. Just like their Protestant WCTU sisters, they employed the movement to secure a place in the male public sphere and to feminize that sphere.

Between 1900 and 1908, the membership of the CTAU of St. Paul decreased from 3,160 to about 1,000 members. John Ireland tried desperately to halt this decline and to reinvigorate the Irish Catholic temperance movement. He initiated the founding of a Catholic Total Abstinence Lecture Bureau composed of six priests. Their task was to initiate Catholic temperance societies in parishes where none existed and to revive those that had discontinued their work by giving lectures on total abstinence. The archbishop was also present at most conventions of the CTAU and encouraged the pioneer workers to renew their activism and the young people to become more active. Besides such pep talks, Ireland donated money to prize essay contests for Catholic high-school students to heighten their fervor for the temperance cause. In order to reinvigorate the Irish Catholic temperance work, he said, he was willing "to suspend any other work, even if necessary, the permanent completion of the new cathedral," which was the project most dear to his heart at the time.[58]

Despite the archbishop's efforts, he could not revitalize the Irish Catholic temperance movement in Minnesota. At the 1901 meeting of the state's CTAU in St. Paul, only eighty-six delegates from fifteen societies were present. Nine of these fifteen societies were located in the Twin Cities, mostly in Minneapolis. In other parts of Minnesota, the work had largely ceased. The CTAU's income during that year was $78. President A. W. Gutridge sarcastically commented that this sum was the measure of Irish Catholic enthusiasm for the temperance cause. In 1907, the number of delegates and members had shrunk so much that even the CTAU's officers conceded that "the palmiest days of the movement were over." In 1910, the CTAU's state annual convention was shortened to one day, and in 1911, due to the low attendance, only routine business was transacted and all musical entertainment and the reading of papers were dispensed with. By 1915, the annual convention had grown so marginal that even the Irish newspapers did not report it any more.[59] After 1915, the CTAU of St. Paul fell into complete oblivion, as it refused to cooperate with the temperance societies striving for prohibition and turned down their invitations to get-togethers. Whereas on the national level some radical Catholic reformers founded a Catholic Prohibition League in 1914, Minnesota's Catholics never established a branch. While individual Irish Catholics time and again displayed prohibitionist leanings, the CTAU refrained from endorsing prohibition for fear of offending many of its members. Most Irish temperance advocates also remained skeptical of the Prohibition Party, as it was said to be anti-Catholic in character. Those of Minnesota's Irish Catholics who were still greatly enthusiastic about temperance reform and in favor of more stringent liquor laws became members of the ASL, such as A. W. Gutridge, who was one of the ASL's trustees. Ireland himself had been instrumental in the founding of the ASL of America, acted as one of its vice presidents, and spoke frequently at its meetings.[60]

The *Catholic Bulletin*, the newly established archdiocesan newspaper, complained about the "deplorable lack of interest in temperance among Catholics in Minnesota." The movement's decline in the state was due to several facts, the *Bulletin* argued. Most importantly, many Irish believed that there was no need for such a movement any more, as the severe intoxication among the Irish had allegedly ceased. In addition, the editor and other Irish leaders, such as the CTAU of St. Paul's President James M. Reardon, claimed that Catholics had missed the chance to adapt their movement to the new and more scientific methods of the Progressive era. Emotional appeals simply did not suffice to attract followers any more but had to be accompanied by "[e]ducation along scientific lines."[61]

This contemporary analysis of the reasons for the Irish Catholic temperance movement's decline appears remarkably accurate. The Progressive movement with its trend toward rationalism and scientific analysis had indeed pushed the CTAU to the margins, and the ASL appeared far more attractive and efficient than the Irish Catholic union. In addition, by the turn of the century, many of the state's Irish had become part of the middle and upper echelons of society and held interethnic business partnerships and powerful political positions. In St. Paul, 30 percent of the city's foreign-stock attorneys were Irish-born, and first-generation Irish held 15 percent of the city's government jobs. Moreover, one-third of all police officers of St. Paul's police force were of Irish background. The 1900 census also shows a slight increase of the second-generation Irish within the professional category, a sign of upward mobility. Even though 43 percent of the city's Irish remained unskilled laborers, these workers greatly profited from their upwardly mobile fellow Irish, who secured them jobs and political leverage.[62] Irish American temperance activism had largely been a means to an end. Once this end—social uplift and integration into Anglo-American society—had been achieved, the means became increasingly superfluous. Moreover, by the 1900s, a large number of the Irish movement's old-time leaders had passed away, and most of its young members, such as the Crusaders, enjoyed it as a social club and job exchange rather than as a force promoting total abstinence. The Crusaders' decision not to pledge their members for total abstinence any more reflects this perceptional shift. Instead, they defined their society as "a union on perfectly equal terms between those who use [liquor] moderately and those who abstain entirely from intoxicating liquors as beverages."[63] What sped this downward trend was the Vatican's increasingly critical stance toward Americanist prelates, such as John Ireland. As early as 1895, Pope Leo XIII had issued *Longinqua oceani*, a letter warning American churchmen not to assume that America's system of church-state separation should be viewed as a model for other countries. Papal criticism climaxed in 1899, when Leo condemned certain aspects of Americanism in his letter *Testem benevolentiae*. Since the temperance movement was a constituent part of the Americanist agenda, it was automatically called into question through the papal writings.[64]

In those years, it was the Irish Catholic women, St. Paul's Sacred Thirst Society in particular, who kept up the Irish fight against liquor in city and state. In 1902, the society enrolled six hundred new members even though it is doubtful that these were permanent gains. The women put a strong emphasis on work among children and charitable work. They also established a temperance society for girls, the Angels of the Home. The name of this society illustrates that many Irish temperance women continued to adhere to traditional conceptions of female identity. After all, the idea of women as Angels in the House was deeply rooted in the ideology of the two spheres.[65]

While most Irish American women seem to have preferred such traditionally female temperance activities, the sparse records documenting female temperance activism in Minnesota illustrate that individual members of the capital's Sacred Thirst Society, like their Anglo-American sisters, ventured into the public sphere. Margaret J. Kelly was one of the few Irish women who decided to emphasize her female over her ethnic identity. Her wish to enter and reshape the public sphere was so great that she left the teachings of the Catholic Church aside. Soon after the Irish-born Kelly and her husband had arrived in

St. Paul in 1891, she started engaging in the city's Irish Catholic temperance movement and rapidly advanced to one of the Sacred Thirst Society's leaders, becoming its president for many years. Furthermore, she, together with Mary I. Cramsie, helped to keep the CTAU of St. Paul alive by serving as officers, giving addresses at conventions, representing the union at the conventions of the CTAU of America, and taking over offices in the national CTAU. Through her offices and a wide range of public agitation, Kelly became a well-known community organizer in St. Paul and popular among temperance reformers all over Minnesota.[66]

Kelly was also one of the few Irish temperance women who was not put off by the WCTU's militant Protestantism and its women's rights approach. Seeking to enhance collaboration between the groups, she encouraged Irish women to champion selected WCTU goals, such as the introduction of Scientific Temperance Instruction into St. Paul's parochial schools. Around 1905, she even became a member of the Lady Somerset and Merriam Park Unions of the WCTU. Due to her popularity in the WCTU, she functioned as Superintendent of Scientific Temperance Instruction on the state level between 1900 and 1918. Kelly's dual membership is a proof of the chances the temperance movement offered for interethnic and interdenominational work. Her activism within the WCTU also exposed her to the women's rights rhetoric of that organization and forced her, in her function as Superintendent of Scientific Temperance Instruction, to negotiate with legislators and principals across the state.[67]

It seems therefore not surprising that in 1902 Margaret J. Kelly was reported to have played an active role in the annual convention of the MWSA. Her advocacy of the democratization of the public sphere through female participation made her slated to become one of St. Paul's first policewomen in 1913. Due to her interest in municipal reform, she became responsible for the enforcement of the law in immoral resorts and saloons. In the last quarter of 1913 alone, Kelly and her colleague Minnie Moore paid almost 2,800 visits to dance halls, theaters, winerooms, and saloons. They were so successful that St. Paul's police soon hired more women and thereby officially sanctioned women's entrance into a previously strictly male domain.[68]

Through her temperance work, a completely new world opened up for Kelly, who had previously been disadvantaged by both her ethnic background and her sex. In the context of her agitation in the Sacred Thirst Society and the WCTU, she learned about poverty, immorality, crime, and the discrimination of women in urban St. Paul. Her extensive temperance activism made her competent, experienced, courageous, and respected enough to enter the city's police department. Through her work as a policewoman, Kelly "reconceiv[ed] the city with public space for women" and "enhanced the possibility for [her] own political empowerment."[69]

Archbishop Ireland realized that Irish Catholic women were mainly responsible for keeping the state's Irish Catholic temperance movement alive and increasingly praised their temperance agitation. In one of his speeches, he argued that if he had to begin temperance work again, he would first enlist the women. Only through the women, he stressed, could temperance reform reach the men. By 1913, most Irish Catholic men had ended their involvement in the temperance cause in Minnesota, a fact that even women's activism could not change. When at that year's state convention Ireland had to announce that the old Father Mathew Society of St. Paul, a bastion of Irish Catholic temperance activism all over the United States, had ceased its work, everyone present realized that the era of Irish Catholic temperance work in Minnesota had finally come to an end.[70]

The Crumbling of the German American Opposition

Whereas in those years the Irish Catholic temperance movement gradually fell into ruin, German American opposition to temperance reached its zenith only to similarly crumble a short time later. With the founding of the German-American Central Alliance of St. Paul (*Deutsch-Amerikanischer Zentralbund von St. Paul*, ZB of St. Paul) in 1899 and its statewide counterpart, the German-American Central Alliance of Minnesota (*Deutsch-Amerikanischer Zentralbund von Minnesota*, ZB of Minnesota) in 1908, the state's German Americans for the first time created long-lasting organizations that protected their interests. These organizations also admitted German American women to their ranks, an innovation in German American anti-temperance work. The founding of these societies marked an apparent stabilization of the newly invented German American ethnicity and a growth of ethnic cohesion. Dreams of ethnic consolidation were shattered, however, when Minnesota's German Catholics refused to join the ZB of Minnesota in 1908. The ensuing intraethnic debate about the ZB and its strategies was, in essence, a discussion about the shape of German American ethnic identity: Was it based on significant cultural icons, such as language, religion, and tradition, or was it just an interest group mentality constructed upon the symbolic vocabulary of personal liberty? The temperance movement, as this debate reveals, had not been able to produce ethnic unity and long-term alliances among the state's heterogeneous German Americans.

Around the turn of the century, Minnesota's German American community felt culturally besieged from all sides. The work of the ASL—its multifaceted law enforcement and Local Option campaigns—struck at the heart of German American drinking culture. The state's German Catholics in particular felt "discriminated" and "hurt" by their archbishop, whom they considered to be one of those American bishops with the least sympathy for German American culture. In addition, they considered their Irish American coreligionists to be in league with the Anglo-American temperance reformers and accused them of abusing the temperance cause for atrocious attacks on their culture.[71] In order to better defend themselves, the leaders of the St. Paul War Veterans' Association (*Kriegerverein*) initiated the founding of an umbrella organization of all the city's German societies in January 1899. The ZB of St. Paul was to protect and preserve German traditions, language, and culture and to unite St. Paul's German Americans "into a strong whole" "in order to position themselves against all sides and to protect the interests of German Americans." More specifically, the ZB was founded to fight against the Anglo-Americans' "silly figments," first and foremost against "all coercive laws, which want to ban body and soul into constraint and yoke." The ZB of St. Paul was thus conceptualized as a major weapon against the temperance movement and as a promoter of German American ethnic identity. The organization quickly entered the political arena. Its members advocated the repeal of coercive laws, such as Sunday Laws, and tried to prevent anti-liquor bills from being passed. They also formed a legislative committee, which lobbied among prospective political candidates and thus tried to act as a counterforce to the ASL.[72]

The ZB of St. Paul seems to have been the first organization of its kind in the United States. It has been generally held that the first ZB was founded in Pennsylvania, but the Pennsylvanian society was established on April 16, 1899. Scholars also generally attribute the founding of the German-American National Alliance of America (*Deutsch-Amerikanischer Nationalbund von Amerika*, NB of America) in Philadelphia in June 1900 to the Pennsylvania ZB alone, but sources prove that the members of the St. Paul ZB were also involved in its formation. Not only did St. Paul's ZB send a delegate to Philadelphia to partake in the founding, but it also became one of the NB's first member organizations. Thus, it was in St. Paul and not in much larger German American centers as, for instance, Milwaukee or Cincinnati, that a movement for greater unity among German Americans first took root. The efforts of St. Paul's Germans and their compatriots from other states were of far-reaching significance: The NB of America became the largest German American society in the United States. As early as 1905, it extended over thirty states and by 1914 laid claim to more than two million members. It soon acquired the reputation of being concerned almost exclusively with opposition to the temperance movement and of being an ethnic counter-organization to the ASL.[73]

Until 1908, the ZB of St. Paul, as its name suggests, was limited almost exclusively to the city of St. Paul. It had about two thousand members, mostly from German fraternal organizations, singing societies, the Turners, the War Veterans' Society, and the manifold homeland associations. However, in 1908—and not as early as 1902, as one scholar has claimed[74]—St. Paul's Germans felt that the reformers' success on the state level and their imposition of lids on St. Paul and other cities necessitated the formation of a state association. Therefore, they drafted a long appeal to all German American citizens of Minnesota, in which they warned them against the "agitation of a cohort of blinded zealots," who endangered free political elections, destroyed municipal self-government, and sought to hand over Minnesota to nativism and prohibition. In order to preserve personal liberty and to defend the German American community against the attacks of these "fanatics" and "nativists," the appeal argued, Minnesota's German Americans needed to found an ethnic organization. "United we are strong; divided, however, we are easy bait for our enemies," the writers of the appeal argued and asked for the founding of a state ZB. The appeal bore fruit, and on September 28, 1908, after a series of preparatory meetings, ZB of Minnesota came to life.[75]

Over the next two years, the ZB grew into Minnesota's largest German American organization, having a membership of 27,000 and consisting of 13 county branches and 137 societies. St. Paul became its operational base, as most of its leaders were St. Paulites. The legislative committee of St. Paul's ZB came to represent the ZB of Minnesota in total. It recommended which bills the association should support, had legislators introduce its own bills, and worked against the passage of temperance bills. ZB leaders especially condemned County Option, the ASL's most ardent goal, as being harmful to the economy and public morality as well as being contrary to the spirit of autonomous municipalities.[76]

The ZB's greatest innovation was, however, its admission of German American women. Up to that point, German American women had hardly been involved in anti-temperance work due to its political nature. The German Americans' great reticence with respect to female anti-temperance activism had mainly to do with their perceptions of gender. Whereas some of them subscribed to a gender ideology similar to that of the Anglo-American two-sphere model, most of them had, in the process of migration, reconstructed their families along the lines of an older model, the household patriarchy, in which all power and decision making rested with the male head of household. Most German American men frowned upon the female public and political activism of Anglo-American temperance women and were strongly opposed to the extension of suffrage to women.[77]

The ZBs of St. Paul and Minnesota became Minnesota's first politically active German American organizations in which men and women fought side by side. Encouraged by their admission, German American women occasionally took stands on the temperance question. In 1910, for instance, thirty women's societies belonging to the ZB filed a report with the Minneapolis School Board complaining about the WCTU essay contests in public schools.[78] In 1914, the ZB of Minnesota even decided in favor of admitting female delegates. Consequently, about forty women appeared at the next meeting and even gave speeches. In order to distance themselves from the Anglo-American women's emancipatory ideology, however, these female delegates hastened to assure listeners that most German American women were opposed to woman suffrage and that, were women ever to be enfranchised, they would willingly vote along with their men. German American women, it seems, put a greater emphasis on their ethnic than on their female identity. The maintenance of German American ethnic culture and traditions dictated women's absence from the political sphere, as the majority of Anglo-American women were intent on voting for the prohibition of alcohol once given the ballot. Against this backdrop, German American women largely abstained from political involvement or downplayed their political ambitions.[79]

The ZB of Minnesota had been founded in order to achieve a durable institutionalized cooperation among Minnesota's German Americans, which would heighten their clout in the fight against temperance. In the wake of its founding, however, the fissures that had continued to exist in the German American community despite its decade-long anti-temperance agitation quickly widened into rifts and shattered German Americans leaders' dream of unity. As the result of a slow process of strategic repositioning that had begun in the 1890s, the state's German Catholics, under the leadership of Joseph Matt, a recently immigrated young German and since 1899 the editor of *Der Wanderer*, became highly critical of their non-Catholic compatriots' anti-temperance agitation. Even though he published the appeal for the founding of a ZB in Minnesota in his *Wanderer*, Matt vented against the ZB and its superficial arguments against temperance. Instead of presenting German Americans as bulwarks of personal liberty and as "standing with a big stick in front of the saloon" blocking any reform efforts, Matt believed that Minnesota's ZB should fight for reasonable reforms of the liquor business and seek to win Anglo-Americans for its position. "[O]ne-sided primordial Teutonic railing against any attempt at reform," Matt argued, was of no use and disadvantageous to the reputation of German Americans. He also resented the ZB's promotion of ethnic separatism. Such an insistence on German habits and cultural traditions, he reasoned, was responsible for relegating German Americans to the margins of American society. For all these reasons, Matt was strongly opposed to the participation of Catholic societies in the ZB of Minnesota.[80]

Due to his critique of ethnic separatism and the emphasis of German culture, non-Catholic Germans considered Matt a fanatic, "narrow and ungerman." However, he was widely supported by German Catholics all over the United States, who wrote him enthusiastic letters. St. Louis's *Die Amerika*, the most influential Catholic German-language newspaper in the United States, published long extracts from Matt's articles. Minnesota's German American Catholics overwhelmingly followed their young rebellious editor's advice. In October 1908, the German Roman-Catholic State Alliance of Minnesota (*Deutscher Römisch-Katholischer Staatsverband von Minnesota*) adopted a resolution against joining the ZB's radical anti-temperance agitation and advocated "true moderation" and "efforts aiming at the promotion of Catholic abstinence societies, for the purpose of good example and for the hardening of one's own character." Instead of fighting against prohibition with "empty catchphrases" such as personal liberty, its members deemed the suppression of the liquor business's immoral practices more appropriate countermeasures against radical temperance reform. The root of all temperance activism—thus was the novel argumentation of Minnesota's German Catholics—was not so much Anglo-American fanaticism or nativism but the depravity of the liquor business in the United States.[81]

On the one hand, this criticism was rooted in the traditional antagonism between the religious Germans (*Kirchendeutsche*) and secular Germans (*Vereinsdeutsche*). In his function as one of the leaders of the German Roman-Catholic Central Association of North America (*Deutscher Römisch-Katholischer Central-Verein von Nordamerika*), Matt elaborated in 1909 on the "difference in principles" between this Catholic organization and the NB of America: "We stand in all things upon the basis of the Christian-Catholic weltanschauung, while the Alliance supports and furthers atheistic and humanistic ideas and ideals."[82] On the other hand, the verbal exchanges between German American Catholics and non-Catholics quickly turned into a discussion about the conceptualization of German American ethnic identity. Matt, as well as many of his German Catholic contemporaries, criticized that German American leaders had exploited the temperance movement in order to form a German American ethnic identity and to unify Germans. He considered love of alcohol weak cultural glue and questioned its ability to generate ethnic cohesion. He also claimed to "value the German name too highly to join in this call" and not to be "in the mood for a unified Germanness that was inspirited by no higher ideals." "Truly," Matt vented, "if there is not better filler to keep Germans in the United States together than the endangered 'personal liberty'—malicious people understand by this the dear German thirst—then the German Americans can bury themselves, together with their 'cultural mission'!" Matt did nothing less than to protest against the invention of a German American ethnicity based on alcohol rather than on more profound cultural commonalities. Not only did he consider alcohol an inappropriate "cultural icon," to use Joane Nagel's term, but he also criticized the "symbolic vocabulary" established by St. Paul's German Americans in the context of the temperance movement and prophesied that an ethnic identity created on the basis of a catchphrase would always remain fragile. Matt was not alone in his assessment: Catholic Germans in other American cities similarly started criticizing the fight for personal liberty.[83]

What had happened in the first decade of the twentieth century that convinced German American Catholics to break out of the anti-temperance coalition? The German Americans' uncomfortable position in the American Catholic Church certainly lies at the heart of the matter. Enmities between Minnesota's Irish and German Catholics had subsided considerably due to the decline of the American-ization movement and John Ireland's recent efforts to reconcile with the German portion of his flock. Minnesota's German Catholics rejoiced that the conflicts and misunderstandings within the archdiocese increasingly vanished. While "in the past the diocese's German Catholics were more on the defensive, today it is possible for them . . . to involve themselves and to see their wishes fulfilled." They especially emphasized that Ireland had recently given ample evidence of "his trust and will to compromise" and that it was now the duty of German Catholics to be similarly cooperative in order to be "of one mind" with their archbishop. Even though the Irish Catholic temperance movement had come to an almost complete standstill, Ireland himself still agitated for the cause, and the issue of temperance was very dear to his heart. German Catholics' participation in the radically anti-temperance ZB would have affronted him and ruined what had become a more cordial relationship. Given their love for their religion and their great loyalty to the Catholic hierarchy, St. Paul's German Catholics had to weigh the pros and cons of radical anti-temperance activism carefully. Strategic considerations thus dominated their decision to emphasize religious over ethnic identity and to opt out of the ethnic coalition against temperance.[84]

Another reason for the German Catholics' unwillingness to join the ZB was the association's entanglement with the liquor business. Both the NB of America and its branches received subsidies from the United States Brewers' Association. In addition, the ZB of Minnesota consulted with the Traveling Men's Liberty League about which candidates to endorse and how to fight the lids. A close connection with the liquor interests also existed in terms of personnel. ZB President Julius Moersch, for instance, was simultaneously the legislative agent of the National Liquor Dealers' Association. Such an entanglement in terms of finances and staff convinced many German American Catholics that the ZB served the interest of a wealthy, professional few rather than the interests of the entire German American community.[85]

A transnational component also encouraged German American Catholics in their criticism of the ZB of Minnesota: the second German temperance move-ment, gathering momentum in Germany since the 1880s.[86] Minnesota's German Americans took note of the anti-liquor agitation in their homeland. Whereas the majority of German Americans argued that the temperance movement in Germany was moderate in character and not comparable to its Anglo-American counterpart, the city's German American Catholics were startled by the growing activism of their coreligionists in Germany and began to question their own attitude toward temperance. Matt, who had himself until recently witnessed temperance agitation in Germany, even presented German Catholics as role models for their German American coreligionists because they approached the question of temperance "in a similarly unbiased manner."[87]

The leaders of the ZB of Minnesota knew that the German Catholics' decision not to join the organization severely hampered its power and influence and therefore made great efforts to involve them. In 1909, they asked Matt to give the keynote address at the German Day in St. Paul, the ZB's major festivity, which was attended by more than 10,000 German Americans. Matt, however, refused and even managed to convince the German Roman-Catholic State Alliance of Minnesota to prohibit its member societies to take part in the celebration. Rather than declaring their solidarity with the ZB, Minnesota's German Catholics preferred to celebrate the new unity among Catholics in the archdiocese. They began to advocate "true temperance," that is, moderate temperance agitation with the aim of reforming drinking habits and abolishing compulsory social drinking. They also decided not to sell intoxicating liquor at Bonifacius Day, an important German Catholic festivity in St. Paul. German American Catholics had chosen a middle path—opposition to radical temperance as well as to radical anti-temperance efforts—in order to improve their relationship with their coreligionists.[88]

Despite its gender inclusiveness and great degree of public and political agitation, the ZB of Minnesota was not able to stem the temperance tide. Without the German American Catholics and with only delayed and comparably meager support by Minnesota's unions, the anti-temperance coalition was not powerful enough to avert the passage of County Option and its implementation in many counties. While the objective of prohibition had successfully welded together the many different reform groups into a rather stable coalition, alcohol had caused only surges of ethnic identification and a temporary fixing of divides among Minnesota's German Americans. As Matt correctly stated, it was too weak a glue for German Americans to construct a durable ethnic identity and to overcome their disunity.

The WCTU—For Gender Justice and "A Clean St. Paul"

The WCTU of Minnesota entered the new century as one of the state's three most active and influential temperance societies, along with the Prohibition Party and the ASL. By 1915, its membership had passed the seven thousand mark. The temperance women's increased numerical strength and the optimistic reform spirit of the Progressive era added to their enthusiasm and heightened their presence in the public sphere. As by now almost all WCTU members were in favor of women's suffrage, the women's rights rhetoric and suffrage agitation of the WCTU and the MWSA finally converged. The women's open demands for equal rights and suffrage not only prevented fruitful collaboration with the

ASL but also led to attacks by supporters of the race-suicide theories that were very prominent at that time. Besides fighting for their rights and engaging in discussions about eugenics, Minnesota's WCTU women placed a major focus on St. Paul in those years. Minnesota's capital, they surmised, was in a deplorable state with respect to reform and therefore deserved their full attention. The diary of St. Paul's WCTU leader Eva Jones is one of the few surviving archival treasures recording in detail how much impact the temperance movement could have on the biographies and mindsets of individual women, how much women's work became inflected by Progressive methods, and which ramifications on environment and people the activism of one person could have.[89]

By the turn of the century, Minnesota's legislators had become used to seeing WCTU representatives hurry up and down the halls of the State Capitol throughout the legislative sessions, talk to legislators, and try to push some bills while protesting against others. In general, temperance women fought for all laws advancing women's rights, protecting children, and restricting smoking and drinking. The Minnesota WCTU's major legislative goals, however, were still suffrage and prohibition. Within the WCTU, sentiments in favor of suffrage continued to increase in the new century. When in 1913 Julia Bullard Nelson asked the unions whether their members were in favor of woman suffrage, there was not one reply in the negative, with most unions, even the small unions from rural areas, stating that the majority of or all their members advocated the ballot. Therefore, in the first decade of the twentieth century, WCTU women "played the franchise department in the very foreground." They repeatedly stressed that the "mere accident of sex is an unfair qualification for citizenship" and that "taxation without representation" was "tyrannical." Women needed the ballot to protect their property, person, and children, and in order to abolish the saloon.[90]

In its work for suffrage, the WCTU further expanded its cooperation with the MWSA, and the overlap in membership between the WCTU and organizations fighting for suffrage intensified. Internal dissensions within the MWSA considerably weakened the suffrage organization and catapulted the efficiently organized WCTU to the front lines of the suffrage battle.[91] In those years, the MWSA seems to have been dependent on the WCTU's organizational and numerical strength and therefore increasingly included it in its campaigns for suffrage. In 1902, the WCTU women not only attended the MWSA's suffrage convention, but they also joined forces with the suffragists in circulating petitions in favor of presidential suffrage. In 1914 and 1915, St. Paul's WCTU women marched in the parades organized by the suffragists and carried banners saying "Not privilege, but justice!" Naturally, WCTU members also continued to support laws in favor of suffrage, both in the state legislature and in Congress, engaged in petition work, and attended legislative sessions to exert political pressure. By the twentieth century, the majority of Minnesota's temperance women had developed into ardent suffrage workers, fighting for suffrage on the basis of justice and equal-rights arguments. The rights discourses of the suffrage and temperance organizations as well as much of their membership had finally converged.[92]

Their decision to fight for prohibition, rather than for County Option, allied the Minnesota WCTU even more closely with the Prohibition Party. While throughout the period WCTU representatives appeared at the Prohibition Party's annual conventions and banquets and gave speeches there, the WCTU's relationship with the ASL remained lukewarm. This was partly due to the women's skepticism about County Option, which they considered a "halfway measure" and a "spotted license." More importantly, however, some of the ASL men voiced their concern about the WCTU women's radicalism, calling them "erratic." While such statements could be read as referring to the women's endorsement of radical temperance reform, that is, prohibition, it is more likely that they expressed the alienation of many ASL members by the WCTU's fight for gender justice.[93]

Criticism of women's rights rhetoric and agitation in the public sphere also caused debates throughout the nation at the time. While women, such as Minnesota's WCTU members, made their influence felt in the public sphere and agitated for equal rights and woman suffrage, they neglected their reproductive duties—thus the complaint of many so-called race-suicide theorists. Fears of race suicide had been rampant since the antebellum years and were based on thoughts of racial superiority, of which WCTU women were also guilty. Due to their greater procreation, immigrants, nonwhites, and the poor, many Anglo-Americans surmised, would soon numerically dominate the "Yankee stock." In the first decade of the twentieth century, President Theodore Roosevelt became the major promoter of such race-suicide scenarios. In March 1905, he attacked birth control, condemned the tendency toward smaller families as decadent, and inaugurated a campaign against race suicide that would last until 1910. Roosevelt declared that childless white Anglo-Saxon women, with their selfish demands for birth control, smaller families, and self-determination, were responsible for this racial decline. By insisting on educational opportunities and on leaving the domestic sphere, he argued, these women sought to rebel against their primary social duty—motherhood. Such arguments reveal that the race-suicide campaign was also a movement for upholding and politically implementing traditional notions of gender. Its leaders "transposed the Cult of True Womanhood . . . into a medical and scientific dogma" and interpreted it as the only way to preserve the nation's racial health and to secure the very survival of Anglo-Saxon Protestant America. The president's attacks on many women's desire for independence and individualism in the context of the race-suicide campaign led to their radicalization and their utter alienation from the Cult of True Womanhood.[94]

Minnesota's WCTU leaders felt personally attacked by Roosevelt's statements. Whereas since the early 1880s they, too, worried about the health of the
race in their Department of Hygiene and Heredity, they naturally attributed
the supposed racial decline to intemperance rather than to female women's
rights advocates and turned fears about race suicide into arguments in favor of
temperance. Julia Bullard Nelson wondered whether it made sense "to bring a
numerous progeny into a rum-cursed world." She also claimed that "the woman
who has never added to the population a fool, a drunkard, or a criminal has
more reason to thank the Lord than many good mothers have." Bessie Laythe
Scovell similarly argued that the alcohol abuse of mother and father was responsible for the racial decline rather than independence-seeking women. Whereas
education, exercise, and careers were sources of strength, alcohol consumption
weakened women's bodies and minds and was the true reason for genetically
inferior offspring. Accordingly, WCTU women were not traitors but saviors of
the race, as their work for the suppression of liquor was largely responsible for
improving the race genetically.[95]

Aside from fighting for prohibition and women's rights, Minnesota's temperance leaders directed much of their attention to St. Paul in the first decades of
the new century. In a truly Progressive manner, the women conceptualized
intemperance as largely a product of the urban environment. As the state's
capital, the women thought, St. Paul should display a greater affinity toward the
temperance movement. WCTU activism in St. Paul was strategically planned
and coordinated by Eva Jones. Like many of her coworkers, such as Julia Bullard Nelson, Jones had migrated to Minnesota from the East Coast with her
parents at some moment in the 1850s. Until 1903, she worked as a schoolteacher
in various Minnesota towns and took a course at Oberlin College, Ohio, a
stronghold of Progressive reform. After the death of both her parents, she moved
to Hamline, which was part of the Midway area, St. Paul's temperance suburb,
in 1908. In part, her move seems to have been motivated by the deplorable
state of WCTU work in the city. Of the three unions with their eighty-nine
members, only the Hamline Union seems to have done regular work, laboring
among children and seeking to suppress blind pigging. As a consequence, Jones
declined a position offered to her by the State Central Committee in order to
dedicate all of her time as a State Organizer to the state capital. Operating out
of Hamline, where she was surrounded by people sharing her alienation with
St. Paul, Jones immediately began her work by placing herself "at the head of
practically every organized campaign against vice in St. Paul." Being childless
and unmarried—one of Roosevelt's independence-seeking, selfish specters—and
having inherited some wealth, she could afford to pursue her temperance work
full time and cover her own expenses. Her ardent campaigns to reform the city
and to give it a new image gained her fame as "the best known temperance and
reform worker in Minnesota."[96]

The list of objectives cited earlier, which she noted down in her journal, displays the ambition, courage, self-confidence, and organizational talent of women at the time. It can also be read as the meticulous plan of an outsider to immerse herself in the city—its demographics, its economic, cultural, social, political structures, and its residential patterns—in order to eventually reshape it. Jones, like many Progressives, must have felt that a scientific approach to social problems would be much more efficient than moral or religious arguments. Therefore, she aimed at organizing St. Paul district by district, at acquainting herself with its social, economic, political, and cultural specificities, and sought to collect evidence for its wide-open policy and toleration of lawbreaking. Besides seeking like-minded collaborators, she also tackled "hard things which others shrank from," as WCTU President Bessie Laythe Scovell remarked about her. Jones was determined to "[v]isit the courts, juvenile, municipal, every kind, and learn the city government." "The Little Mother of the Lost," as she soon came to be called, was also eager to approach groups many middle-class reformers avoided: immigrants and workers.[97]

Jones accomplished most of her goals over the next years. In the first ten months of her work, she got in touch with numerous St. Paulites concerning the temperance cause in the city, visited thirty-five churches, attended thirty-eight meetings of local unions, and gave addresses at twenty-three churches, three Sunday Schools, the jail, three young people's meetings, the MWSA and CTAU conventions, and various other WCTU events and meetings (see figure 4.8). She worked in many of the city's districts—making 947 calls in the interest of the WCTU, gaining 234 new members, and organizing six new unions. It took

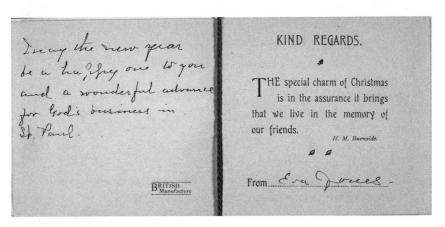

Figure 4.8. Even Eva Jones's Christmas cards bear evidence of her investment in the "wonderful advance for God's business in St. Paul." Card from Woman's Christian Temperance Union of Minnesota Records, 1886–1992. Courtesy of the Minnesota Historical Society.

Jones about six weeks to dig through one of St. Paul's districts. Her house-to-house canvassing was a novelty in the WCTU, whose unions mostly emerged in the context of church work. In 1910, Jones hired a district organizer, Lucy Uhl, who supported her canvassing work. Besides founding new unions, she also repeatedly visited existing unions, encouraging them to further activism and advising them on how to increase their membership. She also attracted more attention to women's temperance work by writing weekly columns for St. Paul's Sunday edition of the *Pioneer Press*.[98]

Jones sought to increase the WCTU's commitment to immigrants. She gave addresses in the Swedish Baptist and Lutheran churches with a special focus on the East Side, the city's Scandinavian enclave. As a result, Scandinavian women joined English-speaking unions and founded the Arlington Hills WCTU, which became one of the city's largest and most active WCTUs. Jones also managed to convince individual German women, most of them belonging to the city's Methodist and evangelical churches, to join English-speaking unions, such as the Dayton's Bluff Union. In order to make up for the meager efforts of the state WCTU, she also actively labored among African Americans. In October 1911, she initiated the founding of the L. M. N. Stevens Union. Due to Jones's constant presence and aid, this union flourished and engaged in several law enforcement campaigns.[99]

Jones's work was guided by her great visions of a "moral cleansing" of and the "revival of religion" in the state capital. She summarized these visions in a slogan, which soon became the motto of all WCTU women: "A clean St. Paul." "[R]eal city cleansing, city transformation," Jones emphasized, was "a not easy task." No place was more "difficult to organize and hold as the big, brewery ruled and beer soaked city," as "[t]he mutterings of city rebellion against state anti-liquor laws and the cry for 'city home rule' are constantly heard." In 1910, in order to heighten motivation, Jones translated the aforementioned slogan into a song about a clean, temperance-oriented St. Paul and distributed its lyrics throughout the city (see figure 4.9).[100]

This song encapsulated Jones's "vision" of St. Paul's remodeled civic identity. With God's help, she and her fellow workers wanted to free the city from the shackles of liquor not only to promote happier homes but also to feel more at home themselves, to overcome their sense of displacement. In the years to come, St. Paul's WCTU women sang this song in their meetings and at the state conventions. As they said themselves, they rejoiced in the hope and faith of it. When, at the annual convention of 1911, other delegates teased St. Paul's WCTU workers by singing "St. Paul Isn't Dry," they countered with their new song, singing it "with a convincing earnestness."[101]

Through Jones's work, the number of St. Paul's unions had increased to nineteen with a membership of 327 by 1913. There were also nine LTLs with about

A SONG FOR ST. PAUL

Words by Eva Jones   Tune—My Old Kentucky Home."

O, a clean St. Paul, how it fills our souls with joy,
   As the vision, by faith we can see,
Of our city fair lifted up from drink's despair,
   In the coming happy time to be.
Now a shadow dark shuts the joy from many a home,
   While staggers some loved one along,
And the heart grows chill with the fear and grief and shame,
   Crushed, are life and hope beneath that wrong

CHORUS

Sound the word, my comrades,
St. Paul shall yet be free,
We will work and pray for that happy, happy day,
And our God himself shall lead the way.

Now the brewer great, rules the city for his greed,
   But surely as God is on high,
Every brewery shall cease, each saloon its doors shall close,
   And that traffic, wicked traffic shall die.
So we'll work right on in our blessed Temperance Cause,
   Our courage in God and the Right,
Till St. Paul is free, and it's homes are full of joy,
   And forever gone, is drink's dark night.

Figure 4.9. WCTU leaflet with the lyrics of Eva Jones's "A Song for St. Paul." Leaflet from Woman's Christian Temperance Union of Minnesota Records, 1886–1992. Courtesy of the Minnesota Historical Society.

two hundred members. Since Jones had not covered a third of the city yet, she went on with undiminished fervor. By then, she had moved from Hamline to central St. Paul and become a member of the Central and newly founded Happy Homes WCTUs. In contrast to many other Midway reformers, she did not remain in her geographically separate temperance enclave but moved right into the city's heart, seeking change from within rather than from without.[102]

Her ambitious goal to reform St. Paul forced Eva Jones, and the women she carried along, to penetrate several of the city's public spheres, in particular the city administration and the city's courts. They voiced their opinions in the St. Paul City Council and repeatedly asked city authorities to enforce the liquor laws and to cease the practice of tacitly sanctioning prostitution. Jones herself informed the women of how the system of prostitution functioned in St. Paul—knowledge she must have gained through thorough investigation.[103] She also supported the city's Law Enforcement League in its efforts to initiate trials against saloon owners violating the Sunday Law. In January 1909, she confided to her diary to have called on Judge W. Finehout and to have copied court records. Between December 1909 and February 1910, Jones noted down to have "planted" a suit against two famous St. Paul saloon owners, Alderman Frank J. Huber and the former sheriff Anton Miesen, for selling liquor on Sunday, and to have written "150 letters to secure the attention of the court." She was the only woman present during the trials, which ended—in typical St. Paul fashion—with a nonguilty verdict. In all of these law enforcement activities, Minneapolis came to be the role model of St. Paul's temperance women. While for the majority of St. Paulites Minneapolis acted as their constitutive outside, the women's admiration of the sister city shows that they had developed an identity running counter to that prevalent in the state capital.[104]

St. Paul's male establishment, of course, resented the women's political activism and showered them with ridicule. In the fall of 1910, Eva Jones had suggested that the women of the Central WCTU go to the chief of police and complain about open saloons on Sundays and about the sale of liquor to minors. At a subsequent meeting, "Mrs. Johnson told of her trip to Chief Police in regard to sloons [sic] and how he just laughed in her face." Courage and stamina were the most important prerequisites for female temperance and suffrage activism in St. Paul's public sphere.[105]

In 1914, St. Paul's WCTU unions faced a major blow. On March 24, at the age of sixty-two, Eva Jones passed away in the wake of an operation on an abscess in her head. Her temperance coworkers unanimously agreed that she had literally worked herself to death. An obituary in the *Pioneer Press* points to the central role she had played in the city's reform movement. It called her a "citizen-soldier" and the "St. Paul Joan of Arc" based on her broad spectrum of reform activism. The WCTU unions deeply mourned their loss. In anticipation of her death, Jones had written a letter to all of the city's unions, asking them "not [to] let this work go back in the city." One-fourth of St. Paul was still uncovered, and some of the existing unions were weak and needed help. "If I stay with you, what I am and have goes into this cause. If I should leave you, close up ranks and shout a word of cheer and triumph and brave determination to all the city and press to capture the city." To protect the women from lack of funds, Jones had left a considerable amount of her $13,000 fortune to St. Paul's district WCTU and to the Minnesota Civic Reform Association, which Jones had helped to found with other WCTU members, the Prohibition Party, and the ASL in 1906. The St. Paul WCTU honored its most active member by paying for her life membership and by erecting a memorial fountain in her honor at Rice Park.[106]

Between 1898 and 1915, activists such as Eva Jones further strengthened woman's role in Minnesota's social and political life. The majority of temperance women were getting ready for the plunge into full citizenship and full participation in the political life of the country. While still causing national and local debates on the role of women and evoking male criticism, their agitation demonstrated that on the ground the ideological construct of the two spheres became increasingly obsolete and that a paradigm shift was at hand.

5. Equating Temperance with Patriotism

The Great War and the Liquor Question (1916–1919)

The Final Fight for a Dry Minnesota

> This war also taught to a great extent, probably more than
> anything else, the need of the restriction of the liquor traffic
> and the elimination of alcohol from our State and Country.

Governor Joseph A. Burnquist's statement neatly summarizes the developments between the passage of the County Option Law in 1915 and the beginning of prohibition in the United States on July 1, 1919.[1] International developments were greatly responsible for the rapid passage and ratification of the Eighteenth Amendment. The American entry into World War I and the ensuing war hysteria directly played into the hands of the country's drys, as the reformers came to be called in those years. In the course of the war, alcohol became increasingly viewed as unpatriotic and as a waste of resources, food, and labor, both on the national scene as well as in Minnesota. Public sentiment also turned against the liquor manufacturers, especially those of foreign descent, who were accused of collaborating with the enemy in order to weaken the U.S. military. In addition to the general war climate, the fight about liquor in Minnesota was particularly intense due to the workings of the Minnesota Commission of Public Safety (MNCPS), which had been created by the 1917 state legislature. Conceptualized as an emergency war government, the commission soon became the accomplice of the drys in wiping out the state's liquor culture.

Within two and a half years after the passage of County Option, the reformers succeeded in gradually drying up large parts of the state by Indian treaty and County or Local Option. Most notably, on June 19, 1916, Duluth, Minnesota's third largest city, went dry through a successful Local Option election, which had

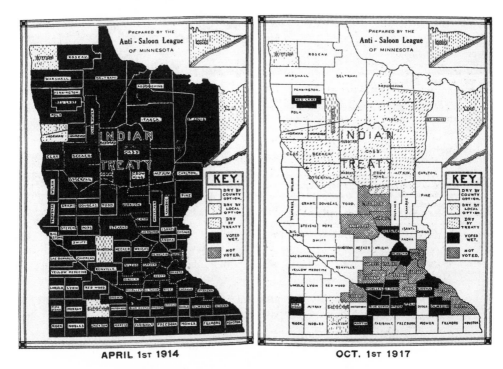

APRIL 1st 1914   OCT. 1st 1917

Figure 5.1. These wet and dry maps prepared by the Anti-Saloon League of Minnesota compare the status of the liquor question in Minnesota on April 1, 1914, with that of October 1, 1917. Maps from Anti-Saloon League of America, "The Minnesota Campaign Manual for a Dry State," Pamphlets Relating to the Liquor Problem in Minnesota. Courtesy of the Minnesota Historical Society.

been held under the provisions of its charter and been successfully concluded through the ASL's intense agitation in the city (see figure 5.1).

While the reformers' continuous progress suggests that prohibition was at hand in Minnesota, such seems not to have been the case. Even the ASL conceded that much had to be done before prohibition in either of its forms—statutory or constitutional—would have a realistic chance to become a reality in the state and considered it dangerous to rush forward.[2] However, international events began to dominate American politics and to influence the course of the temperance movement, both on a national scale and in Minnesota. In August 1914, due to the assassination of Archduke Franz Ferdinand of Austria and Europe's intricate system of alliances, a war had broken out in Europe. For nearly three years, the United States officially stayed neutral, but American economic and political considerations, effective British propaganda, and the more than one hundred American casualties resulting from the German submarine warfare caused American public opinion to take an anti-German turn from 1915 on. The nation became increasingly inclined to enter the war, which it finally did on April 6, 1917.[3]

The Great War, as Ronald Schaffer has argued, "marked one of the high points of social reform in the twentieth century." Progressives saw the war as an opportunity to muster up all their organizational strength and resources to bargain with the federal government about an efficient management of the American nation at war. With respect to alcohol, reformers employed the war to their advantage in a twofold manner. First, they fought for the preservation of military discipline in army camps throughout the United States. Military efficiency, they argued, could be achieved only through young soldiers' abstinence and purity. This argument convinced the majority of Congress members to pass the Selective Service Act in May 1917, which required the establishment of dry zones around every military camp and forbade anyone to sell or serve liquor to any member of the military, not even in a private home. This banishment of liquor from the army was supplemented by a social purification campaign, conducted by Progressive reformers in cooperation with the War and Navy Departments and seeking to uplift the young soldiers morally and personally. Besides the promotion of personal hygiene and literacy, the improvement of soldiers' health was the main objective of these social purifiers, which is why alcohol consumption came under attack.[4] Second, when it became increasingly evident that the United States would enter the war, the struggle for prohibition became deeply entangled with the nation's looming military efforts. "The war," as Schaffer has claimed, "encouraged the prohibition movement by stirring idealism, heightening the national sense of mission, and encouraging a cult of purification—the cleansing of physical and social poison from mind and body, community and nation." In particular, reformers argued convincingly that the conservation of food and fuel was vital for the winning of the war. In response to such argumentation, in August 1917 Congress, pushed by the ASL of America, passed the Lever Food and Fuel Control Act, which prohibited the use of food in the production of distilled spirits for beverage purposes and authorized the president to regulate or prohibit the use of foodstuffs in the manufacture of wine or beer and to limit their alcoholic content. In December 1917, President Woodrow Wilson reduced the alcoholic content of beer to 2.75 percent and limited the amount of grain to be used in the manufacture of beer to 70 percent of that of the previous year. In July of the following year, Wilson reduced the coal consumption of breweries by 50 percent.[5]

The specter and, consequently, the reality of military involvement enhanced the tolerance of many Americans toward restrictive liquor laws they would otherwise not have accepted. This proved true for the Hobson-Sheppard bill, which was drafted by the ASL and introduced into Congress on April 4, 1917. In contrast to its predecessors, which Congress had rejected or protracted, it not only prohibited the commercial liquor traffic but also the home manufacture of alcohol. Despite its radicalism, which even the ASL criticized, Congress eagerly passed it and submitted it to the single states for ratification in December 1917. Within the next seven years, three-fourths of them, or thirty-six states, would have to ratify it in order for it to become the Eighteenth Amendment to the U.S. Constitution. War had made "federal action acceptable to the nation." Rather than being criticized as a curtailment of individual or states' rights, federal anti-liquor legislation had come to be perceived as a "way of managing the nation at war."[6]

In September 1918, Congress passed the National Prohibition Act, which would function as the enforcement act of the Eighteenth Amendment. While it was largely the work of Wayne Wheeler, Superintendent of the ASL of America, it became popularly known as the Volstead Act. Andrew Volstead, congressman from Minnesota, had revised and steered it through Congress, past President Wilson's veto. Volstead's activism in favor of the bill established a putative link between Minnesota and prohibition and created the false impression that the state was a dry stronghold. The Volstead Act defined intoxicating liquor as anything containing more than 0.5 percent alcohol. Whereas it forbade anyone to "manufacture, sell, barter, transport, import, export, deliver, furnish or possess any intoxicating liquor," it permitted people to possess and use intoxicating liquors acquired before the law took effect, provided such liquors were consumed at home. It also allowed the sale of alcoholic liquor for medicinal, sacramental, and industrial purposes and the manufacture of "nonintoxicating" cider, fruit juices, and "near beer"—a brew containing 0.5 percent alcohol—for private use. Volstead's major accomplishment was to help Wheeler phrase the act in a way that it would withstand all later constitutional charges (except, of course, repeal).[7]

The war climate also had a devastating effect on the liquor manufacturers. It was mainly the German brewers—"the redoubtable Generals Pabst, Schlitz, Lemp, Anheuser-Busch 'unser veiter' [sic]"—whom many Americans suspected being tools of the German government and pro-German in their sympathies. These suspicions culminated in and were sustained by the Senate Resolution 307, which was introduced into Congress in September 1918 and authorized an investigation of the United States Brewers' Association and allied interests by the Senate Committee of the Judiciary. The investigation dealt a deadly blow to the brewers' reputation and greatly contributed to the demise of liquor. Liquor, after all, was not merely a waste of resources but came to be increasingly associated with disloyalty.[8]

World War I also played into the hands of Minnesota's temperance reformers. The state's drys also appropriated the war effort to stigmatize liquor as a waste of resources, food, and labor and put pressure onto legislators to quickly stop such waste: "Not in the interest of 'temperance'; not to speed prohibition; not to make men sober by law; not for sentimentalism—BUT TO WIN THE WAR."⁹ The war and the anti-liquor sentiment it generated also facilitated the elimination of the majority of wet candidates, so that Minnesota's 1917 legislature was predominantly prohibitionist. Whereas two years earlier prohibition did not have the slightest chance, in 1917 the only question concerning the legislators seems to have been whether the envisioned prohibitory bill should allow the shipment of liquor or whether it should make Minnesota bone-dry, either prohibiting all shipment or even the personal ownership of liquor.¹⁰

In contrast to the WCTU and the party prohibitionists, the members of the ASL spoke out in favor of the shipment of liquor, as they thought such generosity would lead to a wider support of the amendment. None of these organizations seem to have favored the bone-dry variant banning the personal ownership of liquor. Minnesota's brewery interests tried to save their businesses by dissociating themselves from the saloon owners and by working for a saloonless Minnesota. They proposed to limit the production of liquor to beer and light wines and to confine themselves to home deliveries. If prohibition were to be adopted, they opted for the bone-dry version banning shipment, as permission of shipment would enable out-of-state brewers to reap the profit to the detriment of Minnesota's economy. In the spirit of the time, both House and Senate passed one of the more radical variants, a bone-dry prohibitory constitutional amendment bill prohibiting the manufacture, sale, and shipment of liquor into the state. In case of successful ratification in November 1918, the law would go into effect on July 1, 1920.¹¹

Between the passage of Minnesota's bone-dry amendment in early 1917 and the ratification election in November 1918, a "prohibition wave," as one St. Paul German newspaper called it, "flooded" the state. All of the state's temperance organizations conducted educational campaigns at the grass roots in order to convince voters to decide in favor of the prohibitory constitutional amendment. The ASL generated lists of people in favor of prohibition, who could be mobilized to labor among the opponents of the amendment. The WCTU campaigned among women, seeking cooperation from all kinds of women's organizations. The Prohibition Party organized prohibition picnics and sent around speakers in automobiles to give pep talks in towns and villages.¹²

Aside from such individual campaigns, this prohibition wave gained particular momentum through the unprecedented collaboration of the state's numerous temperance organizations across class, gender, ethnic, and generational lines. The channeling of organizational power took the form of a "Get-Together-Movement," initiated by the Prohibition Party in order to heighten the efficiency of the prohibition campaign. Except for the ASL, all the state's temperance organizations were favorable to such concerted action and organizational convergence. On November 17, 1917, delegates of the WCTU, the IOGT, the Minnesota Total Abstinence Association, the Prohibition Party, the Young People's Citizenship Committee, the Intercollegiate Prohibition Association, the CTAU, the Finnish Total Abstinence Society, the Scandinavian Grand Lodge of the Good Templars, and the Duluth Dry Ordinance Committee organized the Minnesota Dry Federation. The overall purpose of this federation was to harmonize and coordinate the efforts of all the state's anti-liquor organizations in the 1918 prohibition amendment campaign. This combined force of women, Scandinavians, Irish Catholics, Protestant Anglo-American men, young adults, and party prohibitionists was strengthened by two labor organizations: the Trade Union Dry League and the Employees' Anti-Liquor League. The formation of these two organizations brings to the fore the significance of class for the temperance movement. The reformers were aware that the constitutional amendment would be ratified only if a large number of the state's laborers could be won for the prohibitionist cause. Under the leadership of Senator Richard Jones, a Progressive lawyer from Duluth, the reformers, for the first time, attempted to organize labor. Jones, who was experienced with the concerns of labor through his work in the Senate's Labor Committee, functioned as the president of the Trade Union Dry League, while the nonunion laborers were to assemble in the Employees' Anti-Liquor League. The strength of these organizations is difficult to assess, however, as they left no individual records.[13]

In Minnesota, the fight against liquor was also greatly promoted by a commission that had been established by the state legislature—with only one dissenting vote—in April 1917, in order to "safeguard the peace and quiet of the commonwealth so long as the war shall last." Many people felt that the state government was not equipped to deal adequately with the exigencies of war, especially due to Minnesota's allegedly pivotal position as a provider of four-fifths of the ore produced in the country and of a large percentage of the wheat and other food crops. The Minnesota Commission of Public Safety (MNCPS) consisted of seven members: the governor, the attorney general, and five members appointed by the governor.[14] It was authorized

> to do all acts and things non-inconsistent with the constitution or laws of Minnesota or of the United States which . . . are necessary or proper for the public safety and for the protection of life and public property or private property requiring protection; and all acts and things necessary or proper so that the military, civil and industrial resources of the state may be most efficiently applied toward maintenance of defense of the state and nation, and toward the successful prosecution of the war.[15]

This authorization gave the MNCPS sweeping powers and turned it into Minnesota's emergency war government. A federal court decision of July 16, 1917, held that the commission possessed the authority to issue orders having the force of law and thereby gave it even greater power. After April 1918, the MNCPS defined the violation of its orders as a misdemeanor punishable by a county jail sentence or a monetary fine. Its central body was located in St. Paul, but local safety commissions were soon established in every county.[16]

The MNCPS was endorsed by a broad coalition of Minnesotans, who willingly accepted the curtailment of their civil rights for the greater good and out of patriotic fervor. The composition of the commission, however, indicates that rather than advocating the interests of a wide array of Minnesotans, it "represented organized capital from start to finish," as the Minnesota Federation of Labor complained, and was deeply influenced by Minneapolis's corporate interests. It therefore proved a formidable tool for halting all the dangers that were supposedly threatening that city's dominant economic position in the Northwest. Through their work, commission members, such as John Lind, Charles W. Ames—and more blatantly—John F. McGee, intended to eradicate "pro-Germans but also trade unionists (whether moderate or radical), members of the Nonpartisan League, Socialists, pacifists, and all who entertained the slightest doubt with respect to the wisdom of America going to war," as Carl H. Chrislock phrased it. From hindsight, it becomes apparent that under the cloak of patriotism and by fomenting fears of subversive labor radicalism the MNCPS tried to rid Minnesota of all oppositional groups posing a danger to the existing economic and political order.[17]

Some of the commissioners, such as Governor Burnquist and John McGee, were active in, or at least disposed favorably to, the dry cause. McGee, in particular, would become the driving force behind most of the commission's anti-liquor agitation. Such personal affinities notwithstanding, sources suggest that the commission as such initially did not want to become entangled in the dry-wet debate. Nevertheless, twenty-one of its fifty-nine orders restricted the serving or selling of liquor. On the one hand, the MNCPS—thoroughly in line with national purity campaigns and efforts to heighten war efficiency—explicitly justified its anti-liquor orders as patriotic measures, arguing that the saloon interests defied the laws and that saloons demoralized laborers, debauched young people, and were sources of constant disorder and crime, especially among soldiers. The commission downplayed, however, the inextricable link between its suppression of the saloon—the acknowledged focal point of working-class culture, the cherished ethnic institution of most German Americans, and the meeting place of organized labor—and its goal to eradicate pro-Germanism, organized unionism, and radical labor. The MNCPS's intention to oust the saloon curiously intersected with that of the temperance reformers and turned the commission into the temperance workers' most valuable tool, an irony of history considering that it had largely been created through the efforts of George H. Sullivan, the wet leader in the legislature.[18]

Of the eight MNCPS orders issued between April 24 and June 5, 1917, five related to liquor. Three of these orders, Orders 2, 6, and 7, can be read as aiming primarily at the protection of soldiers. Order 2 prohibited the sale of intoxicating liquor in an area surrounding the Fort Snelling Military Reservation, while Order 6 required the closing of all saloons on registration day, June 5, 1917. Order 7 was the MNCPS's response to a letter from Secretary of War Newton D. Baker, who worried that the saloons and the prostitutes frequenting them would tempt the numerous men who would soon enlist in the army. It therefore ordered all saloons, restaurants, and cafés selling liquor and being located in cities of over fifty thousand to remain closed from 10 P.M. to 8 A.M., prohibited cabaret and dancing performances in any saloon or place where liquor was sold, and declared saloons off limits to women and girls. Order 7 was the MNCPS's first liquor-related order affecting the liquor trade all over Minnesota and therefore generated "much dissension." Organized labor felt attacked by this "drastic order," as it deprived many cooks, waiters, musicians, and bartenders of their livelihoods. A Minneapolis saloon owner even petitioned the Federal District Court of St. Paul for an injunction that would bar the MNCPS and the City of Minneapolis from enforcing Order 7, arguing that his property rights were impaired by a decree not within the scope of the commission's constitutional jurisdiction. The presiding judge, however, ruled in favor of the order, seeing it as clearly within the MNCPS's competence.[19]

Orders 1 and 8, however, had nothing to do with the preservation of military efficiency. They instead reveal the commission's intent to eradicate organized labor, the Industrial Workers of the World (IWW), and the Nonpartisan League. Order 1, passed on April 24, 1917, closed the saloons, pool halls, and moving-picture theaters in the Minneapolis Bridge Square District, which had evolved from a bustling city center to an amusement area in which a great number of seasonal harvest hands and timber workers competed for employment. Moreover, in 1915, the Agricultural Workers Organization of the IWW had established its central office in this area. Not surprisingly, the strong presence of "the rough people who do rough work, the amusement places," as well as "the I.W.W. and the crooks" supposedly operating in such areas were thorns in the side of the commission, whose first order therefore deprived them of many of their meeting places. Order 8 was the first of numerous MNCPS orders striking at saloons in counties constituting the heart of, or being adjacent to, the Iron Range and the lumber camps of northern Minnesota. These were the areas favorably visited by the Agricultural Workers Organization in order to organize miners and lumberjacks into unions. Order 8, passed on June 5, 1917, and initiated by McGee, decreed that in all of St. Louis County except in the city of Duluth, liquor was to be sold only in duly licensed saloons and drug stores. While the MNCPS justified it by military necessity, emphasizing the essential nature of ore and timber for war purposes, its actual choice of St. Louis County is by no means surprising, as this county had witnessed a strike of miners and lumberjacks only a few months earlier. At the end of May, shortly before the passage of the order, Commissioner Lind presented a report from an agent that the MNCPS had sent to investigate labor conditions on the Iron Range a short time earlier.[20]

The MNCPS's first round of orders against the liquor trade was interpreted by the temperance reformers as an indicator of its inclination to support the dry cause in Minnesota. Therefore, the ASL, the WCTU, Protestant churches, and individual drys bombarded it with 226 complaints about blind pigging and other infractions on the liquor laws in the state; many of the complainants asked the commission to prohibit the sale of liquor in the state entirely. Most of the complaints came from towns that were dry under Local Option but located in so-called wet counties, or from wet counties serving as oases for the surrounding dry counties. After all, the patchwork solution created by County Option had not succeeded at curbing the consumption of alcohol and was therefore unsatisfactory to the drys.[21] The commissioners were overwhelmed. They feared the wet coalition consisting of breweries, distilleries, unions affiliated with the Minnesota Federation of Labor, and powerful individual businessmen, who had the money and the power to challenge the MNCPS in the courts. On June 19, 1917, they unanimously approved a statement issued by Commissioner Lind announcing to the public that the MNCPS could not "fritter away its time in prosecuting violations of the license laws in this State" due to a host of other, more important duties. However, "[i]f [manufacturers and licensed dealers in intoxicants] continue to encourage and sustain blind pigging there is no recourse left to the commission but to issue an order prohibiting the manufacture and sale of liquor in the State or to urge the Governor to call an extra session . . . to pass a bone-dry law." Not only did this statement display the commissioners' frustration about the flood of complaints, but it also reflected their actual openness toward prohibition.[22]

From September 1917 on, the MNCPS passed another series of orders seeking to restrict liquor consumption in Minnesota. One group of orders (Orders 11 and 12), prohibiting the shipment of liquor within or into the dry counties Koochiching, Beltrami, and Clearwater, can be read in light of the St. Louis County order passed in June. These counties were also part of, or adjacent to, the Iron Range and the home of several lumber mills and had witnessed labor conflict throughout the summer. Over the next couple of months, the MNCPS passed further orders drying northern Minnesota up, applying Order 11 to Polk and Clay Counties (Orders 19, 20) and prohibiting the shipment and sale of liquor into the sole remaining wet spot in northern Minnesota, Red Lake County (Order 43).[23]

Another set of commission orders, however, resulted neither from military necessity nor from the MNCPS's antilabor tendencies. They rather prove that the commission—pressured by Burnquist and McGee—began to move away from its initial unwillingness to engage in the wet-dry question. Martin was the only county located at the Iowa border in which liquor was still sold. Pipestone was sandwiched between dry South Dakota on the west and three dry Minnesota counties on the east. These wet "oases," as they were called by contemporaries, attracted so-called "joy riders," that is, people who traveled long distances in automobiles and bought large amounts of liquor in order to transport them back to their dry counties. In their complaints to the MNCPS, officials and citizens from the neighboring states and southern Minnesota strategically appropriated the war jargon, emphasizing that these oases "interfered with food production," were a "menace to the military," and allowed for a "rendezvous of the I.W.W." The MNCPS's disagreements on the shape of the subsequent Order 10 reflect the qualms of some of the commissioners about entering wet-dry battlegrounds. While McGee and Burnquist readily spoke out in favor of prohibiting the sale of liquor in the two counties, the other commissioners voted against it and adopted a far more moderate solution—the limitation of liquor sales to alcohol consumed on the premises of licensed saloons. It was once again McGee who did not let up and pushed through an amendment shutting the saloons between 5 P.M. and 9 A.M. against the opposition of John Lind, Charles W. Ames, and Anton C. Weiss, who obviously felt reluctant about paying lip service to the dry coalition.[24]

When the MNCPS proceeded to apply Order 10 to another liquor oasis, Blooming Prairie, Steele County, on December 5, 1917 (Order 17), however, it provoked a controversy between wets and drys that would strengthen the MNCPS's position even more. All the efforts made by the town's saloon owners and residents to fight the order—through noncompliance and through the help of the courts—came to naught when on August 9, 1918, the Minnesota Supreme Court emphasized the constitutionality of the Blooming Prairie Order. Strengthened by this decision, the MNCPS released Order 48 that made Blooming Prairie bone-dry for the duration of the war and three months after the ratification of the peace treaty. The MNCPS was at the height of its power.[25]

The MNCPS's ever-increasing stringency when handling questions related to alcohol became also visible in the passage of Order 24 on January 31, 1918, which made bone-dry the state's fifty-nine counties that were dry under Local or County Option and the Indian lid. Delivering liquor into dry territories, the commission argued in a memorandum it obviously felt obliged to attach to the order, undermined the County Option Law and thus was against "the will of the people expressed at the polls." This line of argumentation shows that the MNCPS did not even try to justify its order as a wartime necessity.[26]

Sources remain silent on the reasons for the MNCPS's greater stringency. The saloon owners' law defiance and resistance at Blooming Prairie might have provoked the commission to emphasize the extent of its power. The constant flood of complaints and the growing sentiment in Minnesota and the nation in favor of prohibition could be another reason for the commissioners' increasing willingness to engage in the liquor question. Be that as it may, after the passage of Order 24, the advocates of a dry Minnesota—in particular the ASL—felt they had a powerful and reliable ally in the MNCPS and repeatedly asked the commissioners to decree prohibition for the state as a whole.[27] While the MNCPS was willing to aid the prohibition movement in Minnesota, it declined to decree prohibition, out of respect for the power of the state legislature. In December 1917, McGee declared in a letter that the state legislature had decided to have Minnesota's electorate vote on the prohibition question in November 1918. The MNCPS, he believed, should not interfere with this decision. On February 5, 1918, Commissioner McGee issued a lengthy statement explaining why the MNCPS would not close saloons and breweries in Minnesota. He considered

> the general closing of saloons in this state and nation . . . a war measure upon which the Federal Government has already acted. . . . The President, through legislation, has now the power to eliminate the liquor traffic throughout all of the states and, if he deems it advisable . . . , he will undoubtedly do so. Unless additional causes should develop justifying a course which now appears inconsistent with the present policy of the Federal Government, . . . the Commission does not feel it should act in this matter. It takes this position without regard to its own views, which are clearly disclosed by the course it has heretofore followed.[28]

As their latest orders had shown, the commissioners were clearly in favor of prohibition but were concerned that steps toward implementing prohibition would exceed their power.

Through its numerous anti-liquor orders, the MNCPS had paved the way for a dry Minnesota and encouraged dry activism. The ASL and the Minnesota Dry Federation worked at full speed—separately yet efficiently. The WCTU, the largest organization in the Dry Federation, was responsible for mobilizing women and distributing literature. By November 5, 1918, the women had put up 6,500 posters and distributed 190,000 leaflets, 145,000 pink ballots, 150,000 window signs, 200,000 voters' tags, 50,000 door tags, 25,000 song leaflets, and 23,775 campaign buttons (see figure 5.2). They also held street meetings, engaged in house-to-house canvassing, and involved children in the campaign teaching them campaign cries such as: "Who wants Minnesota dry? I! I! I! Who will help to make it so? I! I! I!" and "Minnesota, peerless, fearless, beerless." The Finnish Total Abstinence Society was the Federation's richest society and financed many campaigns. The Minnesota Total Abstinence Association was the best-organized Scandinavian group and therefore largely responsible for mobilizing their fellow countrymen. The party prohibitionists covered the state four times with their speakers, held 3,116 automobile street meetings, and organized three to five picnics in each county (see figure 5.3).[29]

Figure 5.2. St. Paul signboard asking Minnesotans to cast their ballot in favor of constitutional prohibition on November 5, 1918. Courtesy of the Minnesota Historical Society.

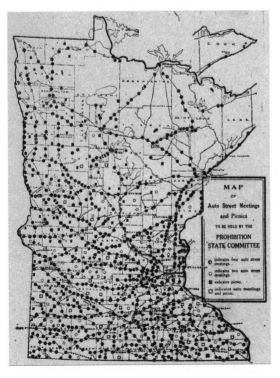

Figure 5.3. This map of the Prohibition Party's auto street meetings and picnics, which took place in the context of the 1918 election, visualizes the fervor of Minnesota's dry forces and the intensity of their campaign. Map from *Warren Sheaf* 10 July 1918: 8. Courtesy of the Minnesota Historical Society.

In light of such efficient campaigning, the antiprohibition coalition could not afford to be idle, but their agitation was not nearly as well organized, efficient, and fervent as the reformers'. While the German Americans were effectively silenced by the doings of the MNCPS and the hostilities experienced in the context of World War I,[30] a great number of laborers, in particular those employed by the liquor industry, actively worked against prohibition by supporting the Minnesota Trade Union League to Prevent Unemployment and Promote the Principle of Home Rule, about whose doings, however, not much is known.[31] The liquor interests, first and foremost the brewers, tried to put into place organizational structures similar to those of the temperance advocates. They established a Minnesota Brewers' Bureau in St. Paul, whose secretary Thomas H. Girling stood in close contact with the MNCPS and regularly traveled all over Minnesota, asking individual brewers and saloon owners to respect the laws. The brewers also organized a Law Enforcement Committee, headed by William Hamm, to stamp out blind pigs.[32] In order to offset the reformers' massive campaigns for prohibition, they reunited with the saloon owners and, through the Brewers' Bureau, sent out letters asking Minnesotans to vote against prohibition. To popularize their arguments against prohibition and to unify the many different branches of the liquor business, the liquor interests began publishing their own newspaper, *Our Side*, in the Twin Cities. After 1915, its editor constantly urged his readers to establish an organization of liquor dealers, sellers, and producers as strong and efficient as the ASL. This suggestion, however, seems to have come to naught. Although all people involved in the liquor business understood that only "[u]nited we stand—divided we fall," jealousies and lethargy prevailed among them, immobilized them, and undermined all efforts to form a state organization.[33]

Considering the war hysteria, the anti-liquor agitation of the MNCPS, and the efficient campaign of the temperance organizations, it is surprising that on November 5, 1918, only 189,614 Minnesotans voted in favor of ratifying the prohibitory constitutional amendment, whereas 173,665 still spoke out against it. Maybe it was the amendment's bone-dry feature that made many Minnesotans decide against it. Although ratification had received more votes, since 1897 Minnesota's constitution required a majority of all people casting a ballot in the election to vote in favor of the amendment. Prohibition had, however, received only 49.8 percent of the votes, and another 689 votes would have been needed for the ratification of the amendment.[34]

Disappointment did not prevail for long among Minnesota's temperance reformers. National events came to help, and within eight months, liquor became a thing of the past within the United States. President Wilson proclaimed that beginning on December 1, 1918, in order to save foodstuffs and coal, no beer was to be produced containing more than 0.5 percent alcohol. On November 21, 1918, Congress passed the War Prohibition Act, which forbade the manufacture of beer and wine after May 1, 1919, and outlawed the sale of all intoxicating beverages after June 30, 1919, with both provisions remaining in effect until the termination of demobilization. The race for the ratification of the Eighteenth Amendment was also at full speed. On January 16, 1919, Nebraska was the thirty-sixth legislature to vote in favor of the Amendment. The ratification process, for which Congress had allowed seven years, had been accomplished in little more than a year.[35]

Minnesota ended up being the fortieth state ratifying the Eighteenth Amendment with a comfortable majority on January 17, 1919. Even some of the wet legislators voted in favor of ratification, as they considered it a foregone conclusion. They jokingly declared that this was the first dry measure they had ever supported. In early April 1919, the Minnesota legislature also passed the Norton Dry Enforcement bill, enforcing the National Prohibition Amendment in Minnesota by prohibiting the manufacture and sale of liquor except for medicinal, sacramental, scientific, or industrial purposes. In the context of this enforcement bill, the state's drys once more proved their strength. After a heated debate and due to the agitation of the ASL, an amendment to the bill permitting the manufacture and sale of beer containing 2 percent alcohol was killed in the Senate.[36]

Thus, the course was set for prohibition in Minnesota. On July 1, 1919, Wartime Prohibition set in, drying up the state as well as the rest of the United States. Saloons could remain in business but had to sell soft drinks or liquor containing less than 0.5 percent alcohol. Some breweries were able to shift their production to near beer and soft drinks, while others had to close. On January 16, 1920, Wartime Prohibition seamlessly passed into National Prohibition. After almost seventy years of struggle, the state's temperance advocates had reached their goal of ousting liquor in Minnesota.[37]

St. Paul—Finally on the Water Wagon?

Before the American declaration of war, life went on as usual in Minnesota's capital with respect to alcohol. The state liquor laws, such as the Sunday Law and the 11 P.M. closing law, were largely ignored, with lack of implementation being backed by the mayor, the chief of police, the liquor producers and sellers, as well as the many residents who dubbed such strategies of law evasion as "a healthy antagonism to the Anglo-American reign of ministers" and a way of "boosting" the city.[38] Between 1915 and 1917, the pietistic reformers from the Midway area continued to fight for law enforcement. Under the leadership of Norman T. Mears, a wealthy St. Paul businessman, they established a Vigilance Committee with the aim of producing evidence for the lack of civic liquor law enforcement. The end result of the work of this "snooping committee" and "Smears," as some St. Paulites came to refer to them, were personal attacks, both verbal and physical, and ruined political careers, while the liquor laws continued to be ignored.[39]

Within a few months, however, the historical tide turned, and developments on the national and state levels greatly played into the hands of Mears and his fellow vigilantes. With the entry of the United States into the Great War and the formation of the MNCPS, St. Paulites could not uphold their predilection for alcohol and their aversion to temperance, at least not openly. The city's business community, in particular, cooperated with the MNCPS in wiping out all suspicions of disloyalty associated with Minnesota's state capital. The doings of the MNCPS, the communal tensions and suspicions created by the war, and the suppression of the city's strong German American heritage shattered the capital's antireformist coalition and led to civic fragmentation. This development intensified after the war when a wave of strikes pitted employers and workers against each other. The state capital became a divided city. When it came to questions concerning liquor consumption, however, the majority of St. Paulites were of one mind and embraced long-practiced problem-solving strategies. Alcohol and joie de vivre made up the glue that held together a disintegrating community.

The war and the ensuing campaigns for loyalty and "100 percent Americanism," a conception of American nationality leaving less and less room for ethnic and political pluralism, also affected St. Paul. Until the close of 1915, the overwhelming sentiment of St. Paulites, along with most other Americans, was that the United States should stay neutral. "It is not our quarrel, so let us keep out of it," the *Pioneer Press* emphasized. This attitude is especially understandable if one considers the demographics of the city. Of the 223,675 people living in Ramsey County in 1910, 70 percent were of foreign birth or parentage. 49,327 people were either born in Germany or had German parents. 34,608 were of Scandinavian birth or parentage, and 13,213 had an Irish background. These three immigrant groups abhorred a war against the Central Powers due to their Old-World ties, or, in case of the Irish Americans, their anti-British sentiments.[40]

However, when U.S. policy took an anti-German turn and official rhetoric shifted from an emphasis of neutrality to one of preparedness, public opinion in St. Paul fragmented in multiple ways, which divided the city along class and ethnic lines. The immigrant communities remained steadfast in their opposition to entering the war. St. Paul's Trades and Labor Assembly also openly declared their opposition to military involvement. The city's small number of Socialists and a significant segment of St. Paul's middle class, especially women, students, and clergymen, joined the laborers and agitated for peace. Some of these peace activists founded a Peace and Neutrality Association and a Peace League. St. Paul's business community, by contrast, was in favor of the interventionist policy of the U.S. government, believing that, in case of an American intervention, the city's economy would be boosted and employment created. In order to demonstrate their patriotism, the members of the St. Paul Business and Commerce Association founded the Patriotic League of St. Paul. The League sought to influence public sentiment by questioning the loyalty of anyone refusing to join it, by suppressing antiwar protests, and by prohibiting antiwar speakers to address audiences in the city. Its members also put local politicians under pressure who spoke out against an American entry into the war. Many leading St. Paulites felt obliged to join the League. The faculty of various colleges and clergymen, such as John Ireland, entered the organization in droves.[41]

Thus, by March 1917, St. Paul had—like in the context of the Maine Law debates of 1852—once again become a divided city. The creation of the MNCPS even widened the rifts in the civic fabric. St. Paul's business leaders, together with their Minneapolis counterparts, had actively lobbied for the establishment of the commission. It was even claimed at the time that the idea of a commission had originated within the Patriotic League. Once the MNCPS was in operation, however, St. Paul's businessmen suddenly found themselves caught up in a campaign against enemies that were nonexistent in St. Paul. The Nonpartisan League, union labor, and Socialists did not carry any threat for St. Paul's economy. Moreover, the liquor and entertainment industries were pillars of the city's economy and the only area in which St. Paul outdistanced Minneapolis. In addition, liquor consumption was a constituent part of the city's civic identity and an integral part of its social life. Nevertheless, St. Paul's business community decided to continue to support the commission. It aided in the strict regulation of the liquor business and the suppression of German American culture in the city, actions that would have been unthinkable before the war. The businessmen were motivated by the hope that by regulating the liquor business in St. Paul more strictly, nearby Fort Snelling might be chosen as a major military cantonment, which would have great economic benefits for the city. "Certain moral conditions must obtain in this community," the editor of the *Pioneer Press* argued, "before it can hope to secure the selection of Fort Snelling as the site of the big military encampment and training ground. The assurance has been given that as a first condition to the selection the youthful soldiers must be exposed to the least possible temptation." Besides such economic considerations, liquor as well as German Americans became more and more associated with disloyalty. As both liquor and German American culture were deeply embedded in St. Paul's social and physical landscape, the city itself appeared disloyal—an impression the businessmen aimed to dispel at all cost.[42]

The debates surrounding the enforcement of the MNCPS's Order 7, closing the city's saloons from 10 P.M. to 8 A.M., prohibiting the serving of women and girls at any time, and banning cabaret performances where liquor was sold, reflect that the businessmen's considerations did not find much support on the ground. While the city's women's clubs, WCTUs, and evangelical churches strongly supported the order, the saloon, cabaret, and theater owners were naturally frustrated about this regulation and its support by the businessmen, as it caused severe economic loss and even forced some of them out of business. However, the anti-liquor order was certainly not merely resented for economic reasons. Feeling alienated by such a stringent anti-liquor policy, the majority of city residents tried to alleviate the situation by circumventing the order. Many saloons ignored the closing hours and gave liquor to soldiers and women, and the city's police did not always act on the information and evidence presented to them. Consequently, drunken soldiers became a common sight in the city.[43]

Such behavior, of course, endangered the city's standing with the War Department. In November 1917, the Inspector General of the U.S. Army visited the city and declared in a press interview: "The information reported to me shows conditions worse here than anywhere I know of. . . . If I had my way I would withdraw the soldiers, lock the doors on the Snelling barracks. . . . I have inspected practically every military camp of any size in the country in the past four months and in no place have I found conditions as bad as reported here." St. Paul's clergymen and reformist citizens fumed and bombarded the commission with petitions asking it to prohibit the sale of liquor in city and state.[44]

In response to this law breaking, the MNCPS threatened to prohibit the liquor traffic in the Twin Cities. Fearing the total loss of liquor revenues on the one hand and the withdrawal of troops on the other, St. Paul's businessmen, supported by the city's evangelical churches, redoubled their efforts to enforce Order 7. The Ramsey County Safety Commission employed more than a hundred special policemen in order to suppress vice and closed several German American liquor outlets, such as the famous *Rathskeller*, an old-style beer garden. From April 1918 on, the military authorities of Fort Snelling even began to patrol downtown St. Paul at night to prevent soldiers from becoming intoxicated. The MNCPS itself also strove to whip Minnesota's capital in line by assigning four companies of the Home Guard to St. Paul alone. By having the guardsmen serve without pay, the commissioners made sure that they came overwhelmingly from the wealthy business community. The commission also endorsed the establishment of Civilian Auxiliaries, mainly consisting of businessmen. Whereas in Minneapolis all these forces enforced the orders, suppressed dissent, intimidated labor, and forced radicals to leave town, in St. Paul the civilian army was less effective. In the summer of 1918, Home Guard captain Robert Rice confessed the utter failure of his men to police the Payne Avenue saloons. This lack of efficiency may have derived from the businessmen's reluctance to further strain civic relations by using force.[45]

By mid-1918, after a severe labor war in the Twin Cities, which ended—completely atypical of St. Paul—with the victory of the open shop and further harassment by the commission, civic alliances in St. Paul seemed irrevocably broken. Businessmen and laborers found themselves on different sides of the fence, and the suppression of the city's German American culture had left a cultural vacuum. It had also become clear to St. Paulites that they no longer had a say in the administration of their city. The state government, acting through the MNCPS, had intruded into St. Paul's civic affairs to an unprecedented degree. St. Paul's mayor had become a mere pawn of the commission. It was bitter for St. Paulites, who had put so much emphasis on home rule and civic independence, to adjust to a new order imposed from outside and starkly contradicting St. Paul's civic identity and economic interests.[46]

In such a climate of war, suspicion, and oppression, St. Paulites could no longer openly uphold their aversion to temperance and became apathetic and dissatisfied.[47] Even though the city's Police Department, despite its close surveillance by the MNCPS, more than once turned a blind eye to the doings of the liquor business, the war hysteria and the workings of the commission with its numerous spies and agents severely affected the city's saloon culture.[48] Whereas in December 1917 there were still 401 saloons in St. Paul, by October 1918 their number had dropped to 306. Many people preferred consuming liquor in clubs or at home rather than going to saloons. Many saloon owners also seem to have begun operating as blind pigs. Blind pigging seems to have been rampant in the city, as the MNCPS contacted various in- and out-of-state breweries, asking them to stop delivering beer to unlicensed saloons in the city.[49]

The Ramsey County Dry Federation, supported by the ASL and the Minnesota Dry Federation, mobilized the churchgoers, many businessmen, and some laborers to work for prohibition. While Archbishop John Ireland had mostly retreated from public life due to serious illness and would soon pass away, the city's Irish Catholic clergymen allied themselves with the dry campaigners, especially since they had been assured that wine for sacramental purposes would be excluded from prohibition. In the name of the younger Catholic clergy and the CTAU members, Reverend James Donahoe, the president of what was left of the CTAU, petitioned the MNCPS in favor of a bone-dry Minnesota. The *Catholic Bulletin* also advocated prohibition and asked the state's Catholics "to play a significant part in a movement which promises so much for individual and social betterment." At the end of October 1918, the *Bulletin* even published a call to prayer in favor of prohibition, which was signed by representatives of various denominations, notably by James C. Byrne, the Administrator of the Archdiocese of St. Paul. Byrne's signature signified the approval of prohibition by the Catholic Church. Such support from the Catholic hierarchy, the doings of the MNCPS, and the campaigns of the drys easily offset the effect of the posters touting personal liberty, with which the liquor dealers had placarded the city.[50]

Despite all this agitation in favor of prohibition, the majority of St. Paulites could not be convinced of its value. On June 30, 1919, the night before Wartime Prohibition went into effect, they threw a wild farewell party in honor of John Barleycorn. The *Tägliche Volkszeitung* reported that the traditional New Year celebrations were harmless compared to the hustle and bustle of that night. Never-ending throngs of people populated the city's main streets. All cafés, cabarets, and saloons were filled to the brim, and the waiters could barely satisfy their customers' liquid needs. In numerous saloons, customers turned back the clocks or threw them out altogether because these relentlessly approached the eleventh hour. John Barleycorn, the newspaper solemnly announced, was buried with much noise, fireworks of all kinds, laughter, and tears. Thousands of St. Paulites also stocked alcohol in their homes, seeking to alleviate the impact of the dry spell.[51]

Similar to the frantic celebration of the repeal of the Maine Law in 1852, the 1919 celebration in honor of John Barleycorn signified much more than merely a salute to alcohol. Whereas in 1852 St. Paulites had felt that they had triumphed over the "Yankee" temperance reformers and had saved their city from becoming a "New England of the West," almost seventy years later the signs were far less promising. Prohibition had become reality, and chances of repeal were bleak. The ban on alcohol deprived the city and its residents of one of their major markers of identity and of one of its most profitable sources of income. The war had also made the restoration of pre–World War I conditions in St. Paul impossible. It had created suspicions, tensions, and communal rifts and had left the city in social ruins. Like Minneapolis, St. Paul had, at least temporarily, turned into an open-shop town, in which class functioned as the defining feature of the city's identity. While the 1852 celebration signified triumph, the 1919 celebration sounded a note of despair and helplessness.

Despite this great transformation of St. Paul's social fabric and the official ban on alcohol, St. Paulites managed to save significant constituents of their city's prewar identity over the war years. Although the war had pitted them against each other and had made negotiation much more difficult, the majority of the city's residents agreed on the importance of joie de vivre and alcohol. Alcohol was maybe the single issue on which St. Paulites were in almost unanimous agreement in the 1920s. The Eighteenth Amendment had not only hurt the city's economy but also crippled many of its cultural traditions. Not surprisingly, St. Paulites fell back on long-practiced patterns of resistance: They simply ignored the amendment and established an illegal but glamorous culture of moonshining, bootlegging, and illicit liquor selling in speakeasies. In August 1920, the *St. Paul Dispatch* reported that federal agents were "in despair" because St. Paul was "wringing wet," with the illicit liquor traffic flourishing to an "alarming degree." Local authorities were unwilling to enforce prohibition unless they were explicitly asked to do so by the federal government. As a consequence, liquor was sold almost openly not only in saloons but also by a "multitude of bootleggers." The whiskey on sale was either produced at home or smuggled in from Canada. The police department estimated that at least 75 percent of city residents were either distilling whiskey or making wine or beer for consumption at home or for sale to consumers or speakeasy owners. St. Paul also became a major distribution point for illegal liquor in the United States. In 1926, federal investigators broke a major bootlegging ring operating from Cleveland; 41 of the 112 people indicted lived in St. Paul. Instead of hopping on the water wagon, by the early 1920s the "Saintly City" had once again gained national renown as one of the wettest cities in the country.[52]

The German American Temperance Opposition Crushed

With their decades-long espousal of alcohol as an inextricable constituent of German American ethnic identity, German American leaders had—unconsciously—contributed to the precarious situation of their community during World War I. Their deep cultural and ethnic entanglement with liquor, an item of consumption now associated with disloyalty, even heightened the suspicions German Americans had to endure on grounds of their ethnic origin. The war hysteria and, in Minnesota, the actions of the MNCPS made it impossible for the German American community to continue its fight against prohibition and thus effectively eliminated one of the major oppositional forces to the dry cause. Official war policies served as the basis of discrimination and repression and led to a transformation of German American ethnic identity. While the war at first heightened ethnic identification among the various groups of German Americans, in the long run, it led to a retreat of German American ethnicity from public view and deeply affected its private expressions. Even though in the 1920s public and private expressions of German American ethnic identity would reappear, they would be, as historian Russell A. Kazal termed it, "subdued."[53]

Before the American involvement in World War I, Anglo-Americans did not mind the rhetorical defense of Germany in the German American press and campaigns for war relief and American neutrality within Minnesota's German American community. *Der Wanderer* argued that the war had been forced onto Germany and Austria and criticized St. Paul's Anglo-American newspapers for their "venomous treatment of Germany." A large number of St. Paul's German and Austrian Americans also adopted resolutions justifying the actions of their home countries and asked for American neutrality. In September 1914, Julius Moersch of the ZB and the Catholic leader Joseph Matt, together with other German American St. Paulites, founded the German and Austro-Hungarian Red Cross Society of the Northwest (*Deutsche und Österreichisch-Ungarische*

Rote-Kreuz Gesellschaft des Nordwestens), a war relief organization. The ZB of Minnesota, in cooperation with the Minnesota Catholic Aid Association, also launched large-scale agitation in favor of Germany, sending letters to American government officials that advised them how to proceed diplomatically. In the context of the war, all intra–German American quarrels subsided, ethnic identification increased, and Minnesota's German Catholics cooperated with other German American societies in working for war relief.[54]

When with the sinking of the Lusitania in May 1915, however, press and community attitudes took a vehement anti-German turn, German American activists increasingly came under suspicion of acting on behalf of the German government (see figure 5.4). By the fall of 1915, worries about the allegedly divided loyalties of "hyphenated" Americans had escalated into a nationwide "anti-hyphenate" campaign with Theodore Roosevelt at its head. President Wilson also lent this campaign moral authority, propagating "100 percent Americanism." From 1915 onward, the so-called National Americanization Commit-

Figure 5.4. After the sinking of the Lusitania, "Hoch der Kaiser" soon turned into "Hook the Kaiser." Loyalty parades, such as the one in the photograph, became a common feature in St. Paul's civic life. Besides seeking to demonstrate the city's unswerving loyalty, the parade was to suppress dissent within the city's German American community. Courtesy of the Minnesota Historical Society.

tee implemented Wilson's antipluralistic agenda by promoting naturalization, English-language training, and loyalty to America among the nation's immigrants. Wilson also directly attacked German Americans. In December 1915, he insinuated that German Americans "have poured the poison of disloyalty into the very arteries of our national life."[55]

By 1917, *Der Wanderer* wrote, "to throw stones at German Americans" had become "a fashionable sport," and a "boundless hunt against anything German" had begun. German Americans had to endure job discrimination, social ostracism, and intimidation. Even Minnesota's legislature and state officials threatened and discriminated against them. The former passed bills prohibiting nonnaturalized Germans, so-called alien enemies, from possessing firearms and explosives and from living within half a mile of armories, butcher's shops, or factories working for the government.[56] And Governor Burnquist wrote to a fellow politician that

> [o]ur pro-German friends are at last learning, that to be quite [*sic*] may be the best policy for them. As late as three days ago the "kaiser" [a nickname for a German American politician] came in on purpose to give me the same old German song or argument. I cut the argument short by telling him that if he was not enough of an American to, at least keep quite [*sic*] that we would make him do so.[57]

The state's English-speaking newspapers also did their share to increase the hostility toward German Americans by constantly reporting about the "German pestilence" and the "German beast" and by encouraging their readers to drive all German American editors out of their offices. Due to such hate speech, the number of complaints against individual German Americans skyrocketed. At the end of April 1917, U.S. Attorney for Minnesota Alfred Jacques reported to Governor Burnquist that a German American state weigher, residing at Merriam Park, had used violent and unpatriotic language. Jacques asked Burnquist to locate this man and to silence him. In November 1917, the parish house of St. Agnes German Catholic Church was bombed. Moderate voices asking to stop this "fierce agitation" were assiduously ignored.[58]

The major force promoting this anti-German hysteria in Minnesota was the MNCPS. Already in 1917, it sent out a circular announcing that "[a]nyone who talks and acts against the government in times of war, regardless of the 'Constitutional right of free speech' which has been so sadly abused, is a traitor and deserves the most drastic punishment." Similar propaganda material, asking German Americans to Americanize and to renounce their ties to Germany, was distributed by the MNCPS throughout the war. Violent speeches, which were Commissioner McGee's specialty, increased suspicions of German American disloyalty. In an interview before the U. S. Military Affairs Committee on April 19, 1918, he expressed his personal opinion on German and Swedish Americans very explicitly: "The disloyal element in Minnesota is largely among the

German-Swedish people. The nation blundered at the start of the war in not dealing severely with these vipers."[59]

In order to root out this alleged disloyalty, the commission embarked on an Americanization campaign. Its first target was the core of German American culture: the German-language press and German language. On August 1, 1917, the MNCPS exacted a promise of cooperation from F. W. Bergmeier of the *Volkszeitung* and Joseph Matt of *Der Wanderer* and began to scrutinize their editorials closely and to harass them.[60] In November 1917, the commission "recommended" to schools in Minnesota to use foreign languages only as a medium for the study of those languages or for religious instruction. It also published a black list of German books that could not be used for teaching any more. In April the following year, the MNCPS decreed that non-American citizens could not work as teachers in Minnesota's schools any more.[61]

In its campaign against disloyalty, the MNCPS also sent its own investigators as well as Pinkerton agents all over Minnesota to search for subversion. In the first half of 1917, twelve agents investigated German localities in St. Paul in order to shake German Americans "into a proper frame of mind." "CH," who was fluent in German, visited saloons patronized by German Americans. He discovered that "all the Germans are very careful what they say and there does not seem any effort on their part to evade or prevent registration." Other documents reveal that individual German Americans were repeatedly investigated relative to statements they had made on the war. Editors of patriotic newspapers also sent lists to Burnquist with the names of those German Americans who had canceled their subscriptions, so that the governor could instruct the detectives to check on them.[62]

More than such investigations, however, German Americans feared to be drafted. On June 5, 1917, all men between twenty-one and thirty-one had been asked to register. Representatives of the German American community pleaded with Governor Burnquist to spare their fellow countrymen from "fratricide" by offering them other options to serve their country. Fears of fratricide also lay at the heart of the gathering of more than eight thousand people, most of them German Americans, at New Ulm, Minnesota, on July 25, 1917. Those present formulated a request to Congress and the government not to force the draftees to fight in Europe against their will. Many native-born Americans perceived this meeting as a "traitors' meeting" and expressed their regret that the Sioux had not done a better job at New Ulm during their attack on the city in 1862.[63] After several investigations, the MNCPS removed the leaders of the New Ulm meeting—all politicians and prominent figures in the German American community—from their offices, a traumatic experience for German Americans all over Minnesota. Governor Burnquist himself held a speech at New Ulm in August 1917, in which he declared it the duty of any American to put aside pro-German feelings. Those who failed to support the cause of America, Burnquist argued, should be deprived of their right of franchise and of the privileges and property they had acquired through the American government. Such citizens should be interred during the war and sent back to the country they preferred to America after the war. He emphasized that "so long as I am governor of Minnesota I am going to do everything in my power to assist in smashing any such damnable propaganda."[64]

Burnquist's speech, the detectives' activities, and the events in New Ulm "had a decidedly quieting influence": Most German Americans ceased voicing their opinions publicly and put up an air of patriotism. German American newspapers advised their readers to bridle their passions and to remain quiet in order not to be persecuted. "Retreat" and "quiet seclusion" rather than celebrations and a forced display of patriotism were the reactions *Der Wanderer* suggested.[65] As so often, German American Catholics were especially under pressure due to Archbishop Ireland's fervent loyalty and patriotism. To him the war provided an exceptional opportunity for Catholics to prove "to be the first patriots of the land." If Catholics agitated against the war, the Church itself would be tainted in the process. Therefore, he argued in a great number of speeches that it was the duty of every Catholic to be "a true American" and to joyfully support nation and government and that he did not approve of any "reservation of mind" and any "slackening of earnest act." He encouraged his flock to serve in the military and suggested deporting the disloyal to those countries they loved more than the United States. Despite scholarly insinuations to the opposite, there is no evidence that Archbishop Ireland participated in the anti-German campaigns. When contacted by the MNCPS in May 1917, concerning the ban of the German language as a vehicle of instruction, Ireland spoke out against such a ban. Upon Ireland's death on September 25, 1918, Joseph Matt asserted his readers that, had he not fallen ill, he would have protected his German American flock from the anti-German attacks, especially as their relationship had continued to improve within the last decade. Matt stated that Ireland had even considered publishing a statement in that direction.[66]

In contrast to John Ireland, many other temperance advocates openly rejoiced at the suspicions and actions against German Americans and greatly supported the MNCPS in its loyalty campaign. As German Americans had for years thwarted their temperance success in Minnesota, many dry leaders felt that they had an ax to grind with them and eagerly joined in the tune of unconditional loyalty. George H. Sutherland from Fairmont, chairman of the Temperance Legislation Committee of 1918, voiced privately and publicly to be getting very "impatient with these people who have come from foreign lands and then repudiate this country" and "who would hand a dagger to the monster or stab our boys in the back by shouting 'Hoch der Kaiser.'" "The question for every American citizen to decide now is," Sutherland argued, "whether he is for this country and its ideals or for the kaiser. There are those who claim Germany is a better country to live in than the United States. Bless their hearts, I want to tell them there will be a lot of dry eyes in this old town if they pack up and go back to their first love." If they wished to stay here, however, they should be convicted of disloyalty and sentenced to jail.[67]

The reformers rejoiced even more when, in the context of the war hysteria, the NB of America and its branches—major instruments of anti-temperance agitation—were forced to disband. As the German Americans' largest organization, the NB of America increasingly became the target of enmity and suspicions, and consequently, in July 1918, Congress repealed the act that had granted the association its charter. The NB of America, it was argued, had operated in favor of the German general staff and worked against the wartime demand of national unity. By that time, however, the NB of America had already ceased to exist, having turned over its assets to the American Red Cross in April 1918. A similar fate seems to have befallen the ZB of Minnesota, which ceased to be mentioned by the German American press after August 1917. Since involvement in such organizations had become too risky for Minnesota's German American community, the ZB had obviously withered.[68]

The war had led to the harassment of the state's German Americans by the federal government, Minnesota's legislature, state officials, an omnipotent MNCPS, and many overly zealous Minnesotan patriots. It had deprived them of their major instrument against the temperance forces, the ZB of Minnesota. It had also caused a close surveillance of the German American press, the engine of all anti-temperance campaigns. Finally, it had considerably weakened the German American brewers by insinuations of disloyalty. All these attacks brought about a standstill of German American social life. In St. Paul, long-established German American beer gardens and restaurants closed, and German composers were removed from the playbills of orchestras. Non-German St. Paulites sought to expunge all traces of Germanness and German culture, the most notable and traumatic act being the removal of the prominent statue of Germania, symbol of German pride, from the city's Germania Life Insurance Building on April 1, 1918 (see figure 5.5).[69]

Thus cornered and deprived of their ethnic self-confidence, cultural symbols, and major oppositional tools, Minnesota's German Americans had no chance to uphold their fight against the temperance movement. Even though German American newspapers and leaders time and again pointed at the injustice of the prohibition of liquor, their appeals became less frequent and took on a note of resignation. In the context of the prohibition election of 1918, the *Volkszeitung* admitted that the lack of activism among the opponents of prohibition "can be mostly traced back to the current conditions."[70]

Instead of continuing their anti-liquor agitation, some of Minnesota's German Americans tried to improve their image by asserting their loyalty. They

Figure 5.5. On April 1, 1918, the statue of Germania was removed from the old Germania Life Insurance Building, whose name was also changed to Guardian Life Insurance Building. Courtesy of the Minnesota Historical Society.

contributed to Liberty Loan drives, made public statements in support of the war, and founded a League of Patriotic Americans of German Origin in St. Paul on April 2, 1918. Many of them also believed that the only way to protect their families and businesses was to comply with erasing every German trace from public life. Between 1910 and 1920, nearly seven thousand residents of German birth disappeared from St. Paul's census rolls, some of them having returned to Germany but most of them having changed their names in order to hide their German descent. German Americans also moved out of the traditionally German fifth and eighth wards in St. Paul in order not to be accused of ethnic separatism. Some of them even started turning on each other. Father Alois Kastigar of the Assumption parish made accusations of disloyalty against eight fellow German priests who had recently arrived in the city.[71]

Anxious, intimidated, and at odds with each other, Minnesota's German Americans accepted the introduction of prohibition with resignation bordering on indifference. German American newspapers did not even mention the ratification of the National Prohibition Amendment any more. A few days later, however, the *Volkszeitung* clearly attributed the ratification to the war, which had encouraged people to sacrifice everything, even their thirst: "All individual rights had to be subordinated to the common welfare, and everything had to happen through the largest exertion of all strengths, as the time was short and the matter urgent." Whereas the *Volkszeitung* asked its readers to appeal against the amendment, *Der Wanderer* was convinced that prohibition would be in effect for decades.[72]

Der Wanderer was to be right. Alcohol, which had become an essential marker of German American ethnicity and a treasured cultural carrier, would be officially banned from the public sphere and relegated to the home or twilight for more than a decade. This relegation deprived many German American celebrations, meetings, and picnics of their traditional sociability—their cultural meaning—and deprived German American ethnic identity of one of its most important supporting pillars. The relegation of alcohol to the private sphere and the decline of sociability added to the further demise of German American associational culture. Other reasons for this demise were a significant trailing off of immigration from Germany, the rise of the second generation of German Americans, and the lure of mass commercial and consumer culture. Moreover, after the war, many German Americans continued to discard or conceal their German heritage and therefore abandoned many of their ethnic associations and cultural practices. Due to the war, Wingerd argues, "the distinctive culture of *Deutschtum* . . . [was] only a weak shadow of its former robust self." Even though German American culture and identity had never been particularly robust but had always been prone to fragmentation, World War I and the Prohibition era were certainly responsible for a transformation of German American ethnicity. The new, "subdued" German American ethnic identity that emerged in the course of the 1920s was based on altered cultural patterns and therefore far more distant from its German origins. Frederick C. Luebke even speaks of a "sort of cultural amnesia" befalling the generations of German Americans growing up between the world wars. Speaking of amnesia might take it too far, but in the 1920s and 1930s, German American ethnicity took on some of the facets that Herbert Gans ascribed to "symbolic ethnicity."[73]

A Female Public Identity Acknowledged

World War I widened opportunities for women in the United States, including Minnesota's temperance women, and won them great respect. Besides continuing its suffrage and prohibition work, Minnesota's WCTU, in particular its Anglo-American members,[74] was one of the numerous women's organizations that eagerly supported the national campaigns for patriotism, food conservation, and Americanization. Since, in the context of the war, Minnesota's women entered occupations in war industries and took on positions in the swelling government bureaucracy, from which they would have been excluded in times of peace, the state WCTU created a new department that aimed at improving working conditions for women and at promoting gender equality in the labor force. Women's professional and administrative engagement and their contributions to the war increased men's respect for them and lent their demands for suffrage great weight. It is therefore certainly no coincidence that the National Suffrage Amendment was passed and ratified shortly after the war. Its ratification marked the first major caesura in the construction of a female public identity.[75]

Shortly after the American entry into the war, the national WCTU asked its branches to work for prohibition even more fervently as "[t]he path of prohibition is the path of patriotism." Minnesota's WCTU leaders therefore encouraged the state's temperance women to work for Wartime Prohibition and sent a telegram to President Wilson asking that the manufacture and sale of liquor be prohibited during the war. "Prohibition," they argued, "will prevent crime, reduce poverty, increase efficiency, safeguard morals, preserve health and conserve human energy. All of these we must secure if we are to win the war." Minnesota's WCTU women also fervently worked for the passage of a prohibitory constitutional amendment for Minnesota and became the largest member organization of the Minnesota Dry Federation.[76] The women also recognized the value of the MNCPS for their own purposes. In the winter of 1917, WCTU women all over the state flooded the commission with petitions asking it to enforce the liquor laws in their communities or, even better, to dry up the state entirely. The Ramsey County WCTU wrote a letter to the MNCPS demanding, in the name of its six hundred members, the closing of saloons, wholesale liquor houses, and breweries in St. Paul during the war for four reasons:

> 1st. The name of our fair city has been brought in contempt by the liquor element and can only be thoroughly cleansed and set right before the World by the closing of all places selling intoxicating liquors.
>
> 2nd. We should conserve every ounce of food stuffs, and using it to debauch our citizens and soldiers is worse than wasting it.

3rd. Revenues spent in the saloons would be used to take care of the families
that charitable institutions are caring for and the sons could join the colors instead
of caring for the families of drunken men.

4th. Thousands of homes would be made happy this Thanksgiving time if all
saloons were closed.[77]

These reasons reflect the women's cunning use of home protection, military
efficiency, and food conservation rhetoric in order to convince the MNCPS to
ban liquor. The third reason, in particular, reveals that through prohibition the
women sought to reform the working class, whose alleged drinking habits led
to impoverishment and the unraveling of familial relations.

In addition to their campaigns against alcohol, the Minnesota WCTU women
engaged in war work. Arguing that their "protection of the home" slogan could
now be applied to the nation itself, they became active in the areas of relief work
and Americanization. All these activities were coordinated by the Minnesota
WCTU's Committee for Patriotic Service, which was composed of the WCTU's
General Officers and the Superintendents of Soldiers and Sailors, Flower Mission, Moral Education, Women in Industry, and Americanization.[78]

In order to accomplish their first goal, relief work, WCTU leaders declared
the Department for the Work among Soldiers and Sailors to be mainly responsible for doing charitable and temperance work among soldiers and for
supporting the war work of the Red Cross. Almost every member of the Minnesota WCTU was also a member of the Red Cross. Individual unions, such
as the Hamline WCTU, even had a Red Cross unit. In order to reach soldiers
and sailors, the women established homelike recreation centers and libraries in
cantonments, camps, naval stations, aviation fields, and battleships; ministered
to army and navy members in hospitals, at the battlefront, in soldiers' homes,
and in life-saving stations; and organized Christian Temperance Unions among
the veterans. In 1916 and 1917 alone, the Minnesota WCTU's 250 unions with
a membership of about 8,000 sewed 2,799 so-called comfort bags, containing
temperance literature, several practical amenities, and a personal note for the
soldiers. Due to their proximity to Fort Snelling, the Ramsey County WCTUs
were in constant contact with the War Department, asking for directions for
further support of the soldiers trained there. They provided the fort with a pho-
nograph for the quarantine ward, a rug for the wounded officers' headquarters,
fifty folding tables to be used on the beds of the wounded soldiers, and jam,
jellies, and magazines. Together with the Red Cross, the women knitted and
sewed hospital supplies and assisted in furnishing base hospitals with these articles. The Minnesota WCTU also contributed to a fund for two White Ribbon
motor ambulances to be used in France and for several stereo-motorgraphs,
with which temperance truths could be presented to soldiers. Throughout the
war, the women "adopted" (that is, financed) ten French orphans and several

dozen French children whose fathers had fallen in the war. They also bought Liberty Bonds, emphasizing their support of the war.[79]

Americanization was another focus of Minnesota's WCTU in those years. The nationwide Americanization campaigns launched in the context of the war suited the agenda of Minnesota's temperance women very well. Since the 1880s, they had argued that immigrants needed to be assimilated quickly and that their immigrant cultures had to be replaced by Anglo-American traditions and values. In May 1917, the national WCTU asked its branches to place greater emphasis on their Americanization work by teaching Americanism and loyalty to immigrants and to cooperate with the Federal Bureau of Immigration and Naturalization and the Americanization Committee of the National Chamber of Commerce. Acting on these suggestions, the Minnesota WCTU declared the Department of Work among Foreign-Speaking People responsible for the Americanization work, renaming it Department of Americanization a short time later. Its newly defined task was "to teach the foreign people in our country the language and customs of America, thus making them more loyal and bringing them in closer contact with each other, with the one purpose, one country, one language, one flag." In order to fulfill this task, many unions established English-language classes for immigrants and set up a "big sister system," assigning several immigrants to each WCTU woman. By 1919, St. Paul's unions alone had three Superintendents of Americanization. The war had turned work among the immigrants from the Minnesota WCTU's most neglected to one of its most cherished fields of activity. The war's emphasis on Anglo-American superiority and cultural dominance was in line with the ethnocentrism of numerous WCTU members, clearly hierarchized their interaction with the immigrants, and made protest unlikely. Under such conditions, most WCTU women seem to have found working among immigrants much more attractive than in previous decades.[80]

Aside from engaging in specific war efforts, the Minnesota WCTU also tried to improve working conditions for women, whose presence in the labor force had tremendously expanded since the beginning of the war.[81] Female laborers, the WCTU women argued, should have the same benefits and wages as their male coworkers. In order to promote equality in the labor force, they established the Department of Temperance and Labor, which was to keep the WCTU membership informed about social conditions in the workplace, all the while trying to enlist laborers in the fight against liquor. It was supervised by the Committee on Patriotic Service of the national WCTU, which in turn cooperated with the Department of Women in Industry of the Woman's Committee, the Woman's Division of the Council of National Defense, and the Federal Department of Labor. Together with all these agencies, the WCTU helped to facilitate women's large-scale entrance into the professional sphere and to protect them from discrimination.[82]

Minnesota's WCTU women also maintained close links with various war agencies in the state. Ella F. Hendrix of the WCTU, for instance, was a member of the State Committee of Moral Education, which was part of the MNCPS's Woman's Division. Individual WCTU women were also represented in other governmental bodies created in the context of the war. WCTU President Rozette Hendrix was appointed vice chairman of the Fifth Congressional District's Woman's Committee of the Council of National Defense, Minnesota Division. Della Mandigo, the WCTU's state treasurer, was a member of said Woman's Committee as well. Their work in the agencies helped the temperance women to influence war policies and to prove their expertise.[83]

Whereas Carl H. Chrislock has questioned whether their war work altered women's status in Minnesota and opened many doors to them, evidence suggests that this is exactly what happened. Multiple newspaper articles reveal that men greatly appreciated women's contributions to the war effort. Governor Burnquist similarly lauded women's war work by emphasizing that they "had vied with the men in patriotic endeavor in every field of service to the country." The praise and respect women had earned through their war agitation led to a greater male endorsement of the constitutional suffrage amendment. In a 1918 speech, Burnquist drew a connection between women's war efforts and the adoption of woman suffrage. Men seem to have felt that after women's great achievements in the war, they could not deny them the ballot. Minnesota's governor thus agreed with President Wilson who announced shortly before the election of 1918: "We have made partners of the women in this war. Shall we admit them only to a partnership of suffering and sacrifice and toil and not to a partnership of privilege and right?" Women were to receive the right to vote as a reward for their patriotic services but also to ensure their continued participation in the war effort. In addition, the war rhetoric of democracy was convincingly appropriated by activists to argue in favor of suffrage. Just like prohibition, suffrage had, to a great extent, become a war measure.[84]

In his inaugural address of 1919, Governor Burnquist recommended to the legislature the adoption of a resolution requesting Congress to submit a national suffrage amendment to the states. Pressured by seventy-one organizations in the Twin Cities, including the Minnesota Dry Federation, the legislature passed it. The bill for a constitutional suffrage amendment for Minnesota was voted down again, but this time at the request of various women's organizations, including the WCTU, whose leaders considered it "unwise and inexpedient." They wanted to wait for a federal suffrage amendment rather than passing a state suffrage amendment. By June 1919, Congress had passed the proposed amendment and gave it to the states for ratification. Therefore, in mid-August, at the request of Minnesota's female suffrage supporters, Governor Burnquist issued a call for a special session of the state legislature on September 8, 1919. "The proposed

Woman Suffrage Amendment," he declared, "involves the electoral rights of five hundred thousand persons within our commonwealth and millions of the citizens of our country." After this emphatic appeal and floods of petitions from the WCTU and various suffrage organizations, the Minnesota legislature ratified the National Suffrage Amendment with a vote of 120 to 6 (House) and 60 to 5 (Senate). Even longtime suffrage opponents, such as Senator George H. Sullivan, advocated it. By August 18, 1920, the amendment was ratified by a sufficient number of states. For the first time, women's public identity was formally and officially acknowledged.[85]

The ratification of the National Suffrage Amendment marked a caesura in women's struggle for emancipation. Making women official players in the dominant public sphere, it signified a paradigm shift in gender relations. Historical developments, such as the war, had greatly boosted women's formal admission to the public sphere and tipped the scales in favor of suffrage. However, it had been the decade-long activism of the WCTU and similar organizations that had laid the groundwork for the emergence of a female consciousness, solidarity, self-confidence, and expertise. It had facilitated women's gradual entrance into the male public sphere, first blurring the boundaries between the spheres only to render them virtually obsolete by the twentieth century. Temperance activism had indeed been a stepping stone toward emancipation.

Conclusion

The battle about temperance reform in Minnesota has revealed that the temperance movement influenced and was influenced by a large number of complexly interwoven and constantly interacting identity discourses, among them ethnic identity, gender, class, civic and religious identity. While being connected to (inter)national historical, social, political, and economic developments, this movement was an intensely local experience, negotiated by social actors on the ground. Greater (inter)national developments and particular local circumstances thus coalesced in a movement that greatly impacted the daily lives of a great variety of actors—men and women, young people, laborers and members of the middle and upper classes, immigrants and native-born Americans, liquor manufacturers and sellers, rural and urban residents, African Americans and Native Americans, ritualists and pietists. Are we really what we drink? This question will now be answered conclusively by reviewing the insights gained from the exploration of the construction and interaction of the aforementioned identities within Minnesota's temperance movement and by reflecting on the repercussions of these insights on our understanding of identity.

As this study has argued, the temperance movement served as a catalyst of ethnic identity construction and negotiation for both German and Irish Americans. It caused German Americans to invent and Irish Americans to renegotiate their ethnic identities and to reposition themselves in the Anglo-American society. The temperance movement was one of the real-life contexts in which negotiations of ethnic identities took place.

While the majority of Minnesota's Irish Americans did not join the movement in person, it still had strong reverberations among the Irish as a group. Intense intraethnic debates on the role of liquor and liquor consumption and the many exhortations and appeals of Irish American temperance reformers fractured long-held beliefs that excessive whiskey consumption was respectable and an integral constituent of Irishness. The "hunger of the Irish to be accepted as Americans"[1] was so great that many of them were willing to renegotiate Irish American ethnic identity, putting a strong emphasis on sobriety. The Irish American temperance societies' welfare provisions, their educational and cultural impetus, the professional successes of their members, and their strengthening of intraethnic networks turned them into motors of Irish American community building and social, intellectual, and cultural uplift. Besides encouraging many Irish Americans to strive for social advancement, the Catholic temperance movement also succeeded in engendering the formation of cross-class and cross-ethnic alliances that further enhanced its members' social and professional standing.

While the temperance movement inspired many Irish Americans to renegotiate their ethnicity, it helped Minnesota's Germans to invent a German American identity. Offending German American cultural sensibilities and endangering their economic well-being, the temperance movement bound German Americans together in the defense of their interests and helped them to realize their commonality in ethnic terms. Their anti-temperance activism can be interpreted as a cradle of ethnicity because it forced German Americans to define the contents of their ethnic identity and strengthened their ethnic consciousness—at least temporarily. It was thus an effective defense against rapid absorption by the Anglo-American society.[2]

The fight against temperance and the newly created German American ethnic identity proved unable to eradicate the many internal divisions within the German American community and to weather historical developments. Mostly due to the intersection of ethnicity and religion, the German American anti-temperance coalition crumbled from the turn of the century on. Additionally, the German American associational world witnessed a slow decline beginning in the 1890s, when German immigration had passed its peak and the second generation gradually turned away from its parents' culture. World War I and the concomitant anti-German hysteria and the harassment by the MNCPS at first heightened ethnic unity among Minnesota's German Americans but in the long run made the public expression of German American ethnicity virtually impossible. After the war, German Americans had to reinvent their German American ethnic identity. This "subdued" ethnicity, as Russell A. Kazal has called it, was, however, based on altered cultural patterns and was far more distant from its German origins.[3]

Besides impacting the formation of ethnic identities, the campaigns for or against liquor were one factor that, along with a variety of other reform movements and historical circumstances, ultimately contributed to the construction of a female public identity. While antebellum female temperance activism was not about identity politics for the majority of Minnesota women, from the 1880s on, the all-female Minnesota WCTU increasingly offered a space to them to address their exclusion from the male public sphere, to encourage society and the state to improve women's economic and social situation, and to establish a female voice in the public sphere, which would not accept being ignored again. The WCTU functioned as a counterpublic in which Minnesota's Anglo-American middle-class women could engage in counter-discourses that made them question their socially assigned roles and conceptualize themselves as political and public beings. In this counterpublic, women trained themselves as leaders, gained confidence as agitators, and were politicized, which over time made them confident and experienced enough to work alongside men. It thereby provided an institutional base permitting female reformers to gradually enter the realm of the male public sphere and was an access route to political life. While a considerable number of Minnesota's WCTU leaders were suffragists and belonged to the leadership and rank and file of the state's various suffrage organizations, many of its members did initially not question existing gender roles and were intimidated by women's rights rhetoric. What greatly contributed to the WCTU's success was its strategic appropriation of conventional gender images in order to gradually acquaint the grass roots with women's right arguments and to slowly move them along the path of emancipation.

Besides ethnicity and female identity, civic identity is the third category of identification this book has put center stage in the context of the temperance movement. In St. Paul, the temperance movement consolidated the city as an anti-temperance space, and aversion to temperance became an integral part of being a St. Paulite. The debates about alcohol consumption caused different urban cultures with their specific cultural, religious, political, and social ideologies to clash. Through these clashes, a discursive space emerged, in which St. Paul's civic identity could be discussed and negotiated, a process that could at times be rather tedious and painful. Despite the social tensions that were temporarily created, in the long run the struggles over temperance strengthened the antireformist culture assigned at the city's founding, shared by the majority of city residents, and rhetorically perpetuated and politically implemented by civic leaders in response to the city residents' cultural and economic needs. The debates about liquor turned St. Paul into the acknowledged bulwark of liberality throughout Minnesota. The supporters of reform, by contrast, identified with Minneapolis. From the 1880s on, Minneapolis was increasingly employed by St. Paulites in order to define what they were not, as St. Paul's constitutive outside.

Until World War I, St. Paul's antireformist camp far outnumbered the reformers and therefore managed to ward off their attacks on the city's liquor culture, making only minor concessions. The reformers achieved temporary successes only when the state intervened on their behalf and forced St. Paul's authorities to locally implement the state liquor laws by defining the limits of home rule. The forces of global history finally brought about what the temperance reformers had failed to accomplish. In the wake of World War I, St. Paul's civic alliances unraveled, and St. Paulites could not uphold their predilection for alcohol and their aversion to temperance, at least not openly.

Finally, my close-grained study of contemporaries' agitation for or against temperance on the ground has brought to light the constant interactions between people's multiple layers of identity. The temperance movement forced individuals and groups to make strategic decisions of identification, emphasizing one identity over the other(s) or reformulating single identities. Such strategic repositioning often resulted in a changed or modified attitude toward the temperance movement. The temperance movement often caused ethnic and religious identities to conflict. Catholic and pietistic German Americans were cross-pressured between their ethnocultural and religious identities, emphasized their religious over their ethnic identity, and consequently modified their attitude toward the temperance movement. Female and ethnic identities could also collide within the temperance movement. German American and most Irish American women put a greater emphasis on their ethnic than on their gender identity and largely abstained from political involvement or downplayed it if necessary. Class also intersected with ethnic or religious identities in the context of the fight against liquor. Many workers, even if they were pietistic or belonged to an ethnic group generally supportive of temperance, were opposed to the movement either out of economic interest or solidarity with their coworkers. The ranks of the Irish Catholic temperance movement, by contrast, featured a large number of laborers who were driven by a longing for upward mobility and greater cultural accommodation. These ethnic longings superseded their class loyalties.

Identities could, however, also reinforce each other and the individual's or group's attitude toward the temperance movement. Being Anglo-American and middle class or Anglo-American and female tended to strengthen activism in favor of temperance. The same applied to belonging to a pietistic denomination and being female or Anglo-American or Scandinavian American. Being German American and liturgical or nonsectarian increased the opposition to the temperance movement.

All ethnic, class, religious, and gender identities influenced the shape of St. Paul's civic identity. St. Paul's liberal alcohol culture and joie de vivre was reinforced by the presence of a large number of German Americans and by the city's Catholicism. Moreover, the great number of workers employed by the liquor industry also strengthened the state capital's infatuation with liquor. St.

Paul's civic identity, in turn, had an impact on its residents' attitudes toward the temperance movement. It had at least a moderating influence on the majority of its residents if it did not encourage outright opposition to the temperance movement. St. Paul's civic identity reinforced the opposition to temperance of most German Americans, some Anglo-Americans, and all those employed in the liquor business. It had a moderating influence on the Irish temperance supporters, whose civic consciousness and wish to climb the civic social ladder made a comparably moderate course obligatory. Even many of the more radical Anglo-American reformers often stepped back from their radicalism arguing that it was uncalled for or premature in a city like St. Paul. Some of them also tried to keep their radical temperance activism secret in order not to risk their reputation and political and economic careers in the city.

While St. Paul's civic identity could temper reformers, it more often radicalized them, acting as the engine behind their agitation. The city's supposed moral laxness and cultural openness provoked women to enter the traditionally male spheres of the saloon, the courts, and the town hall. It also often led to a lack of identification with the city and to a salience of other identities. Many of the most radical temperance reformers were latecomers and thus largely oblivious to the city's internal workings. Appalled by what they perceived and unable to place it within their framework of identities, they emphasized their religious and ethnic identities. Many radical reformers also used the city as a foil against whose cultural implications they defined themselves. As the Midway area, St. Paul's only reformist enclave, demonstrates, such counter-identities often caused a sense of alienation and resulted in spatial and social segregation.

What do all these findings contribute to our understanding of identity? The interpretation of the temperance movement as a catalyst of identity construction and negotiation enhances our conceptualization of identity itself. The choices of what to drink, the forms of consumption—moderate, excessive drinking, or total abstinence—as well as spaces, places, and practices of drinking are constituent elements of one's self-definition and figure prominently in the construction of a wide variety of identities, such as gender, ethnic, civic, religious, and social identities.

Scholars have often dismissed food and, by implication, drink as inferior to "other kinds of social acts or cultural expressions." Food has by now managed to shed much of its inferior status. Whereas before the 1930s, it was not regarded "as a legitimate subject of historical enquiry," in 1988 Claude Fischler stated: "Food is central to our sense of identity."[4] An ever-growing body of scholarship has interpreted food as a significant element in processes of identification and cultural differentiation, in the past as well as in the present, and as a sign of group identity and social cohesion. In their introduction to a compilation of interdisciplinary essays on food, Tobias Döring, Markus Heide, and Susanne Mühleisen have emphasized that

> [f]ood has always operated to define homes as well as cultural otherness. It is an essential part of the discursive practices that determine a community's insiders and outsiders. Eating, in this ethnic sense, does not only produce cultural meaning; it also draws boundaries between "us" and "them" and defines notions of "here" and "there." In its very materiality, food seems to bind cultural identities locally.[5]

Although food and drink are closely related to each other, the role of drink, in particular alcohol, in such processes of identification and cultural differentiation has long been neglected or inappropriately subsumed under the heading of food. While there has been an increasing but variable interest in the study of alcohol and culture by anthropologists and ethnographers since the 1970s, alcohol and drinking behavior have mostly not been the primary focus of research but, as Dwight Heath has termed it, a "felicitous by-product" of other research interests. In addition, induced by the American political war on alcohol and drugs since the late 1980s and the ensuing funding imperatives, many anthropologists have adopted a problem perspective, that is, they have largely focused on drinking problems and suggested preventive measures. An exception is Mary Douglas's 1987 edited collection *Constructive Drinking*, in which she stresses the significant role alcohol plays in marking the boundaries of personal and group identities.[6]

Since the beginning of the twenty-first century, calls by anthropologists for a reevaluation of studies on alcohol and drinking have become increasingly loud and have led to the publication of several excellent studies, mostly by anthropologists but also by historians.[7] In particular, anthropologist Thomas M. Wilson's edited volumes on the relationship between alcohol and ethnic, local, and national identities have demonstrated that alcohol "is not a peripheral or easily discarded menu item in the preparation of many identities" but rather "a main course, of food, of action, and of value." "[D]rink," Wilson has argued, "is one of the most noticeable, emotional and important ways in which people express and discuss their identities and culture." Drinking is "an act of identification, of differentiation and integration." Due to the centrality of drink for the construction, maintenance, and transformation of identities, Wilson has called for more research exploring the multiple facets of people's drinking behavior and practices and their acts of self-definition.[8]

In response to his call, this book has shed light on the role of liquor as a marker of identity in nineteenth- and twentieth-century Minnesota. It has demonstrated that the decision of what to drink was directly connected to the economic, cultural, political, religious, and social aspirations of the various people and groups involved in the struggles for or against temperance and had a great impact on the constructions of their respective identities and their making and unmaking of group boundaries. Therefore, following Donna Gabaccia's catchy slogan "we are what we eat," I would similarly argue that "we are what we drink." Of course, there is much more to one's identity than food or drink, and not all kinds of food and drink bear the same symbolic meaning. Nevertheless, in nineteenth- and early-twentieth-century Minnesota, liquor—its use or the abstinence from it—was a building block in the construction of a wide variety of identities. It is therefore high time for more scholars to take a closer look at precisely this "discarded menu item."[9]

Notes

Introduction

1. Throughout this book, *liquor* refers to alcoholic drinks in general and does not merely refer to alcoholic beverages made by distillation.

2. WCTU of MN Records, box 5: Eva Jones journal, 1908–1914, 26 Sept. 1908.

3. Throughout this book, the terms *temperance* and *total abstinence* are used synonymously. Although the first American temperance societies, founded on the East Coast from 1808 on, interpreted temperance as moderation and accepted the moderate use of liquor, from the mid-1830s on, temperance activists generally promoted total abstinence from all sorts of liquor. In Minnesota's temperance movement, which began in the late 1840s only, temperance almost always took the form of total abstinence. If temperance is to be understood as moderation in the book, it will be explicitly mentioned. Blocker, *Cycles* 32–33, 38–39, 53; Lender and Martin 66–68.

4. Blocker, *Cycles* xii; Rosenzweig 117. Cf. Gusfield; Tyrrell, *Sobering Up.*

5. Murdock; Parsons; Martin. While Bruce Dorsey's and Holly Berkley Fletcher's studies need to be praised for their achievement of "locat[ing] within temperance competing discourses based on race, class, . . . generational conflict," and gender, their analyses mostly pertain to the development of categories of manhood and womanhood within the reform context. Other categories of identity are only taken into account in relation to gender. Fletcher 4.

6. Fletcher 5.

7. Only two scholars have dedicated one chapter of their books to Irish American temperance activism: Moloney, *Lay Groups*; Quinn, *Father Mathew's Crusade.* Irish American temperance activism is also addressed by Meagher, *Inventing Irish America.* For an institutional history of the national CTAV, see Bland.

8. Vecoli, "Inter-Ethnic Perspective" 234.

9. Dyer; Mattingly; Dunlap; Boyle; Fletcher; Martin.

10. Examples of such feminist approaches are DuBois 66, 68–69; Epstein 133, 146, 148; Bordin, *Woman and Temperance* xv, xvii, xxiv, xxvi, 158–59.

11. McCammon and Campbell 241.

12. Most of the existing studies with a microscopic approach have concentrated on the Eastern United States (P. Johnson; Rosenzweig; Meagher, *Inventing Irish America*; Dorsey), while a few have investigated the alcohol question in the South or West (Coker; Noel; Klein). So far, there has been only one study on the Midwest, Jed Dannenbaum's monograph on Cincinnati. Dannenbaum, however, does not use "place" as an analytical category, treats ethnic identity only in passing, and ends his survey with the founding of the WCTU, so that the most significant facets of female temperance activism in the Midwest elude him.

13. Cayton and Gray 4, 26.

14. There is not much literature on the temperance movement in Minnesota. Besides the insightful yet short chapter in Hoverson, see Reardon, "Beginning," "Total Abstinence"; Scovell; Ellingsen; Carmody; Kerr; Samuels; Tikalsky. The latter contributions are either outdated or unpublished and limited in scope.

15. Trounstine 611, 612.

16. Hall 3, 4. Cf. Huntington 27; Cerulo 387; Brubaker and Cooper 1.

17. I will use the terms *Germans* and *German Americans*, *Irish* and *Irish Americans*, and *Scandinavians* and *Scandinavian Americans* interchangeably throughout this study. Their use does not express differences between first- and second-generation ethnics.

18. This conceptualization of ethnicity is drawn from the various theoretical approaches to ethnicity by Vecoli, "Ethnicity"; Barth; Sollors, *Beyond Ethnicity*, "Invention," "Theories"; Nagel, *Ethnic Renewal*; Cornell and Hartmann.

19. Glazer and Moynihan 17–19. Cf. Cohen 83. For a discussion of instrumentalism, see Cornell and Hartmann 58–66.

20. Vecoli, "Ethnicity" 161. For a discussion of primordialism, see Geertz, 41–42; Cornell and Hartmann 51–58; Spickard 20–22.

21. Conzen et al. 4–6, 13, 15, 31–32.

22. Staggenborg 8–11, 32–35.

23. Ryan, "Public Access" 269, 273, 281, 286; Fraser 59, 61, 62, 67, 73.

24. Kerber 27.

25. Ibid.

26. Gieryn 464–65.

27. Fullilove 1520; Gieryn 466, 473, 479. Cf. ibid. 479–80, 482; Fullilove 1516–17; Abbott 698; Burgess 654–55.

28. Czaplicka 375.

29. Wingerd, *Claiming* 4. For similar emphases on the significance of culture as an interpretive paradigm, see Gilfoyle 180, 184, 188; Connolly 262.

30. Wingerd, *Claiming* 9.

31. Gilfoyle 189–90. For a similar opinion, see Ryan, *Civic Wars* 3, 11, 18, 308.

32. Hall 4.

33. Ibid.; Huntington 23; Kazal 3–4.

34. The number of African American women in the Minnesota WCTU was extremely small, and I did not uncover material reflecting independent African American female temperance activism. By contrast, Scandinavian American women were active players

in the Minnesota WCTU. Even though the WCTU records themselves do not inform us about the activities and mindset of single Scandinavian American WCTU reformers, Minnesota's Scandinavian newspapers might be of value for a study on the role of Scandinavian American women in the state's temperance movement. This book mostly focuses on Anglo-American, German American, and Irish American women. I leave it to future scholars to examine the role of other ethnic groups in the temperance movement.

35. All articles from the German-speaking press cited in this book are my own translations.

Chapter 1. "Westward the Jug of Empire"

1. Twain 505.

2. Wingerd, *North Country* 57–58. Cf. ibid. 25, 44, 53, 55, 59, 66–68, 83–84; Frank, Moore, and Ames 348.

3. Hansen 141. Cf. Folwell 1: 86, 138; Mancall 12–13, 16, 21.

4. Ellingsen 2, 5; Wingerd, *North Country* 82, 95; Hansen 140, 144–45; Folwell 1: 165–66.

5. *MN P* 2 Aug. 1849: 2; Folwell 1: 209, 211; Letterman 13.

6. *MNCR* 20 Oct. 1849: 2; *MN P* 8 Nov. 1849: 1; Folwell 1: 166; Seymour 45–47; *MN P* 23 Aug. 1849: 2; Ellingsen 8–9.

7. Frank, Moore, and Ames 348.

8. Qtd. in Jones 70 and Wingerd, *North Country* 58.

9. *MN P* 12 May 1849: 2; 23 Aug. 1849: 2; 8 Nov. 1849: 1; Carmody 41–42; Ellingsen 10–11; Hansen 145; Seymour 45–47.

10. Rumbarger 69–71, 82, 85; Martin 106–23.

11. Qtd. in Wingerd, *North Country* 240. Cf. *MN Democrat* 24 Dec. 1851: 3; 28 Jan. 1852: 2; *w Minnesotian* 3, 31 Jan. 1852: 2, 3; Rice 58; Tyrrell, *Sobering Up* 252–78.

12. Ahlstrom 422.

13. Jarchow 21–22; *w Minnesotian* 16 Oct. 1852: 2; *Minutes of the Minnesota Baptist Association 1852* 6–7; Congregational Association of Central Minnesota 1, 5, 11.

14. Kleppner, *Cross* 71, 73; Gusfield 35, 55, 85, 196; Tyrrell, *Sobering Up* 125–26, "Economic Change" 46, 55, 61; Blocker, *Cycles* 36, 54–58.

15. *St. Anthony Express* 24 Jan. 1852: 1. Cf. Ellingsen 37; *MN Democrat* 24 Dec. 1851: 3; 28 Jan. 1852: 2; *w Minnesotian* 3 Jan. 1852: 3.

16. *w Minnesotian* 21 Feb. 1852: 2. Cf. *MN P* 3 Mar. 1853: 2; *St. Anthony Express* 7 Feb. 1852: 2; John W. North and Family Papers, reel 1, Ann Loomis North, letter to her grandmother, 20 Feb. 1852; Minnesota Legislative Assembly, folder: Legislative Assembly, Petitions 1851; Castle 1: 33. The signature of Joseph R. Brown, a prominent fur and whiskey trader, can be found on one of the pro-prohibition petitions from Ramsey County.

17. *Journal of the House of Representatives during the Third Session* 126–27; *MN P* 11 Mar. 1852: 2; Ellingsen 44–45; *w Minnesotian* 28 Feb. 1852: 2; Carmody 65.

18. *Session Laws 1852* 12–18; Le Duc 20–21.

19. Alexander Ramsey Family Papers, box 32, folder: Ramsey Diary 1852, 4 Apr. 1852; *w Minnesotian* 21 Feb. 1852: 2; *MN P* 4 Mar. 1852: 2; 1, 15 Apr. 1852: 2; *MN Democrat* 19 May 1852: 2.

20. *MN Democrat* 3, 17 Mar. 1853: 2, 3.

21. Alexander Ramsey Family Papers, box 32, folder: Ramsey Diary 1852, 4 Apr. 1852. Cf. Benson, "New England" 93; Bushrod W. Lott Correspondence, letter from L. Robberts [*sic*] and C. Cohn to Bushrod and Murray [*sic*], 2 Mar. 1852.

22. *MN P* 8 Apr. 1852: 2. Cf. Ellingsen 53; *MN Democrat* 1 Dec. 1852: 2; *MN P* 6 May, 9 Dec. 1852: 2.

23. John W. North and Family Papers, reel 2, Ann Loomis North, letter to her parents, 13 Feb. 1853; Ann Loomis North, letter to her grandmother, 9 Jan. 1853; Minnesota Legislative Assembly, Joint Committee, folder: Legislative Assembly, MSA, Petitions 1851, 1853; Benson, "New England" 97; *St. Anthony Express* 17 Dec. 1852: 3; *MN P* 30 Dec. 1852: 2; 13 Jan., 3 Mar. 1853: 2; *Journal of the Council of Minnesota* 41, 62, 74; Folwell 1: 283; *MN SZ* 28 Sept. 1867: 3; *Report of the Executive Committee of the American Temperance Union* 8, 9; *w Minnesotian* 4, 11 Mar., 1854: 2; *MN Republican* 5 Oct. 1854: 2; 18 Jan. 1855: 2; *Journal of the Council of the Territory* 195, 277, Appendix; *Journal of the House of Representatives during the Fifth Session* 188, 215–16, 227.

24. *w Minnesotian* 17 Apr. 1852: 2. Cf. *MN Democrat* 14 Apr. 1852: 3; 19 May 1852: 2; *MN P* 3 Mar. 1853: 2; *St. Anthony Express* 25 Feb. 1853: 2.

25. Anderson and Blegen, box 1, folder 1849–1860, Party Platform 1854. Cf. Gilfillan 171; *MN P* 30 June 1853: 2; *St. Anthony Express* 24 June 1853: 2; 9 July 1853: 2; *North-Western Democrat* 13 July 1853: 2, 3; Minnesota Legislative Assembly, Joint Committee, folder: Legislative Assembly, Petitions 1851, 1853; Wingerd, *North Country* 91, 226, 243.

26. Folwell 1: 374–75; Gilfillan 171; Chrislock, "German-American Role" 104.

27. Gilman 19.

28. Ames 171.

29. *SP d Times* 28 July 1855: 2. Cf. Gilman 19; *MN Republican* 5 Oct. 1854: 2; 11 Jan., 26 July, 2 Aug. 1855: 2; *w Minnesotian* 26 July 1855: 2; Folwell 1: 375; Ellingsen 29, 81; Anderson and Blegen, box 1, folder 1849–1860, Party Platform 1855; Wingerd, *North Country* 243–44.

30. Anderson and Blegen, box 1, folder 1849–1860, Party Platform 1856.

31. Castle 1: 38.

32. Qtd. in Castle 1: 33 and Neill 509. Cf. ibid. 458–59; Folwell 1: 166, 213–21; Kunz 5–6; Schaefer 35; Wingerd, *Claiming* 19–20, *North Country* 157–60.

33. Wingerd, *Claiming* 19–20; Williams 66. Cf. ibid. 64–65; Schaefer 35; Kunz 5–6; Stevens 11; Neill 64–65, 478–80; Folwell 1: 219.

34. Schaefer 35, 44; Kunz 9, 13; Neill 481; Williams 109, 111; Folwell 1: 223–24; Castle 1: 120; Bishop 53; Wingerd, *Claiming* 28; Wills 54.

35. Qtd. in Williams 113. Cf. ibid. 108.

36. Wingerd, *Claiming* 26, 106; Schaefer 53–55, 63–64; Rudnick 114–49; Kunz 13.

37. *MNCR* 4 Aug. 1849: 2. Cf. Hathaway 35; William Pitt Murray and Family Papers, box 3, folder: Biographical Data, "Hon. William Pitt Murray," 1–8; Wingerd, *Claiming* 39.

38. Rice 55, 57–59; Castle 1: 120; Bishop 53; Kunz 13; Wingerd, *Claiming* 28; Wills 54.

39. Gray 2. Cf. Kleppner, *Third Electoral System* 59; Power 5.

40. Qtd. in Rice 59.

41. Qtd. in Berthel 182–83; Conzen, "Swisshelm" 103.

42. Qtd. in Wingerd, *North Country* 240.

43. Qtd. in Marti 5 and Wills 11. Cf. *MN P* 23 Jan. 1850: 2; Rice 58.

44. Qtd. in Marti 4 and Bishop 51. Cf. Berthel 82–83; Benson, "New England" 17; *MN P* 15 Apr. 1852: 2; William Pitt Murray and Family Papers, box 2, folder: vol. 2 Clippings Scrapbook, undated, 1885–1923, "Memories of Early St. Paul" 9–11; Conzen, "Swisshelm" 103, 110; Wingerd, *North Country* 205.

45. *MN P* 23 Jan. 1850: 2; Benson, "New England" 41, 42, 45, 56–61.

46. Fisher, letter to Arthur J. Donnelly; William Pitt Murray and Family Papers, box 2, folder: vol. 2 Clippings Scrapbook, undated, 1885–1923, "Memories of Early St. Paul" 9–11.

47. *MN P* 10 Nov. 1849: 2. Cf. Pegram 12–17; Blocker, *Cycles* 8–11.

48. Bishop 99, 101, 105–7; Shurtleff 29–32.

49. The Sons of Temperance had been founded in New York in 1842. It was the first secret society based on total abstinence principles.

50. Qtd. in Benson, "New England" 88. Cf. ibid. 89; *MN P* 4, 19 May 1849: 2; *MNCR* 10 Nov. 1849: 4; Daniels 195–97; Blocker, *Cycles* 48; Bishop 105; Newson 62, 84, 77, 92; Castle 1: 55–56, 85.

51. *MN P* 1 Nov. 1849: 3; 10 Nov. 1849: 2; *MNCR* 27 Oct. 1849: 2; Newson 66; Ellingsen 29–30.

52. *MNCR* 10 Nov. 1849: 1; Bishop 109; Ellingsen 31; Treasurer's Book.

53. *MN P* 25 Mar 1852: 2. Cf. *w Minnesotian* 3 Apr. 1852: 2.

54. CTAU of St. Paul, box 1, Catholic Temperance Society of St. Paul, Proceedings, Constitution, By-Laws, 1852–1853. Cf. Treasurer's Book; *MN Democrat* 28 Jan. 1852: 2; *w Minnesotian* 24 Jan. 1852: 2.

55. *MN P* 6 May, 8 July 1852: 2; Berthel 174; Ellingsen 53.

56. Williams 323. Cf. Alexander Ramsey and Family Papers, box 32, folder: Ramsey Diary 1852, 8 Apr., 16 Aug. 1852; *MN P* 19 Aug. 1852: 2; Berthel 66; Ellingsen 60–61; *MN Republican* 18 Jan. 1855: 2; Hennessy 79; Le Duc 20–21.

57. Bishop 111.

58. St. Paul City Council, Original Entry Ordinances No. 1 to 80; *w Minnesotian* 29 Apr. 1854: 3; *MN Republican* 15 Feb. 1855: 2; 5 Oct., 9 Nov. 1854: 2. In 1850, the city's population had been 1,338; by 1860 it had leapt to 10,279. In 1860, foreign-born and mixed Germans and Irish made up about 26 percent and 27.4 percent of Ramsey County's population, respectively; Anglo-Americans from New England and the Middle Atlantic states constituted about 23.6 percent of the County's inhabitants. Rice 61–62; Regan, "The Irish" 131, 140; H. Johnson 159; *Eighth Census of the United States.*

59. MN Federal Writers' Project frame 428; Wingerd, *Claiming* 22, 28–29, 32; Kunz 13, 16, 23, 28, 41, 52; Williams 369–81, 467; Folwell 1: 352, 363–64; Neill Appendix; Benson, *Families* 28; Rudnick 8.

60. Wingerd, *Claiming* 40, 41; Regan, *Irish* 2–3, 6, 7–17, "Irish" 132, 140–42; Blessing 545. The Celtic-Irish immigrants were overwhelmingly members of the Roman Catholic Church. The Scotch-Irish, or Ulster-Scots, were mostly uncompromising Presbyterians. Since the latter were very few in number in Minnesota and therefore hard to trace, they will not be considered in this study.

61. Regan, *Irish* 30; Stivers 140–42; Knobel 32, 55, 76, 80, 88. For a detailed overview of Irish employment patterns in St. Paul, see Benson, *Families* 286–89.

62. Qtd. in Regan, "Irish" 140 and O'Fahey 22.

63. Carmody 31–37, 43–45; Reardon, "Beginning" 199–200.

64. Qtd. in Quinn, *Father Mathew's Crusade* 157. Cf. ibid. 47–56, 155–68, 180–83; Quinn, "Father Mathew's Disciples" 624–28; Tyrrell, *Sobering Up* 299; Moloney, "Combatting" 6; Reardon, "Catholic Total Abstinence" 46, 66, 76; Blocker, *Cycles* 70; Bland 8, 17, 33–41, 45–46; Moloney, *Lay Groups* 44–46.

65. Carmody 55–59; Quinn, "Father Mathew's Disciples" 628.

66. CTAU of St. Paul, box 1, Catholic Temperance Society of St. Paul, Proceedings, Constitution, By-Laws, 1852–1853; Newson 261.

67. CTAU of St. Paul, box 1, Catholic Temperance Society of St. Paul, Proceedings, Constitution, By-Laws, 1852–1853.

68. John W. North and Family Papers, reel 1, John North, letter to his parents-in-law, 22 Feb. 1852. Cf. ibid. Ann Loomis North, letter to her grandmother, 20 Feb. 1852; Minnesota Legislative Assembly, folder: Legislative Assembly, Petitions 1853; CTAU of St. Paul Collection, box 1, Catholic Temperance Society of St. Paul, Proceedings, Constitution, By-Laws, 1852–1853.

69. CTAU of St. Paul Collection, box 1, Catholic Temperance Society of St. Paul, Proceedings, Constitution, By-Laws, 1852–1853.

70. *w Minnesotian* 2 Apr. 1853: 2; CTAU of St. Paul, box 1, Catholic Temperance Society of St. Paul, Proceedings, Constitution, By-Laws, 1852–1853.

71. Keller, letter to Archbishop Ireland, 16 Oct. 1895.

72. Bishop 51; Carmody 67–68; Minnesota Legislative Assembly, folder: Legislative Assembly, Petitions 1851, 1853.

73. CTAU of St. Paul Collection, box 1, Catholic Temperance Society of St. Paul, Proceedings, Constitution, By-Laws, 1852–1853; Carmody 73–74.

74. Keller, letter to Archbishop Ireland, 10 Mar. 1895.

75. H. Johnson 159. The Irish element in Minnesota was not nearly as strong as the German element. In 1860, every eighth Minnesotan was Irish-born or of Irish parentage; in 1880, it was only every tenth. Regan, "Irish" 132.

76. Kulas 40–41; Arndt and Olson 220; H. Johnson 158–59, 169; Schmid 132; Conzen, *Germans* 5.

77. H. Johnson 153; Bonney 23; Gross 42–46.

78. *MN Democrat* 28 Apr. 1852: 2. Cf. Wingerd, *Claiming* 36–37; Wills 78; Benson, *Families* 286–89.

79. H. Johnson 169–74; Conzen, *Germans* 4, 51–52, 57; Massmann 215–16; Rudnick 50–65; Mussgang 13–96.

80. For more information on the development of German cultural and national identity, see Dann; Schönemann.

81. Nagel, "Constructing Ethnicity" 162. Cf. Hoverson 288, 292; Brueggemann 8; Conzen, "Germans" 417, *Milwaukee* 157; Gabaccia 78–79, 98–99; Doerries 115–17.

82. Newson 367, 477, 482, 523, 573; Hoverson 17, 28, 287–90.

83. H. Johnson 158–59; Ellingsen 84–85; *MN SZ* 1 Oct. 1859: 2.

84. *SP d Times* 24 Aug. 1855: 2. Cf. *d P* 23, 24, 30 Aug. 1855: 2; *MN Republican* 19 July 1855: 2; Anderson and Blegen, box 1, folder 1849–1860, Party Platform 1855; Wingerd, *North Country* 243–44.

85. Kleppner, *Third* 185–97, *Cross of Culture* 71–75; Jensen 58, 63–68.

86. *MN Deutsche Zeitung* 26 Sept., 3 Oct. 1857: 3; H. Johnson 170; *w Minnesotian* 2 Apr. 1853: 2; Conzen, *Germans* 50; Minnesota Legislative Assembly, folder: Legislative Assembly, Petitions 1851; *MN SZ* 24 Sept. 1859: 2.

87. MN Federal Writers' Project, reel 121, frames 433, 437; *w Minnesotian* 15 May 1858: 3.

88. Rosenzweig 57; Kingsdale 472. Cf. Rosenzweig 35–40, 51, 57; Martin 11, 15–38; Murdock 43–62; Dorsey 99.

89. *d Minnesotian* 22 May 1858: 3. Cf. Rosenzweig 61–63, 95; Powers 11–25.

90. *MN SZ* 31 July, 14 Aug. 1858: 2; 4 Sept. 1858: 3.

91. *MN SZ* 7 Aug. 1858: 4; Ramsey County, St. Paul, City Council, Journals, Council Proceedings 17 Aug. 1858: 165.

92. *d P and Democrat* 18 Aug. 1858: 2. Cf. ibid. 19, 24 Aug. 1858: 1; *d Minnesotian* 28 Aug. 1858: 2.

93. *General Laws of the State of Minnesota, First Session* 186–90; *MN SZ* 3 Mar. 1860: 3; *MN State News* 3 Mar. 1860: 2; *Journal of the House of Representatives, Second Legislature* 574, 581–82; *Journal of the Senate, Second Legislature* 624; *General Laws of the State of Minnesota, Second Session* 184–85, 215; Hathaway 37–38.

94. IOGT Papers, Journal of Proceedings of the Grand Lodge 23, 132.

95. Dorchester 452–71. Cf. Ellingsen 122, 125; Hathaway 37–38; Duis 16–17.

96. *SP d Press* 26 Jan. 1861: 1. Cf. *Minutes of the Minnesota Annual Conference of the ME Church 1860* 27; *d P and Democrat* 18, 27 Jan. 1861: 1.

97. *d P and Democrat* 22, 24, 27 Jan. 1861: 1; *MN SZ* 26 Jan. 1861: 3; *SP d Press* 26, 30 Jan. 1861: 1; *w P and Democrat* 25 Jan. 1861: 3.

98. *General and Special Laws of the State of Minnesota, Fourth Session* 113. Cf. *d P and Democrat* 4 Mar. 1862: 1; *MN SZ* 9 May 1863: 4; *Minutes of the Sixth Annual Session of the General Conference of Congregational Churches in Minnesota* 8.

99. Bordin, *Woman and Temperance* 7–12; Baker 637; Epstein 103; Dorsey 97.

100. Dorsey 109; Fletcher 15, 18. Cf. Dorsey 124, 130–31.

101. *MNCR* 10 Nov. 1849: 1; *MN P* 8 Apr., 25 Mar. 1852: 2; Noel 11–20. See also Tyrrell, *Sobering Up* 21–22; Dorsey 92–93.

102. Bishop 107–8, 110; Minnesota, Legislative Assembly, folder: Legislative Assembly, Petitions 1851, Petitions 1851; John W. North Family Papers, 1849–1938, reel 1, Ann Loomis North, letter to her parents, 6 Feb. 1852, letters to her grandmother, 20 Feb. 1852, 9 Jan. 1853; *w Minnesotian* 21 Feb. 1852: 2; *MN P* 8 July 1852: 2; Berthel 174; CTAU of St. Paul Collection, box 1, Catholic Temperance Society of St. Paul, Proceedings, Constitution, By-Laws, 1852–1853.

103. *MN P* 30 June 1853: 2; *St. Anthony Express* 24 June, 17 Sept. 1853: 2.

104. *MN P* 3 Mar. 1853: 2; *St. Anthony Express* 25 Feb. 1853: 2; Fletcher 16. Cf. *w Minnesotian* 21 Feb. 1852: 2; *MN P* 1, 15 Apr. 1852: 2; *MN Democrat* 19 May 1852: 2.

105. *MN P* 25 Dec. 1851: 3. Cf. Hoffert 18–19. For the role of women on the frontier, see also Riley; Jameson.

106. O'Fahey 2–3, 24–25; IOGT Papers, Journal of Proceedings 4, 8, 19, 50, 53; Daniels 199–200; Ellingsen 104–6.

107. *d P and Democrat* 23 Oct. 1858: 1; 18 Jan. 1861: 1; *SP d Times* 1 Dec. 1858: 2; IOGT, Journal of Proceedings 97.

108. Cf., for instance, John W. North and Family Papers, 1, Ann Loomis North, letter to her grandmother, 20 Feb. 1852.

109. *St. Anthony Express* 17 July 1853: 2, 3.

110. *MN P* 3 Mar. 1853: 2; *St. Anthony Express* 25 Feb. 1853: 2.

111. IOGT, Grand Lodge of MN, Collection of Proceedings, Sixth Annual Session 17; IOGT Papers, Journal of Proceedings 8. Cf. ibid. 43–44, 53, 76–79, 87–88, 95; *Falls Evening News* 5, 7 Apr. 1860: 2; *SP d Press* 8 May 1861: 1; Ellingsen 94, 100, 134; Fletcher 59.

112. *MN SZ* 10 June 1865: 3.

Chapter 2. Organizing into Blocs

1. Cayton and Gray 19; Holmquist 3.

2. Szymanski 19, 25. Cf. ibid. 37; Rumbarger 64, 70.

3. *SP w P* 8 Mar. 1867: 2. Cf. IOGT Papers, Journal of Proceedings of the Grand Lodge 5, 8, 18; *SP w P* 18 May 1866: 5; *Minutes of the Minnesota Annual Conference of the ME Church 1865* 36; *MN SZ* 2, 9 Mar. 1867: 3; *MN VB* 27, 28 Feb. 1867: 1, 2, 5, 6; 8 Mar. 1867: 1; *SP d P* 1 Aug. 1867: 1.

4. *SP w P* 20 Sept. 1867: 2, 3. Cf. *MN SZ* 17 Aug. 1867: 3; 21 Sept. 1867: 4, 6.

5. Kleppner, *Cross of Culture* 169–70, *Third* 235–36.

6. Dannenbaum, *Drink and Disorder* 201, "Origins" 245; *d P and Democrat* 25 Sept., 6, 7 Oct. 1869: 1; 13, 14 May 1869: 1; *MN VB* 14 Oct. 1869: 4.

7. *d P and Democrat* 21 Sept., 3, 4, Nov. 1869: 1; 8 Oct. 1869: 4; 12 Oct. 1869: 1, 4; *SP w P* 20 May 1870: 2; 13 Oct. 1871: 8; *MN VB* 17 Nov. 1870: 4; *WTH* 11, 14 Oct. 1871: 2; *SP d Dispatch* 11 Oct. 1871: 2; Anderson and Blegen, box 1, folder 1861–1872, Party Platforms 1871; White 156–57.

8. Jarchow 32; *MN SZ* triweekly 30 Jan. 1872: 1; *DW* 25 Jan. 1873: 1747; 8 Feb. 1873: 1763; *General Laws of the State of Minnesota, Twelfth Session* 92–93; Dannenbaum, *Drink and Disorder* 81.

9. *WTH* 14 Oct. 1871: 2; Jarchow 30–33; *SP w P* 16 Sept. 1870: 2; 21 Oct. 1870: 3; 10 Nov. 1871: 3, 6; 22 Dec. 1871: 1; *SP d Dispatch* 20 Nov. 1871: 2.

10. *WTH* 29 Aug. 1872: 2. Cf. *MN VB* 25 Jan. 1872: 3; 6, 20 Feb. 1873: 3; *SP d Dispatch* 30 Jan. 1872: 2; 30, 31 Jan. 1872: 4; 12 Feb. 1872: 2; *MN SZ* triweekly 8, 15 Feb. 1872: 1; *Minneapolis d Tribune* 11, 12 Sept. 1872: 4; *MN SZ* 1 Feb. 1873: 1; *SP d P* 23 Jan. 1874: 2; 12 Feb. 1874: 4; 14 Feb. 1874: 2, 4; *DW* 6 Feb. 1875: 2593; 20 Feb. 1875: 2611.

11. The term *liquor interests* was used by contemporaries and in all of the existing literature at the time to refer to both the brewers and hard liquor producers. Due to such contemporary lack of differentiation, it is extremely difficult, if not impossible, to differentiate between the precise involvement of each group in the fight against the temperance movement.

12. For more information about the membership and the activities of these organizations, see the section "German Americans for Personal Liberty" in this chapter.

13. Sons of Temperance, *Minutes of the Grand Division* 3, 15, 16, 19; Jarchow 38; IOGT, Grand Lodge of MN, Collection of Proceedings, 1876: 6, 8, 22–23, 25; *SP d Dispatch* 30 Oct. 1876: 4; 5 Feb. 1877: 2; *d PP* 26 Jan. 1877: 4; 15 Feb. 1877: 6; *Owatonna Journal* 31 Aug., 7 Sept. 1876: 3.

14. *SP d Dispatch* 5 Feb. 1877: 2; *d PP* 26 Jan. 1877: 4; 15 Feb. 1877: 6; 14 Feb. 1878: 3; 15 Feb. 1878: 4, 6; 24 Jan., 20 Feb. 1879: 3; 24 Jan. 1881: 17, 47; Minutes of the WCTU, vol. 1, 1879: 34–35.

15. Marion P. and William W. Satterlee Papers, box 1, Scrapbook and miscellaneous items. Cf. *d P and Democrat* 7 Oct. 1869: 1; *w PP* 10 Nov. 1871: 3, 6; *SP w Dispatch* 27 June 1873: 1; *Temperance Campaign* 18 Oct. 1873: 1; Hudson 88.

16. Austin Willey Papers, folder: Scrapbooks and Miscellaneous Newspaper Clippings Relating to Anti-Slavery and Temperance, 45; Minutes of the WCTU, vol. 1, 1879: 34–35; *d PP* 24 Jan. 1881: 17; 15, 16 Feb. 1882: 6; *Topic* Oct. 1883: 2.

17. *d VZ* 14, 15, 16 Feb. 1883: 3; *DW* 17 Feb. 1883: 6039; *d PP* 12, 15 Aug. 1882: 7; 15 Feb. 1883: 5; 17 Feb. 1883: 10; *Christian Friend* Dec. 1882: 1; Apr. 1883: 1; June 1883: 1; Austin Willey Papers, folder: Scrapbooks and Miscellaneous Newspaper Clippings Relating to Anti-Slavery and Temperance, 88–89, 107–8; *Citizen* 3 Sept. 1890: 1; IOGT, Grand Lodge of MN, Collection of Proceedings, 1860–1902, 1882: 7, 19, 31, 1884: 33.

18. *To-Day* July 1883: 1. Cf. ibid. Aug. 1883: 1; *d PP* 1 Jan. 1883: 4; IOGT, Grand Lodge of MN, Collection of Proceedings, 1884: 9.

19. *w PP* 10 Apr. 1884: 5. Cf. *d PP* 1 Jan. 1883: 4; Woolley and Johnson 178; Christianson 162–63.

20. Bland 269–70; *d PP* 13 Jan., 17, 18 Feb. 1885: 7; *NWC* 19 Feb. 1885: 1.

21. *SP d Globe* 10 Feb. 1887: 4. Cf. *d VZ* 2 Mar. 1883: 3; 1 Nov., 24 Dec. 1884: 3; *d PP* 1 Mar. 1883: 5; 13, 25 Feb. 1885: 7; 3 Mar. 1885: 3, 7; 21 Feb., 3 Mar. 1885: 5; 25 Feb., 3, 6 Mar. 1885: 7; *w PP* 12 Feb. 1885: 1; 26 Feb. 1885: 1, 4; 12 Mar. 1885: 4, 6; 30 July 1885: 2; *DW* 26 Feb. 1885: 1, 5; 7 May 1885: 5; *NWC* 14 Aug., 25 Sept., 2, 16, 30 Oct. 1884: 4; 15 Jan., 19 Feb. 1885: 1, 4; 22 Jan. 1885: 4; 26 Feb., 5 Mar. 1885: 1; 12 Mar. 1885: 1, 4; 19 Mar., 7 May, 4 June 1885: 4; *To-Day* Mar. 1885: 4.

22. Anderson and Blegen, box 1, folder 1883–1894, Party Platform 1886.

23. *NWC* 26 Aug. 1886: 4; 9 Sept. 1886: 2, 4; 23 Sept. 1886: 4; 7 Oct. 1886: 4, 8; *d VZ* 7 Sept. 1886: 3; White 160–64. All of this is not to suggest that the complexities of voting behavior in those years can be reduced to the temperance phenomenon alone. Kleppner, for instance, points out that the effects of the economic depression of the early 1870s, as well as the revival of a redeveloped Democratic Party in the former slave states, were also responsible for cutting into Republican voting support. Kleppner, *Third* 120–40.

24. *Minneapolis Tribune* 10 Feb. 1887: 2. Cf. 8, 9 Feb. 1887: 4; 10 Feb. 1887: 1; *d PP* 10, 12 Feb. 1887: 4; *NWC* 6 Jan. 1887: 4; 27 Jan., 3 Feb. 1887: 4–5; *DW* 3 Feb. 1887: 4, 8.

25. Folwell 3: 175; Downard 111; *d VZ* 25 Jan., 1, 10 Feb. 1887: 2; 28 Jan. 1887: 2, 3.

26. See also Kleppner, *Third* 58, 321.

27. Wingerd, *Claiming* 2–4, 34–36, 66; Wills 120.

28. William Pitt Murray and Family Papers, box 2, folder: 1897–1901, "The Mayors of St. Paul," 4–5. Cf. Writers' Program of the WPA 30–31. Occasional skirmishes about the Sunday Law erupted in 1867 and 1869, but were successfully and quickly negotiated by the respective mayors and the city councils. Cf. *MN VB* 17 July 1867: 4; 18 Oct. 1867: 1; *SP d P* 14 July 1867: 3; 21, 28 July: 1867: 1; 24, 25 July 1867: 2; *MN SZ* 27 July, 17 Aug. 1867: 6; *NWC* 8 May 1869: 4; *d P and Democrat* 27 Apr. 1869: 4; 2 May 1869: 1; 25 May 1869: 2.

29. Doutney 605, 607; *SP d Dispatch* 6 June 1877: 1; 13 June 1877: 4; Anderson H. Wimbish Papers, box 1, folder: Correspondence and Miscellaneous Papers 1870–1877,

letters to his wife 4 June 1876; Neill 416–17; IOGT, Grand Lodge of MN, Collection of Proceedings, 1878: 59–62; Wingerd, *Claiming* 8, 77; Taylor 21–22, 76; Williams 416; Minutes of the WCTU, vol. 1, 1878: 16; *Tenth Census* 538.

30. H. Johnson 159; Wingerd, *Claiming* 49.

31. William Pitt Murray and Family Papers, box 2, folder: 1897–1901, "The Mayors of St. Paul," 7–8.

32. *SP d Dispatch* 2 May 1883: 3; *d PP* 3, 7 June 1883: 8; 6 June 1883: 4, 5; 7 June, 9 Aug. 1883: 7; 11, 17 June 1883: 8; 29 Mar. 1885: 8; 1 Apr. 1885: 4; *Topic* Oct. 1883: 3; Best 94–96; William Pitt Murray and Family Papers, box 2, folder: 1897–1901, "The Mayors of St. Paul," 7–8; Regan, *Irish* 36. For examples of the use of the O'Brien parable, see *d VZ* 27 July 1891: 3; *Our Side* 9 Sept. 1915: 4.

33. *d PP* 12 Aug. 1882: 7; Rice 58; Kleppner, *Third* 206; Methodist Episcopal Church/ Minnesota Annual Conference/Historical Society, box 3, Minutes, St. Paul District 1881–1886.

34. *NWC* 30 Dec. 1882: 4, 8; *d VZ* 20 Dec. 1882: 3.

35. *w PP* 10 Apr. 1884: 5. Cf. ibid. 10 Apr. 1884: 5; *d PP* 6 Apr. 1884: 4; 7, 9, 10 Apr. 1884: 7; *d VZ* 8, 10 Apr. 1884: 2; 9 Apr. 1884: 3; *DW* 10 Apr. 1884: 5; 17 Apr. 1884: 7; Kulas 230; Newson 155. For information on the Minneapolis patrol limits, see Hathaway 5, 89–93.

36. *d PP* 30 Apr. 1884: 7; Wingerd, *Claiming* 32–35; Wills 81–82, 143.

37. *d PP* 2 May 1884: 4.

38. *d VZ* 7 May 1884: 3; *d PP* 31 Mar. 1886: 4. Cf. ibid. 2, 3 May 1885: 4, 6; 4 May, 15 June 1885: 7; 6, 7 May 1885: 4, 7; *DW* 8, 15 May 1884: 5.

39. *DW* 1 Apr. 1886: 8. Cf. ibid. 4 Feb. 1886: 4; 18 Mar., 1 Apr. 1886: 8; *d PP* 14 Mar. 1886: 4; 31 Mar. 1886: 1; *SP d Globe* 30 Mar. 1886: 1; *NWC* 25 Mar. 1886: 5; 1 Apr. 1886: 4–5; *d VZ* 24 Mar. 1886: 3; Newson 415, 456, 529, 262. The first League was founded in Chicago in 1877. In 1886, there existed six hundred local Law and Order Leagues in thirteen states with an aggregate membership of more than 100,000. Since 1883, there was also a Citizens' Law and Order League of the United States, founded by the representatives of twenty-seven Law and Order Leagues. Cherrington, *Evolution* 217; Blair 496, 498; Szymanski 54–56.

40. *DW* 8 Apr., 19 Aug. 1886: 8; *SP d Globe* 6 Apr. 1886: 2; *NWC* 29 Apr., 12 Aug. 1886: 4; 14 Oct. 1886: 4.

41. *d VZ* 7 Aug. 1886: 1. Cf. ibid. 30 Mar., 11 Aug. 1886: 3; 13 Aug. 1886: 2, 3; *Minneapolis Tribune* 11 Aug. 1886: 3; *NWC* 12 Aug., 14 Oct. 1886: 4; *DW* 18 Mar., 1, 8, 15 Apr. 1886: 8.

42. *d PP* 6, 10, 12 Feb. 1887: 4.

43. *d PP* 12, 13 Feb. 1887: 4, 5. Cf. ibid. 3 Mar. 1887: 8; *d VZ* 10 Feb. 1887: 3; *NWC* 3 Mar. 1887: 7.

44. *SP d Globe* 3 Mar. 1887: 2, 5, 6.

45. *SP d Globe* 3 Mar. 1887: 2, 5, 6. Cf. ibid. 4 Mar. 1887: 5; *d VZ* 3 Mar. 1887: 2; *d PP* 3 Mar. 1887: 8.

46. Gusfield 4; Conzen et al. 16.

47. Dorsey 221–22; Quinn, *Father Mathew's Crusade* 42–46; Stivers 17–22; Lender and Martin 59; Barret 18–19, 21–23; Diner 85; Townend 9–11; Malcolm, *Ireland Sober* 1–55, "Rise of the Pub" 55–64; Wittke 48.

48. Diner 136; Stivers 136. Cf. ibid. 53, 65–66, 74, 86–90, 103, 128–29, 140–42, 157–61, 166; Meagher, *Inventing Irish America* 35, *Columbia Guide* 89–90; Hathaway 139.

49. Conzen et al. 12; qtd. in Quinn, *Father Mathew's Crusade* 180. Cf. ibid. 47–56, 155–68, 181–83; Meagher, *Inventing Irish America* 200, *Columbia Guide* 103, 105; Moloney, *Lay Groups* 51; Stivers 166, 158.

50. Qtd. in O'Connell 106. Cf. *NWC* 13 Jan. 1872: 4–5; 7 May 1885: 1; CTAU of St. Paul Collection, box 1, folder: Father Mathew Total Abstinence Society St. Paul, Proceedings and Minutes 1869–1871, 10 Jan. 1869; Reardon, "Total Abstinence" 46, 48; Green 74; Regan, "Irish" 144; Carmody 96.

51. Moloney, *Lay Groups* 55; Newson 732. Cf. ibid. 710; CTAU of St. Paul Collection, box 1, folder: Father Mathew Temperance Society of St. Paul, Constitution and By-Laws 1888, 4, 5, 10; folder: Father Mathew Total Abstinence Society St. Paul, Proceedings and Minutes 1869–1871, 261; *NWC* 27 Feb. 1869: 2, 4; 17 Apr. 1869: 4; Carmody 103.

52. CTAU of St. Paul Collection, box 1, folder: Father Mathew Total Abstinence Society St. Paul, Proceedings and Minutes 1869–1871, 110, 317; folder: CTAU of St. Paul: Meeting Minutes, Convention Proceedings 1872–1882, 1, 4, 5, 13, 25; *NWC* 16 Jan. 1869: 8; Reardon, "Total Abstinence" 60.

53. William Pitt Murray and Family Papers, box 4, folder: Winifred Murry Milne, undated and 1895–1928, "To Name Five Men. . . ." Cf. Wingerd, *Claiming* 106.

54. *NWC* 3 June 1882: n. pag. Cf. ibid. 13 Jan. 1872: 4–5; 18 Jan. 1889: 1, 8; O'Connell 107; Reardon, *Catholic Church* 223.

55. *NWC* 13 Mar. 1869: 4. Cf. ibid. 20 Mar. 1869: 1; Wingerd, *Claiming* 100; O'Connell 108, 112; Reardon, "Total Abstinence" 77, 83; Carmody 99; Green 82.

56. Jansenism came to Ireland through exiled French clerics, who had fled the Revolution in France. These clerics came to staff the Maynooth Seminary, founded in 1795, and were thus greatly responsible for imbuing Irish candidates for priesthood with their teachings. Ahlstrom 60; Shannon 22; Fennell 124–29, 180.

57. See, for instance, *Proceedings of the 8th Annual Convention of the CTAU of the Diocese of St. Paul* 7, 16.

58. Wingerd, *Claiming* 99; CTAU of St. Paul Collection, box 1, folder: Father Mathew Total Abstinence Society St. Paul, Proceedings and Minutes 1869–1871, 15, 21, 29, 32, 155, 163, 227; *DW* 7 Feb. 1884: 5; 14 Aug. 1884: 1; *d VZ* 29 Nov. 1884: 2. See also Reardon, "Total Abstinence" where all the societies founded in St. Paul are listed.

59. CTAU of St. Paul Collection, box 1, folder: Father Mathew Total Abstinence Society St. Paul, Proceedings and Minutes 1869–1871, 205, 207; Carmody 99, 109, 144, 153; Reardon, "Total Abstinence" 58, 71, 77, 83, *Catholic Church* 226; O'Connell 108, 114; Wingerd, *Claiming* 100; Green 82.

60. CTAU of St. Paul Collection, box 1, folder: CTAU of St. Paul: Meeting Minutes, Convention Proceedings 1872–1882, 43; Carmody 150–51.

61. For my calculation, I used the numerical mean of the 1875 and 1876 figures. Two caveats are attached to this percentage. First, the County's slowly emerging third-generation Irish Americans were not captured by either the federal or state census, and their numerical presence on the records would have slightly lowered the percentage of Irish temperance reformers. However, the number of third-generation Irish Americans in

Ramsey County would have been small in the 1880s. Historians assert that the bulk of children of the Catholic immigrants of the 1840s and 1850s would reach maturity in the 1890s and early 1900s only. The lack of data on third-generation Irish is further evened out by the absence of women and girls in the numbers of temperance activists, as they were not allowed to take part in the organized male Irish Catholic temperance movement. Meagher, *Inventing Irish America* 103; Anderson H. Wimbish Papers, box 1, folder: Correspondence and Miscellaneous Paper 1870–1877, letters to his wife 4 June 1876; CTAU of St. Paul Collection, box 1, folder: CTAU of St. Paul: Meeting Minutes, Convention Proceedings 1872–1882, 3, 12, 23, 43, 65; folder: Father Mathew Total Abstinence Society St. Paul, Proceedings and Minutes 1869–1871, 36, 29, 297; Regan, "Irish" 131.

62. O'Brien 35–53; Williams 590; *d PP* 12, 15 Feb. 1874: 4; Newson 627–28; *d P and Democrat* 2, 8 June 1869: 1.

63. CTAU of St. Paul Collection, box 1, folder: Father Mathew Total Abstinence Society St. Paul, Proceedings and Minutes 1869–1871, 32; folder: Knights of St. Paul, Constitution and By-Laws, 1882, 4–5, 28; *SP d Globe* 26 June 1878: 4; 22 Feb. 1886: 2; Conzen, "Festive Culture" 48–49, 58, 66; Meagher, *Inventing Irish America* 176; Williams 416.

64. CTAU of St. Paul Collection, box 1, folder: Father Mathew Total Abstinence Society St. Paul, Proceedings and Minutes 1869–1871, 36, 47, 81, 89, 93, 95, 97, 105, 108, 115, 171, 149, 184, 197, 200, 223, 269; Williams 416; Newson 617; *Proceedings of the 8th Annual Convention of the CTAU of the Diocese of St. Paul* 4; *To-Day* July 1883: 1; *d PP* 13 Jan. 1885: 7.

65. Qtd. in O'Connell 109. Cf. *NWC* 30 Jan. 1869: 4; 13 Jan. 1872: 4–5; 27 Jan. 1872: 1, 5; *SP d P* 13 Jan. 1872: 4; 17 Jan. 1872: 2; Wittke 48; Carmody 103, 157, 162; Tyrrell, *Sobering Up* 300; Stivers 122; Reardon, "Total Abstinence" 49.

66. Moloney, *Lay Groups* 68; CTAU of St. Paul Collection, box 1, folder: Annual Convention Proceedings and Associated Papers, 1874–1909, 1884: 8. Cf. ibid. 1875: n. pag.; *NWC* 20 Mar. 1869: 4; 13 Jan. 1872: 4–5; 13 Apr. 1872: 4; Reardon, "Total Abstinence" 69.

67. *NWC* 23 June 1887: 3–4. For examples of Irish American and Anglo-American cooperation, see the section "St. Paul—From Civic Compromise to Civic Wars" in this chapter. For examples of conflicts between Irish Americans and German Americans, see the section "German Americans for Personal Liberty" in this chapter.

68. *NWC* 8 Apr. 1887: n. pag. Cf. ibid. 5 May 1887: 8; Folwell 3: 178; Bland 140. John Ireland was elected first vice president of the CTAU of America in 1873. Five years later, Bishop Joseph B. Cotter of Winona became its president and was succeeded by Reverend J. M. Cleary of Minneapolis in 1882. Carmody 150–51; Reardon, "Total Abstinence" 72; CTAU of St. Paul Collection, box 1, folder: CTAU of St. Paul: Meeting Minutes, Convention Proceedings 1872–1882, 23, 43; *Catholic Bulletin* 24 June 1911: 4; *NWC* 30 Apr. 1904: 5.

69. *NWC* 26 June 1873: n. pag.; *d PP* 4 Aug. 1882: n. pag.; Wingerd, *Claiming* 39. Cf. CTAU of St. Paul Collection, box 1, folder: Annual Convention Proceedings and Associated Papers, 1874–1909, 1887: 26.

70. See also Conzen, "Festive Culture" 48, 63.

71. *DW* 1 May 1869: 193. Cf. ibid. 8 Apr. 1876: 3077; *MN VB* 25 May 1876: 3; *MN SZ* triweekly 6 Feb. 1872: 2.

72. "Mucker," *Wörterbuch, Handwörterbuch*.

73. *MN SZ* triweekly 11 Feb. 1869: 1.

74. *Journal of the House of Representatives, Ninth Session* 284–85; *MN SZ* 2, 9 Mar. 1867: 3; *MN VB* 27, 28 Feb., 1, 2, 5, 6, 8 Mar. 1867: 1; 5, 6 Mar. 1867: 4.

75. H. Johnson 169; Wingerd, *Claiming* 100; Conzen, *Germans* 32; *DW* 5 Aug. 1876: n. pag.; *SP City Directory 1887–1888* 1360–66.

76. *MN VB* 28 Dec. 1871: 3. Cf. ibid. 25 Jan. 1872: 2; *MN SZ* triweekly 4, 27 Jan. 1872: 4; 11 Jan. 1872: 2; 20, 23, 30 Jan. 1872: 1; *DW* 10 Feb. 1872: 1347.

77. *MN VB* 17 July 1867: 1; *DW* 8 Feb. 1873: 1763. Cf. ibid. 1 Mar. 1873: 1787; *MN VB* 16 Jan., 27 Feb. 1873: 3.

78. *DW* 4 Nov. 1882: 5919. Cf. Nagel, "Constructing Ethnicity" 163; *MN VB* 18 July 1867: 1.

79. *MN SZ* triweekly 1 Feb. 1872: 1. Cf. ibid. 27 Jan. 1872: 4; *DW* 10 Feb. 1872: 1347; Rippley, "Banking" 97, 98; Rudnick 16; Conzen, *Germans in Minnesota* 11, 36, 59.

80. *MN SZ* 30 Jan 1872: 4. Cf. Castle 2: 560.

81. *MN SZ* triweekly 25 Feb. 1873: 1; *d PP* 22 Feb. 1873: 2; *DW* 22 Feb. 1873: 1779; 1 Mar. 1873: 1787; *Journal of the House of Representatives, Fifteenth Session* 229.

82. *SP w Dispatch* 27 June 1873: 1; *MN VB* 27 Apr. 1876: 3. Cf. ibid. 11, 18 May 1876: 3; Prohibition and Temperance Collection, box 4, folder 1: Pamphlets 1874–1882, Circular; *SP d Dispatch* 16 May 1876: 7; *DW* 6 May 1876: 3109; 13 May 1876: 3117; 20 May 1876: 3125; *MN SZ* triweekly 27 Apr. 1876: 4; "George Benz"; *MN SZ* triweekly 27 Apr. 1876: 4.

83. *d VZ* 16 Feb. 1883: 3; Barth 15; Kloß, translation mine.

84. *SP w P* 20 Sept. 1867: 1.

85. *DW* 3, 10 Feb. 1887: 4, 8.

86. *NWC* 7 Oct. 1886: 4, 8; *DW* 14, 21, 28 Oct. 1886: 4.

87. *d VZ* 31 Jan. 1887: 3; 2 Feb. 1887: 2.

88. *d VZ* 30 May 1887: 1. Cf. ibid. 12 Feb. 1887: 3; Wingerd, *Claiming* 106.

89. Fraser 67, 68.

90. Smith-Rosenberg 173; Fletcher 73–74; Cutter 154–95; Martin 151; Scott 58–77; Ginzberg 176; Stuhler, *Gentle Warriors* 19–23; Miscellaneous Records of the Legislature, 185[-]–1891, folder: Suffrage Petitions, undated and 1869; *MN VB* 17 Feb., 4 Mar. 1870: 3; 24, 25 Feb. 1870: 4; *SP w P* 1 Mar. 1867: 2; 1 Apr. 1870: 3, 6; 29 Apr. 1870: 3; *Journal of the House of Representatives, Ninth Session* 27; Nelson 772; Stearns 650–52; Sommerdorf and Ahlbrand 31.

91. Bordin, *Woman and Temperance* 7–12.

92. Ibid. 15, 29–38, 41; Blocker, "Separate Paths" 461–62; Epstein 98, 100; Blocker, *Cycles* 74–85; Dannenbaum, *Drink and Disorder* 212–20.

93. *SP d P* 24 Feb. 1874: 4; 11, 13 Feb. 1874: 1; 15 Feb. 1874: 1, 2; 7 Mar. 1874: 2.

94. *SP d P* 18 Mar. 1874: 4; *SP d Dispatch* 17 Mar. 1874: 5; *Grange Advance* 27 May 1874: 11; *St. Cloud Journal* 23 July 1874: 3; *Goodhue County Republican* 3 Sept. 1874: 4; Jarchow 35; Stearns 652.

95. *SP d Dispatch* 28 Apr. 1875: 4; *SP d P* 29 Apr. 1875: 4; William Pitt Murray and Family Papers, box 3, folder: Biographical Data, 1–8.

96. Qtd. in Sommerdorf, "Harriet Bishop" 13. Cf. *Fourth Annual Meeting, MN Sunday School Temperance League* 3, 9, 11, 12, 19, 23; Scovell 30–31.

97. Qtd. in Scovell 32, 34. Cf. ibid. 39, 40, 42–43.

98. Parsons 168. Cf. Scovell 45; Minutes of the WCTU, vol. 1, 1879: 15, 1881: 40–41; vol. 4, 1902: 30–31; Bordin, *Woman and Temperance* 57–58, 63.

99. Hurd 9; Political Equality Club of Minneapolis, folder: Records, Historical Data, 1905–1906, 1914–1915, 1920–1921, Experiences in Minnesota by Mrs. Alfred H. Bright 4.

100. Minutes of the WCTU, vol. 1, 1879: 15.

101. Ibid., vol. 1, 1879: 24, 1880: 43–45; vol. 2, 1887: 29–30; Epstein 121. The YWCTU was a temperance organization for young single women between fifteen and thirty years of age. Bands of Hope juvenile temperance societies, which had originally emerged in the British temperance movement, were initiated by the WCTU from the mid-1870s on. The first LTL was established by the national WCTU in 1890 and aimed at teaching temperance to children from age six through twelve. Garner 387–88; Cook 38, 154.

102. Minutes of the WCTU, vol. 1, 1879: 15; 1881: 40–41. Cf. ibid., vol. 1, 1879: 24, 1882: 15, 1883: 60–61, 1884: 13–14, 1885: 19; vol. 2, 1887: 29–30; *To-Day* Feb. 1885: 1; Mar. 1885: 4; *w PP* 30 July 1885: 2; Stearns 653–55; Political Equality Club of Minneapolis, folder: Records, Historical Data, 1905–1906, 1914–15, 1920–21, Experiences in Minnesota by Mrs. Alfred H. Bright 3; Stuhler, *Gentle Warriors* 28; Hurd 26; *SP w P* 3 May 1877: 3; *d PP* 22 Feb. 1878: 4; 7 July 1879: 3; 15, 16 Feb. 1882: 6; 21, 22, 24 Mar. 1883: 6; 25 Feb., 3, 6 Mar. 1885: 7; *SP w Globe* 17 May 1883: 2; Scovell 7, 78; *Christian Friend* Apr. 1883: 1.

103. *WTH* 14 Oct. 1871: 2, 3. Cf. Minutes of the WCTU, vol. 1, 1879: 34–35; *d PP* 24 Jan. 1879: 3; Political Equality Club of Minneapolis, folder: Records, Historical Data, 1905–1906, 1914–1915, 1920–1921, Experiences in Minnesota by Mrs. Alfred H. Bright 3; *SP d Dispatch* 20 Feb. 1879: 3.

104. Zimmerman 13–14, 21–22.

105. Minutes of the WCTU, vol. 2, 1887: 76. Cf. vol. 1, 1885: 24; Clifford 47–48.

106. Minutes of the WCTU, vol. 2, 1886: 18, 1887: 7, 29, 76–78; Clifford 50; *SP d Globe* 10 May 1882: 2; *d PP* 10 May 1882: 7. The Scientific Temperance Instruction Law was repealed in 1905 and replaced by a new law with much laxer provisions. Minutes of the WCTU, vol. 2, 1906: 34.

107. Bordin, *Women and Temperance* 95. Cf. Scovell 90.

Chapter 3. *"Talking against a Stonewall"*

1. *Western Leader* 6 June 1894: 2.

2. *NWC* 11 Aug. 1887: 4; 29 Sept. 1887: 6; *d VZ* 4 Aug. 1887: 3; 9 Jan. 1889: 1; *w PP* 14 June 1888: 4.

3. For the arrests for drunkenness and disorderly conduct in 1887, I used the numbers 3,408/2,138 in my calculations. The police year of 1887 had fourteen months. I have population estimates only for the years 1885 (111,397), 1887 (130,000), and 1890 (133,000). My calculations are therefore based on the assumption of a linear population growth in St. Paul (1886: 120,698.5; 1888: 131,000; 1889: 132,000). In 1886, the police arrested 2.13 percent/1.21 percent of St. Paul's total population for drunkenness and disorderly conduct. For 1887, the numbers were 2.62 percent/1.64 percent, for 1888, 2.67 percent/1.81 percent, and for 1889, 2.61 percent/1.84 percent. The per capita production of malt liquors was 9.19 gallons in 1887 and 7.48 gallons in 1889. In 1887, no distilled liquors were produced.

In 1889, however, the per capita production of distilled liquors was 0.87 gallons. "Prohibition, Benefits of" 519, 521; Fanshawe 245. Cf. ibid. 241; Kunz 52; *d PP* 26 Feb. 1887: 4; Woolley and Johnson 197.

4. *d VZ* 22 Jan. 1889: 1; 30 Jan. 1889: 3; *w PP* 4, 5 Apr. 1888: 4; Kleppner, *Third* 329; *d PP* 16, 25 July 1888: 1; *Western Leader* 5 Apr. 1894: 3; IOGT, Grand Lodge of MN, Collection of Proceedings, 1888: 43–44, 1889: 9, 1892: 19, 1893: 10.

5. *MN VB* 17 Nov. 1870: 4.

6. Tikalsky 12–14.

7. Qtd. in Chrislock, *Progressive Era* 209. Cf. ibid., "Protest" 69–70; *d VZ* 18 Jan., 9, 16 Feb. 1893: 2; 21 Mar. 1893: 3; 8 Mar. 1895: 8; IOGT, Grand Lodge of MN, Collection of Proceedings, 1890: 30–32, 1891: 32, 1892: 9, 54; "Scandinavians in Minnesota," *New York Times* 26 July 1886.

8. While the first Farmers' Alliance groups were founded in Minnesota in the early 1880s, since 1886 the Alliance influenced the political scene more directly, fighting for a stringent regulation of transportation, a system of local grain inspection, and mechanisms controlling the markets. While it worked at first with the existing parties, in 1890 and 1892 it put up its own gubernatorial candidates, Sidney M. Owen and Ignatius Donnelly. In 1892, the Alliance split with a large faction joining the Minnesota People's Party. Minnesota's Populist parties drew an impressive amount of votes—in 1894, for instance, 29.7 percent of the gubernatorial vote. The fusion with the Democrats over the issue of "free silver" in 1896 signaled the decline of Populism in Minnesota. Folwell 3: 169, 187, 189; Chrislock, "Protest" 64, 76, 78, 85–86, 100, 124, *Progressive Era* 10–11; Gilman 33–42.

9. Chrislock, "Protest" 70–72. Cf. *d PP* 26 Feb. 1891: 1; *d VZ* 20 July 1892: 3.

10. *d VZ* 7 Mar. 1889: 2. Cf. ibid. 8, 20, 22 Mar. 1889: 3; *d PP* 8 Mar. 1889: 1, 4; *DW* 14 Feb. 1889: 4.

11. *d VZ* 9 Jan. 1889: 1; 30 Jan., 1 Feb. 1895: 8; 1 Mar. 1895: 5; *DW* 21 Nov. 1894: 12; 30 Jan. 1895: 7; *w PP* 5 Apr. 1888: 5.

12. *SP d Globe* 26 Feb 1893: 5. Cf. ibid. 6 June 1893: 8; *d PP* 26 Feb 1893: 8; "Legislators Past and Present."

13. The Young People's Society of Christian Endeavor was an interdenominational youth organization, founded in Maine in 1881. The Epworth League was the youth society of the Methodist Episcopal Church, first established in Ohio in 1889. Boyer 164.

14. *MN White Ribboner* Mar. 1897: 3. Cf. IOGT, Grand Lodge of MN, Collection of Proceedings, 1897: 109–10; *DW* 14 Oct. 1896: 12; *MN Issue* Sept. 1898: 37; *d VZ* 5 Feb., 6 Apr. 1897: 5; *d PP* 6 Apr. 1897: 3.

15. IOGT, Grand Lodge of MN, Collection of Proceedings, 1897: 143.

16. *d PP* 6 Feb. 1887: 4.

17. Massard-Guilbaud 800–1; *d PP* 26 Jan. 1891: 8. Cf. ibid. 12 Jan. 1891: 5; 19 Jan., 9 Feb. 1891: 8; *d VZ* 7 Feb. 1891: 3.

18. Boyer 162. Cf. *NWC* 21 Apr. 1893: 5.

19. *SP d Dispatch* 7 June 1877: 4; *d PP* 13 Jan. 1885: 7; *DW* 8 Apr. 1886: 8; *SP d Globe* 6 Apr. 1886: 2; Wingerd, *Claiming* 60. In the late nineteenth and early twentieth centuries, the term *Midway* was freely used to describe the area "midway" between Minneapolis

and St. Paul, that is, the so-called interurban district including such neighborhoods as Hamline, Merriam Park, Como Park, Macalester Park, Groveland Park, and St. Anthony Park. "Hamline Midway."

20. *NWC* 24 July 1891: 1; *d PP* 25 July 1891: 1. Cf. *d VZ* 2, 16 June 1890: 3; 27 July 1891: 3.

21. *d PP* 26 July 1891: 4; 28 July 1891: 1, 8; 30, 31 July 1891: 5; *d VZ* 2, 16 June 1890: 3; 28 July 1891: 2. Smith was mayor in St. Paul from 1887 to 1892, from 1894 to 1896, and from 1900 to 1908. Writers' Program of the WPA 45

22. *d VZ* 28 July 1891: 2; *d PP* 25 July 1891: 4. Cf. ibid. 25, 27 July 1891: 3.

23. *d PP* 3, 10 Aug. 1891: 5; *DW* 6, 13 Aug. 1891: 8; *SP City Directory 1890–1891*.

24. Brøndal 71–72.

25. Wingerd, *Claiming* 108. Cf. ibid. 79, 107; Anderson and Blanck 4–5; Lanegran 48; LeSueur 31–41; Chrislock, *Progressive Era* 33; Kleppner, *Third* 250.

26. *SP d Globe* 22 Apr. 1892: 6; *DW* 27 Apr. 1892: 9. Cf. *d PP* 22, 23 Apr., 4 May 1892: 4; *d VZ* 29, 30 Apr. 1892: 2, 3; Writers' Program of the WPA 47; *NWC* 29 Apr. 1892: 4. The term *wide-open* implies that the municipal authorities and the police had become deaf to any kind of regulation of the liquor traffic.

27. *d PP* 2 Aug. 1892: 8; 3 Aug. 1892: 4; *d VZ* 5 July 1892: 8; 2 Aug. 1892: 3; *SP d News* 2 Aug. 1892: 5; *DW* 13 July 1892: 8; *NWC* 24 June, 15 July, 5 Aug. 1892: 4.

28. *NWC* 3 Mar. 1893: 5; *d VZ* 21 Jan., 22, 24 Mar. 1893: 3; 18 Apr. 1893: 2.

29. *d PP* 21 Feb. 1893: 1. Cf. *d VZ* 21 Feb. 1893: 3.

30. Boyer 70; *d VZ* 3 May 1890: 3. Cf. also the letter from a German from Minneapolis: *d VZ* 26 Apr. 1890: 3.

31. *d DW* 8, 29 Mar. 1893: 8; *d VZ* 3 Mar. 1893: 3; *d PP* 3 Mar. 1893: 2; Wingerd, *Claiming* 301.

32. *d VZ* 12 Mar. 1894: 8; *DW* 9 May 1894: 12.

33. The Christian Citizenship League had been founded in November 1895 by the radical members of the Law and Order League. It aimed at enforcing all laws, especially those relating to saloons and gambling houses. *NWC* 22 Nov. 1895: 5.

34. *d PP* 18 Apr. 1897: 2; 16, 20 Apr. 1897: 10; 21 Apr. 1897: 5; *d VZ* 19, 20, 24 Apr. 1897: 5; 29, 30 Apr. 1897: 4, 5, 6; 21 May 1897: 5; 27 May, 13 Sept. 1897: 8; 18 June 1897: 6; 19 Apr. 1898: 5.

35. The Paulist Fathers constituted a quasi-pietistic, Jansenist wing of the Roman Catholic Church and therefore provided most of the leadership of the Catholic temperance movement. Between 1870 and 1900, the Paulists claimed to have administered the pledge to roughly thirty thousand men and women during their parish missions. Dolan 147–58, 241; Quinn, "Father Mathew's Disciples" 629, 631.

36. Reardon, "Total Abstinence" 76, 91–92; *Proceedings of the 17th Annual Convention of the CTAU* 14–16, 26, Appendix 2; *Proceedings of the 18th Annual Convention of the CTAU* 5, 15; *NWC* 8 Mar., 21 June, 12 July 1889: 1; 5 Dec. 1890: 7; *Proceedings of the 20th Annual Convention of the CTAU* 19–20; CTAU of St. Paul Collection, box 1, folder: Annual Convention Proceedings and Associated Papers, Proceedings 1892: 17–18.

37. *NWC* 8 Mar., 21 June 1889: 1; Regan, *Irish* 6; Meagher, *Columbia Guide* 176. Sources do not mention the precise date of this informal meeting at Stillwater.

38. *Proceedings of the 18th Annual Convention of the CTAU* 16. Cf. *NWC* 17 July 1891: 7; 24 June 1892: 1; 30 June 1893: 7.

39. Moloney, *Lay Groups* 62–64; Meagher, *Inventing Irish America* 167.

40. *NWC* 31 Jan. 1890: 4. Cf. ibid. 21, 28 Feb. 1890: 4; Moloney, *Lay Groups* 63–64; Meagher, *Columbia Guide* 180–81.

41. CTAU of St. Paul Collection, box 1, folder: Annual Convention Proceedings and Associated Papers, Proceedings 1892: 27. Cf. *Proceedings of the 18th Annual Convention of the CTAU* 43; *Proceedings of the 20th Annual Convention of the CTAU* 34.

42. *Proceedings of the 17th Annual Convention of the CTAU* Appendix 2; *Proceedings of the 20th Annual Convention of the CTAU* 15–16.

43. *NWC* 13 Apr., 2 Mar., 23 Mar., 7 Dec. 1888: 5; 18 Jan. 1889: 1, 8; 21 June 1895: 2; *Proceedings of the 17th Annual Convention of the CTAU* Appendix 3.

44. *NWC* 7 Dec. 1888: 5; 5, 18 Apr. 1889: 5; 3 Jan., 5, 19 Apr. 1890: 5; 25 Apr. 1890: 1; 2 May 1890: 1; 27 June 1890: 1, 4, 5, Supplement; 21 Oct. 1892: 5; 21 Apr. 1893: 5; 18 Jan. 1895: 3; 13 Dec. 1895: 5; CTAU of St. Paul Collection, box 1, folder: Crusaders' Total Abstinence Society, Playbills, Announcements, Invitations, etc., 1890–1903; *Proceedings of the 17th Annual Convention of the CTAU* Appendix 4. At the time, there were not many black Catholics in St. Paul. Only one parish, St. Peter Claver Church in the Rondo neighborhood, served African American parishioners since 1892. In the mid-1890s, the parish founded its own temperance society. Wingerd, *Claiming* 78; *SP City Directory 1895*; *DW* 8 Aug. 1894: 6; *d PP* 13 Jan. 1891: 10.

45. *NWC* 27 June 1890: 1, 4, 5, Supplement. Cf. ibid. 18 June 1897: 4.

46. *Proceedings of the 17th Annual Convention of the CTAU* 14–16; *NWC* 3 Aug. 1894: 9; 18 Jan. 1895: 2; 28 Feb. 1896: 2; 21 Oct. 1900: 5; CTAU of St. Paul Collection, box 1, folder: Catholic Total Abstinence Benefit Association 1899; box 2, folder: Convention Proceedings, Proceedings 1898: 93.

47. *NWC* 26 June 1896: 2; 1 Sept. 1900: 5.

48. *d VZ* 1 Oct. 1889: 3. Cf. ibid. 8 Oct. 1889: 3; Kazal 67–78.

49. CTAU of St. Paul Collection, box 1, folder: CTAU of St. Paul: Meeting Minutes, Convention Proceedings 1872–1882, 59; *DW* 21 July 1898: 1. Cf. ibid. 14 Mar. 1889: 1, 4; 18 June 1891: 1; Gleason, *Conservative Reformers* 29–45, *Keeping the Faith* 41; Bland 61; Moloney, "Combating 'Whiskey's Work'" 2, 11; Quinn, *Father Mathew's Crusade* 9, 172; Green 83; Doerries 278; Wittke 93.

50. *DW* 21 July 1898: 1; *d VZ* 3 Aug. 1894: 8. Cf. *NWC* 18 Jan. 1889: 1, 8.

51. *DW* 18 Feb., 5 Mar., 8 Oct., 19 Dec. 1891: 1; Wolkerstorfer, *"You shall be my people"* 35; Kleppner, *Cross of Culture* 123–40, 145–46, 159–60; O'Connell 290, 304–6. For John Ireland's advocacy of state schools, see *DW* 7 July 1890: 1.

52. *DW* 10 Apr. 1890: 4. Cf. ibid. 19 Dec. 1889: 1; 17 Apr. 1890: 1; 5 May 1890: 3.

53. *DW* 19 Dec. 1889: 1. For an example of German Americans' complaints about Ireland's Americanizing rhetoric against them, see *DW* 20 Oct. 1897: 1.

54. *DW* 8 Aug. 1894: 6; Bland 182–83.

55. *DW* 7 Nov. 1894: 2. Messmer suggested that this organization should be a temperance rather than a total abstinence organization, so that all Catholics could identify with

it. However, the CTAU was not ready to accept any proposition short of total abstinence. Bland 191–93.

56. Evangelical Association of North America, MN Conference, reel 1, 1873: 8, 1875: 5, 1881: 4, 1882: 9–10, 1883: 9, 1884: 9, 1885: 6, 1886: 6, 1887: 5; reel 2, 1889: 5–6, 30, 1890: 25, 1891, 1892: 20, 1896: 21, 1896: 25–26, 1897: 29, 1898: 29; Utzinger 15–16, 37.

57. *SP City Directory 1890–1891*; *d VZ* 9 Mar. 1889: 3. The German Total Abstinence Society of Minnesota, initiated by the WCTU and founded in St. Paul in November 1900, was claimed to be the first German American state temperance society in the country. The Edelweiß Lodge of the IOGT was established in the Twin Cities in 1911. *d PP* 26 Nov. 1900: 4; *DW* 28 Nov. 1900: 12; *d VZ* 2 Nov. 1911: 10.

58. Minutes of the WCTU, vol. 2, 1891: 95–96.

59. Ibid., 1892: 69–73. Cf. ibid. 1888: 55–56, 1889: 60, 74, 1890: 18–19, 1891: 18, 105; vol. 3, 1894: 17–21, 1897: 68; *d VZ* 18 Jan. 1893: 2. In 1891, the WCTU consisted of 250 unions and 25 YWCTUs, with a membership of 3,633 and 546, respectively. Their 121 LTLs and Bands of Hope had an aggregate membership of 5,099. Considering that there were 610,928 women in Minnesota in 1890, the WCTU constituted a small but efficiently organized corps of workers that could certainly not wipe out all social, economic, and political inequalities but through its activism was able to achieve smaller successes and to influence the mindset of men, women, young people, and children. *Eleventh Census 1890*; Minutes of the WCTU, vol. 2, 1891: 101.

60. Minutes of the WCTU, vol. 2, 1888: 73; vol. 3, 1895: 17–18. Cf. ibid., vol. 2, 1890: 101–2.

61. *MN White Ribboner* 1 July 1890: 5; Minutes of the WCTU, vol. 3, 1891: 101, 1895: 63, 67; *d VZ* 11 Mar., 18 Apr. 1891: 2; 8 Apr. 1891: 3; 9, 11 Apr. 1895: 8; *DW* 17 Apr. 1895: 7. See also Julia Bullard Nelson's satirical poem "Hans Dunderkopf's Views of Equality," parodying German Americans' view on woman suffrage. *MN White Ribbon* Nov. 1905: 3.

62. Stuhler, "Organizing for the Vote" 295; "Nelson, Julia Bullard" 364–65; Minutes of the WCTU, vol. 3, 1893–1896; Scovell 7; *MN White Ribboner* 1 July, 1 Sept. 1890: 1; Deo 44; K. Kerr 18. For examples of Nelson's progressive views, see her poem "That Certain Sphere" in the *MN White Ribbon* Sept. 1904: 1.

63. Minutes of the WCTU, vol. 4, 1900: 28.

64. Smith-Rosenberg 176–77, 256–57.

65. Deutsch 4. Cf. *d VZ* 20 Feb., 6, 7, 18, 28 Mar. 1896: 5; 3, 19 Mar. 1896: 8; 4 Mar. 1896: 1; 21 Apr. 1896: 1; *d PP* 21 Apr. 1896: 4; *MN Issue* May 1900: 37; Minutes of the WCTU, vol. 3, 1896: 82.

66. Minutes of the WCTU, vol. 2, 1888: 60–61; 1891: 101, 1892: 57–58.

67. Ibid., vol. 3, 1890: 19. Cf. ibid. 1889: 12; vol. 5, 1909: 36; Pamphlets Relating to the Liquor Problem, folder: HV5006–5298, "An Open Letter from the Minneapolis Non-Partisan Woman's Christian Temperance Union"; IOGT, Grand Lodge of MN, Collection of Proceedings, 1895: 7, 10, 1897: 109.

68. Minutes of the WCTU, vol. 3, 1894: 7, 17–21; Bordin, *Willard* 168–70; Moloney, *Lay Groups* 66.

69. Minutes of the WCTU, vol. 1, 1883: 44–45; 1884: 59–61. Cf. ibid. 1883: 44–45; vol. 2, 1886: 27, 1890: 110–11, 1889: 88–89, 1891: 106, 1892: 67.

70. *DW* 8 Apr. 1896: 12; 9 Nov. 1905: 4. Cf. Minutes of the WCTU, vol. 2, 1886: 44, vol. 3, 1898: 68; vol. 4, 1900: 19, 32, 33, 70–71, 1902: 78, 105, 1903: 62, 1905: 71–72, 1906: 74; vol. 5, 1912: 6; vol. 6, 1913: 57; *MN White Ribbon* Aug. 1902, Feb. 1903: 4; Bordin, *Woman and Temperance* 86.

71. Minutes of the WCTU, vol. 1, 1885: 41; vol. 3, 1893: 48, 1894: 68, 1898: 79–80; vol. 4, 1902: 30–31, 1903: 63, 1905: 72; vol. 5, 1909: 80; K. Kerr 23, 48.

72. Minutes of the WCTU, vol. 4, 1900: 19; 1902: 36.

73. Minutes of the WCTU, vol. 4, 1900: 28, vol. 6, 1914: 65–66. Cf. ibid., vol. 4, 1902: 36; vol. 6, 1913: 56–57, 1915: 66.

74. *d PP* 8 Mar. 1889: 1, 4. Cf. ibid. 14 Nov. 1889: 4; 29 June 1893: 4; *d VZ* 18 July 1894: 8.

75. Minutes of the WCTU, vol. 3, 1895: 32. Cf. ibid., vol. 2, 1891: 98–99; vol. 3, 1896: 82.

Chapter 4. *"Putting on the Lid"*

1. Blegen and Jordan 345. Cf. Haynes 361–65; Chrislock, *Progressive Era* 1–14.

2. Haynes 361–62, 365; Timberlake 4–124; Boyer 196–99.

3. K. Kerr 7–9; Chrislock, *Progressive Era* 1–3, 256; Pegram 85–108.

4. *MN Issue* June 1898: 5–6; Szymanski 4–5. Cf. Pegram 116.

5. *MN Issue* June 1898: 2–6; Aug. 1898: 20, 24–25; Sept. 1898: 33; Dec. 1898: 37, 60, 62; Aug. 1899: 5; Nov. 1900: 78; June 1902: 46.

6. *MN Issue* Aug. 1898: 29. Cf. ibid. June 1898: 2–6; Aug. 1898: 20, 24–25; Sept. 1898: 33, 42; Dec. 1898: 37, 60, 62; Oct. 1899: 13; Nov. 1899: 20–21.

7. *MN Issue* Sept. 1898: 42. Cf. ibid. July 1898: 1; Sept. 1898: 34–35, 37, 42; Dec. 1898: 60; Bland 241.

8. *MN Issue* Dec. 1899: 26–27; Apr. 1900: 28; May 1900: 34.

9. *MN Issue* July 1900: 52; Oct. 1900: 69; Jan. 1902: 3; *Minneapolis Journal* 12 Apr. 1900: 7; Haines, *1909* 15.

10. *Minneapolis Journal* 24 Jan. 1907: 6. Cf. ibid. 21 July, 7 Aug. 1902: 6; 21 Jan. 1905: 5; 24 Jan. 1905: 7; *d PP* 22 Mar. 1900: 6; 26 Mar. 1902: 5; 27 Mar. 1902: 3; *Backbone* Jan. 1906: 2; Prohibition Party (Minnesota), State Committee, vol. 2, Dorsett's Parlor, 27 Feb. 1905.

11. *Minneapolis Journal* 30 Oct. 1906: 2; 6 Nov. 1907: 5; Prohibition Party (Minnesota), State Committee, vol. 2, Plan of Campaign for 1907–1908, 17 Dec. 1906; Dorsett's Parlor, 9 Apr. 1906; 4 Feb. 1907; White 180.

12. *MN Issue* Nov. 1899: 21; Jan. 1901: 6–7; Jan. 1907: 4; *Minneapolis Journal* 13 May 1905: 7.

13. *Minneapolis Journal* 7 Sept. 1905: 14; 8 Sept. 1905: 1; 4, 5 Apr., 12 May 1909: 1; 5 Dec. 1909: 9; 21 Dec. 1909: 1; 12 Apr. 1910: 1; 19 July 1910: 9; 25 July 1910: 12; 28 July 1910: 9; 13 Nov. 1910: 2; 28 Nov. 1910: 1; 23 Dec. 1910: 13; 19 Feb. 1911: 8; 20 Apr. 1912: 1; 21 Apr. 1912: 13; 10 June 1914: 2; 19 Oct. 1914: 1; 12 Nov. 1914: 8; *MN Issue* 26 Nov. 1910: 3; *Bemidji d Pioneer* 8 Sept. 1905: 4; 9 Dec. 1915: 22; 11 Mar. 1918: 4; McKenzie 112–21; Soderstrum 340–41.

14. Duis 20–28, 35, 63; Hoverson 65, 75–88; Hathaway 82–83; William Pitt Murray and Family Papers, box 4, folder: Miscellaneous Addresses, etc., undated and 1891, "Saloon and the Sale of Intoxicating Liquors" 5–8; *MN Issue* Feb. 1902: 12; Aug. 1902: 61; *American Issue MN Edition* Mar. 1913: II.11, 1–3.

15. Haines, *1909* 13, 15–19, 24–26, 59–60, 75–77, 81, 89; ibid., *1911* 4, 6–7, 23, 35, 43, 51, 53–54, 60; *American Issue MN Edition* Nov. 1912: II.7, 3. Cf. ibid. Aug. 1911: I.4, 1–3; Dec. 1911: I.8, 1. For attempts to curb the liquor interests' power, see *Minneapolis Journal* 2, 18 Feb. 1909: 1; 3 Apr. 1913: 1.

16. *MN Union Advocate* 14 July 1916: 2; Blocker, *Cycles* 69; Meagher, *Columbia History* 110; Rosenzweig 98, 116; Epstein 137–39; Moloney, *Lay Groups* 55.

17. *MN Union Advocate* 29 May 1908: 1. Cf. *Minneapolis Journal* 7 June 1908: 6.

18. *Winona Republican Herald* 10 June 1908: 3; 20, 21, 22 July 1914: 1; 24 July 1914: 4; 19 July 1915: 7; *Minneapolis Journal* 10 June 1908: 2; *MN Union Advocate* 3 July 1908: 1; 23 Oct. 1908: 4; 24 July 1914: 1; 28 May 1915: 1, 4; 23 July 1915: 3.

19. *Minneapolis Journal* 10 Oct. 1910: 1; 9 Nov. 1910: 18; *d VZ* 21 June 1910: 8; 22 June 1910: 1, 7; 21 July, 3 Nov. 1910: 8; 26 Oct. 1910: 1; *DW* 23 June 1910: 12; 7 July 1910: 10; 4 Aug. 1910: 4.

20. *Minneapolis Journal* 19 May 1910: 7; *MN Issue* 6 Aug., 20 Aug., 29 Oct. 1910: 2, 6; 12 Nov. 1910: 4; *d VZ* 9 May 1910: 8; "Traveling Men's Liberty League of Minnesota." For the founding of the ZB of Minnesota, see the section "The Crumbling of the German American Opposition" in this chapter.

21. *MN Patriot* Jan. 1914: 3. Cf. ibid. Oct. 1913: 1; *DW* 20 Feb. 1913: 12; Chrislock, *Progressive Era* 20, 33–35, 39, 60; *MN Issue* Mar. 1910: 2.

22. Hoverson. Cf. *MN Issue* Jan. 1907: 6; Cherrington, *Yearbook 1909* 40, *Yearbook 1915* 163, *Yearbook 1914* 155; Oscar Christgau Papers, box 3, folder 9: *American Issue MN Edition* Oct 1913, III.6: 1–2.

23. *MN Patriot* Mar. 1913: 1, 2; Apr. 1913: 1, 3; June 1913: 1, 3; Sept. 1913: 1; Dec. 1913: 1; Feb. 1914: 1–4; June 1915: 1; *Minneapolis Journal* 16, 26 Feb. 1914: 8; 27 Feb. 1914: 11; *MN White Ribbon* June 1914: 3; Prohibition Party (Minnesota), State Committee, box 1, folder: Minutes, Financial Records, Jan. 5–June 30, 1914, Meeting of the Prohibition Executive Committee 10 Mar. 1914.

24. Qtd. in Anderson and Blegen, box 1, folder: 1906–1914, Party Platform 1914; *Minneapolis Journal* 5 Oct. 1914: 10. Cf. ibid. 21 Sept. 1914: 9; 25 Sept. 1914: 1; 5 Oct. 1914: 10; 1 Nov. 1914: 1; *MN Issue* 19 Oct. 1914: 3; Chrislock, *Watchdog* 12–13.

25. *MN White Ribbon* Feb. 1915: 1, 2; *d VZ* 24 Feb. 1915: 8; *Catholic Bulletin* 6 Mar. 1915: 4. Cf. Chrislock, *Watchdog*; *Minneapolis Journal* 22 Apr. 1915: 8.

26. *American Issue MN Edition* Apr. 1915: IV.12, 1, 2; Minutes of the WCTU, vol. 1, 1885: 41; vol. 6, 1915: 79; *Minneapolis Journal* 10 June 1914: 1; *Bemidji d Pioneer* 9 Dec. 1915: 22; 11 Mar. 1918: 4. For an analysis of the relationship between the success of a County Option election and factors such as religion, ethnicity, and location of the county in urban or rural areas, see Tikalsky 32–34.

27. *American Issue MN Edition* Nov. 1915: V.7, 1, 3; *Minneapolis Journal* 22 Apr. 1915: 8; *MN Patriot* Apr. 1915: 3; Prohibition Party (Minnesota), State Committee, box 1, folder: Minutes, Financial Records, Aug. 2–Sept. 18, 1915, Meeting of the Prohibition Executive Committee 16, 23 Aug. 1915.

28. *MN Issue* Jan. 1901: 6–7.

29. Wingerd, *Claiming* 32. Cf. ibid. 29, 31; Wills 49–50, 63–64.

30. Wingerd, *Claiming* 14–16, 88; Wills 199.

31. Of course, one needs to take Minneapolitan assertions of straitlaced morality with a grain of salt. Just like its neighbor across the river, the city was the home of a thriving vice industry. However, Minnesota's temperance advocates asserted that, in comparison to other cities of the same size, Minneapolis deserved praise for the reform eagerness with which city authorities attempted to keep this vice industry at bay. Between 1890 and 1915, numerous temperance organizations established headquarters in Minneapolis. A large number of Minneapolitans welcomed these initiatives, advocated a tighter regulation of the liquor trade, and pushed the city administration toward stricter reforms.

32. Wingerd, *Claiming* 3; *Minneapolis Journal* 22 May 1905: 4; Steffens 64. Cf. *d PP* 22 Aug. 1904: 1.

33. *MN Issue* Feb. 1899: 76; Mar. 1899: 82–83; Jan. 1900: 1–2; Feb. 1900: 11; Jan. 1901: 6; *Minneapolis Journal* 6 July 1899: 6.

34. The business elites' degree of involvement in the vice industry is exemplified by the fate of John M. Fulton, minister of the Central Presbyterian Church, whom his wealthy parishioners forced to resign as he "had been telling too many plain truths from his pulpit in the course of his sermons advancing municipal reform." *SP d Globe* 23 Apr. 1905: 1. Cf. ibid. 4 Apr. 1905: 1; *DW* 12 Apr. 1905: 12; *d VZ* 24 Apr. 1905: 5; 29 Apr., 1 May, 4 Aug. 1905: 4; 23 June 1905: 6; Wingerd, *Claiming* 88; Schmid 18–19.

35. Chrislock, "Rand"; *Minneapolis Journal* 12 Mar. 1900: 5; 13 July 1900: 7; 31 Aug. 1900: 7; *MN Issue* Feb. 1900: 10; Mar. 1900: 17–18; Apr. 1900: 25–26; Sept. 1900: 58; Jan. 1901: 6.

36. *MN Issue* July 1900: 54; Dec. 1900: 84; Jan. 1901: 2; *Minneapolis Journal* 14 Feb. 1901: 10.

37. *MN Issue* May 1901: 36; *d VZ* 17 Jan., 17 Apr. 1901: 8; 14 May 1901: 5; *d PP* 4, 11, 21 Feb. 1902: 6; 5 Feb., 13 Mar. 1902: 7; 7 Feb. 1902: 2; 16 Feb. 1902: 1; 23 Feb. 1902: 2nd sect., 1; 27 Feb. 1902: 4; 27 Mar. 1902: 4; 4 May 1902: 2nd sect., 2.

38. *SP PP* 28 Sept. 1969: leisure sect.

39. *To-Day* March 1885: 1; *Minneapolis Journal* 13 Dec. 1902: 6; McClure 5–7; Bakeman 19–20; Corrigan 38–43; Tierney 7–11, 14.

40. See, for instance, *d VZ* 13, 20 July, 6, 7 Nov. 1895: 8; 12 Nov., 19, 31 Dec. 1895: 5; 12 Feb. 1901: 5; *DW* 13 Feb. 1901: 12; *MN Issue* Apr. 1901: 29; *Minneapolis Journal* 13 Dec. 1902: 6; *d PP* 2 Sept., 7, 20 Oct. 1903: 2; 6, 9, 23 Oct. 1903: 3; 9 Dec. 1903: 1; 17 Apr. 1904: 1, 2. For legislative attempts to deprive the Midway area of its status, see *d VZ* 13 July 1895: 8; *Minneapolis Journal* 15 Mar. 1899: 9; 28 Jan., 13 Feb. 1901: 4; *d PP* 15 Mar. 1899: 3.

41. *Minneapolis Journal* 5 June 1903: 8; 22 Apr. 1904: 6. Cf. ibid. 16 Apr. 1904: 7; *d PP* 16 Apr. 1904: 1, 6; 17 Apr. 1904: 1, 2; *d VZ* 16 Apr. 1904: 9.

42. *SP d Globe* 30 Apr. 1905: 1; *d PP* 16 Apr. 1904: 6; *d PP* 15 July 1903: 3. Cf. *Minneapolis Journal* 14 July 1903: 10.

43. *Minneapolis Journal* 22 Apr. 1904: 6.

44. The Ames mayoralty was the result of Minneapolis's unhappy experiment with the open primary system in 1900. Large numbers of Democrats participated in the city's Republican primaries and put former Democrat Ames into office. Nathanson 39–66.

45. Steffens; Chrislock, "Rand"; Minutes of the WCTU, vol. 4, 1902: 34, 1903: 34, 68.

46. *Minneapolis Journal* 5 Nov. 1905: 6. Cf. *d VZ* 1 Nov. 1905: 5.

47. *Minneapolis Journal* 21 Nov. 1905: 6. Cf. Minutes of the WCTU, vol. 4, 1906: 30; *d PP* 6 Nov. 1905: 2.

48. *MN Issue* July 1907: 2–3.

49. Qtd. in Nathanson 17; *SP d Globe* 8 Apr. 1900: 17.

50. Rachie 74, 77. Cf. *MN Issue* July 1907: 2–3.

51. *d VZ* 10 June 1907: 5. Cf. ibid. 19 June 1907: 6; 22 June 1907: 3; *d PP* 9 June 1907: 1, 6; *DW* 20, 27 June 1907: 12; *MN Issue* July 1907: 5.

52. *Minneapolis Journal* 30 Oct., 4 Nov. 1907: 1; 3 Nov. 1907: 4; 29 Nov. 1907: 20; *DW* 28 Nov. 1907: 12; *d VZ* 25, 27, 29 Nov. 1907: 8.

53. *MN White Ribbon* Feb. 1908: 2. Cf. *d VZ* 16, 17 Dec. 1907: 5.

54. *Minneapolis Journal* 19 Dec. 1907: 7; 26 Jan. 1908: 5; 24 Feb. 1909: 6; 15 Mar. 1909: 1; 8 Feb. 1911: 7; 3 Mar. 1911: 1, 2; 1 Apr. 1911: 12; *d VZ* 21 Dec. 1907: 3; 12 Mar. 1909: 7; *w VZ* 26 Dec. 1907: 5; 9 Jan. 1908: 3; *DW* 26 Dec. 1907: 12; 16 Jan. 1908: 12; 18 Mar. 1909: 12; *American Issue MN Edition* Nov. 1912: II.7, 3; Minutes of the WCTU, vol. 6, 1913: 77.

55. *d VZ* 1 May 1911: 8.

56. *Minneapolis Journal* 13 Aug. 1912: 1; *d VZ* 23 Apr. 1914: 5; 9 Aug. 1915: 8; *d PP* 9 Aug. 1915: 1, 10; 14 Aug. 1915: 1.

57. Salisbury 51. Cf. Prohibition Party (Minnesota), State Committee, box 1, folder: Minutes, Financial Records, June 1–July 31, 1915, Meeting of the Prohibition Executive Committee 1 June 1915; *MN Patriot* June 1915: 1, 3; *d VZ* 1 June 1915: 5; 18 June 1915: 8; *SP PP* 18 June 1915: 6; 19 June 1915: 7; 3 July 1915: 5, 9.

58. *NWC* 26 July 1913: 5. Cf. ibid. 1 Sept. 1900: 5; 20 June, 8 Aug. 1908: 5; *MN Issue* Mar. 1900: 18; *Catholic Bulletin* 24 June 1911: 1; 20 Apr., 6 July 1912: 5.

59. *NWC* 22 June 1907: 5. Cf. ibid. 24 June 1911: 1; *Minneapolis Journal* 26 June 1901: 7; *DW* 26 June 1901: 12; *d VZ* 26 June 1901: 5; *Irish Standard* 28 June 1901: 4; 15 June 1907: 4; 20 June 1908: 1; *NWC* 11 June 1910: n. pag.; 6 July 1912: 5.

60. *DW* 16 July 1914: 1; 30 Sept. 1915: 22; Prohibition Party (Minnesota), State Committee, box 1, folder: Minutes, Financial Records, July 1–Dec. 31, 1914, Meeting of the Prohibition Executive Committee 21 Dec. 1914; *SP PP* 9 July 1915: 5; *NWC* 30 June 1893: 7; *MN Issue* Dec. 1898: 62, 1900: 42; Quinn, *Father Mathew's Crusade* 188, "Father Mathew's Disciples" 635; Odegard 2–7; *Catholic Bulletin* 29 July 1916: 4. For examples of prohibitionist leanings among Minnesota's Irish, see the debate about John Ireland's prohibitionist speech in 1889. *Proceedings of the 18th Annual Convention of the CTAU* Appendix 2, 4; James M. Reardon Papers, box 6, folder: Publications, Correspondence, Notes: Archbishop Ireland, "Archbishop Ireland and Prohibition"; *NWC* 18 Jan. 1889: 1, 8; 3 Aug. 1894: 9; 18 Jan. 1895: 3.

61. *Catholic Bulletin* 24 June 1911: 4. Cf. ibid. 10 Oct. 1914: 4; *Irish Standard* 16 June 1906: 4; James M. Reardon Papers, box 5, folder: Writings and Research: Temperance Movement, Catholic Total Abstinence Movement 1905–1918, "A New Crusade."

62. Wingerd, *Claiming* 40–41; Flanagan 248–49, 267–74.

63. CTAU of St. Paul Collection, box 1, folder: Crusaders' Total Abstinence Society, Playbills, Announcements, Invitations, etc., 1890–1903, Total Abstainers Pledge Card. Cf. *Catholic Bulletin* 22 June 1912: 4; 21 June 1913: 4; 26 July 1913: 1; 10 Oct. 1914: 4.

64. O'Connell 217; Quinn, "Father Mathew's Disciples" 636–37.

65. *NWC* 31 Jan. 1903: 5; 27 Feb. 1907: 5; 30 Apr. 1904: 5; *d VZ* 26 June 1901: 5.

66. *d PP* 14 June 1903: 2; *NWC* 15 Aug. 1903: 5; 30 Apr. 1904: 5; *Irish Standard* 27 June 1903: 8.

67. Minutes of the WCTU, vol. 3, 1899: 32; 1900: 75; vol. 5, 1907: 90–91; *NWC* 7 Oct. 1898: 5.

68. *d VZ* 13 Mar. 1913: 5; *Catholic Bulletin* 5 Apr. 1913: 1; 10 Jan. 1914: 4; *SP PP* 29 Mar. 1914: 3rd sect., 9; Foster 161; *SP d Globe* 4 June 1902: 6; "In the Beginning." For other examples of Irish women's temperance work in the public sphere, see *NWC* 1 Nov. 1895: 3, 4; 18 June 1895: 6; 20 Mar. 1896: 7; 1 May 1896: 2.

69. Deutsch 24.

70. *NWC* 30 Apr. 1904: 5; 12 June 1909: 5; *Catholic Bulletin* 26 July 1913: 1.

71. *DW* 30 May 1907: 1–3. Cf. ibid. 2 May 1907: 4; 7, 21 July 1898: 1.

72. *d VZ* 20 Feb. 1899: 5. Cf. ibid. 19, 23 Jan. 1899: 5; 19 Mar., 22 Oct. 1900: 5; 15 Oct. 1901: 5.

73. Godsho 7; *d VZ* 29 Aug. 1913: 6; 17 Apr. 1899: 5; 19 Mar. 1900: 5; 18 Mar. 1901: 5; 20 Mar. 1901: 2; Heinrici 780–84, 791; Kazal 2; Luebke, *Bonds of Loyalty* 98.

74. Conzen, *Germans in Minnesota* 66.

75. *DW* 16 Jan. 1908: 12. Cf. *d VZ* 29 Aug. 1913: 6.

76. *d VZ* 20 July 1908: 5; 28 Oct. 1908: 4; 31 May 1910: 8; 26 Apr. 1913: 7; 1 Jan., 1 June 1914: 5; *w VZ* 1 Oct. 1908: 3; 11 Feb. 1909: 3; *SP PP* 30 Oct. 1910: 1; *Minneapolis Journal* 8 Feb. 1910: 8.

77. Kazal 84–90; Harzig 141–57.

78. *d VZ* 23 Jan. 1899: 5; 17 June 1910: 9; 4 Feb. 1914: 7; *DW* 23 Jan. 1908: 1; *Minneapolis Journal* 17 June 1910: 13.

79. *d VZ* 19 Jan., 23 Feb. 1914: 8.

80. *DW* 16 Jan. 1908: 1; 26 Mar. 1914: 1. Cf. ibid. 16 Jan. 1908: 12.

81. Matt 98–99. Cf. *DW* 5 Sept. 1907: 12; 16, 23 Jan., 16 Apr. 1908: 1; 13 Feb., 8 Oct. 1908: 4; 16 Mar. 1914: 1; Luebke, *Bonds of Loyalty* 108; Gleason, *Conservative Reformers* 57, 100.

82. Gleason, *Conservative Reformers* 156. Cf. ibid. 154, 158; Luebke, *Germans in the New World* 15.

83. *DW* 16 Jan., 16 Apr. 1908: 1; Nagel, "Constructing Ethnicity" 163. The Catholic Illinois *Vereinsbund*, for instance, also decided against joining the NB of America. *DW* 6 Feb., 11 June 1908: 1.

84. *DW* 28 July 1910: 1. Cf. O'Connell 466–67, 510.

85. Matt 96–99; Luebke, *Bonds of Loyalty* 99; Gleason, *Conservative Reformers* 154; *MN Issue* 29 Oct. 1910: 2; *DW* 18 June 1908: 1; *d VZ* 28 Oct. 1908: 4; 23 Nov. 1908: 8; *MN Union Advocate* 16, 23 Apr. 1915: 5; 14 May 1915: 4; 29 Oct. 1915: 1.

86. The first temperance movement in Germany had begun around 1830 and ebbed away during the 1848 Revolution. While Catholics did not play a significant role in this movement, they figured more prominently in the second German temperance movement that emerged in the 1880s. Tappe 141–43, 154, 156, 175, 181, 287, 343, 354–55, 371.

87. *DW* 24 Sept. 1908: 4. Cf. ibid. 3 May 1905: 4; 2 May 1907: 4; 30 May 1907: 1; 18 Mar. 1909: 1; *d VZ* 24 Oct. 1911: 6.

88. *DW* 15 Jan. 1914: 1. Cf. ibid. 3 Feb. 1910: 1; 18 June 1914: 5; 16 July 1914: 1.

89. Scovell 92.

90. *MN White Ribbon* May 1906: 3; Dec. 1908: 3. Cf. Minutes of the WCTU, vol. 4, 1905: 87; vol. 5, 1907: 87, 1909: 94, 1910: 94, 1912: 42, 68–69, 88; vol. 6, 1913: 41–42.

91. In 1910, Maud Stockwell stepped down from her decade-long presidency in the MWSA. Her resignation inaugurated an internal crisis, resulting in the founding of a rival organization, the Minnesota Equal Franchise League. Stuhler, *Gentle Warriors* 76–77.

92. *MN White Ribbon* Apr. 1915: 1. Cf. Yearbook of the SP Political Equality Club; Minutes of the WCTU, vol. 4, 1902: 39, 82, 95. For a detailed overview of the legislative struggles about woman suffrage between 1898 and 1915 and the WCTU's involvement in them, see Stuhler, *Gentle Warriors* 111; Minutes of the WCTU, vol. 5, 1907: 22, 90–91, 1911: 24; *MN White Ribbon* Apr. 1909: 1; May 1909: 1, 3; Feb. 1911: 1; Mar. 1913: 1; Stockwell 324–25.

93. *MN White Ribbon* Apr. 1910: 1; *MN Patriot* Jan. 1915: 2; *MN Issue* Nov. 1902: 8. Cf. Minutes of the WCTU, vol. 5, 1907: 2, 1912: 34–35; *MN White Ribbon* Oct. 1911: 1; *d PP* 27 July 1898: 10; *Minneapolis Journal* 20 Mar. 1900: 6; 22 Mar. 1902: 7; 24 Jan. 1912: 9; Prohibition Party (Minnesota), State Committee, box 1, folder: Minutes, Financial Records, Jan. 5–June 30, 1914, Meeting of the Prohibition Executive Committee 21 June 1914.

94. Smith-Rosenberg, *Disorderly Conduct* 23. Cf. ibid. 24, 258, 262; Gordon 133–55.

95. Qtd. in K. Kerr 41–42, 44.

96. *New Ulm Review* 1 Apr. 1914: 2. Cf. Minutes of the WCTU, vol. 4, 1900: table, 1901: table, 1902: 104, 1904: 65, 1905: 35, 71–72, 96–97, 1906: 71, 1908: 40–41.

97. WCTU of MN Records, box 5: Eva Jones journal, 1908–1914, 26 Sept. 1908, obituaries. Cf. Minutes of the WCTU, vol. 5, 1908: 40–41.

98. WCTU of MN Records, box 5: Eva Jones journal, 1908–1914; Minutes of the WCTU, vol. 5, 1909: 77, 1910: 81, 1911: 68, 122–23; vol. 6, 1913: 42, 53; *MN White Ribbon* Dec. 1908: 4; *SP PP* 15, 29 Oct. 1911: 4th sect., 7; 10 Aug. 1913: 4th sect., 10; 7 Mar., 18 Apr. 1915: 3rd sect., 6; Central WCTU, Organization Records, vol. 1, 28 Oct. 1908.

99. *SP PP* 26 Feb., 26 Mar. 1911: 3rd sect., 8; 19 Mar., 21 May 1911: 6th sect., 8; 23 July 1911: 4th sect., 3; 15 Oct. 1911: 4th sect., 7; 9 Oct. 1910: 3rd sect., 8; 22 Jan. 1911: 3rd sect., 10; 16 July 1911: 4th sect., 6; 13 Aug. 1911: 4th sect., 2; 15, 29 Oct. 1911: 4th sect., 7; 24 Mar. 1912: 4th sect., 12; 19 Jan. 1913: 3rd sect., 24; WCTU of MN Records, box 5: Eva Jones journal, 1908–1914, 6 Dec. 1908, 23 Sept. 1910, 17 Aug. 1913.

100. *SP PP* 15 Oct. 1911: 4th sect., 7; 29 Oct. 1911: 4th sect., 7; *MN White Ribbon* Nov. 1910: 1; Minutes of the WCTU, vol. 5, 1910: 81. Cf. *SP PP* 27 Nov. 1910: 3rd sect., 10.

101. *SP PP* 27 Aug. 1911: 4th sect., 6. Cf. ibid. 27 Nov. 1910: 3rd sect., 10.

102. Minutes of the WCTU, vol. 5, 1910: 59, 105; vol. 6, 1913: 77, 119–20; *SP PP* 4, 18 Dec. 1910: 3rd sect., 10.

103. *DW* 28 July 1910: 12; *SP PP* 11 Dec. 1910: 3rd sect., 12; 29 Jan. 1911: 3rd sect., 10; 17 Nov. 1912: 3rd sect., 28; Central WCTU, Organization Records, vol. 1, 18 Aug. 1910; Minutes of the WCTU, vol. 4, 1901: 111; vol. 5, 1911: 122–23.

104. WCTU of MN Records, box 5: Eva Jones journal, 1908–1914, 15 Jan.1909, 21 Dec. 1909, 28 Feb. 1910. Cf. *d VZ* 25 Feb. 1910: 9; 24 Feb. 1910: 6; 26 Feb. 1910: 3; 28 Feb. 1910: 8; *DW* 3 Mar. 1910: 12; *SP PP* 16 Apr. 1911: 2nd sect., 6; 14 May 1911: 6th sect., 6; 21 May

1911: 6th sect., 8; 20 Aug. 1911: 4th sect., 6; 11, 18 Aug. 1912: 4th sect., 32; 25 Aug. 1912: 5th sect., 40; Minutes of the WCTU, vol. 4, 1904: 88–89; vol. 5, 1910: 81.

105. Central WCTU, Organization Records, vol. 1, 19 Oct. 1910.

106. *SP PP* 25 Mar. 1914: 1; 5 Apr. 1914: 1st sect., 4; Pratt Appendix B. Cf. WCTU of MN Records, box 5: Eva Jones journal, 1908–1914, obituaries; Prohibition Party (Minnesota), State Committee, folder: Minutes, Financial Records, Jan. 5–June 30, 1914, Meeting of the Prohibition Executive Committee 3 Apr. 1914; folder: Aug. 2–Sept. 18, 1915, Meeting of the Prohibition Executive Committee 13 Sept. 1915; ibid. vol. 2, Articles of Incorporation of Minnesota's Civic Reform Association, Dorsett's Parlor, 25 June 1906; Central WCTU, Organization Records, 1906–1917, vol. 1, 23 Apr. 1914; Foster 154.

Chapter 5. Equating Temperance with Patriotism

1. J. A. A. Burnquist Papers, box 12, folder: Correspondence and Miscellaneous Papers, undated, 1918, "Since the Commencement of the War" 17–18.

2. *MN Patriot* Mar. 1916: 5; *American Issue MN Edition* Nov. 1915: V.7, 1–3; Prohibition Party (Minnesota), State Committee, box 1, folder: Minutes, Financial Records, Oct. 4–Dec. 15, 1915, Meeting of the Prohibition Executive Committee 5 Oct. 1915; newspaper article 4 Oct. 1915; Cherrington, *Yearbook 1917* 154–56.

3. Doenecke 44, 58–92, 263–68; Chrislock, *Watchdog* 40, 46.

4. Schaffer 108. Cf. ibid. 96–103.

5. Schaffer 97. Cf. Timberlake 173–75; *MN Patriot* 2nd Quarter 1917: 2; 3rd Quarter 1917: 4; 4th Quarter 1917: 1–2; *Our Side* 12 Sept. 1918: 1; K. Kerr 199–208; Pegram 142–44; *DW* 28 June, 5, 12 July 1917: 4; *MN White Ribbon* Sept. 1917: 2.

6. Schaffer 97, 98. Cf. Timberlake 173, 175, 178.

7. Timberlake 182. Cf. ibid.181, 183; James 6, 7; Chrislock, *Progressive Era* 200; Pegram 150–52.

8. Oscar Christgau Papers, box 3, folder 9, *American Issue MN Edition* July 1917: VIII.3, 6. Cf. Prohibition and Temperance Collection, box 8, folder 4: Pamphlets 1917–1919, "Brewing and Liquor Interests and German and Bolshevik Propaganda" 1–7.

9. *MN Patriot* 2nd Quarter 1918: 2. Cf. *DW* 5 July 1917: 4; MNCPS Papers, box 8, folder 123.1, letter from the Minnesota Dry Federation to the MNCPS, 19 Aug. 1918; folder 123.3, letter from McCall's Resort to the MNCPS, 13 May 1918; leaflet "WASTE!"

10. *DW* 11 Jan. 1917: 8; *SP PP* 20 Jan. 1917: 3; 21 Jan. 1917: 1st sect., 4; 25 Jan. 1917: 5; *MN White Ribbon* Feb. 1917: 1, 3; Mar. 1917: 1, 2; Apr. 1917: 1, 2. "Bone-dry" had become a prohibitionist watchword in the wake of the Webb-Kenyon Act, passed in 1913 by Congress under the pressure of the ASL. By prohibiting liquor shipments into or through a dry state, the act facilitated the passage of sweeping state laws prohibiting personal-possession or personal-use shipments of liquor. In December 1917, the Supreme Court upheld the Webb-Kenyon Act, a heavy blow to the liquor interests. Hamm 235–36.

11. *SP PP* 24 Jan. 1917: 10; 25, 27 Jan. 1917: 6; 26, 31 Jan. 1917: 1; 1 Feb. 1917: 1, 10; 3 Feb. 1917: 5; 5 Feb. 1917: 8; 7 Feb. 1917: 6, 10; *d VZ* 24, 26, 27, 31 Jan., 17 Feb. 1917: 6; 25 Jan., 1, 16 Feb., 7 Mar. 1917: 5; 22 Feb. 1917: 8; *MN White Ribbon* Feb. 1917: 1, 3; Mar., Apr. 1917: 1, 2.

12. *d VZ* 26 Jan. 1917: 6. Cf. ibid. 20 Mar. 1917: 8; *MN Patriot* 3rd Quarter 1917: 3; Prohibition Party (Minnesota), State Committee, box 1, folder: Minutes, Financial

Records, Jan. 8–Mar. 31, 1918, Meeting of the Prohibition Executive Committee 26 Mar. 1918; *MN White Ribbon* Mar. 1917: 1, 2; Oct. 1917: 4.

13. *MN Patriot* 3rd Quarter 1917: 1, 3, 4; *Bemidji d Pioneer* 11 Sept. 1918: 1.

14. *MN White Ribbon* Apr. 1917: 1, 2. Its original members were, besides Governor Burnquist and Attorney General Lyndon A. Smith, John Lind and John F. McGee of Minneapolis, Charles W. Ames of St. Paul, Charles H. March of Litchfield, and Anton C. Weiss of Duluth. Ames and Lind left the commission in early December 1917 and were replaced by Henry W. Libby of Winona and Thomas E. Cashman of Owatonna.

15. J. A. A. Burnquist Papers, box 2, folder: Correspondence and Miscellaneous Papers, "Description of the Powers of the MNCPS" 1–2.

16. Chrislock, *Watchdog* 68, 93.

17. Qtd. in ibid., 77, 86. Cf. ibid. 14–17, 31, 33, 62–63, 82; Wingerd, *Claiming* 136–43, 145, 149, 151. The Nonpartisan League, a farmer protest organization that had established headquarters in St. Paul in 1917, sought to politically implement state ownership and operation of the intermediary sector of the agricultural economy. It was also opposed to the United States' entry into World War I. Since 1910, the Socialist vote had steadily increased, particularly in Minnesota's northern counties and several working-class wards in Minneapolis. Moreover, the Industrial Workers of the World (IWW), founded in Chicago in 1905, established their presence in Minnesota, primarily in the northern mines and forests, in order to organize unions for migratory workers.

18. *MN Patriot* 1st Quarter 1917: 3; J. A. A. Burnquist Papers, box 2, folder: Correspondence and Miscellaneous Papers, "Description of the Powers of the MNCPS" 1–2.

19. MNCPS Papers, box 10, folder 102, letter from the TLA of Minneapolis to the Chairman of the Council of National Defense, 8 June 1917. Cf. ibid. letter from the MNCPS to O. H. O'Neill, 8 June 1917; Chrislock, *Watchdog* 97–98, 109–12, 213; J. A. A. Burnquist Papers, box 2, folder: Correspondence and Miscellaneous Papers, "Description of the Powers of the MNCPS" 1–2; box 13, folder: Feb. 21–Mar. 4, 1918, "Official Orders and Resolutions of the MNCPS"; *d VZ* 26, 30 Apr. 1917: 3; *DW* 14 June 1917: 8; Holbrook and Appel 2: 58–59; Wingerd, *Claiming* 158–59.

20. MNCPS, Minutes, 24 Apr. 1917, 5 June 1917. Cf. ibid. 29 May 1917; Wingerd, *Claiming* 141; Chrislock, *Watchdog* 32–33, 97–98, 109–12, 213; J. A. A. Burnquist Papers, box 13, folder: Feb. 21–Mar.4, 1918, "Official Orders and Resolutions of the MNCPS."

21. MNCPS, Minutes, 19 June 1917; *d VZ* 20 June 1917: 7; J. A. A. Burnquist Papers, box 10, folder: Correspondence and Miscellaneous Papers, undated, June 11–31, 1917, letter from the Pastor of St. Mark's Church to Burnquist, 11 June 1917; Tikalsky 54; Wolkerstorfer, "Anti-German Nativism" 5. For examples of complaints and prohibition requests, see the letters in MNCPS Papers, box 103 L8 1B, folder 80.

22. MNCPS, Minutes, 19 June 1917. Cf. Chrislock, *Watchdog* 213.

23. MNCPS, Minutes, 19, 20, 21 June, 28 Aug. 1917, 6, 13 Aug. 1918; J. A. A. Burnquist Papers, box 13, folder: Feb. 21–Mar.4, 1918, "Official Orders and Resolutions of the MNCPS"; Chrislock, *Watchdog* 123–25; 215, 219–21; *Bemidji d Pioneer* 15 Aug. 1918: 1.

24. *Bemidji d Pioneer* 11 Mar. 1918: 1; MNCPS, Minutes, 16, 24 July, 28 Aug., 4, 11 Sept. 1917. Cf. Chrislock, *Watchdog* 213–15; J. A. A. Burnquist Papers, box 13, folder: Feb. 21–Mar. 4, 1918, "Official Orders and Resolutions of the MNCPS."

25. MNCPS, Minutes, 14 May 1918; Chrislock, *Watchdog* 217–20; J. A. A. Burnquist Papers, box 2, folder: Correspondence and Miscellaneous Papers, "Description of the Powers of the MNCPS"; box 15, folder: Correspondence and Miscellaneous Papers, Aug. 3–16, 1918, letter from the citizens of Blooming Prairie to Burnquist, 8 Aug. 1918; *d VZ* 5 July 1918: 7; 12 July 1918: 5, 8; 13, 24 July, 9 Aug. 1918: 5; *SP PP* 9 Oct. 1918: 14; *Our Side* 10 Oct. 1918: 1.

26. J. A. A. Burnquist Papers, box 13, folder: Correspondence and Miscellaneous Papers, Apr. 1–16, 1918, "Official Orders and Resolutions of the MNCPS." Cf. Chrislock, *Watchdog* 220; Hilton 10; Holbrook and Appel 2: 62–63.

27. J. A. A. Burnquist Papers, box 12, folder: Correspondence and Miscellaneous Papers, Dec. 14–17, 1917, letter from W. D. Ferguson to J. McGee, 18 Dec. 1917; *d VZ* 28 Nov. 1917: 8; 28 Jan. 1918: 6; 30 Jan. 1918: 8.

28. MNCPS, Minutes, 5 Feb. 1918. Cf. MNCPS Papers, box 8, folder 110.1, MSA, letter from the MNCPS to the Masonic Observer, 29 Dec. 1917. The Commission's orders remained in force until February 5, 1919. The commission itself ceased to exist on December 15, 1920. Chrislock, *Watchdog* 314, 323.

29. *MN White Ribbon* Oct. 1918: 6. Cf. Prohibition Party (Minnesota), State Committee, box 1, folder: Minutes, Financial Records, Jan. 8–Mar. 31, 1918, Meeting of the Prohibition Executive Committee 26 Mar. 1918; folder: Apr. 9–June 29, 1918, Minutes of the Executive Committee Meeting 20 Apr. 1918; *MN Patriot* 1st Quarter 1918: 3; 2nd Quarter 1918: 1.

30. Cf. the section "The German American Temperance Opposition Crushed" in this chapter.

31. *MN Union Advocate* 19 May, 21 July 1916: 1; 5 Jan., 11 May 1917: 1; 19 Jan. 1917: 4; 8 Feb. 1918: 3; 29 Mar. 1918: 5; 1 Nov. 1918: 1, 4; *Labor Review* 21 July 1916: 1, 2.

32. J. A. A. Burnquist Papers, box 11, folder: Correspondence and Miscellaneous Papers, Dec. 2–7, 1917, letter from O. Seebach to Burnquist, 6 Dec. 1917; *d VZ* 20, 30 June 1917: 7; *MN Patriot* 2nd Quarter 1916: 1; 3rd Quarter 1917: 3.

33. *Our Side* 12 Oct. 1916: 1. Cf. ibid. 22, 29 June 1916: 1; 13 July 1916: 1, 4; 17 Aug. 1916: 1, 5; 30 Nov. 1916: 4.

34. *MN White Ribbon* Dec. 1918: 2; *Our Side* 21 Nov. 1918: 1; *d VZ* 7 Nov. 1918: 5; 8 Nov. 1918: 8; 13 Nov. 1918: 6; Tikalsky 71, 73.

35. *Catholic Bulletin* 5 July 1919: 4; *Minneapolis Journal* 19 Apr. 1919: 8; Minutes of the WCTU, vol. 7, 1919: 36; Timberlake 178, 180.

36. *Minneapolis Journal* 17 Jan. 1919: 1, 2; *MN White Ribbon* Feb. 1919: 2: May 1919: 1; *w VZ* 20 Mar., 6 Apr. 1919: 6; *DW* 27 Feb., 17 Apr. 1919: 8.

37. *SP PP* 1 July 1919: 1; *Our Side* 3 July 1919: 4. For the reaction of Minnesota's breweries to national prohibition, see Hoverson 115–21.

38. *d VZ* 10 Aug. 1915: 8; *Our Side* 31 Aug. 1916: 1. Cf. *d VZ* 9 Aug. 1915: 8; *d PP* 9 Aug. 1915: 1, 10.

39. *d VZ* 26 Aug. 1915: 6; *Our Side* 31 Aug. 1916: 1. Cf. *d VZ* 20 Mar. 1916: 8; *DW* 24 Aug. 1916: 12; "Abstract of Votes, 1904–1932." Mears had cofounded the Buckbee-Mears Company, a small firm engaged in photo-engraving, commercial photography, art, and design, but he was also an early member of St. Paul's Rotary Club No. 10 and the First Baptist Church of St. Paul.

40. Qtd. in Holbrook 2–3. Cf. Wolkerstorfer, "Persecution" 3–4.

41. Wingerd, *Claiming* 117–18, 125–26, 132; Chrislock, *Watchdog* 47; Holbrook 11. Contrary to Wingerd, I would not argue that one reason for Ireland to support the war was his conflict with his German American flock. By then most conflicts had subsided. Ireland rather interpreted the war as a chance for Catholics to prove their patriotism and thus to improve their image.

42. Qtd. in Holbrook 231. Cf. Wingerd, *Claiming* 136, 143–45; Chrislock, *Watchdog* 53.

43. MNCPS Papers, box 103 L8 2F, folder 102, letter from L. Gilosky to the MNCPS, 30 July 1917; box 8, folder 110.1., letter from "A Woman" to the MNCPS, 13 Dec. 1917; Memorandum; letter from the MNCPS to J. J. O'Connor, 17 Nov. 1917; letter from A. Chapman to the MNCPS, 30 Aug. 1917; box 8, folder 110.2, letter from W. Envin to the MNCPS, 5 Aug. 1917; box 103 L8 4F, folder 132, letter from the *SP d News* to the MNCPS, 18 Aug. 1917; box 103 L8 7B, folder 168, letters from the MNCPS to T. Girling, 31 July 1817, 17 Sept. 1917; *d VZ* 28 Aug. 1917: 6; 1 Nov. 1917: 8.

44. Qtd. in Holbrook 233. Cf. e.g., MNCPS Papers, box 8, folder 110.1, Petition from St. John the Evangelist Parish, 8 Nov. 1917; letter from the WCTU to the MNCPS, 9 Nov. 1917; box 8, folder 110.3, letter from Mrs. Charles P. Noyes to the MNCPS, 22 Jan. 1918.

45. Wingerd, *Claiming* 159, 166–69; Holbrook 219–20, 233; Wolkerstorfer, "Nativism in Minnesota" 151.

46. Wingerd, *Claiming* 138, 176–205, 208–9.

47. *d VZ* 11 May 1918: 4; *MN White Ribbon* Jan. 1919: 4.

48. MNCPS Papers, box 8, folder 110.6., letter from the MNCPS to J. J. O'Connor, 23 June 1918, letter from the St. Paul Federation of Churches to the MNCPS, 22 Apr. 1918; folder 110.1, letter from Agent #51 to the MNCPS, 31 Jan. 1918; box 103 L9 2F, folder 217, letter from "A Woman" to the MNCPS, 6 Mar. 1918.

49. *d VZ* 27 Dec. 1917: 5; *DW* 31 Oct. 1918: 10; *SP PP* 24 Oct. 1918: 12; MNCPS Papers, box 8, folder 110.1, letters from the MNCPS to Gund Brewing, Casanova Brewing, Jung Brewing, Schmidt Brewing, 11 Jan. 1918; folder 110.4, letter from A. N. Vannuff to the MNCPS, 29 Oct. 1918; folder 110.6, MSA, letter from C. B. Wheeler to the MNCPS, 17 June 1918.

50. *Catholic Bulletin* 19 Oct. 1918: 1, 4. Cf. ibid. 10 Feb., 7 July 1917: 4; 26 Oct. 1918: 8; 2 Nov. 1918: 4; *d VZ* 23 Apr. 1918: 4; 16 Sept. 1918: 6; *MN Patriot* 3rd Quarter 1918: 3; *SP PP* 18 Oct. 1918: 7; 9 Oct. 1918: 14; MNCPS Papers, box 8, folder 110.1, letter from James Donahoe to the MNCPS, 29 Jan. 1918.

51. *d VZ* 1 July 1919: 5; *SP PP* 1 July 1919: 14.

52. *SP Dispatch* 27 Aug. 1920: 1. Cf. Wingerd, *Claiming* 252–54; Maccabee 25–44.

53. Kazal 197.

54. *DW* 29 Oct. 1914: 4. Cf. ibid. 6 Aug. 1914: 1; 27 Aug. 1914: 22; 8 Oct. 1914: 5; 29 Oct. 1914: 4; 21 Sept. 1916: 10; *d VZ* 18 Aug. 1914: 1; 5 Aug., 7 Sept. 1914: 5; 24 Oct. 1914: 6; Wolkerstorfer, "Anti-German Nativism" 59, "Nativism in Minnesota" 126; Kazal 156, 159.

55. *DW* 23 Dec. 1915: 4. Cf. ibid. 20 July 1916: 1; 22 June 1916: 4; *d VZ* 18 May 1915: 4; 31 May 1915: 5; Wolkerstorfer, "Persecution" 3–4; Kazal 160–64, 166; Chrislock, *Progressive Era* 98.

56. *DW* 6 Sept. 1917: 4; 26 Sept. 1918: 1. Cf. *d VZ* 23 May 1917: 5; Chrislock, *Watchdog* 57; Wolkerstorfer, "Nativism in Minnesota" 130; Rippley, "Conflict" 181. Congress passed

similarly discriminating acts, seeking to root out disloyalty and to protect the United States. The Espionage Act of 1917 threatened those with severe fines who obstructed recruiting and attempted to cause "insubordination, disloyalty, mutiny, or refusal of duty" in the armed forces. The Sedition Act of May 1918 outlawed any "disloyal, profane, scurrilous, or abusive language about the form of government of the United States, or the Constitution of the United States, or the flag of the United States," or language that might bring them into "contempt, scorn, contumely, or disrepute." Kazal 175.

57. J. A. A. Burnquist Papers, box 10, folder: Correspondence and Miscellaneous Papers, April 1917, letter from Burnquist to P. H. Konzen, 8 Apr. 1917.

58. Qtd. in *DW* 30 Aug., 27 Sept. 1917: 4; J. A. A. Burnquist Papers, box 10, folder: Correspondence and Miscellaneous Papers, undated, August [?]–28, 1917, letter from A. B. Kaercher to Burnquist, 23 Aug. 1917. Cf. folder: Correspondence and Miscellaneous Papers, April 1917, letter from A. Jacques to Burnquist, 30 Apr. 1917; Wolkerstorfer, "Anti-German Nativism" 63. During 1917 and 1918, the commission received 974 complaints directed against Germans. H. Johnson 176.

59. Qtd. in Wolkerstorfer, "Persecution" 5, and in Chrislock, *Progressive Era* 171–72. Cf. Hagedorn; J. A. A. Burnquist Papers, box 12, folder: Correspondence and Miscellaneous Papers, undated, 1918, "The Kaiserite in America," "What the Kaiser Says."

60. MNCPS, Minutes, 1917–1920, 1 Aug., 2, 11 Oct. 1917. Bergmeier was soon interned by federal authorities, as he had violated the alien enemy proclamation of April 6, 1917, which forbade alien enemies to write, print, or publish attacks on the government. The *Volkszeitung* continued publication under his sister-in-law, Clara Bergmeier. Chrislock, *Watchdog* 160; Holbrook 229.

61. J. A. A. Burnquist Papers, box 2, folder: Correspondence and Miscellaneous Papers, "Description of the Powers of the MNCPS" 23; box 11, folder: Correspondence and Miscellaneous Papers, Nov. 6–Dec. 1, 1917, MNCPS, 22 Nov. 1917. Cf. ibid. box 2, folder: Correspondence and Miscellaneous Papers, "Description of the Powers of the MNCPS" 32; box 11, folder: Correspondence and Miscellaneous Papers, Nov. 6–Dec. 1, 1917, Report of Special Committee on German Textbooks in Public Schools of Minnesota; Rippley, "Conflict" 175–77.

62. J. A. A. Burnquist Papers, box 11, folder: Correspondence and Miscellaneous Papers, Sept. 1–20, 1917, letter from TG Winter to CW Ames Sept. 20, 1917; qtd. in Chrislock, *Watchdog* 121. Cf. ibid. 117; Wingerd, *Claiming* 169; J. A. A. Burnquist Papers, 1884–1961, box 11, folder: Correspondence and Miscellaneous Papers, Sept. 21–Oct. 9, 1917, letter from F. Hopkins to H. E. Samuelson, 8 Oct. 1917; letter from F. Clague to Burnquist, 9 Oct. 1917; box 15, folder: Correspondence and Miscellaneous Papers, July 22–Aug. 2, 1918, letter from P. Liesch to Burnquist, 29 July 1918; letter from Burnquist to P. Liesch, 1 Aug. 1918.

63. J. A. A. Burnquist Papers, box 10, folder: Correspondence and Miscellaneous Papers, undated, June 11–31, 1917, letter from S. S. Viereck to Burnquist, 15 June 1917; qtd. in Chrislock, *Watchdog* 138. Cf. ibid. 137; *DW* 31 May 1917: 4.

64. J. A. A. Burnquist Papers, box 10, folder: Correspondence and Miscellaneous Papers, undated, August, 28, 1917, "Our Present War" 1, 5. Cf. Chrislock, *Watchdog* 137–38, 152; H. Johnson 176.

65. J. A. A. Burnquist Papers, box 11, folder: Correspondence and Miscellaneous Papers, Sept. 21–Oct. 9, 1917, letter from H. C. Hess to Burnquist, 4 Oct. 1917; *DW* 19 Apr. 1917: 1. Cf. ibid. 5 Apr. 1917: 4; 19 Apr. 1917: 1; *d VZ* 25 Aug., 24 Sept. 1917: 4.

66. *Winona Republican Herald* 28 Aug. 1917: 6. Cf. ibid. 13 Oct. 1917: 10; MNCPS, Minutes, 22 May 1917; *DW* 6 Sept. 1917: 4; 26 Sept. 1918: 1. By contrast, Wingerd speaks of Ireland's "apparent complicity" in the anti-German campaigns without giving any evidence for this claim. Wingerd, *Claiming* 132–33.

67. J. A. A. Burnquist Papers, box 12, folder: Correspondence and Miscellaneous Papers, undated, Jan. 1–16, 1918, clipping from *Fairmont Sentinel.*

68. Prohibition and Temperance Collection, box 8, folder 4: Pamphlets 1917–1919, "Brewing and Liquor Interests and German and Bolshevik Propaganda" 4–5; Kazal 182; *Our Side* 12 Aug. 1915: 5; Luebke, *Bonds of Loyalty* 98, 269–70.

69. Conzen, *Germans in Minnesota* 69; Wingerd, *Claiming* 162–63.

70. *d VZ* 4 Nov. 1918: 5. Cf. ibid. 30 Jan. 1917: 6.

71. *d VZ* 3, 11, 22, 24 Apr. 1918: 6; Wolkerstorfer, "Nativism in Minnesota" 120, 165, 172, "Persecution" 12, "Anti-German Nativism" 4–5; Wingerd, *Claiming* 162–65, 210.

72. *d VZ* 27 Feb. 1919: 4. Cf. ibid. 20 Jan. 1919: 4; *DW* 20 Mar. 1919: 4.

73. Wingerd, *Claiming* 210; Kazal 197; Luebke 329; Gans. Cf. Wingerd, *Claiming* 211; Kazal 79–108; Luebke, *Bonds of Loyalty* 319; Conzen, *Germans in Minnesota* 72, 74.

74. Due to a dearth of records, nothing is known about Minnesota's Irish American, Scandinavian American, and the few German American temperance women's contributions to the war. If they participated in war efforts alongside their Anglo-American WCTU sisters at all, which is rather unlikely due to their Old-World ties, they must have been affronted by the intensive campaigns for Americanization, all of which held implicit assumptions of Anglo-American superiority.

75. Bingham 442–45; Schaffer 90–95.

76. *MN White Ribbon* Feb. 1918: 1; Oct. 1918: 6. Cf. ibid. May 1917: 1; June 1917: 4; Minutes of the WCTU, 1878–1920, vol. 6, 1917: 22–23, 38; vol. 7, 1918: 20–21.

77. MNCPS Papers, box 8, folder 110.1, letter from the Ramsey WCTU to the MNCPS, 9 Nov. 1917.

78. Scovell 95.

79. Minutes of the WCTU, vol. 6, 1917: 34–38, 40, 49–50; vol. 7, 1918: 38, 80; *MN White Ribbon* Feb. 1918: 1; July 1917: 2; *SP PP* 19, 26 May 1918: 3rd sect., 12; 10 Nov. 1918: 10; 22 Dec. 1918: 3rd sect., 7; Scovell 95.

80. Minutes of the WCTU, vol. 7, 1918: 87. Cf. ibid. 1920: 37, 80; *SP PP* 26 Aug. 1917: 3rd sect., 8.

81. In 1918, the records of the Women's Division of the Federal Employment Service reported that 10,595 of St. Paul's women had been placed into jobs. Holbrook 213–17.

82. *MN White Ribbon* Feb. 1918: 1; *SP PP* 17 Nov. 1918: 3rd sect., 12.

83. MNCPS, Minutes, 19 June 1917; Minutes of the WCTU, vol. 6, 1917: 34–36; *SP PP* 23 Sept. 1917: 3rd sect., 8; 9 June 1918: 3rd sect., 12; Stuhler, *Gentle Warriors* 152; Wolkerstorfer, "Nativism in Minnesota" 138; Scovell 96.

84. J. A. A. Burnquist Papers, box 2, folder: Correspondence and Miscellaneous Papers, "Description of the Powers of the MNCPS"; Wilson qtd. in Schaffer 94. Cf. ibid. 92;

Chrislock, *Watchdog* 247; J. A. A. Burnquist Papers, box 12, folder: Correspondence and Miscellaneous Papers, undated, 1918, "Since the Commencement of the War" 18. For more male praise of women's wartime work, see *MN Patriot* 1st Quarter 1918: 1.

85. Qtd. in Stuhler, *Gentle Warriors* 169, 175. Cf. ibid. 171; *d VZ* 26 June 1919: 6; 13 July 1918: 5; Minutes of the WCTU, vol. 7, 1919: 23, 31–32.

Conclusion

1. Fuchs 46.

2. See also Conzen, "Festive Culture" 48, 63, 75–76.

3. Kazal 197.

4. Wild 881; Fischler 275.

5. Döring, Heide, and Mühleisen 7. For key examples of this growing scholarship on food, see Caplan; Counihan and van Esterik; Gabaccia; Lentz; Scholliers; Diner; Sutton; Watson and Caldwell; Wilson, *Food*.

6. Qtd. in Hunt and Barker 167. Cf. ibid. 166, 168, 169, 171; Gefou-Madianou 1–6; Douglas 8–12; Heath.

7. Hunt and Barker; Marcus. Recent examples of such studies are Scholliers; deGarine and deGarine; Wilson, *Food, Drinking Cultures*.

8. Wilson, "Drinking Cultures" 5, 7, 10. Cf. ibid. 9.

9. Gabaccia 9; Wilson, "Drinking Cultures" 5.

Bibliography

*Newspapers, Government Documents, Minutes/Proceedings,
Archival Collections*

"Abstract of Votes, 1904–1932." MSA.

Alexander Ramsey and Family Papers, 1838–1965. MNHS.

The American Issue Minnesota Edition [Westerville, Ohio] 1911–1916. MNHS.

Anderson H. Wimbish Papers, 1838–1906. MNHS.

Anderson, William, and Theodore C. Blegen, comps. Minnesota Political Party Platforms, 1849–1942. MNHS.

Austin Willey Papers, 1827–1896. MNHS.

Backbone [St. Paul] 1897–1906. MNHS.

Bemidji Daily Pioneer 1896–1903. MNHS.

Bushrod W. Lott Correspondence, 1849–1855. MNHS.

The Catholic Bulletin [St. Paul] 1911–1919. MNHS.

Catholic Total Abstinence Union of St. Paul Collection. AASPM.

Central Woman's Christian Temperance Union. Organization Records, 1906–1917. MNHS.

The Christian Friend [Minneapolis] Dec. 1882–June 1883. MNHS.

The Citizen [St. Paul] 1890. MNHS.

Congregational Association of Central Minnesota. Association Record Book, 1853–1872. MNHS.

The Daily Minnesotian [St. Paul] 1854–1858. MNHS.

The Daily Pioneer [St. Paul] 1854–1855. MNHS.

The Daily Pioneer and Democrat [St. Paul] 1855–1860, 1869. MNHS.

The Daily Pioneer Press [St. Paul] 1876–1909. MNHS.

The Eighth Census of the United States: 1860. Washington, D.C.: GPO, 1864.

The Eleventh Census of the United States: 1890. Washington, D.C.: GPO, 1890–1896.

Evangelical Association of North America, Minnesota Conference. Minnesota Conference Minutes, 1868–1887. MNHS.

The Falls Evening News [St. Anthony] 1857–1861. MNHS.

Fisher, Daniel J., Letter to Arthur J. Donnelly. Undated. Box: Catholic Historical Society A–Z Files D–Ge. Folder: Fisher, Daniel J., Letters, 1852, 1853. AASPM.

Fourth Annual Meeting of the Minnesota Sunday School Temperance League. St. Paul: Ramaley and Cunningham, 1877.

General and Special Laws of the State of Minnesota: Passed and Approved during the Fourth Session of the Legislature. St. Paul: Wm. R. Marshall, 1862.

General Laws of the State of Minnesota: Passed and Approved during the First Session of the Legislature. St. Paul: Earle S. Goodrich, 1858.

General Laws of the State of Minnesota: Passed and Approved during the Second Session of the Legislature. Faribault: Orville Brown, 1860.

General Laws of the State of Minnesota: Passed and Approved during the Twelfth Session of the State Legislature. St. Paul: Press Printing Company, 1870.

Goodhue County Republican [Red Wing] 1874. MNHS.

The Grange Advance [Red Wing] 1873–1877. MNHS.

Independent Order of Good Templars, Grand Lodge of Minnesota. Collection of Proceedings, 1860–1902. MNHS.

Independent Order of Good Templars Papers. Journal of Proceedings of the Grand Lodge of Minnesota, 1856–1866. MNHS.

The Irish Standard [Minneapolis] 1886–1920. MNHS.

J. A. A. Burnquist Papers, 1884–1961. MNHS.

James M. Reardon Papers. AASPM.

John W. North and Family Papers, 1849–1938. MNHS.

Journal of the Council of Minnesota during the Fourth Session of the Legislative Assembly of the Territory of Minnesota. St. Paul: Joseph R. Brown, 1853.

Journal of the Council of the Territory of Minnesota during the Fifth Session of the Legislative Assembly. St. Paul: Brown and Olmstead, 1854.

Journal of the House of Representatives during the Fifth Session of the Legislative Assembly of the Territory of Minnesota. St. Paul: Brown and Olmstead, 1854.

Journal of the House of Representatives during the Third Session of the Legislative Assembly of the Territory of Minnesota. St. Paul: Owens and Moore, 1852.

Journal of the House of Representatives of the Fifteenth Session of the Legislature of the State of Minnesota. St. Paul: Press Printing Company, 1873.

Journal of the House of Representatives of the Ninth Session of the Legislature of the State of Minnesota. St. Paul: M. J. Clum, 1867.

Journal of the House of Representatives of the Second Legislature of the State of Minnesota. St. Paul: Newson, Moore, Foster, 1860.

Journal of the Senate of the Second Legislature of the State of Minnesota. St. Paul: Newson, Moore, Foster, 1860.

Keller, George. Letters to Archbishop Ireland. 10 Mar., 16 Oct. 1895. Box: Catholic Historical Society, A–Z Files H–Se. Folder: Keller, George, Fr., Papers, 1872–1897. AASPM.

Labor Review [Minneapolis] 1907–1917. MNHS.

Marion P. and William W. Satterlee Papers, 1878–1937. MNHS.

Methodist Episcopal Church/Minnesota Annual Conference/Historical Society. Methodist Episcopal Church Records, 1840–1909. MNHS.

Minneapolis Daily Tribune 1867–1876. MNHS.

Minneapolis Journal 1888–1919. MNHS.

The Minneapolis Tribune 1886–1909. MNHS.

Minnesota Chronicle and Register [St. Paul] 1849–1851. MNHS.

Minnesota Commission of Public Safety. Minutes, 1917–1920. MSA.

Minnesota Commission of Public Safety Papers. MSA.

Minnesota Democrat [St. Paul] 1850–1855. MNHS.

Minnesota Deutsche Zeitung [St. Paul] 1855–1858. MNHS.

Minnesota Federal Writers Project. Annals of Minnesota: Chronological, Subject, and Geographical Files, 1849–1922, 1941–1942. Reel 121: Subject Files for Suffrage, Temperance. MNHS.

The Minnesota Issue [Minneapolis] 1898–1902, 1907–1911. MNHS.

Minnesota Legislative Assembly. Joint Committee Reports and Miscellaneous Records, 1849–1857. MSA.

Minnesota Patriot [Minneapolis] 1913–1919. MNHS.

Minnesota Pioneer [St. Paul] 1849–1855. MNHS.

The Minnesota Republican [St. Anthony] 1854–1858. MNHS.

Minnesota Staats-Zeitung [St. Paul] weekly 1858–1877, triweekly 1867–1877. MNHS.

Minnesota State News [St. Anthony] 1859–1863. MNHS.

The Minnesota Union Advocate [St. Paul] 1897–1919. MNHS.

Minnesota Volksblatt [St. Paul] 1861–1877. MNHS.

The Minnesota White Ribbon [St. Paul] 1901–1919. MNHS.

The Minnesota White Ribboner [Minneapolis] 1890–1901. MNHS.

Minutes of the Minnesota Annual Conference of the Methodist Episcopal Church 1860. St. Paul: Pioneer Book and Job Printing, 1860.

Minutes of the Minnesota Annual Conference of the Methodist Episcopal Church 1865. St. Paul: St. Paul Press Printing, 1865.

Minutes of the Minnesota Baptist Association 1852. St. Anthony: St. Anthony Express Print, 1852.

Minutes of the Sixth Annual Session of the General Conference of Congregational Churches in Minnesota. St. Paul: Press Printing Company, 1861.

Minutes of the Woman's Christian Temperance Union of Minnesota, 1878–1920. 7 Vols. SWHA.

Miscellaneous Records of the Legislature, 185[?]–1891. Folder: Suffrage Petitions, Undated and 1869. MSA.

New Ulm Review 1892–1922. MNHS.

Northwestern Chronicle [St. Paul] 1869–1919. MNHS, AASPM.

North-Western Democrat [St. Anthony] 1853–1856. MNHS.

Oscar Christgau Papers, 1900–1978. MNHS.

Our Side [Minneapolis, St. Paul] 1915–1920. MNHS.

The Owatonna Journal 1888–1906. MNHS.

Pamphlets Relating to the Liquor Problem in Minnesota, 1882–[?]. MNHS.

Political Equality Club of Minneapolis. Records, Undated and 1883–1921. MNHS.

Proceedings of the 8th Annual Convention of the Catholic Total Abstinence Union of the Diocese of St. Paul, Minnesota, Minneapolis, June 18–19, 1879. St. Paul: Northwestern Chronicle, 1879.

Proceedings of the 17th Annual Convention of the Catholic Total Abstinence Union of the Diocese of St. Paul, Held at Winona, Minnesota, June 13–14, 1888. Minneapolis: Irish Standard Job Printing, 1888.

Proceedings of the 18th Annual Convention of the Catholic Total Abstinence Union of the Diocese of St. Paul, Minnesota, Minneapolis, June 5–6, 1889. St. Paul: Northwestern Chronicle, 1889.

Proceedings of the 20th Annual Convention of the Catholic Total Abstinence Union of the Archdiocese of St. Paul, Held at St. Paul, Minnesota, June 17–18, 1891. St. Paul: P. M. Maroney, 1891.

"Prohibition, Benefits of." *The Cyclopaedia of Temperance and Prohibition: A Reference Book of Facts, Statistics, and General Information on All Phases of the Drink Question, the Temperance Movement and the Prohibition Agitation.* Ed. Walter W. Spooner. New York: Funk and Wagnalls, 1891. 499–559.

Prohibition and Temperance Collection, 1786–1960. SWHA.

Prohibition Party (Minnesota), State Committee. Prohibition Party Records, 1876–1919. MNHS.

Ramsey County. St. Paul. City Council. Journals. MSA.

Report of the Executive Committee of the American Temperance Union 1853. New York: American Temperance Union, 1853.

"Scandinavians in Minnesota." *The New York Times* 26 July 1886: n.p. *The New York Times,* n.d. Web. 30 Sept. 2013.

Session Laws of the Territory of Minnesota Passed by the Legislative Assembly at the Session Commencing Wednesday 7 Jan. 1852. St. Paul: James Goodhue, 1852.

Sons of Temperance of North America, Grand Division of Minnesota. *Minutes of the Grand Division of the Sons of Temperance, State of Minnesota: From Its Organization, February 22, 1870, to the Close of Its First Annual Session, October 26, 1870.* Minneapolis: Tribune Printing Company, 1870.

St. Anthony Express 1851–1860. MNHS.

St. Cloud Journal 1866–1876. MNHS.

St. Paul City Council. Ordinances City of St. Paul, 1854–1858. MSA.

St. Paul City Directory 1887–1888. St. Paul: Polk and Co. Publishers, 1887.

St. Paul City Directory 1890–1891. St. Paul: R. L. Polk and Co., 1890.

St. Paul City Directory 1895. St. Paul: R. L. Polk and Co., 1895.

St. Paul Daily Dispatch 1868–1885. MNHS.

St. Paul Daily Globe 1884–1896. MNHS.

St. Paul Daily News 1887–1894, 1900–1919. MNHS.

The St. Paul Daily Pioneer 1867–1876. MNHS.

St. Paul Daily Press 1861–1864. MNHS.

St. Paul Daily Times 1854–1859. MNHS.

St. Paul Dispatch 1920. MNHS.

St. Paul Pioneer Press 1909–1920. MNHS.

St. Paul Weekly Dispatch 1868–1903. MNHS.
St. Paul Weekly Globe 1880–1883. MNHS.
St. Paul Weekly Pioneer 1865–1875. MNHS.
Tägliche Volkszeitung [St. Paul] 1882–1920. MNHS.
The Temperance Campaign [Minneapolis] 1873. MNHS.
The Tenth Census of the United States: 1880. Washington, D.C.: GPO, 1883.
To-Day [Minneapolis] 1883–1886. MNHS.
The Topic [Minneapolis] 1883. MNHS.
"Traveling Men's Liberty League of Minnesota." Pocket Binder. c. 1909. Doug Hoverson's Collection.
Treasurer's Book: Excelsior Club No. 1 of Temperance Watchmen St. Paul, Minnesota. MNHS.
Der Wanderer [St. Paul] 1867–1920. MNHS, University of Notre Dame.
Warren Sheaf 1880–1922. *Chronicling America*, Library of Congress.
Weekly Globe [St. Paul] 1878–1883. MNHS.
The Weekly Minnesotian [St. Paul] 1852–1858. MNHS.
The Weekly Pioneer and Democrat [St. Paul] 1855–1865. MNHS.
The Weekly Pioneer Press [St. Paul] 1876–1906. MNHS.
The Western Leader [Minneapolis] 1892–1894. MNHS.
Western Temperance Herald [Minneapolis] 1870–1872. MNHS.
William Pitt Murray and Family Papers, 1836–1944. MNHS.
The Winona Republican Herald 1901–1919. MNHS.
Wöchentliche Volkszeitung [St. Paul] 1907–1919. MNHS.
Woman's Christian Temperance Union of Minnesota Records, 1886–1992. MNHS.
Yearbook of the St. Paul Political Equality Club, 1911–1912. MNHS.

Secondary Literature

Abbott, Carl. "Thinking about Cities: The Central Tradition in U.S. Urban History." *Journal of Urban History* 22.6 (1996): 687–701.
Ahlstrom, Sidney E. *A Religious History of the American People.* 2nd ed. New Haven: Yale University Press, 2004.
Ames, Charles G. *A Spiritual Autobiography: With an Epilogue by Alice Ames Winter.* Boston: Riverside Press, 1913.
Anderson, Philip J., and Dag Blanck. Introduction. *Swedes in the Twin Cities: Immigrant Life and Minnesota's Urban Frontier.* Ed. Philip J. Anderson and Dag Blanck. St. Paul: Minnesota Historical Society Press, 2001. 3–13.
Arndt, Karl J. R., and May E. Olson. *German-American Newspapers and Periodicals 1732–1955: History and Bibliography.* Heidelberg: Quelle and Meyer, 1961.
Bakeman, Mary H. *Casting Long Shadows: 125 Years at Hamline United Methodist Church.* St. Paul: Hamline United Methodist Church, 2006.
Baker, Paula. "Women and the Domestication of Politics, 1780–1920." *American Historical Review* 89 (1984): 620–47.
Barrett, James R. "Why 'Paddy' Drank: The Social Importance of Whiskey in Pre-Famine Ireland." *Journal of Popular Culture* 11.1 (1977): 17–28.

Barth, Fredrik. Introduction. *Ethnic Groups and Boundaries: The Social Organization of Culture Difference.* Ed. Fredrik Barth. Bergen: Universitetsforlaget, 1969. 9–38.

Benson, James K. *Irish and German Families and the Economic Development of Midwestern Cities, 1860–1895.* Diss. University of Minnesota, 1980. European Immigrants and American Society: A Collection of Studies and Dissertations. New York: Garland, 1990.

———. "The New England of the West: The Emergence of American Mind in Early St. Paul, MN, 1849–1855." MA Thesis. University of Minnesota, 1970.

"George Benz." *Genealogy Trails*, n.d. Web. 12 Jan. 2013.

Berthel, Mary Wheelhouse. *Horns of Thunder: The Life and Times of James M. Goodhue, Including Selections from His Writings.* St. Paul: Minnesota Historical Society Press, 1948.

Best, Joel. *Controlling Vice: Regulating Brothel Prostitution in St. Paul, 1865–1883.* History of Crime and Criminal Justice Ser. Columbus: Ohio University Press, 1998.

Bingham, Marjorie. "Keeping at It: Minnesota Women." *Minnesota in a Century of Change: The State and Its People since 1900.* Ed. Clifford E. Clark Jr. St. Paul: Minnesota Historical Society Press, 1989. 433–71.

Bishop, Harriet E. *Floral Home, or, First Years of Minnesota: Early Sketches, Later Settlements, and Further Developments.* New York: Sheldon, Blakeman and Co., 1857.

Blair, Henry W. *The Temperance Movement, or, the Conflict between Man and Alcohol.* Boston: Smythe, 1888.

Bland, Joan. *The Hibernian Crusade: The Story of the Catholic Total Abstinence Union of America.* Washington, D.C.: Catholic University of America Press, 1951.

Blegen, Theodore C., and Philip D. Jordan. *With Various Voices: Recordings of North Star Life.* St. Paul: Itasca Press, 1949.

Blessing, Patrick J. "Irish." *Harvard Encyclopedia of American Ethnic Groups.* Ed. Stephen Thernstrom, Ann Orlov, and Oscar Handlin. Cambridge: Belknap-Harvard University Press, 1981. 524–45.

Blocker, Jack S., Jr. *American Temperance Movements: Cycles of Reform.* Social Movements Past and Present. Boston: Twayne, 1989.

———. "Separate Paths: Suffragists and the Women's Temperance Crusade." *Signs* 10 (1985): 460–76.

Bonney, Rachel A. "Was There a Single German-American Experience?" *A Heritage Deferred: The German-Americans in Minnesota.* Ed. Clarence A. Glasrud. Moorhead: Concordia College, 1981. 20–31.

Bordin, Ruth. *Frances Willard: A Biography.* Urbana: Chicago University Press, 1986.

———. *Woman and Temperance: The Quest for Power and Liberty, 1873–1900.* Philadelphia: Temple University Press, 1981.

Boyer, Paul S. *Urban Masses and Moral Order in America, 1820–1920.* Cambridge: Harvard University Press, 1992.

Boyle, Sarah. "Creating a Union of the Union: The Woman's Christian Temperance Union and the Creation of a Politicized Female Reform Culture, 1880–1892." Diss. SUNY Binghamton, 2005.

Brøndal, Jørn. *Ethnic Leadership and Midwestern Politics: Scandinavian-Americans and the Progressive Movement in Wisconsin, 1890–1914.* Northfield: Norwegian-American Historical Association, 2004.

Brubaker, Rogers, and Frederick Cooper. "Beyond 'Identity.'" *Theory and Society* 29.1 (2000): 1–47.

Brueggemann, Gary. "Beer Capital of the State: St. Paul's Historic Family Breweries." *Ramsey County History* 16.2 (1981): 3–15.

Burgess, Patricia. "Discovering Hidden Histories: The Identity of Place and Time." *Journal of Urban History* 26.5 (2000): 645–56.

Caplan, Pat, ed. *Food, Health and Identity*. London: Routledge, 1997.

Carmody, Charles J. "Rechabites in Purple: A History of the Catholic Temperance Movement in the Northwest." MA Thesis. St. Paul Seminary, 1953.

Castle, Henry A. *History of St. Paul and Vicinity: A Chronicle of Progress and a Narrative Account of the Industries, Institutions, and People of the City and Its Tributary Territory*. Vols. 1–2. Chicago: Lewis, 1912.

Cayton, Andrew R. L., and Susan E. Gray. "The Story of the Midwest: An Introduction." *The Identity of the American Midwest: Essays on Regional History*. Ed. Andrew R. L. Cayton and Susan E. Gray. Bloomington: Indiana University Press, 2001. 1–26.

Cerulo, Karen A. "Identity Construction: New Issues, New Directions." *Annual Review of Sociology* 23 (1997): 385–409.

Cherrington, Ernest H., ed. and comp. *The Anti-Saloon League Yearbook of 1909*. Columbus: ASL, 1909.

———. *The Anti-Saloon League Yearbook of 1914*. Westerville: American Issue Press, 1914.

———. *The Anti-Saloon League Yearbook of 1915*. Westerville: American Issue Press, 1915.

———. *The Anti-Saloon League Yearbook of 1917*. Westerville: American Issue Press, 1917.

———. *The Evolution of Prohibition in the United States of America: A Chronological History of the Liquor Problem and the Temperance Reform in the United States from the Earliest Settlements to the Consummation of National Prohibition*. Montclair: Smith, 1969.

Chrislock, Carl H. "The German-American Role in Minnesota Politics, 1850–1950." *A Heritage Deferred: The German-Americans in Minnesota*. Ed. Clarence A. Glasrud. Moorhead: Concordia College, 1981. 104–17.

———. "The Politics of Protest in Minnesota, 1890–1901: From Populism to Progressivism." Diss. University of Minnesota, 1955.

———. "Profile of a Ward Boss: The Political Career of Lars M. Rand." *Norwegian-American Studies* 31 (1986): 35–72. *NAHA online*. Norwegian-American Historical Association, n.d. Web. 1 Jan. 2009.

———. *The Progressive Era in Minnesota, 1899–1918*. St. Paul: Minnesota Historical Society Press, 1971.

———. *Watchdog of Loyalty: The Minnesota Commission of Public Safety during World War I*. St. Paul: Minnesota Historical Society Press, 1991.

Christianson, Theodore. *Minnesota Becomes of Age*. Chicago: American Historical Society, 1935.

Clifford, Eileen Jean. "The Impact of Selected Organizations on Health Education in the State of Minnesota." Diss. University of Minnesota, 1986.

Cohen, Abner. "Ethnicity and Politics." *Ethnicity*. Ed. John Hutchinson and Anthony D. Smith. Oxford Readers. Oxford: Oxford University Press, 1996. 83–84.

Coker, Joe L. *Liquor in the Land of the Lost Cause: Southern White Evangelicals and the Prohibition Movement.* Religion in the South. Lexington: University of Kentucky Press, 2007.

Connolly, James. "Bringing the City Back In: Space and Place in the Urban History of the Gilded Age and the Progressive Era." *Journal of the Gilded Age and the Progressive Era* 1.3 (2002): 258–78.

Conzen, Kathleen Neils. "Ethnicity as Festive Culture: Nineteenth-Century German America on Parade." *The Invention of Ethnicity.* Ed. Werner Sollors. New York: Oxford University Press, 1989. 44–76.

———. "Germans." *Harvard Encyclopedia of American Ethnic Groups.* Ed. Stephen Thernstrom, Ann Orlov, and Oscar Handlin. Cambridge: Belknap-Harvard University Press, 1981. 405–25.

———. *Germans in Minnesota.* The People of Minnesota. St. Paul: Minnesota Historical Society Press, 2003.

———. *Immigrant Milwaukee, 1836–1860: Accommodation and Community in a Frontier City.* Cambridge: Harvard University Press, 1976.

———. "Pi-Ing the Type: Jane Grey Swisshelm and the Contest of Midwestern Regionality." *The Identity of the American Midwest: Essays on Regional History.* Ed. Andrew R. L. Clayton and Susan E. Gray. Bloomington: Indiana University Press, 2001. 91–110.

Conzen, Kathleen Neils, David A. Gerber, Ewa Morawska, George E. Pozetta, and Rudolph J. Vecoli. "The Invention of Ethnicity: A Perspective from the U.S.A." *Journal of American Ethnic History* 12.1 (1992): 3–41.

Cook, Sharon A. *Through Sunshine and Shadow: The Woman's Christian Temperance Union, Evangelicalism, and Reform in Ontario, 1874–1930.* Montreal: McGill-Queen's University Press, 1995.

Cornell, Stephen, and Douglas Hartmann. *Ethnicity and Race: Making Identities in a Changing World.* 2nd ed. Sociology for a New Century. London: Pine Forge Press, 2007.

Corrigan, Joseph A. *The History of St. Marks and the Midway District.* St. Paul: Church of St. Mark, 1939.

Counihan, Carole, and Penny van Esterik, eds. *Food and Culture: A Reader.* London: Routledge, 1997.

Cutter, Barbara. *Domestic Devils, Battlefield Angels: The Radicalism of American Womanhood, 1830–1865.* DeKalb: Northern Illinois University Press, 2003.

Czaplicka, John J. "Conclusion: Urban History after a Return to Local Self-Determination—Local History and Civic Identity." *Composing Urban History and the Constitution of Civic Identities.* Ed. John J. Czaplicka, Blair A. Ruble, and Lauren Crabtree. Baltimore: Johns Hopkins University Press, 2003. 372–410.

Daniels, William H. *The Temperance Reform and Its Great Reformers: An Illustrated History.* New York: Nelson and Phillips, 1878.

Dann, Otto. *Nation und Nationalismus in Deutschland, 1770–1990.* München: Beck, 1993.

Dannenbaum, Jed. *Drink and Disorder: Temperance Reform in Cincinnati from the Washington Revival to the WCTU.* Chicago: University of Illinois Press, 1984.

———. "The Origins of Temperance Activity and Militancy among American Women." *Journal of Social History* 15.2 (1981): 235–52.

deGarine, Igor, and Valerie deGarine, eds. *Drinking: Anthropological Approaches*. New York: Berghahn, 2001.

Deo, Swati. "Julia Bullard Nelson." *The Privilege for Which We Struggled: Leaders of the Woman Suffrage Movement in Minnesota*. Ed. Heidi Bauer. St. Paul: Upper Midwest Women's History Center, 1999. 42–47.

Deutsch, Sarah. *Women and the City: Gender, Space, and Power in Boston, 1870–1940*. Oxford: Oxford University Press, 2000.

Diner, Hasia R. *Hungering for America: Italian, Irish and Jewish Foodways in the Age of Migration*. Cambridge: Harvard University Press, 2001.

Doenecke, Justus D. *Nothing Less than War: A New History of America's Entry into World War I*. Lexington: University of Kentucky Press, 2011.

Doerries, Reinhard R. *Iren und Deutsche in der Neuen Welt: Akkulturationsprozesse in der amerikanischen Gesellschaft im späten neunzehnten Jahrhundert*. Vierteljahrschrift für Sozial- und Wirtschaftsgeschichte 76. Stuttgart: Steiner, 1986.

Dolan, Jay. *Catholic Revivalism: The American Experience, 1830–1900*. Notre Dame: University of Notre Dame Press, 1978.

Dorchester, Daniel. *The Liquor Problem in All Ages*. New York: Phillips and Hunt, 1888.

Döring, Tobias, Markus Heide, and Susanne Mühleisen. "Introduction: Writing/Eating Culture." *Eating Culture: The Poetics and Politics of Food*. Ed. Tobias Döring et al. American Studies: A Monograph Ser. 106. Heidelberg: Winter, 2003. 1–16.

Dorsey, Bruce. *Reforming Men and Women: Gender in the Antebellum City*. Ithaca: Cornell University Press, 2002.

Douglas, Mary, ed. *Constructive Drinking: Perspectives on Drink from Anthropology*. Cambridge: Cambridge University Press, 1987.

Doutney, Thomas N. *Thomas N. Doutney, His Life-Struggle, Fall, and Reformation, also a Vivid Pen-Picture of New York, Together with a History of the Work He Has Accomplished as a Temperance Reformer*. Boston: Franklin Press, 1886.

Downard, William L. *Dictionary of the History of the American Brewing and Distilling Industry*. Westport: Greenwood Press, 1980.

DuBois, Ellen. "The Radicalism of the Woman Suffrage Movement: Notes toward the Reconsideration of Nineteenth-Century Feminism." *Feminist Studies* 3 (1975): 63–71.

Duis, Perry R. *The Saloon: Public Drinking in Chicago and Boston, 1880–1920*. Urbana: University of Illinois Press, 1983.

Dunlap, Leslie Kathrin. "In the Name of the Home: Temperance, Women and Southern Grass-Roots Politics, 1873–1933." Diss. Northwestern University, 2001.

Dyer, Dawn Michele. "Combating the 'Fiery Flood': The Woman's Christian Temperance Union's Approach to Labor and Socialism." Diss. Auburn University, 1998.

Ellingsen, Agnes E. "A History of the Temperance Movement in Minnesota to 1865." MA Thesis. University of Minnesota, 1933.

Epstein, Barbara Leslie. *The Politics of Domesticity: Women, Evangelism and Temperance in Nineteenth-Century America*. Middletown: Wesleyan University Press, 1981.

Fanshawe, Evelyn Leighton. *Liquor Legislation in the United States and Canada: Report of a Non-Partisan Inquiry on the Spot into the Laws and Their Operation, Undertaken at the Request of W. Rathbone, M.P.* London: Cassell, 1893.

Fennell, Desmond. *The Changing Face of Catholic Ireland.* Washington, D.C.: Corpus Books, 1968.

Fischler, Claude. "Food, Self, and Identity." *Social Science Information* 27 (1988): 275–92.

Flanagan, Kieran Denis. "Emigration, Assimilation, and Occupational Categories of the Irish Americans in Minnesota, 1870–1900." MA Thesis. University of Minnesota, 1969.

Fletcher, Holly Berkley. *Gender and the American Temperance Movement of the Nineteenth Century.* Studies in American Popular History and Culture. New York: Routledge, 2008.

Folwell, William Watts. *A History of Minnesota.* 4 Vols. St. Paul: Minnesota Historical Society Press, 1956–1969.

Foster, Mary Dillon, comp. *Who's Who among Minnesota Women.* St. Paul: M. D. Foster, 1924.

Frank, John W., Roland S. Moore, and Genevieve M. Ames. "Historical and Cultural Roots of Drinking Problems among American Indians." *American Journal of Public Health* 90.3 (2000): 344–51.

Fraser, Nancy. "Rethinking the Public Sphere: A Contribution to the Critique of Actually Existing Democracy." *Social Text* 25/26 (1990): 56–80.

Fuchs, Lawrence H. *The American Kaleidoscope: Race, Ethnicity, and the Civic Culture.* Hanover: University Press of New England, 1990.

Fullilove, Mindy Thompson. "Psychiatric Implications of Displacement: Contributions from the Psychology of Place." *American Journal of Psychiatry* 153 (1996): 1516–23.

Gabaccia, Donna R. *We Are What We Eat: Ethnic Food and the Making of Americans.* Cambridge: Harvard University Press, 1998.

Gans, Herbert J. "Symbolic Ethnicity: The Future of Ethnic Groups and Cultures in America." *On the Making of Americans: Essays in Honor of David Riesman.* Ed. Herbert J. Gans. Philadelphia: University of Pennsylvania Press, 1979. 193–220.

Garner, Nancy Gail. "Loyal Temperance Legion (LTL)." *Alcohol and Temperance in Modern History: An International Encyclopedia.* Ed. Jack S. Blocker Jr. et al. Santa Barbara: ABC-Clio, 2003. 387–88.

Geertz, Clifford. "Primordial Ties." *Ethnicity.* Ed. John Hutchinson and Anthony D. Smith. Oxford Readers. Oxford: Oxford University Press, 1996. 40–44.

Gefou-Madianou, Dimitra. Introduction. *Alcohol, Gender and Culture.* Ed. Dimitra Gefou-Madianou. London: Routledge, 1992. 1–34.

Gieryn, Thomas F. "A Space for Place in Sociology." *Annual Review of Sociology* 26 (2000): 463–96.

Gilfillan, Charles D. *The Early Political History of Minnesota.* Collections of the Minnesota Historical Society 9. St. Paul: Minnesota Historical Society Press, 1901.

Gilfoyle, Timothy J. "White Cities, Linguistic Turns, and Disneylands: The New Paradigms of Urban History." *Reviews in American History* 26.1 (1998): 175–204.

Gilman, Rhoda R. *Stand Up: The Story of Minnesota's Protest Tradition.* St. Paul: Minnesota Historical Society Press, 2012.

Ginzberg, Lori D. *Women and the Work of Benevolence: Morality, Politics and Class in the Nineteenth-Century United States.* New Haven: Yale University Press, 1990.

Glazer, Nathan, and Daniel Patrick Moynihan. *Beyond the Melting Pot: The Negroes, Puerto Ricans, Jews, Italians, and Irish of New York City.* Cambridge: MIT Press, 1963.

Gleason, Philip. *The Conservative Reformers: German-American Catholics and the Social Order.* Notre Dame: University of Notre Dame Press, 1968.

———. *Keeping the Faith: American Catholicism Past and Present.* Notre Dame: University of Notre Dame Press, 1987.

Godsho, Albert. *Chronological History of the National German American Alliance of the United States.* Philadelphia: National German American Alliance, 1911.

Gordon, Linda. *Woman's Body, Woman's Right: Birth Control in America.* Rev. ed. London: Penguin, 1990.

Gray, Susan E. *The Yankee West: Community Life on the Michigan Frontier.* Chapel Hill: University of North Carolina Press, 1996.

Green, James J. "The Organization of the Catholic Total Abstinence Union of America, 1866–1884." *Records of the American Catholic Historical Society* 61.2 (1950): 71–97.

Gross, Stephen J. "Family, Property, Community, Class and Identity among German-Americans in Rural Stearns County, Minnesota, 1860–1920." Diss. University of Minnesota, 1999.

Gusfield, Joseph. *Symbolic Crusade: Status Politics and the American Temperance Movement.* 2nd ed. Urbana: University of Illinois Press, 1986.

Hagedorn, Hermann. *Where Do You Stand? An Appeal to Americans of German Origin.* St. Paul: Publicity Dept. Commission of Public Safety, n.d.

Haines, Lynn. *The Minnesota Legislature of 1909: A History of the Session, with an Inside View of Men and Measures.* Minneapolis: L. Haines, 1910.

———. *The Minnesota Legislature of 1911.* Minneapolis: L. Haines, 1911.

Hall, Stuart. "Introduction: Who Needs 'Identity'?" *Questions of Cultural Identity.* Ed. Stuart Hall and Paul du Gay. London: Sage Publications, 1996. 1–17.

"Hamline Midway." Ramsey County Historical Society Saint Paul, n.d. Web. 31 Mar. 2008.

Hamm, Richard F. *Shaping the Eighteenth Amendment: Temperance Reform, Legal Culture, and the Polity, 1880–1920.* Chapel Hill: University of North Carolina Press, 1995.

Hansen, Marcus Lee. *Old Fort Snelling, 1819–1858.* Minneapolis: Ross and Haines, 1958.

Harzig, Christiane. "The Ethnic Female Public Sphere: German-American Women in Turn-of-the-Century Chicago." *Midwestern Women: Work, Community, and Leadership at the Crossroads.* Ed. Lucy Eldersveld Murphy et al. Bloomington: Indiana University Press, 1997. 141–57.

Hathaway, James T. "The Evolution of Drinking Places in the Twin Cities: From the Advent of White Settlement to the Present." Diss. University of Minnesota, 1982.

Haynes, John E. "Reformers, Radicals, and Conservatives." *Minnesota in a Century of Change: The State and Its People since 1900.* Ed. Clifford E. Clark Jr. St. Paul: Minnesota Historical Society Press, 1989. 361–95.

Heath, Dwight B. "Anthropology and Alcohol Studies: Current Issues." *Annual Review of Anthropology* 16 (1987): 99–120.

Heinrici, Max. *Das Buch der Deutschen in Amerika.* Philadelphia: Walters Buchdruckerei, 1909.

Hennessy, William B. *Past and Present of St. Paul, Minnesota: Being a Relation of the Progressive History of the Capital City of Minnesota from the Earliest Historical Times down to the Present Day, Together with an Exposition of the Lives of the Makers of History.* Chicago: S. J. Clarke, 1906.

Hilton, Ora A. *The Minnesota Commission of Public Safety in World War I, 1917–1919.* Stillwater: Oklahoma Agricultural and Mechanical College, 1951.

Hoffert, Sylvia D. "Jane Grey Swisshelm and the Negotiation of Gender Roles on the Minnesota Frontier." *Frontiers: A Journal of Women Studies* 18.3 (1997): 17–39.

Holbrook, Franklin F. *St. Paul and Ramsey County in the War of 1917–1918.* St. Paul: Ramsey County War Records Commission, 1929.

Holbrook, Franklin F., and Livia Appel. *Minnesota in the War with Germany.* 2 Vols. St. Paul: Minnesota Historical Society Press, 1928–1932.

Holmquist, June. Introduction. *They Chose Minnesota: A Survey of the State's Groups.* Ed. June Holmquist. St. Paul: Minnesota Historical Society Press, 1981. 1–16.

Hoverson, Doug. *Land of Amber Waters: The History of Brewing in Minnesota.* Minneapolis: University of Minnesota Press, 2007.

Hudson, Horace B. "Churches and Philanthropies." *A Half Century of Minneapolis.* Ed. Horace B. Hudson. Minneapolis: Hudson Publishing, 1908. 69–89.

Hunt, Geoffrey P., and Judith C. Barker. "Socio-Cultural Anthropology and Alcohol and Drug Research: Towards a Unified Theory." *Social Science and Medicine* 53 (2001): 165–88.

Huntington, Samuel P. *Who Are We? The Challenges to America's National Identity.* New York: Simon and Schuster, 2004.

Hurd, Ethel Edgerton. *Woman Suffrage in Minnesota: A Record of the Activities in Its Behalf from 1847.* Minneapolis: Inland Press, 1916.

"In the Beginning." St. Paul Police Historical Society, 2000. Web. 26 Mar. 2008.

James, Carol L. *Andrew J. Volstead: A Summary of Research.* St. Paul: C. L. James, 1978.

Jameson, Elizabeth. "Women as Workers, Women as Civilizers: True Womanhood in the American West." *The Women's West.* Ed. Susan Armitage et al. Norman: University of Oklahoma Press, 1987. 145–64.

Jarchow, Merrill E. "Social and Cultural Aspects of the Methodist Church in Pioneer Minnesota." MA Thesis. University of Minnesota, 1933.

Jensen, Richard. *The Winning of the Midwest: Social and Political Conflict, 1888–1896.* Chicago: University of Chicago Press, 1971.

Johnson, Hildegard Binder. "The Germans." *They Chose Minnesota: A Survey of the State's Groups.* Ed. June Holmquist. St. Paul: Minnesota Historical Society Press, 1981. 153–84.

Johnson, Paul E. *A Shopkeeper's Millennium: Society and Revivals in Rochester, New York, 1815–1837.* New York: Hill and Wang, 1978.

Jones, Evan. *Citadel in the Wilderness: The Story of Fort Snelling and the Old Northwest Frontier.* New York: Coward-McCann, 1966.

Kazal, Russell A. *Becoming Old Stock: The Paradox of German-American Identity.* Princeton: Princeton University Press, 2004.

Kerber, Linda K. "Separate Spheres, Female Worlds, Woman's Place: The Rhetoric of Women's History." *Journal of American History* 75.1 (June 1988): 9–39.

Kerr, Austin K. *Organized for Prohibition: A New History of the Anti-Saloon League.* New Haven: Yale University Press, 1985.

Kerr, Kathleen Edith. "Female Empowerment: A History of the Minnesota Woman's Christian Temperance Union, 1900–1910." Hon. Paper. Macalester College, 1992.

Kingsdale, John M. "The 'Poor Man's Club': Social Functions of the Urban Working-Class Saloon." *American Quarterly* 25.4 (1973): 472–89.

Klein, James E. *Grappling with Demon Rum: The Cultural Struggle over Liquor in Early Oklahoma*. Norman: University of Oklahoma Press, 2008.

Kleppner, Paul. *The Cross of Culture: A Social Analysis of Midwestern Politics, 1850–1900.* New York: Free Press, 1970.

———. *The Third Electoral System, 1853–1892: Parties, Voters, and Political Cultures.* Chapel Hill: University of North Carolina Press, 1979.

Kloß, Heinz. *Um die Einigung des Deutschamerikanertums: Die Geschichte einer unvollendeten Volksgruppe*. Berlin: Volk und Reich, 1937.

Knobel, Dale T. *Paddy and the Republic: Ethnicity and Nationality in Antebellum America*. Middletown: Wesleyan University Press, 1986.

Kulas, John S. Der Wanderer *of St. Paul, the First Decade, 1867–1877: A Mirror of the German Catholic Immigrant Experience in Minnesota*. Diss. University of Minnesota, 1988. New German American Studies 9. New York: Lang, 1996.

Kunz, Virginia Brainard. *St. Paul: Saga of an American City*. Woodland Hills: Windsor, 1977.

Lanegran, David A. "Swedish Neighborhoods of the Twin Cities: From Swede Hollow to Arlington Hills, from Snoose Boulevard to Minnehaha Parkway." *Swedes in the Twin Cities: Immigrant Life and Minnesota's Urban Frontier*. Ed. Philip J. Anderson and Dag Blanck. St. Paul: Minnesota Historical Society Press, 2001. 39–50.

Le Duc, William G. *Minnesota Yearbook for 1853*. St. Paul: W. G. Le Duc, 1853.

"Legislators Past and Present." Minnesota Legislative Reference Library, n.d. Web. 10 Oct. 2011.

Lender, Mark Edward, and James Kirby Martin. *Drinking in America: A History*. New York: Free Press, 1982.

Lentz, Carola, ed. *Changing Food Habits: Case Studies from Africa, South America, and Europe*. Amsterdam: Harwood, 1999.

LeSueur, Meridel. "Beer Town." *Life in the United States*. New York: Scribner's, 1933. 31–41.

Letterman, Edward J. "St. Paul's Early Settlers and the Indians among Them: Foolish and Childlike or Fierce and Savage?" *Ramsey County History* 2.2 (1965): 11–17.

Luebke, Frederick C. *Bonds of Loyalty: German-Americans and World War I*. Dekalb: Northern Illinois University Press, 1974.

———. *Germans in the New World: Essays in the History of Immigration*. Urbana: University of Illinois Press, 1999.

Maccabee, Paul. *John Dillinger Slept Here: A Crooks' Tour of Crime and Corruption in St. Paul, 1920–1936*. St. Paul: Minnesota Historical Society Press, 1995.

Malcolm, Elizabeth. *"Ireland Sober, Ireland Free": Drink and Temperance in Nineteenth-Century Ireland*. Syracuse: Syracuse University Press, 1986.

———. "The Rise of the Pub: A Study in the Disciplining of Popular Culture." *Irish Popular Culture, 1650–1850*. Ed. James S. Donnelly and Kerby A. Miller. Dublin: Irish Academic Press, 1998. 55–64.

Mancall, Peter C. *Deadly Medicine: Indians and Alcohol in Early America*. New York: Cornell University Press, 1995.

Marcus, Anthony. "Drinking Politics: Alcohol, Drugs and the Problem of US Civil Society." *Drinking Cultures: Alcohol and Identity*. Ed. Thomas M. Wilson. Oxford: Berg, 2005. 255–76.

Marti, Donald. "The Puritan Tradition in a 'New England of the West.'" *Minnesota History* 40.1 (1966): 1–11.

Martin, Scott C. *Devil of the Domestic Sphere: Temperance, Gender, and Middle-Class Ideology, 1800–1860*. DeKalb: Northern Illinois University Press, 2008.

Massard-Guilbaud, Geneviève. "The Genesis of an Urban Identity: The Quartier de la Gare in Clermont-Ferrand, 1850–1914." *Journal of Urban History* 25.6 (1999): 779–808.

Massmann, John C. "German Immigration to Minnesota, 1850–1890." Diss. University of Minnesota, 1966.

Matt, Joseph. "The Catholic City Federation of St. Paul." *Acta et Dicta* 7.1 (1935): 95–103.

Mattingly, Carol. *Well-Tempered Women: Nineteenth-Century Temperance Rhetoric*. Carbondale: Southern Illinois University Press, 1998.

McCammon, Holly J., and Karen E. Campbell. "Allies on the Road to Victory: Coalition Formation between the Suffragists and the Woman's Christian Temperance Union." *Mobilization: An International Journal* 7.3 (2002): 231–51.

McClure, Jane. "The Midway Chamber and Its Community: The Colorful History of an 'Unparalleled Feature' of St. Paul." *Ramsey County History* 29.3 (1994): 4–20.

McKenzie, Fred A. *"Pussyfoot" Johnson: Crusader—Reformer—A Man among Men*. New York: Revell, 1920.

Meagher, Timothy J. *The Columbia Guide to Irish American History*. New York: Columbia University Press, 2005.

——. *Inventing Irish America: Generation, Class, and Ethnic Identity in a New England City, 1880–1928*. Notre Dame: University of Notre Dame Press, 2001.

Moloney, Deidre M. *American Catholic Lay Groups and Transatlantic Social Reform in the Progressive Era*. Chapel Hill: University of North Carolina Press, 2002.

——. "Combating 'Whiskey's Work': The Catholic Temperance Movement in Late Nineteenth-Century America." *U.S. Catholic Historian* 16.3 (1998): 1–23.

"Mucker." *Englisch-Deutsches und Deutsch-Englisches Wörterbuch*. Ed. Friedrich Grieb. Philadelphia: Weik, 1857.

——. *Handwörterbuch der deutschen Sprache*. Ed. Daniel Sanders and Ernst Wülfing. Leipzig: Wigand, 1910.

Murdock, Catherine Gilbert. *Domesticating Drink: Women, Men, and Alcohol in America, 1870–1940*. Baltimore: Johns Hopkins University Press, 1998.

Mussgang, Margaret. "The Germans in St. Paul." MA Thesis. University of Minnesota, 1932.

Nagel, Joane. *American Indian Ethnic Renewal: Red Power and the Resurgence of Identity and Culture*. New York: Oxford University Press, 1994.

——. "Constructing Ethnicity: Creating and Recreating Ethnic Identity and Culture." *Social Problems* 41.1 (1994): 152–76.

Nathanson, Iric. *Minneapolis in the Twentieth Century.* St. Paul: Minnesota Historical Society Press, 2010.

Neill, Edward D. *The History of Minnesota: From the Earliest French Explorations to the Present Time.* Minneapolis: Johnson, Smith and Harrison, 1878.

Nelson, Julia B. "Minnesota." *History of Woman Suffrage.* Ed. Susan B. Anthony and Ida Husted Harper. Vol. 4. New York: Susan B. Anthony, 1902. 772–82.

"Nelson, Julia Bullard." *Women of Minnesota: Selected Biographical Essays.* Ed. Barbara Stuhler and Gretchen Kreuter. Rev. ed. St. Paul: Minnesota Historical Society Press, 1998. 364–65.

Newson, Thomas M. *Pen Pictures of St. Paul, Minnesota, and Biographical Sketches of Old Settlers: From the Earliest Settlement of the City, up to and Including the Year 1857.* St. Paul: T. M. Newson, 1886.

Noel, Thomas. *The City and the Saloon: Denver, 1858–1916.* Lincoln: University of Nebraska Press, 1982.

O'Brien, Thomas D. "Dillon O'Brien." *Acta et Dicta* 6 (1933): 35–53.

O'Connell, Marvin R. *John Ireland and the American Catholic Church.* St. Paul: Minnesota Historical Society Press, 1988.

Odegard, Peter H. *Pressure Politics: The Story of the Anti-Saloon League.* New York: Columbia University Press, 1928.

O'Fahey, Charles J. "John Ireland's Rhetorical Vision of the Irish in America." MA Thesis. University of Minnesota, 1973.

Parsons, Elaine Frantz. *Manhood Lost: Fallen Drunkards and Redeeming Women in the Nineteenth-Century United States.* Baltimore: Johns Hopkins University Press, 2003.

Pegram, Thomas R. *Battling Demon Rum: The Struggle for a Dry America, 1800–1933.* Chicago: Ivan R. Dee, 1998.

Power, Richard Lyle. *Planting Corn Belt Culture: The Impress of the Upland Southerner and Yankee in the Old Northwest.* Westport: Greenwood Press, 1983.

Powers, Madelon. *Faces along the Bar: Lore and Order in the Workingman's Saloon, 1870–1920.* Chicago: University of Chicago Press, 1998.

Pratt, Randall A. "Miss Eva Jones: The Biography of a State Leader of the Women's Christian Temperance Union." Major Paper, n.p., 1968.

Quinn, John F. *Father Mathew's Crusade: Temperance in Nineteenth-Century Ireland and Irish-America.* Amherst: University of Massachusetts Press, 2002.

———. "Father Mathew's Disciples: American Catholic Support for Temperance, 1840–1940." *Church History* 65.4 (1996): 624–40.

Rachie, Elias. *The Temperance Crusade.* Minneapolis: Holter, 1908.

Reardon, James M. "The Beginning of the Catholic Total Abstinence Movement in Minnesota." *Acta et Dicta* 1 (1908): 199–209.

———. *The Catholic Church in the Diocese of St. Paul: From Earliest Origin to Centennial Achievement.* St. Paul: North Central, 1952.

———. "The Catholic Total Abstinence Movement in Minnesota: Period of Growth, 1869–1876." *Acta et Dicta* 2 (1909): 44–93.

Regan, Ann. "The Irish." *They Chose Minnesota: A Survey of the State's Groups.* Ed. June Holmquist. St. Paul: Minnesota Historical Society Press, 1981. 130–52.

———. *Irish in Minnesota*. The People of Minnesota. St. Paul: Minnesota Historical Society Press, 2002.

Rice, John G. "The Old-Stock Americans." *They Chose Minnesota: A Survey of the State's Groups*. Ed. June Holmquist. St. Paul: Minnesota Historical Society Press, 1981. 55–72.

Riley, Glenda. *The Female Frontier: A Comparative View of Women on the Prairie and the Plains*. Lawrence: University of Kansas Press, 1988.

Rippley, La Vern J. "Conflict in the Classroom: Anti-Germanism in Minnesota Schools, 1917–1919." *Minnesota History* 47.5 (1981): 170–83.

———. "German-American Banking in Minnesota." *A Heritage Fulfilled: German-Americans*. Ed. Clarence A. Glasrud. Moorhead: Concordia College, 1984. 94–115.

Rosenzweig, Roy. *Eight Hours for What We Will: Workers and Leisure in an Industrial City, 1870–1920*. Interdisciplinary Perspectives on Modern History. Cambridge: Cambridge University Press, 1983.

Rudnick, Oskar H. *Das Deutschtum St. Paul's in Wort und Bild: Eine historische Beleuchtung deutsch-amerikanischer Tätigkeit in St. Paul*. St. Paul: n.p., 1924.

Rumbarger, John R. *Profits, Power, and Prohibition: Alcohol Reform and the Industrialization of America, 1800–1930*. SUNY Ser. in New Social Studies on Alcohol and Drugs. Albany: State University of New York Press, 1989.

Ryan, Mary P. *Civic Wars: Democracy and Public Life in the American City during the Nineteenth Century*. Berkeley: University of California Press, 1997.

———. *Cradle of the Middle Class: The Family in Oneida Country, New York, 1790–1865*. Cambridge: Cambridge University Press, 1981.

———. "Gender and Public Access: Women's Politics in Nineteenth-Century America." *Habermas and the Public Sphere*. Ed. Craig Calhoun. Cambridge: MIT Press, 1992. 259–88.

Salisbury, Harrison E. "The Victorian City in the Midwest." *Growing Up in Minnesota: Ten Writers Remember Their Childhoods*. Ed. Chester G. Anderson. Minneapolis: University of Minnesota Press, 1976. 49–78.

Samuels, Jason. "From Temperance to Prohibition: The Development of Restrictive Alcohol and Drug Policies in the United States and in the State of Minnesota." History Term Paper. University of Minnesota, 2003.

Schaefer, Francis J. "The History of the Diocese of St. Paul." *Acta et Dicta* 4.1 (1915): 32–71.

Schaffer, Ronald. *America in the Great War: The Rise of the Welfare State*. Oxford: Oxford University Press, 1991.

Schmid, Calvin F. *Social Saga of Two Cities: An Ecological and Statistical Study of Social Trends in Minneapolis and St. Paul*. Bureau of Social Research: Monograph Ser. 1. Minneapolis: Bureau of Social Research, the Minneapolis Council of Social Agencies, 1937.

Scholliers, Peter, ed. *Food, Drink and Identity: Cooking, Eating and Drinking in Europe since the Middle Ages*. Oxford: Berg, 2001.

Schönemann, Bernd. "Frühe Neuzeit und 19. Jahrhundert." *Geschichtliche Grundbegriffe: Historisches Lexikon zur politisch-sozialen Sprache in Deutschland*. Ed. Otto Brunner, Werner Conze, and Reinhart Koselleck. Vol. 7. Stuttgart: Klett, 1992. 281–380.

Scott, Anne Firor. *Natural Allies: Women's Associations in American History*. Urbana: University of Illinois Press, 1991.

Scovell, Bessie Laythe. *A Brief History of the Minnesota Woman's Christian Temperance Union from 1877 to 1939*. St. Paul: Bruce, 1939.

Seymour, E. Sandford. *Sketches of Minnesota: The New England of the West: With Incidents of Travel in That Territory during the Summer of 1849: In Two Parts*. New York: Harper and Bros., 1850.

Shannon, William V. *The American Irish: A Political and Social Portrait*. 1963. Amherst: University of Massachusetts Press, 1989.

Shurtleff, Malcolm C. "The Introduction of Methodism in Minnesota." MA Thesis. University of Minnesota, 1922.

Smith-Rosenberg, Carroll. *Disorderly Conduct: Visions of Gender in Victorian America*. New York: Oxford University Press, 1986.

Soderstrum, T. Jason. "Johnson, William Eugene 'Pussyfoot.'" *Alcohol and Temperance in Modern History: An International Encyclopedia*. Ed. Jack S. Blocker Jr. et al. Vol. 1. Santa Barbara: ABC Clio, 2003. 340–41.

Sollors, Werner. *Beyond Ethnicity: Consent and Descent in American Culture*. New York: Oxford University Press, 1986.

———. "The Invention of Ethnicity." Introduction. *The Invention of Ethnicity*. Ed. Werner Sollors. New York: Oxford University Press, 1989. ix–xx.

———. "Theories of American Ethnicity." Foreword. *Theories of Ethnicity: A Classical Reader*. Ed. Werner Sollors. London: Macmillan, 1996. x–xliv.

Sommerdorf, Norma. "Harriet Bishop." *The Privilege for Which We Struggled: Leaders of the Woman Suffrage Movement in Minnesota*. Ed. Heidi Bauer. St. Paul: Upper Midwest Women's History Center, 1999. 11–15.

Sommerdorf, Norma, and Sheila Ahlbrand. "Sarah Burger Stearns." *The Privilege for Which We Struggled: Leaders of the Woman Suffrage Movement in Minnesota*. Ed. Heidi Bauer. St. Paul: Upper Midwest Women's History Center, 1999. 29–33.

Spickard, Paul. *Almost All Aliens: Immigration, Race, and Colonialism in American History and Identity*. London: Routledge, 2007.

Staggenborg, Suzanne. *Gender, Family, and Social Movements: Sociology for a New Century*. Thousand Oaks: Pine Forge Press, 1998.

Stearns, Sara B. "Minnesota." *History of Woman Suffrage*. Ed. Elizabeth Cady Stanton et al. Vol. 3. New York: Susan B. Anthony, 1887. 649–61.

Steffens, Lincoln. *Shame of the Cities*. New York: McClure, Phillips and Co., 1904.

Stevens, John H. *Personal Recollections of Minnesota and Its People, and Early History of Minneapolis*. Minneapolis: Tribune, 1890.

Stivers, Richard. *A Hair of the Dog: Irish Drinking and American Stereotype*. University Park: Pennsylvania State University Press, 1976.

Stockwell, Maud C. "Minnesota." *History of Woman Suffrage*. Ed. Ida Husted Harper. Vol. 6. New York: National American Suffrage Association, 1922. 317–25.

Stuhler, Barbara. *Gentle Warriors: Clara Ueland and the Minnesota Struggle for Woman Suffrage*. St. Paul: Minnesota Historical Press, 1995.

———. "Organizing for the Vote: Leaders of Minnesota's Woman Suffrage Movement." *Minnesota History* 54.7 (1995): 290–303.

Sutton, David E. *Remembrance of Repasts: An Anthropology of Food and Memory*. Oxford: Berg, 2001.

Szymanski, Ann-Marie E. *Pathways to Prohibition: Radicals, Moderates, and Social Movement Outcomes*. Durham: Duke University Press, 2003.

Tappe, Heinrich. *Auf dem Weg zur modernen Alkoholkultur: Alkoholproduktion, Trinkverhalten und Temperenzbewegung in Deutschland vom frühen 19. Jahrhundert bis zum Ersten Weltkrieg*. Diss. University of Münster, 1992. Studien zur Geschichte des Alltags 12. Stuttgart: Steiner, 1994.

Taylor, David Vassar. *African Americans in Minnesota*. St. Paul: Minnesota Historical Society Press, 2002.

Tierney, Mike. "Merriam Park: A Village between Two Cities." Seminar Paper. College of St. Thomas, 1984.

Tikalsky, Greg. "The Anti-Saloon League and County Option: Reaching Consensus for Prohibition in Minnesota, 1897–1919." MA Thesis. Minnesota State University, 2005.

Timberlake, James H. *Prohibition and the Progressive Movement, 1900–1920*. Cambridge: Harvard University Press, 1963.

Townend, Paul A. *Father Mathew, Temperance and Irish Identity*. Dublin: Irish Academic Press, 2002.

Trounstine, Jessica. "All Politics Is Local: The Reemergence of the Study of City Politics." *Perspectives* 7.3 (2009): 611–18.

Twain, Mark. *Life on the Mississippi*. Boston: Osgood, 1883.

Tyrrell, Ian R. *Sobering Up: From Temperance to Prohibition in Antebellum America, 1800–1860*. Westport: Greenwood Press, 1979.

———. "Temperance and Economic Change in the Antebellum North." *Alcohol, Reform and Society: The Liquor Issue in Social Context*. Ed. Jack S. Blocker Jr. Westport: Greenwood Press, 1979. 45–67.

Utzinger, Albert H. *History of the Minnesota Conference of the Evangelical Association, 1856 to 1922*. Cleveland: Evangelical Press, 1922.

Vecoli, Rudolph J. "Ethnicity and Immigration." *Encyclopedia of the U.S. in the 20th Century*. Ed. Stanley J. Kutler. Vol. 1. New York: Scribner's, 1996. 161–93.

———. "An Inter-Ethnic Perspective on American Immigration History." *Mid-America: A Historical Review* 75.2 (1993): 223–35.

Watson, James L., and Melissa L. Caldwell, eds. *The Cultural Politics of Food and Eating: A Reader*. Oxford: Blackwell, 2005.

White, Bruce M., et al., comps. *Minnesota Votes: Election Returns by County for Presidents, Senators, Congressmen, and Governors, 1857–1977*. St. Paul: Minnesota Historical Society Press, 1977.

Wild, Mark. "Out of Many, Many More: Immigrants and Identity Proliferation." *Journal of Urban History* 33.5 (2007): 873–82.

Williams, John Fletcher. *A History of the City of St. Paul, and the County of Ramsey, Minnesota*. Collections of the Minnesota Historical Society 4. St. Paul: Minnesota Historical Society Press, 1876.

Wills, Jocelyn. *Boosters, Hustlers, and Speculators: Entrepreneurial Culture and the Rise of Minneapolis and St. Paul, 1849–1883*. St. Paul: Minnesota Historical Society Press, 2005.

Wilson, Thomas M., ed. *Drinking Cultures: Alcohol and Identity*. Oxford: Berg, 2005.

——. "Drinking Cultures: Sites and Practices in the Production and Expression of Identity." *Drinking Cultures: Alcohol and Identity*. Ed. Thomas M. Wilson. Oxford: Berg, 2005. 1–24.

——. "Food, Drink and Identity in Europe: Consumption and the Construction of Local, National and Cosmopolitan Culture." *Food, Drink and Identity in Europe*. Ed. Thomas M. Wilson. European Studies Ser. 22. Amsterdam: Rodopi, 2006. 11–29.

——, ed. *Food, Drink and Identity in Europe*. European Studies Ser. 22. Amsterdam: Rodopi, 2006.

Wingerd, Mary Lethert. *Claiming the City: Politics, Faith, and the Power of Place in St. Paul*. Diss. Duke University, 1998. Cushwa Center Studies of Catholicism in Twentieth-Century America. Ithaca: Cornell University Press, 2001.

——. *North Country: The Making of Minnesota*. Minneapolis: University of Minnesota Press, 2010.

Wittke, Carl. *The Irish in America*. Baton Rouge: Louisiana State University Press, 1956.

Wolkerstorfer, John Christine. "Anti-German Nativism in Ramsey County." MA Thesis. University of Minnesota, 1968.

——. "Nativism in Minnesota in World War I: A Comparative Study of Brown, Ramsey, and Stearns Counties, 1914–1918." Diss. University of Minnesota, 1973.

——. "Persecution in St. Paul: The Germans in World War I." *Ramsey County History* 13.1 (1976): 3–13.

——. *"You shall be my people": A History of the Archdiocese of St. Paul and Minneapolis*. Strasbourg: Editions du Signe, 1999.

Woolley, John G., and William E. Johnson. *Temperance Progress in the Century*. London: Linscott, 1903.

Writers' Program of the Works Project Administration in the State of Minnesota, comp. *The Mayors of St. Paul, 1850–1940: Including the First Three Town Presidents*. St. Paul: St. Paul Vocational School, 1940.

Zimmerman, Jonathan. *Distilling Democracy: Alcohol Education in America's Public Schools, 1880–1925*. Lawrence: Kansas University Press, 1999.

Index

Maine Law: German American Methodists'
support for, 42–43; Maine Law campaign,
20–26, 31; repeal of, 32, 184; Temperance
Watchmen founding, 31; women's support
for, 49
Malmros, Oscar, 55
Manahan, James, 109
Mankato, 122
Marshall, William R., 25, 31, 41, 67
Martin County, 175
Massard-Guilbaud, Geneviève, 99
Mathew, Theobald, 34
Matt, Joseph, 154–57, 185, 188–89
McCarthy, C. M., 77
McClure, I. F., 122
McGee, John F., 172, 173, 175–76, 187
McGill, Andrew R., 92, 94
Mears, Norman T., 179–80, 231n39
men: ASL as men's organization, 126;
domestic violence and alcoholism and, 47;
frontier masculinity, 30–31, 48–49; Irish
drinking traditions and, 71; masculinity
in temperance societies, 30–31, 49–50, 86;
saloons as gendered spaces, 40, 44, 119;
temperance movement as generational
conflict, 48–49, 205n5. *See also* gender;
women
Merriam, John L., 141
Messmer, Sebastian, 114–15
Methodist Church: constitutional prohibition
advocacy, 59; Epworth Leagues, 98, 129,
219n13; establishment in St. Paul, 28;
German Methodist Church, 42–43, 115;
High License opposition of, 95; IOGT
alliance with, 54; Maine Law advocacy,
23; MTSU founding, 56–57; New England
settlers and, 28–29; pietistic theology and,
42; pro-temperance views, 21, 42–43, 58;
St. Paul temperance societies and, 30, 46;
support for ASL, 127
Middle Atlantic states (St. Paul settlers from),
28–29
Midway (St. Paul suburb), 14, 138–39, 140–42,
160, 180, 194, 202, 219n19
Miesen, Anton, 164
Minneapolis: Ames mayorality, 142; anti-
wineroom ordinance, 140; as ASL
headquarters, 127–28; Bridge Square
District, 173; demographics, 53, 138; First
Methodist Church, 58; founding and
character of, 137–38, 225n31; High License
initiative in, 66; Minneapolis-St. Paul
differences, 8, 14, 137–40, 139, 146; saloon

closing time laws, 146; St. Paul differences
with, 8, 14, 137–38, 200; Sunday Law
campaign of 1905, 142–44, 144. *See also*
Hennepin County
Minnesota and temperance, 6–7, 46, 206n12
Minnesota Brewers' Bureau, 178
Minnesota Civic Reform Association, 165
Minnesota Commission of Public Safety
(MNCPS), 166, 171–78, 180–85, 187–89, 199
Minnesota County Option League, 98
Minnesota Dry Federation, 170–71, 176, 183,
193, 196
Minnesota Irish Immigration Society, 75
Minnesota People's Party, 97, 219n8
Minnesota State Association for the
Protection of Personal Liberty, 57, 59, 82
Minnesota State Federation of Labor, 133, 172,
174
Minnesota State Temperance Union (MTSU),
56–58
Minnesota Sunday School Temperance
League, 57, 88
Minnesota Temperance Union, 46
Minnesota Total Abstinence Association, 171,
176
Minnesota Trade Union League to Prevent
Unemployment and Promote the Principle
of Home Rule, 133
Minnesota Wholesale Liquor Dealers
Association, 57, 82
Minnesota Woman Suffrage Association
(MWSA), 85, 90, 118, 150, 157–58, 228n91
Missouri Compromise, 25
MNCPS (Minnesota Commission of Public
Safety), 166, 171–78, 180–85, 187–89, 199
Moersch, Julius, 156, 185
Moloney, Deidre M., 72, 77
Montana, 95
moonshine, 184–85
Moore, Minnie, 150
morality: inadequacy of moral suasion,
20; intemperance as religious sin, 21;
middle-class 1890s moral reformism, 100;
moderation as moral achievement, 79–80;
moral cleansing as WCTU motivation,
162; place and, 12, 28–30, 100–101, 140–42;
Progressivist theories and, 124–25; ritualists
vs. pietists and, 41–42; Sunday leisure
practices and, 40; temperance as frontier
civilizing initiative, 17; women as moral
barometers, 49–50. *See also* religion
Morawska, Ewa, 9
Morgan, David, 105